BOSTON
SURVIVING
Y2K

And Other Lovely Disasters

by

Boston T. Party

Published by

To Al —
Stay Healthy in 2000!
Boston T. Party

JAVELIN PRESS

c/o P.O. Box 31F, Ignacio, Colorado. (81137-0031)
(Without any 4 USC §§ 105-110 *"Federal area"* or *"State."*)
www.javelinpress.com

ACKNOWLEDGMENTS

Huge appreciation goes to my graphic artist, proofreaders, and editors--you know who you are. I apologize to you all for being occasionally crabby during the writing of this book.

Thanks go to Dan Chittock and his *Preparedness Expo* crew who host such a unique and valuable forum. Through these Expos, I have met many of my readers and colleagues. Probably 30% of Americans can enjoy an Expo within a day's drive, so I urge you all to attend one in 1999.

I also owe a very special thanks to Amelia Porter, author of *A Common Sense Approach to Farmstead Livestock* (due in spring 1999), who so generously contributed the excellent chapter *Raising Animals for Food*. She dropped her domestic concerns and worked dozens of hours to meet a horrendous deadline. Thank you Amelia, and the best of success to you with all your critters! (Even though you're not wild about them for Y2K, I still want some emus...)

DEDICATION

I dedicate *Boston on Surviving Y2K* to all my readers. Every writer needs his public, and I am very happy that you and I have found each other. Because of your interest in and support of my books, you have made possible a comfortable living by me being *me*. Also, my author career has pulled me into the countryside, unknowingly preparing in advance for Y2K (of which I wasn't even aware until 1997).

Ten years ago, I did not know which direction my life would take, but I now know that I will always be, at least in *some* capacity, an author. Thanks to you, I get to write about topics I'm passionate about, *and* be paid for it. I wish everyone were so blessed. See you on the other side of Y2K.

Other works by
Boston T. Party

Good-Bye April 15th!
Published November 1992. Unfortunately, we are currently out of stock but will reprint soon--details to follow on **www.javelinpress.com**.

You & The Police!
Published January 1996. The definitive modern guide regarding your rights and tactics during police confrontations. Every gunowner needs a copy to avoid seizures under the *Gun Free School Zone Act* (repassed in 1996). Don't lose your freedom through ignorance!
128 pp. Available for Ø15 + Ø4 s&h (cash, please).

Bulletproof Privacy
How to Live Hidden, Happy, and Free! Published January 1997. Our book will explain precisely how to lay low and be left alone by the busy-bodies, snoops, and bureaucrats. Boston has "been there--done that" and shares many of his unique methods. Don't settle for old, fluffy, rip-off titles. Nothing we've seen compares to this book.
160 pp. Available for Ø16 + Ø4 s&h (cash, please).

Hologram of Liberty
The Constitution's Shocking Alliance with Big Government
Published August 1997. The Philadelphia Convention of 1787 and its Constitution was the most brilliant and subtle *coup d'état* in history. The federalist/nationalist framers *wanted* a strong central government, which they guaranteed through purposely ambiguous verbiage.
262 pp. Available for Ø20 + Ø4 s&h (cash, please).

Boston on Guns & Courage
Proven Tools for Chronic Problems
Published March 1998. "What if Thomas Paine had an AR-15, or if Patrick Henry went to Thunder Ranch?" A rousing how-to/*why*-to on modern gun ownership. According to Washington, firearms are *"liberty's teeth"* and it's time we remembered it. A most definitive work.
192 pp. Available for Ø17 + Ø4 s&h (cash, please).

a novel (yet untitled)
Due 1999. If you liked *Unintended Consequences* by John Ross and Ayn Rand's *Atlas Shrugged*, then Boston's novel will be a favorite. It dramatically outlines an innovative recipe for Liberty which neatly bypasses the bureaucracies, the courts and the Congress.

TABLE OF CONTENTS

7 Health

8 Energy

16 People

17 Services During Y2K

18 Raising Animals for Food

19 Recreation

PREFACE

This is going to have implications in the world and in American society we can't even comprehend.
-- Deputy Defense Secretary John Hamre, before a Senate committee on Y2K; *Reuters,* 5 June 1998

It does not pay to leave a dragon out of your calculations, if you live near him.
-- H.R. Tolkien

By disrupting power, transportation, and communications, it is inarguable that Y2K will cause *some* degree of dislocation and discomfort. How *much* is open to wide speculation because we can't predict with 100% accuracy how *long* the power and phones will be out, the railroads dead, and the planes grounded.

While we all desire Y2K disruption be minimal and thus prepared for by a mere "have some extra candles and canned food" level of precaution, do you *really* want to gamble your family's *lives* on that wish? *Boston on Surviving Y2K* was unabashedly written *assuming* a *worst*-case scenario. (If the rollover to 2000 turns out to be a *mild* event, then no hard-core guide was necessary--therefore, why *write* one?) No, I'm willing to risk some professional embarrassment by betting this book on a severe crash, resulting in a depression and martial law.

Recall that lovely little strike by UPS union employees? It bankrupted over 600 businesses in America. Had it gone on for another month it would have shut down thousands. Had it gone on for *two* more months it might have triggered a recession.

My point is that the veneer of civilization is always very thin, and the more sophisticated the civilization, the thinner and more fragile the veneer. Technology demands the division of labor and the specialization of talent. I can't design and manufacture an automobile and build a highway system if I'm spending 70% of my time scratching around for food, as is most of the world. There are individuals who totally support themselves by having become experts in some highly trivial field, such as African tribal dance. (An "expert" is somebody who knows more and more about less and less, until he knows everything about *nothing*. Not that I disparage anyone's career in Asian beetles, however, *I* have only one life down here and cannot in good conscience choose to devote my years to such arcane pursuits. I want to do the most good for the most people.)

As long as the rest of society refines the experts' gasoline, delivers their food, builds their microwave ovens, maintains their phone lines, etc. these people can not only enjoy their specialized passions, but make a *living* at them. Not even general self-sufficiency is practiced any more.

Example: An acquaintance is a corporate executive. She lives in a downtown high-rise apartment building. She eats out exclusively. She has no food in the fridge but some yogurt and coffee cream. She relies on public transportation. She gets paid by automatic deposit and writes checks for most things, or uses ATMs. Because her company is paying for it, she is working on an MBA, to be completed by 2001. I personally do not know *any* individual as dependent on civilization for mere survival. Predictably, she sneers at the Y2K crisis scenario. *"Somebody has to be the optimist, and I won't live in fear!"* (As if living in *denial* is preferable.) On Monday morning, 3 January 2000, she fully expects to go to work as usual.

The eye sees only what the mind is prepared to comprehend.
    -- Robertson Davies

I postulated to her that if *I'm* wrong, *so what*? I've got some extra food, water, a generator, etc.--stuff that I can always use anyway. Noboby's talking about moving to a cave somewhere. However, if *she* is wrong... Even though it's simple logic that one should prepare for Y2K, she subconsciously understands that such preparations would *drastically* change her life--and she won't accept *that*. Fortunately, her parents live in the country an hour away, so she may weekend there on 1/1.

While much of life *does* depend on one's attitude, a sunny disposition cannot reinstate electricity and phone service. Mere cheerfulness alone cannot make food appear on grocery store shelves, much less on restaurant tables. In light of the *mountain* of information on Y2K from hundreds of technical experts, breezy unconcern for 2000 is "whistling past the graveyard."

We seemed to have forgotten that civilization is *not* natural. The *jungle* is natural. The *desert* is natural. **Only *Nature* is natural.** Through technology, civilization purposely defies the "gravity" of nature. Beautiful women in dresses fearlessly walking alone down lit streets are not natural. (If you want to understand a society's sophistication, simply observe their women.) Full stomachs, white teeth, and shampooed hair are not natural. Hunger pangs, rotting mouths, and body odor *are*.

Civilization is *not* natural. Archeologists make a living at combing through the ruins of *failed* civilizations. The point here is that civilizations *do not last*. They are temporary. Why? Because mankind cannot forever hold its ground against Nature. We never have, we never *will*, and only our infinite arrogance prevents us from accepting it. Like a wave, we keep tripping over some unforeseen sandbar and come crashing down to earth. We then claw our way out of that particular Dark Age, convinced that we've made the *last* mistakes, that we'll *finally* get it right the next time. The "sandbar" of our modern age is something so beautifully picayune as a two digit year date field. It's the little things that seem to matter most, as we stumble not over mountains, but on pebbles.

> For the want of a nail the shoe was lost,
> For the want of a shoe the horse was lost,
> For the want of a horse the rider was lost,
> For the want of a rider the battle was lost,
> For the want of a battle the kingdom was lost,
> And all for the want of a horse-shoe nail.
> -- Benjamin Franklin

Don't get me wrong, I'm *not* a Luddite or Stone Age fan. I *like* the scent of perfume. I *like* technology. I enjoy my laptop computer, laser printers, and GPS devices. **Technology is neat-- *while it works*.** Modern society is an intricate motor, precisely balanced and carefully oiled. A failed wrist pin or valve spring, so to speak, will shut the whole thing down. Basically, the motor runs (and runs well) or it does not run at all. High performance items ought to be relegated to luxury use only, but we have made a fatal bargain with technology by relying on it for *everything*. We have utterly no "Plan B."

When it *doesn't* work, technology is worse than useless, it's *harmful* because we have grown to utterly depend on it, daily. (How many of you had dead pagers in May 1998 when one bad chip made the Galaxy IV satellite take a dive?) In short, that's the detrimental thing about technology: it co-opts and buys off our ability to survive in a state of nature.

Running is fine, as long as you *first* learned to crawl and walk, and don't mind crawling or walking for a while if running is for some reason not possible. We have forgotten how to crawl and walk, assuming we ever learned in the first place. If you think about it, machines are sought not just for the *service* they provide, but for the labor we can then *avoid* doing by hand. When muscles are replaced by machinery, the muscles atrophy. (Western civilization is utterly unique in history by developing an entire industry around *productionless* human effort: exercise gyms. People running several miles a day without being chased or delivering an urgent message? Unbelievable!) We are approaching the state of those bodyless alien brains in sapphire cylinders, supported by technology.

What city dweller can walk into the wilderness and, with nothing but a good knife, build shelter, make a fire, and hunt for food? (Once, when nobody else could, I fixed a stereo at big city party, and was treated thereafter like a *god*.)

While I am not totalitarian by nature, it "should have been the law" that citizens were trained and practiced in basic survival and that supplies for such (food, water, generator power, etc.) were mandated to be stored by every citizen. Why not put polling places way out in the wilderness, to be reached by a several day rugged hike. Only if you make it can you cast your vote. (I'm only *halfway* kidding...)

While we *might* not be forced to utterly "crawl" after 1/1/2000, at least "walking" seems assured. I believe this *so* strongly that I've postponed (perhaps indefinitely) several other books (including my novel) that I'm writing.

When the juice goes...

Every test I have seen done on an electrical power plant has caused it to shut down. Period. I know of no plant or facility investigated to this date that has passed without Y2K problems.
-- David Hall, embedded-systems consultant at Cara Corporation, *Netly News*, 13 May 1998

The weakest link in a chain is the strongest because it can break it.
-- Stanislaw J. Lem

I expect a prolonged (weeks to months) power blackout covering 50-95% of the country. In New Zealand, from 22 January to 20

February 1998, Auckland's four old power cables from the hydroelectric plant south of town successively failed, plunging 1.2 million people into darkness. **The total power outage lasted for *over four months*.** Food rotted in dead refrigerators, and garbage rotted in apartment building hallways. High-rise office buildings became saunas as their modern construction dictated non-opening windows. Ships docked in Auckland harbor provided emergency power to hospitals. Diesel fumes from generators choked the city. Auckland's 80,000 commuters stayed home, turning the city into a ghost town. 95% of all downtown businesses failed.

Remember, Auckland had at its disposal not only the resources of all New Zealand, *but of the entire world.* Technicians, generators, cables--all of it available from a planet eager to help, *and it still took over four months to restore power!* If one of the world's 200 largest cities had to flounder in the cold darkness for over four months when everybody else was standing outside the pit with a rope, imagine *thousands* of cities across the globe without heat, A/C, lighting, cooking, showering, elevator service, food, garbage pickup, or fire protection.

Still not convinced? Turn off the power in *your* home and in *your* business for seventeen weeks and see how well *you* fare.

When the food runs out...

I expect food shortages by 15 January 2000. The grocery stores all operate on "Just-In-Time" inventory scheduling and have no more than three days of food during *normal* demand. Having grown up in hurricane-plagued Texas, I have seen grocery stores wiped out of batteries, tape, candles, canned food, etc. in an afternoon by the unprepared hordes. I've lived through power and phones being dead for days, and homes flooded out from streets being underwater up to their stop signs. I assure you that the novelty rather quickly wears off.

Right now, go to your cupboards and pantries and calculate how long your stored food will feed you and your family. There's a 90% chance that it's only 2 weeks or less.

When the big cities self-destruct...

A senior executive at Barclays has warned people to sell their [city] *homes, stockpile cash and buy gold in case of a global economic collapse caused by the millennium computer bug. This extraordinary warning is echoed by other bank managers who fear a run on deposits. "The average man or woman does not appreciate what is going to happen," said the Barclays executive, who wishes to re-*

main anonymous. "I'm going to plan for the absolute worst. I am talking about the need to start buying candles, tinned food and bottled water from mid-1999 onwards. **(If he waits until then, he'll be too late.** BTP) *People think that I am mad, but a company director I met last week is intending to set up a commune and buy a shotgun because of the potential for looting is also quite high."* **(A measly shotgun is all Brits can own these days. BTP)**
-- *London Times*, Sunday Edition, 29 March 1998

I expect the big cities to descend into anarchy. The bee hivers will have no power and no food. Their precarious state of civilization requires regular supply from outside, which will be, at the minimum, erratic. The cities will go down. Los Angeles, for example, is a mess *now*. Imagine its state in 2000...

When the banking system implodes...

Only 8% of economic activity is handled by cash. The rest relies on the phantom "money" supply of checks, electronic and artificial bookkeeping entries--which I call the "MØ." Once the check-based "money" supply goes, instant depression. That's what happened in the 1930s. (The cash, being physical, didn't go away. Only the MØ did.) If the MØ comprised less than 10% of the "money" supply then bank credit contraction could not wield such destructive leverage, **however, the MØ comprises 92%.** We have allowed ourselves to become totally vulnerable to intangible "money" which can (and will) evaporate overnight.

It is our prediction that it will only take five to ten percent of the world's banks payments systems to not work on that one day to create a global liquidity lock-up. I don't think the markets have quite grasped the implications of what will happen if the entire system goes down.
-- Robert Lau, PA Consulting, Hong Kong
    Reuters, 6 October 1997

When the Federal Government collapses...

IRS Commissioner Charles Rossotti said the year 2000 glitch is his top priority. He said that if the IRS doesn't prepare its antiquated computer system for the digital crisis in time, 90 million taxpayers won't get refunds. "It's a very risky situation," he said. Preparing its computers...will cost nearly $1 billion. Rossotti has set a Jan. 31, 1999 deadline for fixing the year 2000 problem. "There's no plan B," he said. "The whole financial system of the United States will come to a halt. It's very serious. It not only could happen, it will happen if we don't fix it right."
-- *USA Today*, 2 April 1998

It barely functions even in the best of times, and once the IRS can no longer collect incomes taxes (which it *admits* as a distinct likelihood), the federal drones' paychecks will cease. They will not then report for work out of mere sense of duty. Clinton will freak and enact Executive Order 12656:

> A national security emergency is any occurrence, including natural disaster, military attack, **technological emergency**, or other emergency, that threatens or seriously degrades the national security of the United States.

This will subsume all communications, transportation, fuel, food, etc.--*even when such is in private hands.* (Congress can do nothing but *review* his actions *only after six months.*) Then the shooting begins and America (which is actually *several* countries under one national roof) unravels at the seams.

Conclusion

> But if the watchman sees the sword coming and does not blow the trumpet to warn the people and the sword comes and takes the life of one of them, that man will be taken away because of his sin, but I will hold the watchman accountable for his blood.
>   -- Ezekiel 33:6 (NIV)

> Twenty six percent of 229 Year 2000 Group computer experts anticipate "political crises within the U.S. and regional social disruptions." Scary. **A tenth of these experts selected "depression, market collapse and local martial law."**
>   -- *Newsweek*, 4 May 1998

Too gloomy? Take heart; other researchers forecast a *80%* city death toll in America from famine and mayhem. Even though this book is *based* on a "Northian" (Gary) utter apocalypse, I *don't* believe that such will occur. Civilization has far too much momentum to suddenly grind to a halt as he projects. Personally, I figure 75% of worst-case. Why then my book's total severity? **Because I can't foretell *which* 75% will collapse.** So, I portray the worst and leave you to reject the implausibly dour.

Coincidentally, a recent survey on comp.software.year-2000 newsgroup asked 39 programmers (with an average 17 years of work experience each) to rate the potential severity of Y2K on a scale of 1 (no problem at all) to 5 (total economic collapse). The average was 3.96--meaning, 80% of total collapse.

Edward Yardeni, chief economist and managing director of Deutsche Morgan Grenfell, has upped his 1997 prediction of a

30% chance of global recession to 60% (in May 1998) and now to 70% (in July 1998). Yardeni was an economist for the New York Federal Reserve Bank and, not surprisingly, advocates globalist/collectivist policies to deal with Y2K.

While I don't expect the *utter* collapse of Western society, I *do* forecast a pre-computer/limited electricity standard of living for a *minimum* of 3 months. More likely this will persist for a few years in many regions. Rand's *Atlas Shrugged* described the gradual devolution of industrial America over several years. Y2K could bring such devolution to pass in a matter of *weeks*. I'd prepare for a disruption in severity somewhere between the USSR's breakup and post-WWII Germany. No kidding.

Western civilization *will* soon see *some* kind of crash, and Y2K is merely the most imminent, credible, and dramatic of triggers. Someday, our "doomsayers" will be right. The odds are that they'll be right on 12:00AM, 1 January 2000.

"The battle is not always to the swift nor to the strong, but that's the way to bet!" Similarly, it may prove foolish to have prepared for Y2K, *"but that's the way to bet!"* Even basic precautions cost under Ø2,000 and will *greatly* increase your chances of survival, but get moving. If no Y2K crash occurs, what has the well-prepared family *lost*? Nothing. Either way, all their gear will be valuable and useful after 2000. But do *something, soon*. To encapsulate *Boston on Surviving Y2K*:

1. *The systems are broken.*
2. *There is not enough time to fix them; many will fail.*
3. *We depend on these systems for our way of life.*
4. *Decide what you need to do to look after yourself and the people you care about.*
5. *Get ready quickly.*
      -- Robert Folsom (robertf@bellsouth.net)

It wasn't raining when Noah built the ark.
      -- Howard J. Ruff

And his neighbors *laughed* at him, *until* it began to rain...

Good luck, and God bless! See you on the other side.

Note on reading my books

Quotations are in this form. Any original emphasis is underlined.
Any added emphasis of mine is in boldface. *When I supplement
a quote, my nonitalicized comments are within ( ) or [ ]--(like this).*

Also, within each chapter, the material is organized into:

SECTIONS,

which are divided into subsections,

and sub-subsections,

and sub-sub-subsections.

Since *Boston on Surviving Y2K* will the first Boston T.
Party book for many of you, you're going to wonder what in the
world the Ø symbol stands for. It's a lone typographic symbol,
quietly pointing a Zolan *J'accuse* finger. **Ø denotes "Federal
Reserve Notes"** which are no longer redeemable in, and
masquerade, as real $ dollars (*i.e.*, weights of gold/silver
money). When you see Ø, think "funny money" which is backed
by nothing more than our foolish confidence. The Federal Government can (and one day *will*) destroy it through monetary inflation, and then replace it with something new (but just as
intrinsically worthless). Such is the history of fiat (Latin for *"let
it be"*) "money." We'll repeat that history in a few years.

For new developments, visit www.javelinpress.com

I *originally* envisioned this book to be about 220 pages,
and it's 132 pages thicker than that, and I *still* wrote it in only 3
months. So, *please*, no whining about the unavoidable typos! I
write faster than my proofers can proof, and this book was an
emergency project. I rushed to get this out before December
1998 on the principle that an imperfect 85% book in *1998* is better than a 99% perfect book in mid-1999, when it's too late to afford many of the items listed herein.

The day after this book goes to press, there will occur to
me a hundred things that I should have mentioned. Such is
inescapable. Hop onto the Javelin Press website for any correc-
tions, new ideas, products, etc. that supplement this book. Also,
drop me a line if you've anything valuable to add, and I'll post it
on the site. We're all in this together. Nobody's a passenger on
this *Titanic*--everybody's crew. Let's get to work, shall we?

Some final words

Please share what you've learned in this book with anybody who will listen. I realize that money is tight for all of us, so don't feel that everybody you know must buy my book, when families and friends can share a common copy. While I'd *love* for the entire country to order my book, I didn't write it for the *money's* sake.

Given the unexpectedly large page count of *Boston on Surviving Y2K*, I had to cut some of the chapters short (*e.g.*, *Communications, Shelter, Transportation,* and *Tools*), else this would have been a 450 page book not seen until March 1999. Besides, I think their brevity is more than made up by the book's best chapters (*e.g.*, *Why Disaster Looms, Y2K Countdown Timetable, Location, Weapons, Food, Health, Energy, Money, Barter, Raising Animals, Rules,* and *Get Going*).

In short, the perfectionist and thorough researcher in me were hampered during this book, but I hope you'll appreciate the time constraints I wrote under.

Also, I urge you to buy every quality book on Y2K, as other authors have their own vital wrinkles on the subject. 1999 will see a *lot* of Y2K hype and hucksters, so make sure that you're getting *unique* information. Beware of the shameless rehash.

Since a technological meltdown might put me out of the book writing business for some time, this could be my "last" book--even though I'm now working on five new titles, including my first novel. I'll try my hardest to put out the novel in 1999, because it's *highly* relevant to our near future.

So, maybe you'll see another Boston T. Party title out before 2000. I hope so, even I hate to rush yet another book. Ayn Rand worked *14* years on *Atlas Shrugged*. (I'd be happy with just 14 *months*...) Enough grousing. Let's get on with this book!

Boston T. Party

WHY DISASTER LOOMS

We are at the end of *three* eras, or cycles: the 50 year Kondratieff wave, Liberty's historically short (*i.e.*, 200 year) cycle (the vast tradition of human history is *bondage*, not freedom), and the 500 year macro-wave.

Also, our economy has been experiencing since 1973 the failure of the "employee model" (*"Work hard at your job and you shall Live Long and Prosper."*):

The fact is that in all the thousands of years of human history, the employee model was really valid only for about 70 years. The employee model works only in a free or almost free industrialized economy based on the principles of Common Law. Because only under those circumstances can companies plan ahead enough to accumulate enormous amounts of savings-- economists call it capital--to build the highly productive big machines, factories and office buildings that provide high paying jobs.

From about the year 1900 to 1970, the groundwork laid by America's founders had finally yielded so much fruit that the employee model was possible. America had become the most free and prosperous land ever known, and you could put your fate into the hands of a good company and be very well taken care of.

But that's all gone now. It's been gone for twenty years. By 1973, the taxes, regulations, inflation and political law had done so much damage that anyone who follows the employee model now is in serious danger of **spending his life going backwards.** We are now on what economist F.A. Hayek called The Road To Serfdom.

We must now revert back to the only model that has a reasonable chance of working under a big, powerful, government.

That's the entrepreneurial model. Don't be an employee, be a business owner, an entrepreneur.

Up until 1776 the entrepreneurial model was the only one an honorable person could use to achieve success. **We're back to those conditions again.** *The family business is the only model I feel comfortable recommending, because the evidence shows that* **teaching a child to be an employee is preparing him for failure.**
But if you teach him to be an entrepreneur you're giving him a good chance to do well in life, to stand on his own two feet and be prosperous enough to take good care of his or her family.
Why be a business owner? It's simple. When the business is doing well, the owner earns more money than anyone else does. When the business is doing poorly, the owner is the last one to be laid off.
   -- Richard Maybury; *"Uncle Eric" Talks About...Personal, Career & Financial Security,"* pp.26-28

Finally, according to Dr. Ravi Batra's Power/Mind/Money cycle of rulers, we are about to leave the rule of Money for the rule of Power--*i.e.*, from under the banksters' FRN thumb to martial law and the M16 (and/or the AK47, if foreign troops arrive). Read Batra's *The Depression of 1999* for a full discussion of this.

Notice that I didn't even mention Y2K? Y2K merely happens to be the most likely of crash triggers, that's all. I'll cover the stock market first as it's inherently precarious even *without* Y2K concerns. Then I'll cover the banking system (vulnerable to bank runs), the power grids (which should be fine until the NRC shuts down the nukes by 12/99), and the Federal Government (which won't survive the crash in its present size).

But first, let me cover the various Y2K scenarios, followed by "Achilles' Heel" of Y2K.

Y2K SCENARIOS

According to the Gartner Group *Year 2000 World Status Update* of July 1998, the *least* prepared industries are: medical and law practices, architectural engineering, construction, farming, and government services. *Best* prepared (comparatively) are: insurance, investment services, banking, computer manufacturing, aerospace, and telecommunications.

I got the following from www.techweb/wire/story/y2k/ TWB19980806S0003. It's a good overview of possibilities.

Best

Government and business code-fixing efforts successful
Few mainframes crash, are rebooted with minimal data loss
Stock market drops a bit, recovers on 3 January 2000
Refugees straggle back to cities after extended vacation

Moderate

Brownouts in a few cities
Prices rise for a few days as some supply lines interrupted
Some hospital systems fail
Stock market drops, stays down on fears of overseas conflicts

Bad

Entire U.S. power grid fails
Water filtration plants fail
Rail transport-control systems crash
FAA air-traffic control systems fail
Widespread hospital equipment failure
Stock market dives, run on banks

Worst

Large-scale outages for months
Telephone network crashes or degrades to unreliability
Rioting in cities
Banking system fails, stock market crashes
Huge shortages in food, medical supplies, other necessities

EMBEDDED CHIPS

There has simply not been enough testing [of embedded systems]
to comment intelligently on what will happen. **What could happen,
though, is plenty scary.**
-- from *Forbes*, 21 September 1998, p. 260

If Y2K were *just* a software problem, then we could have *possibly* fixed it in time. But lines of faulty code are only 20% of the problem. The other 80% lies in embedded microprocessors, of which there are an estimated 25 to 75 *billion* across the globe.

These chips (usually in C-code) are PROMs or EPROMs, which are burned in at the factory and *cannot* be reprogrammed. They are in counters, flowmeters, sensors, transceivers, and hundreds of other important applications.

The average ocean oil rig, for example, has 10,000 such embedded systems, many of them deep underwater.

While perhaps only 5% of these chips are date sensitive, and perhaps only half of *them* are not Y2K compliant, that still works out to as many as 2.5% of the world's microchips (62.5-187.5 *million*) which can somehow fail on 1/1/2000. **Their probability of failure is by no means hypothetical.** As you'll read, mock 2000 rollovers (from DoD to GM to power plants) have caused systems to fail in nearly every instance.

Other problems: Non-Y2K chips are visually indistinguishable from Y2KOK chips, and about a fourth of the chip manufacturers are no longer in business. Either way, detection and replacement are both impossible in time.

[A] *vendor supplies a chip set to a company that makes a motherboard or single board computer. That company modifies the BIOS or CMOS to work with proprietary chips or designs on the board and ships it off to an assembler who changes the configuration settings to suit more add-ons. Then it goes to a distributor...who adds more value and makes more changes. It doesn't take a mathematician to see that the permutations are awesome. How many boards or computers are identical? Even similar? So where do you start to test Y2K compliance? Who has the answers?*
-- Don "Doc" Taylor, Y2K "guru" in Hampton Roads, Va.

Finally, it's not practical to *unsolder* every bad chip--the entire *board* or *device* must be replaced, and there's just not the inventory. You see, ass the entire world is only *now* becoming Y2K alarmed, expect an all out scramble for boards in 1999. Board factories are highly complex, and cannot double output by simply turning up a dial. The replacement boards and chip sets needed by the entire world can not be designed or made in time.

Our modern way of life is made up of concentric circles or systems layers which are independent and interdependent at the same time. It's an *organism,* basically, and one made up of smaller organisms. The power grid is "alive" as is the Internet. All must be *tested organically* (and will be on 1/1/2000), and not merely mechanically on a subsystem level. Very few companies are conducting that kind of testing because they either cannot spare the capacity, or they are concerned that a failure during such Y2K testing will cause too much downtime.

We'll see very few full-blown mock 2000 rollover tests in 1999. There shall be no dress rehearsals--only "opening night."

THE COMING STOCK MARKET CRASH

*The fiercest bear markets maul investors repeatedly: They're characterized by a series of rallies that fail. For instance, while the Crash of 1929 gets all the publicity, the subsequent decline of 1930 to 1932, **a sickening 70% slide,** was the most devastating drop on record and wiped out more wealth. Similarly, a 22% decline in stock prices in 1966 foreshadowed a 37% drop between 1968 and 1970, and a 48% catastrophe in 1973 and 1974.*

-- Kuhn and Kover, *"Will A Bear Market Wreck Your Retirement Plans?,"* 19 August 1996, *Fortune*

irrational exuberance...

-- Alan Greenspan, on the Dow before it had reached 6000

*Traditionally, Wall Street has never been comfortable with the market's ability to sustain a Price to Earnings (P/E) ratio in excess of 16. **We crossed that watermark last year** [in 1996] **when the Dow reached 7300.** I'm nervous.*

While "bears" might seem like a thing of the past, we have had 14 since 1950, with an average decline in stock prices of 24% and an average recovery period of 13 months.

-- Tony Keyes; *The Y2K Computer Crisis*, pp.22, 23

There are just two things you must know about the market:

Markets move in *ANTICIPATION* of *PERCEIVED* events or circumstances.

***Fear* is *3 times* more powerful than greed, which explains why bears are 3 times more intense than bulls.**

If the markets merely reacted *ex post facto* to events or circumstances, then stock investing would be easy. But when would *you* rather leave a building: *after* it's on fire, or *before*? Would you wait until you actually saw flames, or would you trust a credible rumor of fire? My point, I believe, is clear.

Stock market investors will not wait to cry *"Sell!"* until Monday, 3 January 2000 to see if the power grids are down, if the planes are grounded, or if the phones are dead. We will have *many* pre-2000 indicators of Y2K problems, which will begin in spring 1999 and progressively grow more alarming. Below is the most comprehensive list of known "Spike Dates":

Y2K "Spike Dates"

1 January **1999**	first "99" date; FORTRAN *"end of file"* marker
6, 13, 27 March	SIA "Tier I" testing
1 April	N.Y., Japan, Canada, U.K. fiscal 2000 begins
9 April	the 99th day of 1999
10 April	final "Tier I" testing
May	SIA "Tier II" test
1 July	fiscal 2000 for all states but NY, TX, AL, MI
	all 110 nuclear power plants must be Y2KOK
11 August	all nukes must formally yea/nay to the NRC
22 August	GPS interface clocks rollback 1024 weeks
1 September	Texas fiscal 2000
9 September	9/9/99 possibly unintentional program marker
1 October	AL, MI, *and Fed. Govt.* fiscal 2000 rollover
December	the NRC shuts down noncompliant nukes
1 January **2000**	Year 2000 rollover
29 February 2000	century date leap year (only every 4 centuries)
31 December 2000	the 366th day of the year

83% of Y2K transition managers expect the Dow to fall by at least 20% as Y2K begins to unfold. By spring 1999 the market will be getting *very* skittish over Y2K implications, especially if the Securities Industry Association's (SIA) "Tier I" test for Y2K fails, and certainly by 1 April if New York state's year 2000 fiscal rollover has problems. When the public begins to *anticipate perceived* systemic Y2K problems, they will take their profits and run. It's like musical chairs: *when the music stops, the panic begins.*

1999 Y2K repairs will affect the market

❶ Companies divert millions of Ø for Y2K work.
❷ Their profits drop as productive work declines.
❸ Layoffs commence and the market reacts negatively.
❹ Investors begin to bail out, dropping the market further.
❺ Large firms drop noncompliant suppliers. Stocks plummet.
❻ Mutual fund portfolio managers drop the Y2K weak.
❼ Moodys lowers the rating on Y2K weak bonds.
❽ The stampede for the door begins as nervous investors pull out.
❾ Federal, state, and local governments lose huge tax revenue.

Litigation and potential litigation

Beginning in 1999, serious year 2000 noncompliance problems will surface. Harmed consumers file class action suits against manufacturers, which hurts their stock prices. The manufacturers' shareholders sue the directors and officers for allowing such Y2K problems. Manufacturers then sue their suppliers, lowering *their* stock prices. Suppliers sue their software suppliers, lowering *their* stock prices, and so on.

The litigation has already begun. As of October 1998, there have been over two dozen suits filed.

Look to April 1999 for the market crash

By April 1999 there will have been 3 *weeks* of likely failed "Tier I" SIA testing, and problems with New York's rollover. That should sufficiently alarm the market into a brisk sell off, which snowballs into a *big* drop (say 20%). The market will try to rally, unsuccessfully. *Then* will begin the murderous decline, fueled by progressively worse "Spike Date" incidents.

If you want a graphic dramatization of what a stock market crash will be like, read any of Paul Erdman's novels, or *Debt of Honor* by Tom Clancy (all at any used bookstore). Just like 1929, we have a bubble economy created by easy Fed money.

The Dow is *already* turning

By summer 1998, the Dow had *already* dropped *2,000* points from 9,400 to 7,400. Gold has just broken through its Ø300 floor. Nervous money is now flowing into gold. (The days of Ø285 gold, *production cost* for many mines, are gone.)

Also, it is rumored that the Big Boy Insiders are bailing out (*e.g.*, Goldman Sachs going public), and will prop up Clinton (whose ship is sinking) only until after the midterm elections in November 1998. Any impeachment will occur only *after* January 1999 (the halfway point of Clinton's term) to give Gore the ability to seek two elected terms under the 22nd Amendment.

How money will move--a dash for the door
From stocks into *bonds*

(Note: As of October 1998, this is now beginning to happen.) Long rates will drop, meaning mortgage money rates. A good time to dump your urban 2000 deathtrap on some sucker.

From bonds to *near-cash assets*
T-bills, CDs, and money market funds (if the market is still fairly stable at that time).

From money market funds into *bank accounts*
Checking and savings.

From bank accounts to *cash*
Good luck after summer 1999, as I expect cash withdrawal restrictions by then. **If you've shorted the market, *get out early.*** I don't mean just get out of the market, but get out of *all* accounting-based assets into cash, precious metals, safe country/small town land, and usable commodities. Investing has its place, but too many people live in that virtual reality and functionally believe that such is the "real world."

THE COMING BANKING COLLAPSE

Inevitable difficulties are going to emerge. You could end up with... a very large problem. ***Before we reach the year 2000 there is economic loss.*** *(Notice he said "before" and not "after." BTP)*
-- Federal Reserve Chairman Alan Greenspan on Y2K,
USA Today, 26 February 1998

Smith Barney's Y2K testing foul up
During a June 1997 Y2K test, the computers of that well-known stock brokerage and mortgage firm bestowed overnight in each of their 525,000 accounts a glitch gift of Ø19,000,000 This translated to Ø10 *trillion*. Of course, the error was caught immediately and corrected, but the Y2K angle was hushed up.

The GPS connection
On 22 August 1999, the GPS satellite system's clocks will roll back 1024 weeks (20 years), making global synchronization impossible. The interconnected banking system of the western world could have grave problems in the time-sensitive processes of currency transfers and money wires.

It is estimated by banking experts that if the system were to go down for a full week, ***there would be a worldwide global depression that would last at least a decade.***
-- The *McAlvany Intelligence Advisor*, September 1998, p.11

The rush for liquidity

It only takes 3 depositors in 100 demanding their balance in cash to deplete the reserves of most banks. When word gets out that "First Federated" is bone dry, the bank runs will begin. Bank runs are not evil--depositors simply want their own property back (which isn't there and never *was*).

Fractional reserve banking and bank runs explained

Let's say that there is only *one* kind of car in the country, and they are also *identical* in color, age, seat adjustment, radio settings, everything. Every car is exactly the same as any other. An airport long-term parking garage notices that there are always about 50 cars on their lot. Since one is the same as another and there are plenty of perfectly good cars just sitting there, **why not supplement the parking lot business with the car *rental* business?** The parking lot proceeds to rent out 10 cars, then 20, and then 40 cars. This works because cars are identical (the owner doesn't care if he gets his *original* car back), and because the inflow of cars to be parked *exceeds* what the lot rents--until word gets out. Suddenly, owners swarm the lot, claim checks in hand, to get their cars back. The lot cannot quickly enough call back the rental cars, and the police close down the lot for fraud and unlawful conversion. Then, the lot reopens until another name.

Until the Federal Reserve System of 1914, this was the state of independent banking. Then, the big parking lot boys decided to band together for one *national* parking lot system, which would supply each *other* cars during illiquidity. No longer would a single lot be at the mercy of local owners; it could call on "Parking Papa" to cover his car needs. This works until the entire *country* wises up to the fraud. (Such happened first in 1933, and will happen next in 1999--probably in April.)

The "bank holiday" of 1999

Clinton will declare a "bank holiday." (Only in *banking* is the announcement of embezzled goods called a "holiday." Neat.) Cash withdrawals will *"temporarily"* be outlawed by executive order, or limited to Ø50/day. Credit cards will generally be frozen up. Checks and dedit cards only, please.

A banking collapse can cause a market crash (1929), or a market crash can cause a banking collapse (1933). Both are way overdue. Since virtually all American banks have joined, or been co-opted by, the Federal Reserve System, a banking trigger as in 1929 is nearly impossible--*however*, a market crash can initiate a systemic banking system run, as in 1933. I expect just this to occur by mid-July 1999, if not by April.

The Automated Clearing House (ACH)

This is our electronic banking system (consisting of 38 regional ACHs), which handles 3.5 billion yearly transactions totally Ø11 trillion. Participating are 500,000 companies, 22,000 financial institutions, all 50 states and over 1,000 federal agencies. Transactions include all automatic deposits (pensions, payroll, government benefits, etc.), credit cards, tax payments, and ATMs. The ACH is not, and will not be, 2000 compliant.

Maybe it won't be such a bad thing...

Look at it this way: We're all going to suffer through this. **Why not use it as an opportunity to collapse the financial/banking cartel while we're at it and get out from under its yoke?** *The best thing that could happen out of all this is to utterly collapse the Federal Reserve/IMF/World Bank private financial cartel system's stranglehold.* **If this would happen, then it would really all be worth it.** *Yes, that much pain around the globe really would be worth it to get rid of the modern day feudal system.*

-- Roger Voss; fedinfo@halifax.com

WHEN THE POWER GRIDS FAIL

Control computer systems within the bulk electric control centers across North America use complex algorithms to operate transmission facilities and control generating units. Many of these control center software applications contain built-in clocks used to run various power system monitoring, dispatch and control functions. Many energy management systems are dependent on time signal emissions from Global Positioning Satellites, which reference the number of weeks and seconds since 00:00:00 UTC January 6, 1980. In addition to resolving Y2K problems within utility energy management systems, these supporting satellite systems, which are operated by the U.S. government, must be Y2K compliant.

-- North American Electric Reliability Council
www.nerc.com/~filez/scs.html

Electric power is the crucial utility. After more than about three days [of being down] everything just folds up. Trains, heat, refrigeration, water supplies all go. **We'd be straight back to the 18th and 19th**

century, and it would take 20 years to regain the lost economic capability.
-- Ross Anderson, Cambridge University Computer Lab, *Reuters*, 8 June 1998

There are approximately 7,800 power generating and distributing plants in America. There is only 10-15% excess capacity. The nukes will shut down (by law) in late 1999, leaving the rest of the plants vulnerable to malfunction on 1/1/2000.

Nuclear power plants (22%)

Just 110 nukes provide 22% of the nation's electricity, and 40-50% in some regions (*e.g.*, the Northeast) and states. Six states containing roughly 12% of our population (Connecticut, New Jersey, Maine, Vermont, South Carolina, and Illinois) rely on nuclear power for *more than half* their electricity.

The Nuclear Regulatory Commission (NRC) is a federal agency whose mandate is *safety*, not power generation. When their 11 August 1999 deadline for Y2KOK assurance is not met, the NRC *will* shut down nukes operating in an *"unanalyzed condition"* by 12/99. (Sweden has already very clearly promised to shut down their nukes if *any* Y2K doubt remains.)

If local 911 emergency services fail, then that area's nuke *must* by law shut down (10 CFR 50.59). Even if the NRC *allows* post 12/31/99 operation (nearly impossible), then the 2000 rollover will kill the nukes. Assuming the national grid holds up, nearly one fourth of homes and businesses will be plunged into freezing darkness.

When the greens discover by mid-1999 the nukes' precarious situation, they will scream to their political "leader" Al Gore to shut them down. Don't be *anywhere* near a nuclear power plant after 11 August 1999, else you *will* be caught in a blackout, or, worse yet, a domestic Chernobyl in 2000.

O.K., so the nukes go off-line before 2000. Can the rest of the power plants pick up the slack? Certainly not in the Northeast, N.C., Illinois, etc., where the nukes are 50+% of the power.

Coal-fired power plants (40% of total)

They have only 1-3 weeks of coal, and rely on the railroads for resupply. The railroads have long since converted their switching and scheduling ops to embedded electronic systems, which are *notoriously* Y2K noncompliant. So, *assuming they remain on-line after 1/1/2000*--which they won't--the coal-fired plants will *starve* for lack of coal.

Gas-fired power plants (11% of total)

These plants rely on 1,300,000 miles of pipelines. Gas is moved from the Southwest to the highly populated eastern U.S. by four major pipelines. Nobody is coordinating the 288,000 gas wells, 125 pipeline companies, and 1,200 distribution companies for Y2K compliance work. Risk seems very high.

Hydroelectric power plants (27% of total)

Since their turbine's fuel does not have to be supplied over long distance (as in coal and gas plants), there's one less critical component involved. Still, the hydros should go down because of Y2K failed embedded systems, as in the other plants.

Year 2000 simulations are crashing plants

As reported in *MIA* 8/98, two coal-fired plants were simultaneously tested for Y2K compliance and both immediately shut down due to an embedded controller chip:

> *In an attempt to better understand the failure, the rollover test was repeated. In the second test, the plants again failed, but a different embedded controller was determined to be at fault. The rollover test was repeated a third time... In this third test the plant failed from yet a different embedded controller.* **It was determined that this last failure would have caused a portion of the national grid to fail had the plants been on-line. It took 13 days to restore the plants to working condition from the last failure.**

Such progressively worse failures are typical of complex systems in which the *weakest* of the weak links break *first*. Dozens of tests might be needed to finally reach the strongest (and last) weak link. As reported in 2 June 1997 *Newsweek*:

> *When the Hawaiian Electric utility in Honolulu ran tests on its systems to see if it would be affected by the Y2K Bug, "basically, it just stopped working." says systems analyst Wendell Ito. If the problem had gone unaddressed, not only would some customers have potentially lost power, but other could have gotten their juice at a higher frequency, in which case, "the clocks would go faster, and things could blow up," explains Ito.*

Ashley Dunn of the *Los Angeles Times* wrote on 9 August 1998:

Donald LeMaster, president of the Seattle-based TAVA/R.W. Beck, a venture created to deal with embedded Year 2000 problems in utilities, related the story of a power-generating plant that conducted a [Y2K] test while shut down for maintenance. The problem took hours to manifest itself but gradually spread to various parts of the operation like a virus.

"The system just got overloaded," he said, adding that if the failure had occurred for real, the plant would have shut down, since even the backup system would have been affected...

Restarting downed grids is a *real* problem

The *frightening* issue is this: it takes electricity to produce electricity. Downed plants must be "kick started" by backup generators or other plants. That power might not exist for weeks or months, and might not exist in sufficient quantity for *dozens* of testing failures times up to 7,800 plants. Further:

*Extensive blackouts are the nightmare of the power industry. Once power is interrupted in large metropolitan areas, diversity of electric use on the network is lost. When power is restored, all thermostatically controlled electric loads come back on simultaneously. **This stress, added to the higher demands of many devices such as motors and transformers, can draw up to 600% of normal load during restoration procedures.***

-- *Earth in Space*, Vol.9, No.7, March 1997

Remember, it took *over 4 months* to restore electricity to Auckland, New Zealand, and *that* was with the *world's* resources on hand. In 2000, plants may be unable to help out each other.

Conclusion

*Quite honestly, I think we're no longer at the point of asking whether or not there will be any power disruptions, **but...how serious the disruptions will be...** If we don't have power to generate electricity, quite frankly, everything else is moot.*

-- Sen. Christopher Dodd (D-Conn.)

If Y2K hit tomorrow, there is a 100% chance that the [national] grid would fail. With 18 months to go, we may be able to get this down to 40%.

-- Sen. Robert Bennett (R-Utah), 6 June 1998

At the very minimum, I expect half the country will be without power for 3 months. At worst, a new Dark Age lasting years. What experts are concerned about is if the *entire* grid goes down at once, the riots and mayhem could destroy all hope of ever getting it back up again. (Civilization is not natural.)

WHEN THE TELEPHONES FAIL

Make a phone call on Jan. 1, 2000, and there's a good chance that the call won't go through. There's a 50% to 60% chance each major carrier will suffer at least one failure of a mission critical system, says Lou Marcoccio, research director with The Gartner Group. And that's despite the industry spending more than two years and billions of dollars to rid their system of Year 2000 bugs.

    -- USA Today, 19 May 1998

Think of it another way: Won't *you* be calling all your family and friends on Saturday morning, 1 January, to ask if their power is still up, if everything is O.K., etc.? Of *course* you will. That day's sudden extra load of billions of calls will bring down the phones even without Y2K *technical* concerns. I usually can't get through on Mother's Day or Father's Day.

The phone system is *already* vulnerable to a cascade failure, as AT&T's April 1998 software problem demonstrated by failing 44 hubs. Forget about long-distance calls on 1/1/2000, and probably local calls, too.

Have a ham radio (and know how to use it before 2000). When the telephone was invented, some "futurist" of the day was laughed at for suggesting that someday every *town* would have one. In 2000, each town will need at least one ham radio operator. Operating as a local node for national needs could very well prove to be a fine service industry in 2000, and will be worth probably at least a silver dime/minute. (I wouldn't worry too much about not having an FCC license. There's a good chance of the FCC not even being around in 2000. Still, you'll have to put up with the busybody licensees who will *greatly* resent your illegal black market transmitter.)

WHEN BUSINESSES FAIL

Most business operations (such as accounts receivable/payable, payroll, "just-in-time" inventory, purchasing, and shipping) are completely reliant on computers. 44% of American companies have *already* experienced Y2K computer problems. Since only 20-25% of corporate technology projects get done on time, business Y2K compliancy outlook is rather dour.

Date problems/tests are stopping factories

"One British oil refinery identified 94 embedded apps that it needed to research. The vendors for 20 couldn't be found. Of the remaining 74, only three failed the Y2K test. However, two of those three will cause the refinery to shut down on 1/1/00." (Peter de Jager) *That underscores the ultimate issue with Y2K. Even if you're 98% compliant, that last 2% can take you down. And that last 2% will be the toughest to find.*

-- *Pick Postings,* Summer 1998

The 1996 incident at the New Zealand Camalco aluminum smelter is a prime example of how critical are date-related embedded systems. 660 automated process controllers didn't "know" that 1996 was a leap year with 366 days, so at midnight 30 December 1996 they "thought" that it was 1 January 1997, and failed to shut down the heaters, which burned a hole in the reactor. Fortunately, the damaged N.Z. plant warned its sister plant in Australia to expect the same glitch during their midnight. The second plant went to manual until the process controllers could be reprogrammed, thus averting disaster.

GM did a mock 2000 rollover in one of its assembly plants. The entire robotic line simply froze up, and the automatic locks on the plant doors engaged, forcing the personnel trapped inside to radio for outside help to unlock the doors.

The wise thing for factories to do in 1999 is to produce *lots* of excess inventory, yet such assumes that factories will be able to *ship* their product and get *paid* for it. Banking and shipping will both be erratic at best in 2000.

The big economic picture

Caper Jones, founder and chairman of Software Productivity Research in Burlington, Massachusetts, published a study called *The Economic Impact of the Year 2000 Computer Software Problem*, in which it was estimated that:

1% of Fortune 500 companies will fail. That means 5 of them.
5-7% of midsize companies (1,000-10,000 workers) will fail.
That's 1,500-2,100 of an estimated 30,000 companies.
3% of very small companies (<100 workers) will fail.
That's 180,000 of 6,000,000 such companies.

I'd guess that those estimates are somewhat optimistic, but even so, *10-11 million* people will suddenly be out of work in

January 2000. That's about one worker in 12 in the *first* wave. A similar U.K. study estimated 6 million unemployed in the *first* wave of Y2K problems. As we have about 4.3 times more workers than Britain, that means 25.8 million first wave unemployed here, which seems more likely than "only" 10-11 million.

Regardless of the number, 10 million suddenly unemployed Americans means *instant depression*. The *second* wave would take out probably 2-3 times as many. It would take at least 10-15 years to claw our way out.

GOVERNMENT COLLAPSES

Nobody seems willing or able to say it in simple language, so let me be the one: **the federal government is not going to finish its Y2000 project.** *No maybes, no ifs, ands, or buts. No qualifiers, no wishy-washy statements like "unless more money is spent" or "unless things improve." We're not going to avert the problem by appointing a Y2000 Czar or creating a National 2000 Commission. Let me say it again, in plain English: The United States federal government will not finish its Y2000 project.*

How Washington expects to continue functioning after 1/1/2000 is a mystery to me. *How American society expects to continue operating in a "business as usual" fashion, when half of the federal government agencies stop functioning, is a deeper mystery-- and one for which we must all begin planning.*

All of this is so mind-boggling that it falls into the category of "thinking about the unthinkable." Realistically, we can no longer talk about what might happen IF Washington fails to fix its Y2000 problems. **Realistically, we have to start talking about what will happen WHEN the Y2000 problem brings the government to its knees.**

-- Ed Yourdon; *Timebomb 2000: What the Year 2000 Computer Crisis Means To You*

While the cheering is deafening, hold on a second. Government at large employs one American in three (the federal government employs, directly and indirectly, one in five) and the rest of us, like it or not, depend on Government for many areas of our existence. Although Government's *gradual* whittling down is a good thing, it's sudden *collapse* without a ready replacement by the free market would be disastrous.

The Military

In an August 1997 operational exercise, the Global Command Control System failed testing when he date was rolled over to the year 2000. *GCCS is deployed at 700 sites worldwide and is used to generate a common operating picture of the battlefield for planning, executing, and managing military operations.* *The U.S. and its allies, many of whom also use GCCS, would be unable to orchestrate a Desert Storm-type engagement in the Year 2000 if the problem is not corrected.*

-- GAO; *Defense Computers: Year 2000 Computer Problems Threaten DoD Operations,* April 1998, p.5

By September 1998, the DoD had (allegedly) fixed only 27% of its "mission critical" systems. I'm underwhelmed. This 21 June 1998 article from the *Boston Globe* is chilling:

A preview of possible military disaster was the incident in the 1991 Gulf War, when a Scud missile blew up a barracks in Saudi Arabia, killing 28 National Guard troops inside. *A post-mortem of the disaster revealed that the Patriot air-defense battery failed to shoot down the Scud **because the clock in the Patriot's radar system was not properly synchronized.***

The radar had been designed to be left on for only a short while. *Its clock viewed a day as 23 hours and 59 minutes long. However, once this particular Patriot arrived in Saudi Arabia, the radar was left on continuously.* *So its clock drifted away from the actual time by one minute per day.*

When the Patriot system's computer detected an incoming Scud missile, it would see the missile on two radar screens and send both blips to...its fire-control system. *But since the two blips were not synchronized, the fire-control computer could not connect them--could see them as a target.*

The Scud tragedy illustrates why the clocks and calenders inside computers matter so much. *John Pike, a weapons specialist..., explained, "Systems generally require time-synchronization in order to talk to each other.* *A lot of systems use time-synchronization as a way to establish data links.* *So, if one computer says it is 1900 and another says its 2000, 'they can't talk to each other."*

FEMA

At press time, the Federal Emergency Management Agency was (allegedly) only 47% mission critical compliant, which raises an interesting question: *Who* will save *FEMA* during a Y2K emergency? It's like a fire station not being able to put out its own blaze.

The FAA

IBM informed the FAA that:

> [T]*he* [40] *computers at the heart of the control centers, which handle high-altitude, long-distance air traffic,* **were so old that no one at IBM knew how to check them for Y2K problems.**
> -- *New York Times on the Web,* 4 May 1998

The FAA has drugged its heels on Y2K and wasted critical time. I would *not* trust the air traffic control system in 1/2000. I have inside knowledge of one particular American airline that will ground *all* of its flights during 1-3 January 2000. Many pilots in general will refuse to fly on New Year's Eve and Day, so Raymond Long (director of airway services for the FAA) may have difficulty making good on his haughty promise to fly cross-country at midnight 12/31/99. *Bon voyage!*

The IRS

> *It's hard to imagine how things could get much worse for the IRS. It is taking a beating on Capital Hill, it's struggling to keep up with an ever more complicated tax code, its aging computers are falling apart, and it will soon launch a top-to-bottom management overhaul. Now, the Internal Revenue Service faces a potential calamity: a meltdown triggered by the Year 2000 computer glitch--and the guy in charge of keeping the data systems running just quit.* (Heh!)
> - www.businessweek.com/premium/08/b3566148.htm

Arthur Gross, Assistant Commissioner and Chief Information Officer, told Congress that the Ø4 billion/11 year IRS computer upgrade project failed. The IRS cannot keep up with the Ø1 billion/year maintenance of their 63 mainframes. Then, in April 1998, he bailed and left government service. He commented on Y2K at a recent conference in Washington, D.C.:

> *Failure to achieve compliance with Year 2000 will jeopardize our way of living on this planet for some time to come.*

Compliance will begin to plummet in 1999, beginning with the self-employed. (I oughta know...)

> *When word* [of the entrepreneurs' successful noncompliance] *spreads to the general public, there will be a hue and cry--maybe at first against the evaders, but then against the employers who are sending in employees' money when the self-employed people are escaping. Meanwhile, cash-only, self-employed businesses will begin to lure business away from tax-compliant businesses by offering big discounts.*

> *This will start happening all over the world. Once it begins, it will not easily be reversed. The* [income] *tax system rests on this faith: (1) the government will pay us what it owes us; (2) the government can get us if we stop paying. Both aspects of this faith will be called into question in the year 2000 if the governments' computers are not in compliance.*
> -- info@garynorth.com

There is a *very* good chance that the federal income tax will be replaced with a national sales tax in 1999 (or 2000, if technologically possible). If you can postpone tax payments until 2000, then you'll probably be home free. The IRS, of course, will expect this, so count on your IRA, 401k, etc. to be congressionally frozen by fall 1999. No kidding. Believe me, that artificial tax-free corral has an imminent gate just waiting to slammed shut.

The SSA

They are allegedly the first federal agency to discover the Y2K problem, in 1989. They've done the most work in computer repair, and even they won't be ready until 2001. Also, since the Treasury Department's Financial Management Service is responsible for sending out Social Security checks, 42 million elderly and disabled people will likely be cut off.

Medicare

Medicare has *not* renewed the contracts of the 70 companies which administer nearly a billion yearly claims from 38 million people, but is trying to bring their transaction system in-house under one giant computer system.

The IRS spent 11 years and Ø4 *billion* to fail at the same thing. Medicare *knows* that their new computers are not compliant, and they want the 70 companies to fix the Y2K problem before they leave. The chance of that is about the same as you or me putting super unleaded gas in a rental car...

GPS

> The GPS Year 2000 problem has to do with the three parts of the operational system: the space component, the ground control component, and the portable user interface component.
> There are about two dozen satellites mounted on six orbital planes continuously broadcasting navigation signals.
> Ground stations that receive and upload correlation data to the main GPS contractor, with planned deployment in mid-1999. There

> *are six monitor stations, four ground antennas and one master control station, currently using software written in the 1960's that has two-digit [year] dates. This software has been modified and has to be fielded in a way that supports upgrading the satellite uplink interfaces to also handle new four-digit [year] dates.*
> ***The remaining problems are with the user interface component, which has an earlier clock rollover problem.*** *GPS receivers use a 10-bit field for weeks since [6] January, 1980. To get the current date, they compute the days since the base and divide successively to get the increments for year, month, and day. Given the limit to 1024 weeks, input values at receivers using the 1980 base date will roll over on August 22, 1999. Many recent models, including any procured through the JPO, will use the real date of the last reference to compute the current date, rather than the saved 1980.... Some commercial models may still be* (using) *1980....*
>
> -- www.mitre.org/research/cots/GPS.html

Why is GPS so important? Because the vital systems of defense, power, banking, and communications all use GPS to coordinate their operations. Remember, our artificial work has evolved to the point of pseudo-organism, and time-based processes are at the heart of its "nervous system." We call a misfiring nervous system *epilepsy*. Technological "epileptic" seizures are exactly what to expect through 1999, peaking on 1/1/2000.

Final comments

Reading an October 1998 article in *The Free American*, the two-digit year field was purposely mandated by the feds:

> *Warning, logical and maintenance flaws have been discovered in the design of worldwide programming code and databases. These flaws will result in the collapse of the world's computer systems on or before 2000 A.D.*
> *How did it all begin?* ***On November 1, 1968****, the National Bureau of Standards issued a Federal Information Processing Standards Publication (FIPS PUB#4) where it* **specified** *the use of 6 digit dates for all information exchanged between Federal agencies.*
>
> -- Jerome T. Murray & Marilyn J. Murray; *Computers in Crisis--How to Avert the Coming Computer Systems Collapse*

This book (ISBN 089433-223-6; now OP) was written in *1984*! Mr. Murray worked for IBM and Honeywell, and had his warning been heeded *fourteen years ago,* Y2K could have been fixed.

So, don't look to the government to save us. They've known about this since at least 1989 (and maybe as early as 1968). Had President Bush orchestrated a "Manhattan Project" type of Y2K action in 1989, we'd be compliant by 2000. (We certainly wouldn't have a gridlocked military and doomed power plants.)   Clinton has so far uttered only 124 words on Y2K. Gore, 0. They are "leading" us over a cliff. (Newsflash: Gore just mentioned Y2K in a mid-October speech on global communications. Now we can relax.)

"WE'RE COMPLIANT!"

Unless they've done *extensive* mock 2000 rollovers, *nobody* can *truthfully* claim that they are compliant. *"We're compliant"* really means *"We're working on it."*   If they have not finished remedial work by 1998 to reserve *all* of 1999 for testing, then they will *not* be compliant in time. *Period.* Testing is at least *half* the work, and if they are not testing by the time you read this, then they "ain't gonna make it."   Claims to the contrary are mere smoke.

THE POLLYANNAS

We're having a great time now! Why bother with Y2K? I mean, there's money to be made. You can take over other companies. There's the global market place. You know, don't bother me with the Year 2000 problem; it's just annoying.... I've got to give you this analogy. **This is Titanic America.** *They went down to the ocean floor and they found the rivets. They brought the rivets up from the Titanic. They cut them in half. They found crystal in the metal.* **What sank the Titanic was...the rivets were defective! Think of computers as the rivets of our global economy.** *They're defective. And we're going full speed at night, in the middle of the Atlantic where it's freezing cold, and everything is brittle, straight for an iceberg. And we're dancing in steerage and having first class meals on top.*

-- Edward Yardeni, during a 2 June 1998 Y2K symposium

In fact, after a survey of the evidence, the occurrence of such a [Y2K] disaster now is only a very remote possibility, the most likely outcomes ranging from either a spate of annoying systems failures to the worst likely outcome, a moderate recession...

-- The John Birch Society website (www.jbs.org/y2k.htm)

The global telecommunications systems will not fail. The oil industry will not grind to a halt. The financial industry will be one of the most

stable of all industries.   ATM's, Debit cards, credit cards and cheques will not fail. The power grid will not collapse.
   -- Peter de Jager;
      www.year2000.com/archives/timeflies.html

"There's <u>no</u> Y2K problem, and I'm not <u>responsible</u> when everything collapses in 1999 and 2000!"

"Y2K will be serious, but nothing bad will happen.   NOTHING will occur other than inconveniencies or disruptions."
   This kind of thinking is rampant.   Clinton lied to a grand Jury, but he did not commit perjury. (BTP Note: Hey, he was "legally accurate.") Clinton had oral sex but he did not have a sexual relationship. Clinton fabricated cover stories, but did not tell anyone to lie.
   So go ahead, all you "wise" Pollyannas.   Do nothing.   Stay in the cities. Do not prepare.
   -- fedinfo@halifax.com

WILDCARDS

Gee, if that isn't bad enough, here are some others. We're truly between hawk and buzzard between now and 1/1/2000.

Natural disaster

One disastrous flood, hurricane, or earthquake could set off a market crash or bank run. (Don't forget about tidal waves, volcanic eruptions, tornados, major fires, electrical blackouts, wildfires, and riots.) An unusually harsh blizzard or ice storm in winter 99/00 would exacerbate an already gloomy situation.

Another interesting wrinkle will be the Leonid meteor shower in November 1998 (the most severe in 33 years), which peaks on the 17th or 18th with perhaps 100,000 meteors/hr. The shower is the result of passing through comet Temple-Tuttle. While the particles are smaller than a grain of sand, their velocity gives them the power of a .22LR. The 500 satellites are quite vulnerable to this barrage, and we could see communications, navigation, and weather systems knocked out. As O'Malley said, *"Life is just one damned thing after another."*

Terrorist attacks

Experts have long forecasted this. The Trade Center attack very nearly toppled that building and its 100,000 people.

For those interested in Biblical prophesy, Chapter 18 of Revelations is fascinating in which the decadent commercial port city of Babylon is destroyed. Three verses expressly say that the city is consumed by *fire,* and three *other* verses describe that destruction as occurring *in only one hour.* Read it for yourself and see if it doesn't *precisely* fit the scenario of New York City being wiped off the map by a nuclear device.

Surprise nuclear strike

It is projected that when the GPS satellite user interface 10-bit clock system rolls back 1024 weeks on 22 August 1999 that the West's ICBMs will be dead in their silos for lack of effective guidance systems. The missiles could be down only a week, or until 12/99. Boeing was contracted in 1996 to replace our ICBMs' IMOSC (Integrated Mission Operation Support Center), but will not do so until *December* 1999.

The Russian's ICBMs, however, do *not* use GPS. They use an older system known as gravitational mapping, based on mapped minor fluctuations of the earth's gravitational field. While it's not as accurate as GPS, it will be working until 2000. Yes, their military's systems will be toast on 1/1/2000, just like ours, but *they* will have a seventeen week monopoly window of ICBM capability. **From 22 August to as late as 31 December, they will be able to launch with impunity.**

The Russians haven't been our "friends" but for a few years. Could the Russian leadership resist this utterly historic opportunity when MAD (Mutually Assured Destruction) is not only "switched off," but on a date known well in advance? The U.S.A. outpaced the U.S.S.R.'s military expenditures until they couldn't afford to stay in the game. On 22 August 1999, the former U.S.S.R. will have arrived at a "short cut" that will last for up to 4 months. The temptation to use it might just be too great.

At the minimum, I expect some colossal behind-the-scenes nuclear blackmail. If you read of our sudden, massive bailout of Russia, their fall 1999 ICBM monopoly will most likely be the reason. (Note: Just after I wrote this, it was announced that we'd be sending them millions of tons of food for winter 1998.)

I personally will not be in *any* major American city after 21 August 1999. I wouldn't recommend that you be, either.

Studying maps of theoretical fallout deposition, areas which should escape not only nuclear attack, but fallout, are:

> northern California/southern Oregon
> west Texas Mexican border (Del Rio to Marfa)
> south Texas (Rio Grande Valley)

I've been to all three, and could recommend southern Oregon as the most pleasant. It's already well-known for its mild survivalist population, and the country abounds with water and game.

West Texas is big, empty, and *hot.* I don't think Mexico would take it back.

The Rio Grande Valley of Texas might be a cosmically choice spot, as everything there is said to happen 20 years later. Learning Spanish is a must, as the RGV is in truth more a part of Mexico than the U.S.A., and politically destabilized from the *colonias* (Third World squalor in a First World country).

Y2K COUNTDOWN TIMETABLE

Based on the best information possible, here is, *assuming* a full technological collapse, my forecast of probable events in their logical order. Please recall that I am *not* predicting such a full and utter collapse. **I am *extrapolating* likely events *from* an utter collapse.** Nobody can predict exactly *how* bad Y2K will be. I am not really trying to do so in *Boston of Surviving Y2K*. Although I believe that it will be *quite* bad, my position is not 100% Northian. (More like 70-80%.) Still, I wrote this book *assuming* a total meltdown so you'll have that kind of information just in case such happens.

One *very* possible scenario is a stock market crash in 1999, which could easily bring about martial law. The feds would be wise to preposition their troops inside the cities *before* 2000, and a market crash would provide the "best" excuse to do so.

The progression of mental acceptance

People come around to shocking, unpleasant truths at their own pace (if ever). As T.S. Eliot said:

Mankind cannot tolerate too much reality.

In educating your friends and family on Y2K, I would remind you of that well-proven (yet nearly unknown) psychological truth: You can't persuade others of *anything*--they can only persuade *themselves*. So, take it easy with them and serve up the Y2K meal in bite-sized portions.

❶ Ignorance stage
> *"What's 'Y2K'?"* You tell them. Then, they go to ❷ or ❸.

❷ Complacency/denial stage
> *"Oh, the government wouldn't allow things to get that bad"* or *"Somebody will find a fix for it."* They will either harden their denial, or they will let it gradually be eroded by facts.

❸ Awareness stage
> *"Yeah, this 'Y2K' thing may be a problem."*

❹ Growing concern stage
> *"Wow, the power grids might go down! We'd better have some extra food and water by Christmas 1999!"*
> Better, but the issue still hasn't hit home yet.

❺ Deep concern stage
> *"The power, phones, and banking system could be out for weeks or months! My family and friends are now working together on planning and purchasing, for solar energy, generators, food storage, and security."* Correct answer!

❻ Panic stage
> Prepared people rarely panic. It's when folks go from ❶ or ❷ or ❸ to ❺ in less than a week do they panic: *"It's December 31st and New York City's power went dead! The rolling blackout is headed this way! Get in the car--we've got to get to Albertsons before the hordes pick everything clean!"*
> (Nobody ever considers *himself* as part of the hordes...)

THE LOCUSTS

People never believe in volcanos until the lava actually overtakes them.
> -- George Santayana

Locusts are not all alike. If one prepares *early* enough, one is not a ravenous locust. Regardless, I'll lump us all in the locust category, by class, to most easily illustrate a certain progression in the public's attitude towards Y2K.

But nothing we do in 1998 can realistically be characterized as "panic"; panic is what will happen in late 1999 if a significant segment of the population suddenly decides that their money, their jobs, and their physical safety is seriously threatened. Stockpiling extra

food in 1998 might be considered unnecessary or crazy, but it could be labeled "hoarding" in late 1999 and declared illegal. Similarly, withdrawing some or all of one's funds from the bank in 1998 might be considered foolish, but if there is sufficient evidence of a real "panic" in late 1999, it will be declared illegal.
-- Ed Yourdon, www.yourdon.com/articles/y2k

Locust 1st Class

These people, primarily Christians, are the "remnant" that Dr. Gary North writes for. They have stockpiled by mid-1998, long before Y2K has intruded significantly on the public consciousness. Freeze-dried food, gold coins, battle rifles, ammo, generators, etc. were still plentiful and low priced at that time. Only these folks will have a surplus to help others.

Length of self-sufficiency: 6 months to indefinitely
Percentage of population: *infinitesimal* (maybe 50,000 people)

Locust 2nd Class

Stockpiled by December 1998, before Y2K falls within a 12 month horizon (the limit of the public's "long term" perception). As long as something is still "over a year away" people can easily ignore it. Critical goods widely available, though prices began to ratchet upwards.

Length of self-sufficiency: 3-18 months
Percentage of population: less than 1% (about 100,000 people)

Locust 3rd Class

Stockpiled before April 1999, when the public *really* begins to perceive a crisis impending. News on Y2K begins to heat up. There could be a stock market crash that spring, resulting in martial law in the larger cities.

Length of self-sufficiency: 3-12 months
Percentage of population: 1%

Locust 4th Class

Stockpiled before fall 1999, when Y2K anxiety finally became a national issue.

Length of self-sufficiency: 1-6 months
Percentage of population: 2%

Locust 5th Class

Will wait until December 1999 and then try to stockpile during the Christmas shopping rush.

Length of self-sufficiency: 1-3 months
Percentage of population: 5%

Locust 6th Class
Will wait until after Christmas to stockpile (good luck!).
Length of self-sufficiency: 1-4 weeks
Percentage of population: 10%

Locust 7th Class
Will wait until 31 December for actual news of the crash overseas, then rush down to KMart and Albertsons.
Length of self-sufficiency: 1-3 weeks
Percentage of population: 20%

Locust 8th Class
Will wait until his electricity goes out on 1 January before he joins the teeming hordes to pick over the bones of empty stores. He'll start out with less than a week's worth of food at home, and he'll forage maybe another week's worth. He represents about half the population.
Length of self-sufficiency: 1-2 weeks
Percentage of population: 50+%

The Unprepared
He *"won't live in fear"* and hasn't bought so much as an extra can of beans. He thinks Y2K is a hoax propagated by the computer companies, and even if it's not, the government will save him. He represents one out of ten Americans.
Length of self-sufficiency: several days
Percentage of population: 10%

1998 to 12/31/99

1998

Summer 1998
I first heard about Y2K in the summer of 1997, but didn't think much about it until the spring of 1998. I began this book in late July out of a burning sense of urgency to warn people.

The Y2K issue is beginning to simmer in the mainstream press. Even *USA Today* is carrying frequent articles on it.

Klinton's executive ban on imported "assault rifles" has increased their market price by about 50%. The days of the Ø100 SKS and the Ø400 Century Arms FAL are over, forever.

Congress killed Y2K emergency appropriations in June.

Fall 1998
Expect a *vast* multiplication of Y2K books, articles, and Websites. The sheep will begin to really take notice, yet delay most meaningful action until it's far too late.

November 1998
Perhaps the last free national elections to be held for quite a while. Campaigning congressmen will jeer the increasing spirit of survivalism, and assure us that America faces no Y2K crisis. (Don't panic the sheep before their new corral is built.)

December 1998
With Congress safely reelected and back in office, plans for 1999 and 2000 will quickly be implemented. **Remember, government is a disease which masquerades as its own cure.** The Social Security Administration has been working on their own Y2K problems since *1989,* so the feds have known about it for some time. They *need* a crisis to justify their "solution" of martial law and coercive global integration, which explains why they're dragging their feet on Y2K. They seem to *want* a Y2K crash. They want society to become unraveled so they can stitch it together in *their* fashion.

During 1999 government will work to see that the remaining avenues for self-sufficiency are closed off. Expect laws against "hoarding" (food and cash, especially).

The "National Instant Criminal Background Check" system goes on-line 1 December. All FFL *"transfers"* now logged in the FBI's computer. This will greatly hamper the gun shows (if not close many of them down since 60-95% of the exhibitors are FFL dealers). Unpapered private transfers remain lawful in those 24 fortunate states (mostly in the south and west). The public *finally* begins to realize that firearm availability is in a tightening noose. Good luck trying to find a privately sold AR15 or FAL after mid-1999.

1999

January 1999
Y2K now less than 12 months away to at last pierce the bovine consciousness of the public. You will have but a few months to finally acquire critical supplies at affordable prices. Once winter breaks, the masses will turn their attention more towards Y2K preparation.

Spring 1999

[W]hen the outside directors of publicly-traded companies begin re-signing in early 1999, [it's] because they've suddenly discovered that their Directors & Officers (D&O) insurance policies have a Y2K exclusion and that they're personally liable for any [Y2K] lawsuits.
         -- Ed Yourdon, www.yourdon.com/articles/y2k

The SIA Y2K testing fails and New York's 1 April fiscal 2000 rollover downs their many of their systems, bringing a stock market crash. *("April is the cruelest month"* according to T.S. Eliot.)   The feds might then activate their rumored plans for martial law on the 120 largest cities (from NYC to Warren, Michigan). Restrictions on cash withdrawals 80% likely at this time, 95% likely by summer, and 100% likely by fall.

Market crash or not, I would expect precious metals to finally begin their long overdue rebound as people transform checks into gold and silver (cash being limited to Ø50-100/week). Poignant enough, we could then expect the mandatory reporting of bullion purchases.

I forecast that unpapered private sales of firearms will at last be regulated or even banned, plus a return of ammo sale regulation. This will spur the Locusts 3rd Class into action.

Summer 1999

On 1 July, 46 states attempt to rollover to fiscal 2000, unsuccessfully. It is headline news for weeks. The public now *really* begins to panic. The 110 nuclear power plants must by 8/11 certify to the NRC that they are Y2KOK. They are not.

Foreign and domestic travel possibly at an all time high. Could be one's last chance for years to see Venice, or even Yellowstone. Y2K is easily pushed out of the public's focus; it's summertime and January is still 6 months away (an eternity!).

Locusts 4th Class (3% of the population) finish up their stockpiling. Supplies of critical items now quite tight with public awareness growing very quickly from here on.

Fall 1999

A sense of foreboding descends on the land as 1/1/2000 is correctly perceived to be just around the corner. Congress passes "anti-hoarding" laws with toll-free fink lines for snoopy neighbors to call in and report the self-sufficient. Cash withdrawal restrictions are in place by this time. By Executive Order, electricity rates *double* (ostensibly in preparation for Y2K problems, but mainly to decrease demand).

Phone calls and letters will at least triple as people contact their friends and family to deliver conditional "good-byes." (Send yours by *October* to avoid the Christmas/pre-Y2K rush.) Make sincere amends with all required. Have those deep talks you've put off for a lifetime. Work out personal differences. Learn to say *"I'm sorry"* and *"I love you."*

December 1999

1/1/2000 now within the "look-ahead" time of embedded systems and many show early 2000 compliance problems.

Many companies and individuals will not expect the banking system to last into 2000, so they will demand cash payment for their goods and services (even though Congress already restricted cash withdrawals).

Y2K is the topic of all conversation and a "sinking ship" atmosphere begins to form. Gloomy expectations aside, most people *still* have not deigned to prepare. (Close your eyes and maybe the bogeyman will go away. That's why Jews enroute to the concentration camps packed furs, silver, cameras, etc.) For the secular, this Christmas will be *especially* hollow.

The NRC shuts down the nukes on Sunday night, the 26th. Nearly half of the power is gone for the Northeast.

Thursday, 30 December 1999

All the TV and radio news stations will be trumpeting their tomorrow's coverage of the year rollover. Y2K disruptions will have already occurred *months* prior (as early as April) since many companies and countries rolled over on their *fiscal* calenders. Therefore, I expect the planet's mood to be gloomy and skittish. Read about March 1945 Berlin to get the proper flavor. Probably 15% of the population will call in "sick" for Friday.

Huge sarcastic TEOTWAWKI (tee-OH-tawa-kee; *The End of the World as We Know It*) parties will nonetheless be scheduled by the Pollyannas. Ostriches will rent videos and stay home.

The International Date Line was placed between Hawaii and New Zealand. Thus, Fiji and New Zealand will be the first countries to begin the year 2000. Hawaii will rollover 22 hours later, and then finally Midway Island an hour later.

0600 CST -- Friday, 31 December 1999

On Friday morning, 31 December 1999 at 6:00AM Central Standard Time (Chicago and Houston), New Zealand will rollover to 2000. Like a silent plague, the Y2K glitch will begin to sweep across the planet from east to west.

Two hours later, at 8:00AM CST, Sydney and eastern Australia will rollover. At 9:00AM, Seoul and Tokyo. At 10:00AM, Hong Kong and Singapore. Moscow at 3:00PM. Western Europe at 5:00PM. London at 6:00PM. The Labrador coast of North America at 10:00PM. (This is the first chance for cascading North American power blackouts.) New York City at 11:00PM. Chicago and Houston at midnight. Hawaii will enjoy an extra four hours; Midway Island an extra five. After Midway Island, it will be the year 2000 for the entire globe.

From sunrise on that last day in 1999, Americans will have 19 hours to follow the dark cloud of Y2K as it inexorably claims the planet. By breakfast, we will know if the electricity two-thirds around the world is shutting down from Y2K, and we'll know then if the crisis is for real or not. Billions of radios and TVs will be tuned in that morning for Y2K news.

What *will* happen if there's *no* Y2K crash

First of all, the phone lines will be swamped with billions of *"I told you it was all B.S.!"* phone calls. This will probably bring down the phone system temporarily.

The rejoicing will be savagely Bacchanalian. Hangovers to last for days. September will see many additional newborns.

Unneeded crisis supplies will be returned to stores by the carload. A national holiday will likely be declared. The stock market will rebound dramatically as buyers rush in to snap up the corpses. Y2K stocks, however, plummet.

What *will* happen if New Zealand crashes

I guess we can't make fun of their life-style anymore!
        -- from *Tremors*, when the town's "survivalist" couple kills
           one of the four giant worms with massive gunfire

The more savvy Locusts 7th Class will have camped out in the parking lots of the 24hr Walmarts and supermarkets, listening to the radio. When news of New Zealand's crash is confirmed, they will storm the stores for batteries, fuel (Coleman, propane, charcoal, etc.), canned food, fresh fruit, sleeping bags, toilet paper, tampons, guns, ammunition, tools, pharmaceuticals, etc.

(Locusts 6th Class will have already done their "shopping" hours or days *before* the news hits, correctly figuring that they can always return for refund their items if no crash occurs. A logical, no-risk hedge--assuming such goods can be *had* that late in the game.)

Credit cards will first be maxed out (if they're accepted at all, which I doubt), then checks tendered to their max approval limit (if accepted at all, which I doubt), and finally the hidden cash will be used. Prices will be much higher than normal.

Next, the gas stations will be descended upon by thirsty hoarders with huge tanks to be filled. When the hardware stores open up shortly afterwards, they too will be cleaned out. Same for the gun stores (assuming there's no federal/state moratorium on sales), and the drug stores. The liquor stores, however, will most assuredly be open as usual.

Once news *really* gets out, the Locusts 8th Class will leave work and emerge in hordes. Many Locusts 4th-6th Class will get spooked, demote themselves to 8th Class and join their ravenous brethren. The mass exodus from the cities begins, immediately choking up the freeways.

The Unprepared will be trying to phone their local police department, demanding that the cops *"do something."*

The Locusts 1st-3rd Class will sit out the panic at home, gloating over their foresight, sacrifice, and discipline.

Phone lines will be swamped with billions of *"I told you it wasn't all B.S.--hunker down!"* phone calls. This will on its own bring down the phone systems before the stroke of midnight.

Most flights are cancelled, leaving thousands of holiday travellers stranded in airports.

The mourning will be intense. Many suicides. Hangovers to last for days. September will see many additional newborns.

Now the "fun" begins. Here follows my worst-case scenario. I truly hope to God I'm wrong.

2000

Week 1 -- 1-7 January

Electronic banking locks up. Nobody gets paid by automatic deposit. Checks are not delivered by mail, and local checks aren't accepted, anyway. Banks are not open to cash checks, and cash withdrawals have been restricted for months.

Twenty million Americans are immediately out of work, with no gold or silver coins, no power, little cash, and a week of food. Airlines are grounded. The public panics.

Unchecked looting and pillaging. Every ATM is broken open. Highly-skilled robbery crews take planned advantage of failed security alarms and busy police to pounce on banks, jewelry stores, etc. Local police (numbering only 3 for every 1,000 people) are overwhelmed by Day 2. The public begins to comprehend the enormity of the collapse. Martial law is declared with a 5PM curfew, but is too late in arriving and highly erratic.

Return of power is sporadic as new Y2K problems continue to be uncovered. Those with generators must guard them, as they're stolen within minutes of being starting up.

Uneaten food rots in millions of refrigerators (make jerky quickly). As the canned food runs out, the hunger pangs begin for the Locusts 8th Class and the Unprepared--meaning 60% of the population.

The railroads are frozen up from Y2K, and 90% of the planes are grounded.

Week 2 -- 8-14 January

Food begins to run out for Locusts 7th Class (20%). 80% of the population feel shrinking bellies. These people generally have no camping or wood stoves to cook with. Many asphyxiate themselves from cooking indoors with charcoal.

The cities looted and under erratic martial law, the hungry masses now slip into the countryside in desperation. Trees are cut down by the millions for firewood, and wildlife is slaughtered. Some of this is halted by armed countryfolk.

Week 3 -- 9-21 January

Food running out for Locusts 6th Class (10%). 90% of the population are now going hungry to some degree. Situation becoming critical as some people are beginning to starve to death. Deaths by hypothermia increasing dramatically.

Some help from government begins to be felt, but it's too little, too late. The U.S. Army begins to lose control of the inner cities, and many troops desert *en masse*. Permanent despair setting in. Suicides increasing.

Week 4 -- 22-28 January

Locusts 5th Class (5%) now running out of food. 95% of the population now foraging frantically for food. Rumors of cannibalism rampant. 2.8 million, 1% of the population, now dead from cold, starvation, violence, and suicide.

Roving road-warrior gangs begin to form, many from ex-Army units. Military bases now under siege, often by their former comrades.

Month 2 -- February

Locusts 4th Class (3%) begin to run out of food. 98% of the population now going hungry. Cities barricade themselves by zones. Well-stocked towns become city-states.

Things begin to settle down slightly as the initial shock and panic is over. The battle for simple survival is viewed with increasing rationality. "Flea markets" spring up by the tens of thousands, acres in size. Bartering farmers from the country begin to arrive with produce and meat, trading sacks of potatoes for grand pianos.

Month 3 -- March

Society reverts to classic tribalism and race wars begin in the bigger cities. On this issue, *The Coming Race War* by Carl Rowan, or *Civil War 2* by Thomas Chittum. City leaders are killed or have fled, collapsing all metropolitan government.

Total dead now at 8 million, or 3% of the population.

Month 4 -- April

Gardens being planted in the southern states. Some power being restored on a rationed basis to government and industry. Small towns beginning to pull together.

The cities only get worse, being totally controlled by several tribal groups. Their surrounding countryside begins to physically cordon them off with barriers and armed patrols. Countryfolk issue themselves makeshift IDs.

Month 5 -- May

Gardens being planted in the middle states.

The U.S.A. now broken up *de facto* as the Federal Government cannot maintain national cohesiveness.

Month 6 -- June

Gardens being planted in the mountain/northern states.

Massive refugee movement into the western states. Much of this is blocked at the state line by terrified citizens.

Civil war now occurring in a dozen states.

A different perspective...

In Robert A. Heinlein's 1964 novel *Farnham's Freehold*, a family weathers out a devastating nuclear war in their well-stocked bomb shelter. The husband, Hugh, muses to his wife:

"Barbara, I'm not as sad over what has happened as you are. **It** *might be good for us.* *I don't mean us six; I mean our country."*
She looked startled. "How?"

"Well--It's hard to take the long view when you are crouching in a shelter and wondering how long you can hold out. But--Barbara, I've worried for years about our country. **It seems to me that we** **have been breeding slaves--***and I believe in freedom. This war may have turned the tide.* **This may be first war in history which** **kills the stupid rather than the bright and able--where it makes** **any distinction."**

"How do you figure that, Hugh?"

"Well, wars have always been hardest on the best young men. This time the boys in service are as safe or safer than civilians. **And** **of civilians those who used their heads and made preparations** **stand a far better chance.** **Not every case, but on the average,** **and that will improve the breed.** **When it's over, things will be** **tough, and that will improve the breed still more.** **For years the** **surest way of surviving has been to be utterly worthless and** **breed a lot of worthless kids.** **All that will change."**

She nodded thoughtfully. *"That's standard genetics.* *But it seems cruel."*

"It is cruel. **But no government yet has been able to repeal** **natural laws, though they keep trying."** (p.29-30)

Similarly, Y2K may be the first disaster *"which kills the stupid rather the bright and able--where it makes any distinction."* The modern welfare society has elevated sloth and squalor to a higher level than industriousness and prosperity, and such cannot be maintained forever. Every attempted loafer's paradise has turned into a hellhole. Y2K could act as sort of an organic fever to burn off the parasites. The national host will be sick for quite a while afterwards, but it will recover.

❖ 3

Location, Location, *Location!*

If you live within five miles of a 7-11, you're toast.
  -- Paul Milne, chief Y2K alarmist

Where you choose to be in 1999-2000 will be the *most* important decision you can make regarding the Y2K Crash. If, for example, you *knew* a hurricane was approaching Florida, would you stay in Miami? Well, there is a technological *tsunami* scheduled to arrive in summer/fall 1999, which will *peak* in 2000. Why stay in dangerous areas?

LEAVE THE BIG CITIES!

The urban hordes will be hungry and pissed off in January 2000. Looting, rioting, and raping will be common. Pillaging, too. Also, if you believe Carl Rowan's book, *The Coming Race War in America: A Wakeup Call*, then any major city with a high black population will erupt in very ugly violence once food and power are cut off. NYC, for example, is building a Ø15,000,000 emergency control center which is bombproof and bioproof. Sell your Manhattan condo to some sucker and get out. (Programming expert and Y2K "alarmist" Ed Yourdon sold his NYC apartment and moved to New Mexico.)

In combat gunnery it will seldom be a one on one proposition. Humans are a gregarious lot, and they form all kinds of groups and clubs for noble purposes. If the purpose is immoral and violent, we call their group a gang. That's probably what you'll be facing. What will they be like?

Most of these people will be under-educated slow-to-think types who are alive because they compensated for stupidity by becoming street-wise and ruthless. As always, a gang has more power than the individuals who make it up. Underestimating them would be a mistake. **They won't give up. They can't. They are ruled by pride, and they would rather die brave than live as cowards.** *They have lived in fear of dying all their lives and have adjusted; you cannot intimidate them. Once committed to taking your property or your family, they won't back off.*

-- Don Paul; *Great Livin' In Grubby Times,* pp. 37-38

So, if you're too dumb to stay, then maybe you "deserve" the consequences (but your children won't).

Mind you, I'm not suggesting that you [merely] *lock up the house or the apartment or the business and get out of town for a few days while the storm blows over. Your actions must be stronger than that.* Sell all your property within thirty miles *of a major city. Pack up your belongings and your family and get away while it is possible to do so.* **Do this now before property values drop like a rock.** *Start life anew in a small community where welfare programs are a relative rarity. Live in a community where the local churches and charities will be able to take care of the needy if things get really bad because of Y2K.* (at 178)

-- Jim Lord; *A Survival Guide For The Year 2000 Problem*

Food is important, too, but only with this provision: you really do intend to locate a safer place to live than a city of 100,000 or more people. It does no good to store food...for the expected looters. If you say to yourself, "What good is my food when I live here?" you have just provided yourself with a first-rate reason for moving. Don't blame the vulnerability of food; blame your geography. **If you live in an area where the food is too risky to store, then you absolutely have to move. Not maybe; absolutely. Soon.** (at 277)

-- Dr. Gary North; *Government by Emergency* (1983)

How to sell your urban domicile

Do *not* tell people (especially the Realtor) that you're moving away because of Y2K, else you'll be classified as a "motivated seller" who will accept a low offer. Price your property about 10% under market value. Do not owner carry, as you want cash and liquidity, not a note from a stranger. Keep your new destination private and tell the curious that you'll be moving just outside of town, or travelling.

GET TO THE COUNTRY, *NOW!*

I'd go in with a few good families and buy (under an anonymous Nevada corporation, preferably one with tax-free status) at least 50 acres (your per/acre cost goes down dramatically) with plenty of water and timber, and develop it as you all see fit. Each family needs at least 10 acres for privacy.

If 1/1/2000 is a non-event, *so what?* You'll have a self-sufficient country home with good neighbors.

THE UNITED STATES OF AMERICA

The U.S.A. varies greatly in matters important to your Y2K planning, such as climate, cultural attitude, work ethic, politics, and individual responsibility. Some regions and states are more like foreign countries to each other.

The Northeast

Very highly populated, highly socialistic, and a cold climate. Nuclear plants supply 40-50% of its electricity. You'd be better off to move.

If, however, you're stuck in the Northeast there are many rural areas where you can make the best of probably the most vulnerable region in the country. Rural Vermont (no gun control!), New Hampshire (*"Live Free or Die!"*), and Maine (which generates nearly 50% of its electricity from independent sources) are the better choices.

The Deep South

Manageable winters, good ag land and growing seasons, and moderate population density would otherwise make the South a good region except for one thing. It's a racial timebomb which will explode once the food stamps no longer arrive. White flight has been accelerating for years, and for good reasons. Read Thomas Chittum's *Civil War 2* (from Loompanics). South Florida might be vulnerable to Cuba's Soviet-built Chernobyl nuclear reactors. Avoid South Carolina because it relies on nukes for 50% of its power.

The western "panhandle" of Florida, the Ozarks, the Cumberland mountains, and the rural North Carolina would be my picks in the Deep South.

The Midwest

Hot summers, cold winters, and moderate population density. I don't care for the region's topographical indefensibility (*e.g.*, like Poland). Their people are often slavish and obedient, so the mavericks run greater risk of being squealed on for "hoarding" food, fuel, etc.

North Dakota is known as the "Saudi Arabia of wind energy" and the other Plain States are also very windy.

The Rocky Mountains

This is one of my favorite regions. While the winters can be quite harsh (Solution: Wear a coat. Build a greenhouse.), the cold *does* have the advantage of keeping out most of the roaches (whatever their leg count, 2 or 8). **During any post-crash days I'd rather be amongst "Ice People" than "Sun People."** This region is the "Switzerland of America" and would be the *last* to be occupied militarily, if ever. With a good greenhouse, you can grow fresh food year round. With an earth-bermed or underground house, your heating bills are negligible.

It's hard to go wrong in western Montana, western Wyoming, and western Colorado. Avoid Colorado's Eastern slope to keep at least 100 miles west of Denver and the Springs.

The Southwest

Basically, Texas, New Mexico, Arizona, and Nevada. Not as good as the Rockies, but much better than the Northeast and the Deep South. The further north, the better.

The Northwest (Wash., Oregon, Idaho)

Very water rich. While Seattle has far too many people, the Olympic peninsula is less crowded with better weather. The San Juan islands are beautiful, but vulnerable strategically. Eastern Washington north of Spokane is pretty nice. Ditto for Southern Oregon around Medford (where real estate brokers are very busy selling Y2K havens). Northern Idaho is lovely.

California

I wouldn't be south of Redding. Northern California should do pretty well with its southern Oregon neighbor.

If you're *anywhere* near Los Angeles, *get out!* Come 1/2000 there will be 20 million very hungry people seeking food. 100,000 of them will be armed *gangsta* dirtbags. While San Diego is much better than L.A., it borders with Mexico.

Alaska

"The last 'best' place." Unsurpassed terrain, and liberty loving individualists. Lots of privacy. Remote and cold. Expensive. Only the hardest-core folks should consider Alaska. Livable exceptions include the Southeast (from Ketchikan to Yakutat), Price William Sound, and the Kenai Peninsula.

Hawaii

Lovely, lush climate with generally friendly people. Very little domestic manufacturing, so life there will become *very* basic if the Crash lasts longer than 6 months. Oahu contains 91% of the population but less than 10% of the land area, so pick a smaller island.

Non-ethnic residents might experience persecution from native Hawaiians. The Federal Government *did*, after all, steal that sovereign island one hundred years ago.

WHAT ABOUT FOREIGN COUNTRIES?

I'm staying in the U.S.A. It will see the least damage (though not *little* damage) and will recover from the Crash first. According to CIA spokesman Sherry Burns, Canada, Australia, and the U.K. are 6-9 months behind the U.S.A.; Western Europe is 9 months behind; Russia, Japan, China, Hong Kong, and other Pacific nations are 9-12 months behind. The Gartner Group forecasts that 50% of the world's companies in the oil, electrical, and gas utility industry will experience Y2K failures in mission critical systems.

I am comfortable here, can keep my guns, and it's the only country with a significant history of liberty. But, if you've notions to relocate elsewhere, I'll cover the rest of the world.

Canada

If I could take my guns with me, Canada would be a distant option. British Columbia is, I think, the best province.

Their people, however, strike me as rather childlike and naïve. They are also quite socialistic. (Remember, Canada was largely settled by Tories who fled the 1780s U.S.A. It shows.) Most Canadians are urbanites who will be very unprepared for 2000 and beyond. I'd rather be in Montana.

Mexico and Central America

Although we might have to slog through a Mexican standard of living for a few months, we'll rise above it. Latin America never has, and likely never will. If you *want* to live like a Mexican or Central American, then *Adios*. Western Costa Rica is your best bet. Some folks really like Panama and Belize.

The Caribbean

Pick a formerly Dutch island over a British one. They're better run and racial tensions are less pronounced. The Bahamas and Jamaica are out. Avoid Puerto Rico and the Dominican Republic (which borders Haiti!). The Caymans are too close to Cuba for my tastes, and who knows what old Fidel might do. The U.S. Virgin Islands are probably your best choice.

South America

Totally Y2K unprepared--especially Argentina and Venezuela. Too bad, as there are some choice spots, especially in Peru, Chile, and Argentina. Bolivia is known for its civilian gun ownership.

Australia and New Zealand

Y2K unprepared. Aussies can't own guns any more. Crime and drug use are far less than in the U.S.A., however.

New Zealand might be a fine choice. Great people, and lots of fish, game, water, and timber.

The South Pacific

Guam is a crime-ridden mess. Fiji is a good option. There is insufficient space here to cover dozens of islands.

Asia

Y2K unprepared and already suffering from depression. If you want to forever live like a 2nd or 3rd World Asian, then I'd go to Thailand or South Korea. The Philippines are corrupt and crime-ridden. Indonesians are quietly and slowly starving.

Middle East

Only Israel is studiously working on Y2K.

Europe

While I love Europe, I can't imagine being there in 2000. They are *quite* unprepared for Y2K and have chosen to spend all their computer tech time on the *Euro* currency conversion. Fatally silly. Besides, in only Switzerland, Norway, and the Czech Republic may civilians own firearms with any freedom.

Africa

Africa is Africa, and always will be. South Africa has *eight times* the murder rate of the U.S.A., a rape every ten minutes, and is now beginning its long-predicted massacre of whites and Christians. Johnanesburg now has over 2,600 carjackings a year. I know of one white family there whose house is surrounded by a 12' high, 7000V electric fence. God help them (and their two teenage daughters) if the power goes.

The high seas

While I'm not the mariner type, some of you are. If you've decided to ride out Y2K on your sailing yacht, then at least form a flotilla with some friends, as piracy is *already* a problem now and will increase in 2000. Have some firearms on board (*e.g.*, hard-chromed rifle with armor-piercing incendiary ammo). Stick with common *international* calibers (*e.g.*, 9mm, 8x57, etc.)

SO, WHERE *SHOULD* I GO?

In the McKeevers' *Self-Reliant Living*, they suggest:

1. Locate the *area* of the U.S.A. for your country retreat.
2. Find a desirable *town* within that area.
3. Check out *several* properties around that town.
4. Negotiate on 3+ properties for the best deal.
5. **Most important are water, soil, and septic approval.**
   The rest is subjective.

This is good, sound planning. Let's take each in order.

Within an area that:

has mountain valleys with hidden southern exposure.
   Offers privacy, security, and winter sun.

is 200+ miles from major cities and 100+ miles from the Interstate.
   This will keep you away from the motoring urban hordes.

has *abundant* water.
   Not average or "O.K." water, but *abundant*. Water is life.

has a good climate.
   Decent rainfall, growing season, and temp. extremes.

is not prone to floods, hurricanes, tornados, or earthquakes.
   While tornados and earthquakes can happen almost anywhere, avoid "Tornado Alley" or fault lines.

has minimal danger to nuclear blast and fallout.
   A good reason not to live near big cities or military bases.

is not right on the coast.
   Don't be vulnerable to tidal waves and seafaring attack.

From big city to country, from East to West, from South to
North. I'd pick Montana (few people), Wyoming (no people!),
Idaho, Oregon, or Colorado. The Medford, Oregon area is good.

Near a town that:

has 500-5,000 people.
   Large enough to for diversity of talent.

is not a "New Age" or cult-oriented "Mecca."
   Wimberley (Texas), Sedona (Arizona), Taos (New Mexico)
   and others have rather odd reputations. These towns
   have good "harmonics" or "energy" and get swamped by
   "New Age" hippy types. You can do better.

is not a resort area.
That's where many city folks will *first* think of going to.
Besides, these places are too "artsy-fartsy" and full of
puffball, wimpy people (locals and tourists alike).

is *not* dependent on one company or industry.
Some towns in Michigan are totally reliant on the auto in-
dustry. If chocolate sales dried up, so would Hershey, PA.
Look for a town with a mix of industry, ag, and services.

is not *utterly* dominated by a particular church denomination or sect.
Some towns will lean more towards one or another, but a
de facto town religion might persecute newcomers.

does not seem to have a pawn shop on every other corner.
Such implies impoverished, lazy, irresponsible people.

has citizens of hard-working, moral character.
Some areas (often college and resort towns) are magnets
to fleabags. A town is its kids. Look for FFA-types.

produces its *own* varied food supply.
Cattle, orchards, crops, gardens, fishing, and hunting.

has a good hospital, library, schools, and organic farmers market.
Self-explanatory.

has all the basic services and a few luxury ones.
E.g., medical, auto, home, recreation, food, etc.

has nonexistent or conducive zoning/building regulations.
Circumvention is possible, but it's too involved for here.

has tolerable taxes.
Again, lawful circumvention *is* possible, *but...*

has tolerable local politics.
Avoid any town/county with a *hint* of political corruption.

Notice that most of my criteria were *people*-based? Good folks
can make an average area a paradise, while creeps can make
the Garden of Eden a dump.

Again, avoid the modern "hippy" areas near ski resorts.
While these poverty-groveling people are often communal and
self-sufficient, their indifferent personal hygiene and odd beliefs will annoy "normal" folks pretty quickly. Yes, I'm painting
with an unkind and broad brush, but I've been there. Every advanced nation in decline suffers its hippy stage in which perfectly well-fed, educated middle-class youths reject their

parents' culture for paganism. These modern hippies with their incessant drumbeating are nothing new. First records of this are from ancient Rome. 1920s Weimar Germany had its *Wandervoegeln* (Wandering Birds) which sported long, stringy, unwashed hair and blue-tinted glasses. Not to worry. They fade away (or die out) during every depression and famine.

with a property that:

is in a mountain valley with private southern exposure.
> You'll need southern exposure for the winter sun. You want privacy so that nobody sees your solar panels, etc.

is *abundant* in water, both surface and underground.
> An uphill spring feeding a cistern is ideal.
> A good well is vital, preferably one with 10+gpm flow.

has good soil for sufficient growing.
> Have it tested for alkalinity and salt content.

has a septic permit.
> If you can't handle your own sewage, you're in a mess.
> Make your offer contingent on a well and septic approval.

has congenial (or at least very private) neighbors.
> Poor neighbors can make your Paradise a hell.

has good, maintained roads.
> Ask around to know the quality of county maintenance.

is already fenced.
> This will save you ØØØØ and weeks of work.

has a cabin, barn, and other outbuildings.
> Unless you find property with exactly the house you want, you'll have to build. If a cabin and barn are already there, then you have a place to live and work while building. Another option is to install a mobile home or RV.

is large enough for animals, shooting, and privacy.
> 5 acres is considered the *minimum* for raising animals.
> 10 acres is probably the minimum for a 100yd range.
> 20-40 acres are probably necessary for real privacy.

backs up to National Forest or BLM land.
> You then have an almost limitless "backyard" full of game.

offers owner financing.
> This is much more private than mortgage banking, and the terms are usually much more flexible.

❖ **4**

WEAPONS

I want to have extra stuff to help people, but I don't want people to help themselves to my stuff.
  -- my local pastor, on owning guns for the Y2K crash

Weapons are necessary now, and will be *vital* during Y2K. If you can't *defend* your home and food storage, then why *have* it?

FIREARMS

While you should already have my *Boston on Guns & Courage*, I'll reiterate, abridge, and amplify on guns for this chapter. Every person of gunbearing ability needs, *at bare-bones minimum*, a handgun and a rifle. I personally own many guns. Some are spares for myself, friends and family; some are trading *wampum*; and some are rather superfluous collectibles.

I'd get your necessary guns *today*. I'm looking at a July *1988* copy of the *Shotgun News*. All semi-autos were "pre-ban"; mags were cheap and plentiful. The prices will make you weep:

Swedish M38 carbines in exc. condition	Ø 90
FR-7 .308 carbines	Ø115
FN-49s	Ø126
Chinese AK-47s	Ø275
M1 Garands	Ø299
M1As (w/Ø4 mags!)	Ø325
AR15s	Ø395
Belgian FALs (w/Ø4 mags!)	**Ø595!**
AUGs (w/Ø25 mags!)	**Ø870!**
Belgian paratrooper FALs	Ø875

Ten years later in July 1998, AR15s are Ø900+; Belgian FALs are Ø2,500+; and AUGs *begin* at Ø2,800. Even Ø100 SKSs are now getting Ø175+. *Do I have your attention?* Good.

Now listen to me *very carefully*: The queasy wistfulness you feel *right now* over the 1988 prices is *exactly* how you'll feel by fall 1999 over *1998's* prices. You might even feel *worse*.

By 2000, *forget* about acquiring an AR15 or FAL. What you have by mid-1999 is what you'll probably have for many years, or even rest of your life. (At least *plan* on that.)

You can never have your guns *too* early. If you are unarmed, then guns are a bargain at *any* price because defending your family's lives is (or *should* be) worth *all* of your assets. I'd go into *debt* if necessary to arm my family and close friends. The November 1998 issue of *Guns* (p.104) reported that California gun dealers are seeing markedly increased sales to computer and electronics professionals who foresee Y2K disruption.

Your handguns
Q: *"What if I could have only one handgun?"*
A: Get a Glock, in .40S&W, and probably the M23.

Glocks work flawlessly right out of the box and rarely break. Having only 35 parts (versus 57 to nearly 80 for a Colt 1911), there are fewer *to* break, anyway. They are indifferent to poor and abusive conditions. Remember that I can only highlight the *best* equipment in this chapter, so if you're still unconvinced, then get *Boston on Guns & Courage* for more argument on this issue. In a word, you can't go wrong with a Glock.

Which caliber?

It's between the 9mm, .357SIG, .40S&W, 10mm, and .45ACP. Although the **.357SIG** is an excellent caliber, it's far too new to be common enough. The **10mm**, though also excellent, has yet to really catch on and isn't common at all.

While **9mm** *might* have edge in ammo availability, the .40S&W and .45ACP are *significantly* better stoppers in a fight.

Since the **.45** Glock comes only in the full-size Model 21 and the compact Model 30 (too new to appear on the used market in any numbers), I prefer the .40S&W models.

The **.40S&W** is really the best of both 9mm and .45ACP worlds. It's got nearly the mag capacity of the 9mm and nearly the stopping power of the .45. It's also the cops' caliber of choice so ammo is/will be common.

Most cops have gone to the .40S&W, and of them most have chosen the Glock (usually the Model 22). I like the compact Model 23 over the 22. The 23 can use the 15rd mags of the 22, and is more easily concealable. The micro 27 is smaller still, but recoils more than the 23 and is more difficult to train with. **All things considered, I'd choose the Model 23 for my only handgun.** Used, the 23 goes for Ø425-500. If *very* deep concealment is required, then choose the micro Model 27.

Regarding .45 Glocks, if a private sale Model 30 was available, then such would be tied for first with the 23. Model 21s are superb pistols, though quite large and hard to conceal, and concealability will be *quite* important in the near future.

Simply because of the vast ammo stocks, I'd also own Glocks in 9mm and .45ACP. If I were in some foreign country, then 9mm would clearly be the caliber of the realm.

Don't shoot lead bullets in a Glock, as the hexagonal rifling leads badly, which produces unwanted higher pressures.

Glock magazines

Although pre-ban high-cap mags are Ø50-85, post-ban 10rd mags are only Ø18 from CTD. Use high-cap mags for duty, and 10rd mags for training. While I'd love high-cap mags all around, I don't feel significantly underarmed with 10rd mags. Remember, a handgun is only what you use to fight your back to your *rifle.* You don't *go* to a fight with a mere handgun; you only get *caught* in a fight *without* your rifle.

Attend Thunder Ranch for Defensive Handgun 1, *ASAP.*

Q: *"What should be my 2nd handgun?"*
A: A *quality* backup in at least 9mm/.38 Special.

Sometimes, a backup handgun is the quickest way to "reload." Such has saved the lives of countless cops. Ideally, for inventory's sake, it should be in the same caliber as your primary handgun, though this is not absolutely necessary.

Autos: The micro Glock 27 backs up the 23 beautifully. The Makarov in 9x18 is a solid, reliable bargain at Ø175-225.

Revolvers: A *quality* snub-nose .38 Special or .44 Special. (The .357 Mag has too much muzzle flash--*stupefying*, actually--which will temporarily blind you at 2:00AM.)

Q: *"What should be my 3rd handgun?"*
A: Probably a .22LR, such as the Ruger MarkII.
These are excellent for training, plinking and pest control. Younger children can shoot it.

For a full size pistol, get a Ruger MarkII for Ø175-200. For tiny back ups, get a Beretta 21A or Taurus PT-22 for Ø165.

Q: *"What should be my 4th handgun?"*
A: A second model of your *first* handgun.
This is your spare for caching or for a friend, or in case your first handgun is lost or stolen. Remember in the movie *Aliens* when Bishop had a second shuttle brought down from the mother ship to replace the one that had crashed? Inside was an identical full complement of weapons to replace the ones lost. Only then could Ripley lock and load. Have a spare handgun.

Ammo for your handguns

Have several thousand rounds of quality FMJ (full metal jacket) ball. While the specialty defensive ammo (MagSafe, CorBon, etc.) are better stoppers than FMJ, FMJ is the most *reliable* ammo and it's also the least expensive.

Why several *thousand* rounds? Because there's no such thing as "too much" ammo--*ever*. One can easily go through 200rds in an afternoon of practice. You'll shoot 1,000-1,500rds during 5 days of Thunder Ranch. Have oodles of ammo. What you don't need, somebody else *will*. Count on it.

For your .22LR, get 10,000rds (relax, this will cost only Ø200) of copper-plated (to avoid lead on your fingers) ammo. Each brick of 500rds will run you only Ø10 at any WalMart, etc. If there's no such thing as "too much" ammo, then there's *really* no such thing as "too much" *.22LR* ammo because nearly *every* gunowner has a .22LR of some kind. We may be using .22LR shells like nickels after 2000.

Gear and spare parts for your handgun

Kydex® belt holsters and mag pouches from Mad Dog Tactical (520-772-3021/3022fax). They're simply the best.

Have a Model 6Z Sure-Fire flashlight and pouch (from CTD), several spare bulbs, and *dozens* of Duracell 123A 3V lithium batteries (they store for years).

Necessary spare parts are mag springs, mainsprings, firing pins, and extractors. (Glocks rarely break at all. I've *read* of a trigger bar once breaking.) Have an extra set of sights since they can and do break (and always at the worst moments). An extra barrel also couldn't hurt in case yours is damaged from an overpressure load.

Your shotgun

Skeet and dove hunting shotguns have long, unwieldy barrels, 5 shell capacity, and poor sights. Trying to fight with one of these is like trying to take a 4x4 road in a Porsche 911. Why own incapable equipment that works *against* you?

If you live in the city, get one of these "riot" 12 gauge pumps with an extended mag tube: a Remington 870 or a Winchester 1300 Defender. It must have a full-length pistol-grip rear stock (Choate), ghost-ring rear sight, SideSaddle, and sling. A forestock Sure-Fire flashlight is also necessary. CTD has most of these accessories, so shop there first.

Your rifles

If I could have only *one* firearm, it would be a *rifle*. A rifle is what you *go* to a fight with, not a handgun. Your rifle must be able to quickly and reliably deliver an incapacitating blow to distant lethal threats. It must be highly ergonomic and rugged.

Q: *"What if I could have only one rifle?"*
A: Make it a *very* accurate .308 semi-auto battle rifle.

.223 or .308?

*No responsible deer hunter would shoot an animal at 300 yards with [a .223 or 7.62x39], and I find it odd that they are considered suitable for a human--the most dangerous animal on earth (because only a human can inflict injuries from a distance). I do not believe we need to take bear cartridges to war, **but we do need to take white-tail cartridges, at least.** (Here, here! BTP)*
          -- Timothy J. Mullin; *Testing the War Weapons*, p. 410

Since rifles are for neutralizing long-distance threats, choose the .308 over the .223. Although the .223 will sometimes (and even often) suffice as your main battle rifle caliber, it's in all honesty limited to 300yds through light cover, while a .308 will penetrate 12" of tree, or drop a bad guy out to 800yds. You can hunt deer and elk with a .308, but not with a .223. **Get a .308 first.** Its only drawback is increased weight and recoil, although both are easily manageable.

The .308 FAL

I prefer an FAL because of its excellent ergonomics, reliability, accuracy, Ø7 mags, and vast parts availability.

Since the pre-ban Belgian and Argentine FALs are Ø2,500+, the only *affordable* alternative is the America-made FAL by DSA (847-223-4770; www.dsarms.com). They use Austrian Steyr blueprints and CNC equipment to manufacture the metric receivers, and the quality is outstanding.

Which model? *Not* the 16¼"bbl SA58 Carbine, because of reduced velocity and increased muzzle blast. *Not* the SA58 Standard because of the steel handguard (which gets too hot to hold). The bull barrel models are too heavy (but would make a good pseudo-sniper rifle). I'd pick the 21" medium contour barrel (has the cooler synthetic handguard), and in stainless for an extra Ø50. Dealer cost is Ø1,200; retail Ø1,520. (The medium and bull barrels are cryo treated, which is well worth the extra price.) Replace the short, unreachable safety with an L1A1 version (look in *Shotgun News* for FAL parts distributors).

The recent "sporter" FALs (inch pattern uppers on metric receivers) from Century Arms for Ø600 are O.K. I'd replace the awful folding stock with a "Dragunov" version, and the folding bolt handle with a Belgian knob (both from DSA). While such a domestic post-ban semi-auto may have a pistol grip stock, it legally may not also have a flash suppressor.

If my FAL were needed for long-distance work, I'd install (on top a DSA #620-A base) an Elcan scope (Ø650).

DSA offer used Austrian metric mags (will fit in any FAL) for only Ø7 (Ø5 in large quantity). Affordable quality mags are a key issue, as you should have *at least* 30 mags for each battle rifle. 50-100 mags are even better. Why so *many?* Because mags are "consumables." They fail, they break, they get lost, and they are discarded in a firefight. You'll need lots of spares.

The .308 AR10

A close second (because of its superior ergonomics and accuracy) is Armalite's AR10, which is a .308 AR15. I'd pick a flat-top upper model with a 21"bbl. (I'm *not* a fan of short barrel .308s because of reduced velocity and increased muzzle blast. A 16¼"bbl wastes much of the .308's potential, although such short barrels in a .223 is fine, if not preferred.) This means either an AR10(T) target, or the AR10A4.

The **(T)** model has a lovely stainless 24"bbl and National Match trigger. With the right scope, it would make an excellent sniper rifle out to 800yds, although it really is too long and heavy to hump as a true battle rifle. Dealer cost is Ø1,495 and retail is Ø1,995.

The **A4** model has a 20"bbl (add Ø100 for stainless) and weighs nearly a pound less than the (T). With stainless barrel, dealer cost is Ø1,095; retail is Ø1,425. I'd probably put an Elcan scope on it for the closest thing to an all-around rifle (for short and long range, hunting or defense).

While none exist in pre-ban form and are thus without a flash suppressor (helpful for low light work, and *vital* for NVD use), obeying 18 USC §921(30)(B) will probably *not* be one of your higher concerns after 1/1/2000. Have the barrel threaded for a vortex flash suppressor (tell the gunsmith it's for a *muzzle brake*, which is legal on domestic post-ban semi-autos). The M14/M1A 20rd mags can be adapted to the AR10 for Ø20 each, or you can DIY with a steady hand and Dremel tool. Visit Armalite at www.armalite.com.

Between the DSA FAL and the AR10

For a long-range sniper platform, choose the AR10(T) because of its flattop upper (vs. an accessory mount on the FAL), lighter weight, better trigger, and better accuracy. The more expensive mags of the AR10 is not as big an issue with a sniper rifle, as you won't need as many.

For a battle rifle, it's a *very* close call. The AR10 has an edge on accuracy, ergonomics, and adaptability; the FAL has an edge on mag availability and reliability. **It's the mag issue which hurts the AR10.** Suppling Armalite with your M14/M1A mags (Ø20 each) for Ø20 conversion means Ø40 mags at the cheapest. (They're Ø65 retail if bought whole from Armalite.) While owners of other .308 battle rifles (*e.g.*, the H&K91) are used to paying up to Ø70 for their mags, the FAL owner can buy in quantity at only Ø5 each! (Armalite blew it by not using FAL mags for the AR10.)

So, unless you have extra cash to spend on AR10 mags and want to save training time with the FAL system, I'd have to point you to the FAL. It's an excellent combat rifle with very good ergonomics (though the AR10 is best).

I just have a crush on the AR10, which makes the choice difficult for me. Armalite even offers them in .243, which I think is rather neat, though I'd never choose a .243 over .308. If they offered it in 7-08 or *.260* (6.5-08), then I'd probably have to splurge on one to satisfy my frustration of there being no ".264 Boston" battle rifle (read pp. 9/1-6 of *BoG&C* for details).

If you have the money for a *lot* of AR10 mags and seek unmatched versatility, then get an A2 (or A4) rifle for battle work, are replace its upper in 1 minute with a Leupold scoped (T) upper for long-range work (dealer cost Ø820; retail Ø1,000). (Note: It's Ø185 cheaper buying the A2 rifle, (T) upper, and NM trigger (Ø110) versus getting the (T) rifle with NM trigger already installed, and A2 upper.) You could carry your A2 rifle for most work, and if you encounter a long-range target, slip the scoped (T) upper out of your backpack and swap uppers. (You'll have to experiment if the (T)'s zero will hold during the swaps.)

Other .308 battle rifles

While you could make do with an H&K91, this rifle has significant drawbacks (fully discussed in *BoG&C*). The Galil is an *outstanding* rifle, but who can afford a couple of dozen of Ø125 mags? The M1A is fine, but a DSA FAL is much better for only a little more money. (Only because of politics did we not adopt the FAL in the 1950s, even though it proved to be a better rifle.) Stick with the FAL or AR10.

Final comments on your .308 battle rifle

If your rifle can shoot within ¾-1¼MOA, then it will be accurate enough for 6" groups out to 500-800yds. Do not accept iron sight groups larger than 2¼MOA--find a better rifle.

I'd have three sets of spare parts (bolt, sights, firing pin, extractor, ejector, trigger assembly, hammer spring, pins, etc.), an extra barrel or two, *30+* mags (they get damaged and lost easily), and at least 10,000rds of boxer-primed ammo.

Then, I'd get to Thunder Ranch (830-640-3138/3183 fax) *immediately* for Rifle 1 and 2.

Q: *"What should be my 2nd rifle?"*
A: A pre-ban AR15A2.

For your second rifle, get a pre-ban AR15A2 with full A2 sight radius (avoid the "shorty" carbine forestock model). Ideal barrel twist is 1-9" (Colt's 1-7" is too fast for 55gr bullets, and the older A1 1-12" barrels are too slow for the modern SS109 62gr bullets.) Bushmaster is the best, but Colt or PWA are acceptable. Mount a vortex flash suppressor, Tritium front sight, RediMag (with bolt stop), Sure-Fire flashlight, and sling. The trapdoor, full-length A2 buttstock (no fragile/hollow telescoping stocks, please!) should have cleaning rod and gear, oil, and an extra bolt and spare parts.

The Israeli Army likes the C-More sight for their M16s. While it's battery powered, you can still use the iron sights when the batteries go or if the unit fails. Clint Smith raves about the C-More, which is high praise from a High Priest.

If I could build a Bushmaster AR15, it would be a 16" pre-ban Dissipator model, on a flattop receiver, which leaves optical/NVD sights an option. It'd still have a fixed front sight, as iron sights are *vital* on battle rifles. While a carry handle upper is O.K., the flattop receiver lowers any additional sighting device about an inch (which aids accuracy and handling) and is more solid a mount.

As with my FAL, I'd have three sets of spare parts (bolt, sights, firing pin, extractor, ejector, hammer spring, pins, etc.), an extra barrel or two, *30+* mags (they get damaged and lost easily), and at least 10,000rds of ammo.

AR15 mags

Government contract issue 30rd only. No plastic mags.

If you live in the city and plan on staying, or fighting your way out, then get a pre-ban 100rd C-Mag (800-867-7999) for Ø625. The Ø225 post-ban mags are sold only to cops and feds. (The Chinese 120rd drums for the AR15 don't seem to ever work, so their Ø70 price is a false economy. The 90 Rounder mags work O.K. and are still floating about at gunshows.) **Why a *100rd* mag? So you can stay in the fight *longer*.** Even 30rd mags shoot empty quickly, and if you're trying to outrun the inner city hordes you'll kiss that C-Mag afterwards. "Omega Man" stuff? *You* bet.

Q: *"What if I can't find or afford an AR15?"*
A: Try the Daewoo DR-200, or the Bushmaster M17.

The Daewoo

The affordable (Ø650) South Korean Daewoo is a marvelous hybrid AR15/AK47 design. It has generally AR15 controls, and uses AR15 mags. It has an excellent trigger and is highly accurate. With its AK-style gas system (piston, no tube) it is more reliable in adverse conditions than the AR15. The right side bolt handle (perfect for lefties) can be replaced with a custom-made Galil version (which is top operated). I don't care at all for the Daewoo's safety, which, although properly placed, has an awkward 180° counterclockwise throw. (An AR15 90° clockwise version could probably be custom made.)

The Bushmaster M17

This is a *great* little rifle. Post-ban models still have threaded barrels (because of the lock nutted barrel sleeve) and can technically accept a vortex flash suppressor (although this is illegal--your call). The M17 uses the superior AR180 gas piston system, but plentiful AR15 mags. The main drawback to the M17 is the 25yd fixed sights, so an optical sight must be mounted. I recommend the Trijicon A.C.O.G. Reflex gunsight, or other quality *non-battery* optical sight. Besides the poor iron sights, the other drawback of the M17 is that its aluminum receiver becomes too hot to hold after just a couple of mags. Some insulation and heat shielding *must* be installed for the M17 to be a viable combat rifle.

Other .223 battle carbines

I cannot recommend: the Galil (too expensive and exotic, Ø100 mags), the H&K93 (poor ergonomics, expensive mags and parts), the Chinese AK (poor accuracy and ergonomics, uncommon mags), or the Ruger Mini14 (poor accuracy and ergonomics, too fragile).

Gee, have I offended every non-AR15 owner? "Sorry." Stick with the AR15-system rifles for their superior ergonomics, parts availability, and plentiful Ø10 mags.

Q: "What should be my 3rd rifle?"
A: An *extremely* accurate scoped bolt-action .308.

Any accurate Winchester M70, Ruger M77II, or Remington M700BDL will serve well. These are the most common bolt-actions with the best selection of stocks, triggers, scope mounts, and other accessories. (The Finnish Sako is a lovely rifle, but too expensive and exotic for our purposes.)

My preference is a stainless steel rifle in a synthetic stock, camo painted with Bow-Flage paint.

Don't skimp on **barrel** length. Length means velocity (and the .308 isn't a Magnum caliber). 19" is the *minimum*, and 22" is often better. Have a Douglas, Shilen, etc. barrel cryo-treated and professionally installed. Consider adding a BOSS.

The ideal **scope** is the Leupold Mark4 M1-10X with Mil-Dot reticle and BDC. Dope it, dial it, dump it. If you can't spend the Ø1,000, then any 3-9X Leupold or Burris scope will do fine (send it to Premier Reticle, 540-722-0601, for Mil-Dots). Even

___

the Ø100 Tasco World Class 3-9X-40mm scope is pretty decent. Buy the best scope you can *painfully* afford.

For Ø450 you can have a good quality 400yd rifle out of the box (with Tasco scope). For Ø800 you can have a very nice 600yd rifle (Leupold scope, synthetic stock, Timney trigger). For Ø1,200 you can have a truly fine 800yd rifle. For about Ø3,000+ you can have a *really* trick custom rifle from Robar. The question is simple and personal: **How much accuracy can you afford *not* to have?**

In truth, you could do fine with a scoped bolt-action .308 *instead* of the .308 battle rifle. While I certainly wouldn't feel uncomfortably *underarmed* with "only" an AR15 and M70 Winchester in .308, I'd sure miss my FAL. This affordable combination is more sensible for families who just cannot spend Ø1,500+ for an FAL or AR10.

A .30-06 would also be fine. Even though it's another caliber to stock, it's always been *slightly* more common than the .308, gives another 100-150fps, and feeds the 220gr bullets. With a Ø15 chamber adapter, a .30-06 can accurately (1½MOA) fire the shorter case .308. If I could have only *one* bolt-action rifle for uncertain times and remote places, the .30-06 really is more common and versatile than the .308. (I'd stock the odd camper and cabin with .30-06 rifles.)

Still, I'd probably stick with the .308 for your bolt-action, especially if you *also* get an FAL or AR10. If you *can't* do it with a .308, then a .30-06 *won't* make the difference.

Q: *"What should be my 4th rifle?"*
A: Probably a semi-auto .22LR.

These are necessary for training, plinking, and pest control. If you camp or hike often, choose the take-down Marlin M70 Papoose (preferably in stainless). Otherwise the Ø85 tube-fed Marlin M60 or Ø150 mag-fed Ruger 10/22 are the way to go.

Q: *"What should be my 5th rifle?"*
A: Something exclusively for routine travel.

Don't get caught these days away from home without a handgun *and* a rifle. Remember, a handgun is only what you fight your way back to your *rifle*. So you're in L.A., riots break out and you need your rifle but left it at home? *Uh, oh.*

There are substantial high-level rumors of martial law for the 150,000+ population cities in spring/summer 1999, and if you travel often you might get caught in a strange city under sudden martial law or catastrophe. Handguns are fine, but they *cannot* perform a rifle's duty.

Rifles for plane trips

A friend of mine has vowed to *never* get caught in a big city without a rifle. He has a 16"bbl pre-ban folding stock Chinese AK especially for his checked suitcase. (He paid only Ø300 for it ten years ago, though it's worth Ø800+ today. He also has a beautiful Ø1,100 pre-ban Daewoo K2 with folding stock, but considers it far too valuable to risk traveling. I agree.) With it goes 9 30rd mags (one for the rifle and the other 8 in two 4-mag pouches already on their belt) and 270rds of ammo in stripper clips. Naturally, his Colt 1911A1 accompanies him, too. This is a very capable set up, although he takes a *big* chance having an "assault rifle" in the wrong city or state.

I've chosen a No.4 Mk.I Lee-Enfield for *my* travel duty. The barrel has been shortened to 16¼" (¼" over legal minimum) and the buttstock cut down and thinned out. The whole thing is only 27" long (½" over legal minimum) and weighs 6lbs. While muzzle blast and recoil are stout, TANSTAAFL folks. For only Ø120 (which includes the barrel and front sight work) I've got a dependable, accurate, powerful .303 British rifle with detachable 10rd box mag. (If you don't want to add another caliber, then consider the Ø150 No. 6 or 7 Lee-Enfields in .308, which are better quality than I recently believed.) With it goes two extra mags, and 50rds in strippers. Being "only" a bolt-action, there will be much less hassle if caught with it vs. a military-style semi-auto with its nasty "banana clips."

Another good traveling rifle is the Marlin .30-30 (or .44 Mag) lever-action. Its rear stock removes quickly, and ammo can be found anywhere. It's also the least "threatening" rifle of all to officials. Have good pouches to carry 50-100rds of ammo.

I would *not* choose a rifle in a *pistol* caliber (*e.g.*, 9mm and .40S&W). They are just not powerful enough (except for the .44 Magnum Marlin), and if you're going to pack the *weight* of a rifle you might as well enjoy the *power* of a rifle. I don't consider the .30 Carbine to be sufficiently powerful, even though it *is* the equivalent to an autoloading .357 Magnum (110gr at 1,900fps) and performs well enough within 50yds. A *true* rifle caliber will strike an incapacitating blow to at least 300yds.

The point of these rifles with folding or removable butt-stocks is to avoid having to transport them in an obvious rifle case. If the rifle is somehow short enough, then it can fit at least diagonally in most any hard suitcase. Be *anonymously* armed. Choose a hard suitcase with combination lock, which allows quick keyless access. I'd take two handguns: one to pack with your rifle in its case, and the other for the second checked bag. That way, if either bag gets lost you'll still have a handgun.

Although you'll need a hard case for your weapons' security and protection, such is impractical if you have to beat feet, so take also a small backpack for the *"Oh, shit!"* essentials. Don't forget quality tactical boots, as dress shoes won't cut it. Also pack a rugged vest or jacket to conceal your handgun.

By law, checked firearms must be unloaded (mags included, as they are considered part of the weapon), in a locked case, and declared to the counter agent (who will have you sign a tag attesting to their unloaded and locked status--no big deal). Ammo must be packed in their original containers, but plastic ammo boxes (CaseGuard, etc.) will do. All this is still perfectly legal--*unless* you're flying to an anti-gun city or state (*e.g.*, NYC, N.J., etc.). "Assault rifles" are generally illegal in all but the southern and western states. *Cuidado.* Know before you go.

Moral: Don't get caught these days away from home without a handgun *and* a rifle.

Rifles for car trips

To save money, you could use your air travel rifle, say one of the No. 6 or 7 Lee-Enfield "Jungle Carbines" in .308 for Ø150, or a used Marlin .30-30 for Ø150-225. In some states (*e.g.*, Texas) you can drive around with a loaded, accessible long gun but *not* a handgun (unless licensed). In other states your rifle must be unloaded and locked in a case or the trunk. **Know before you go.** Be careful when passing within 1,000' of a "school" to avoid a felony federal arrest and conviction.

Q: *"What should be my 6th rifle?"*

A: A spare AR15 or FAL for yourself or friend.

AR15s and FALs will be worth their weight in gold after 2000. They may be worth a cabin and several acres of property. No other hand-held weapon can effectively neutralize multiple aggressors out to 500yds. Such rifles are the queen of battle. Have at least one spare salted away in a safe place with its own ammo, mags, cleaning kit, and spare parts.

Q: *"What should be my 7th rifle?"*
A: **If in the city, a third AR15 or FAL.**
   If in the country, probably a bolt-action .50BMG.
   If you want to bust up vehicles and equipment at distances up to *2 miles*, then you just *gotta* have a .50BMG. It's the most powerful weapon you can have without a federal license. Unsurpassably serious weapons for unsurpassably serious folks. Get my *Boston on Guns & Courage* for more discussion.

   From River Valley Ordnance (314-926-3076) you can get pulled M20 bullets for about 80¢ apiece. These are API-T, which means armor-piercing, incendiary tracer. This bullet will light up all the way to a car 1,000yds away, punch right through the body, and set the interior on fire. *Tee, hee.* What else can give you so much fun for a mere *80¢*?

"Gee, Boston, that's a lot of rifles!"

   Yeah, it *is*. Rifles are merely tools, and no *one* tool can do it *all* (although a scoped FAL or AR10 comes close...). Think of rifles like shoes: how many pairs of *shoes* do you have? You've got tennis shoes, running shoes, dress shoes, beach sandals, hiking boots, work boots, and house slippers. That's seven pairs of footwear. Now, does seven *rifles* sound so extreme?

   At least three of them could be in .308 (the FAL, the bolt-action, and the Lee-Enfield travel rifle), four if you get a second FAL. The only other calibers are .22LR, .223, and .50BMG.

   I *could* have urged you to get two other bolt-actions (in .300Win Mag and .338 Lapua Mag), an AK47-clone (for training), and a new Steyr Scout Rifle (Jeff Cooper's concept in commercial form). That would have been *eleven* rifles in three additional calibers. A scoped .223 bolt-action would also be nice for the ladies and children.

   Even though an AR15, a scoped .308 bolt-action, and a .22LR rifle can handle 95% of all rifle needs, only your family's *lives* depend on your weaponry. Will three rifles giving 95% be enough? Is that a gamble you can make in good conscience? If those three rifles are all that you can truly afford, then they'll have to suffice, but know in advance that 95% is all they'll give.

It's the *man*, not the gun

   The World War I pilot in his biplane would be no match for the F-18 pilot, but the Pattern 14 Enfield-equipped [WWI] soldier may very well easily kill the soldier of the late 1990s armed with an M16A2 rifle. Certainly, the fighters in Afghanistan showed that their Enfields

were equal to Soviet AK-74 rifles--and served as an example for all of us who are confronted with oppressive governments that seek to limit our ability to acquire current-issue military weapons.
-- Timothy J. Mullin; *Testing the War Weapons*, p. 419

So, if you're "stuck" with an Enfield or .30-30, don't despair. Both are good 200yd calibers, and deadly in the right hands.

Ammo for your rifles

For .223, choose the newer 62gr SS109 ball (it's usually green tipped), *if* your AR15 has a barrel twist rate of 1-9". (1-12" is too slow and good only for 55gr bullets.) Your 1-9" barrel will shoot the cheaper 55gr rounds (for training) quite well, too.

For the .308 FAL, any modern boxer-primed ball is fine. Good bargains are the Venezuelan (Cavim brand) and Portuguese ammo for Ø160ish per 1,000rds. U.S. Lake City is the best ball, but more expensive. Have some black tip AP, too.

For the .308 bolt-action, most BDC scopes are calibrated for the Federal Match load of a 168gr Sierra MatchKing. This is a fine round, very accurate, and easily duplicated in handloads. The 175-190gr bullets, however, buck the wind better over long distances. If I could have only *one* load for *everything* (deer, elk, and bad guys), I'd send the 180gr Sierra GameKing at 2600fps.

Blackpowder guns

Don't laugh. A good man with merely a muzzleloading rifle will challenge (or beat) an average man with better equipment. Even with my Glock and AR15, I don't think I'd happily face a muzzleloader-armed Clint Smith to a gunfight. **It's the man, not the rifle.** The *man* (courage, intellect, stamina, alertness, etc.) is the weapon--his rifle is merely a *tool*.

While some of us may be reduced by circumstance to blackpowder (so know how to fight with them), I'm still acquiring *modern* firearms. Perhaps when I've got some extra money and time to piddle with blackpowder I'll give one a try. I'm *not* discounting muzzleloaders; I'm just saying to *prioritize*.

The originally blackpowder calibers (*e.g.*, .30-30, .30-40, and .45-70) *will* revert to black powder use for many people who might have no choice but to make their own gunpowder. I can't help but mention that Clint Smith has designed an 1880s weapons class for Thunder Ranch. You get to clear the Tower with blackpowder guns, using oil lamps. Cool!

Ruger's modern 77/50 is pretty neat. It uses 2 Pyrodex 50gr pellets, a cap, and plastic-flanged Black Belt Bullet to throw a 405gr bullet at 1348fps (1635fpe) and 2¾MOA at 100yds with very little smoke and fouling. This is .45-70 ballistics, without the expensive brass and reloading of the .45-70, from a 6½lb rifle with a 22" bbl. *Hmmmmm.*

Coating and finishes

Rocky Mountain Arms (800-375-0846) offers DuPont Teflon-S coating for all firearms in many colors.

Robar (602-581-2648) offers NP3 (a satin gray P.T.F.E./electroless nickel, suitable for all gun metals, and best for internal parts), and their excellent proprietary exterior finish, Roguard (available in most colors and camos). Robar also offers blueing, electroless nickel, stainless steel blackening, and parkerizing. All Robar products and services are exemplary.

Even though sending your gun to a smith is not legally a *"transfer,"* the BATF/FBI may *treat* it that way after 30 November 1998 and require an NICBC approval before you get it back. Find out from your dealer *before* sending an unpapered gun.

Training and practice

As I've urged earlier, get to Thunder Ranch (or some near equivalent) *immediately.* The training is priceless. A superb firearm in untrained hands is almost worthless.

Test your guns and zero them *now*, while it's still not a problem to shoot. Later on, you may not *have* a hassle-free location, or the time, or the ammo. Get squared away *now.*

A great new target stand from MTM (937-890-7461) is the Jammit, which stakes into the ground and holds your target a full 3' off the ground. Only Ø13.50. (www.mtmcase-guard.com) They weigh only 2lbs. and can be stuck anywhere. Great for mobile range practice.

Targets should be as realistic as possible, meaning no bullseye target for tactical simulation. Use torso targets, preferably with an armed bad guy on them.

GUN GEAR

Stuff you wear

BDUs (Battle Dress Utilities)

Military camo clothing. Nothing else works as well for patrolling and combat. Rugged and versatile.

Eagle ammo chest pouch for battle rifle

For training, around-the-yard use, perimeter patrol, brief errands, etc. It will hold 8 30rd AR15 mags or 4 20rd FAL mags right next to your body's center of gravity. In time, you'll never know it's there. An absolutely *essential* piece of gear. Have an extra in every vehicle for every person.

SKS ammo chest pouch

These are only Ø2.75 from CTD. They have 10 pockets, each holding (in stripper clips) 20rds of 7.62x39 or 30rds of .223 (though the pocket's third stripper clip is a rather tight fit). All your rifle's unloaded ammo should be in stripper clips to quickly top off mags. With every chest pouch, paracord a mag loading tool. I would have a *minimum* of 3 loaded pouches per rifle.

These chest pouches are also useful as tool/parts kits, first aid kits, etc. Rugged and inexpensive; have *dozens*.

Eagle tactical vest

For extended patrolling, light missions, etc. It has a CamelBak sleeve, mag pouches, and extra pockets. It wears very comfortably. A superb piece of gear.

CamelBak

Indispensable for easy and continuous hydration. Get the 100oz. bladder, and have some extra valves.

2 quart bladder canteen

Use this to replenish your CamelBak. Squeeze out air to eliminate the sloshing sound. (Impossible with hard canteens.)

Survival tabs

Contains 15 days of food energy and nutrition in a pleasant malt ball taste. Their plastic bottles fit in the 1qt canteen pouches. Ø24 per bottle from Nitro-Pak. I'd buy several cases.

Headgear
Boonie hat
Lightweight camo hats that bunch up for packing. Add a couple of feet of camo netting material to break up outline.

PASGAT helmet
Although I probably wouldn't wear one every day (unless under mortar/artillery fire), it might be good to have one.

Kevlar flak vest (Army or Marine Corps issue)
While these are *not* bulletproof, they *do* offer some resistance to rounds, and will stop most shrapnel. Heavy and cumbersome, they are still a necessary bargain at Ø75.

Bulletproof vest
Pistol caliber vests are under Ø350, but Level IV rifle caliber vests are Ø1,275 (from JRH). What's your *life* worth?

If you get head shot, *tough luck*. A PASGAT helmet might deflect a glancing round, but it'll still ring your bell.

Binoculars
A must. Don't skimp on quality--buy a pair of Steiners. Don't skimp on size--get the 7x50s. A 50mm objective lens gathers much more light than 21mm or 35mm lenses, which makes the difference in forests and other low-light environments. Combat vets have convinced me that the superior performance of armored 7x50s is well worth is well worth the extra weight.

If you see a pair of Steiners with *gold* mirror lenses, snap them up immediately! They are laserproof models (to eliminate laser blindness from the enemy) and *very* hard to find. These are not sold on the open market, so any pair you find might be stolen military property. (Don't show them in public.) The gold coating scratches at a harsh word, so don't touch it!

Life Pack
If you're on foot for days or weeks, the Life Pack 100 contains the necessary materials to sustain an individual for 30 days. It's got food, water tablets, cook stove, vitamins, first aid kit, and even a gas mask. A great pack to have in the car, cabin, etc. From Millennium (800-500-9893) for Ø477 + Ø25 S&H.

Stuff you carry
Cleaning gear, caliber converters (from MCA; 907-248-4913), radios, bandanas, socks, sunglasses, camo facepaint, etc.

Quality gun safe

Buy the best you can afford, and bolt it to the concrete. Good brands are Browning, Cannon (www.cannonsafe.com; 800-242-1055), Fort Knox, and Liberty. A.G. English carries most of the above brands (800-222-7233; www.agenglish.com).

Cache tubes

PVC sewer pipe works great. A tube 58"x8" holds four AR15s and 2000rds of ammo. A tube 40"x8" holds three .50 ammo cans. Sealing them with caps is the only critical task.

NIGHT VISION DEVICES

There are several pieces of equipment which will give you what I call an order of magnitude advantage over likely opponents. Encrypted radio communications are one. Bulletproof vests are another. Night vision devices are another.

Zero Generation

Non-U.S. spec stuff made in the U.S.S.R. Very low light gain, and fun-house lens optics. Inexpensive, and not worth it.

First Generation

Our first NVDs. Heavy and bulky, using vacuum tubes.

Second Generation

The minimum standard, in my opinion. Gen II devices use micro-channel plate (MCP) intensifiers, which are lighter, more sensitive, and longer lasting than Gen I tubes. U.S. Gen II NVDs will satisfy most applications. An affordable value. (Note: 2nd gen Russian is often equivalent only to our 1st gen.)

Third Generation

Wow! State-of-the-art, amazing equipment. A gallium arsenide (GaAs) photocathode replaces the Gen II multialkai version, providing increased photosensitivity. An improved MCP greatly enhances resolution, and tube life is extended by an ion barrier. Very expensive and very worth it .

Uses of NVDs

Name it. Gunsights, hand scopes, goggles, and camera applications. Hunting, surveillance, and patrolling.

Shopping for NVDs

Even among identical makes and models, tube clarity varies. Some have more spots, chicken wire, or honeycomb (fixed-pattern noise) than others. Compare, *compare, compare.* I'm don't buying mail-order since I can't compare actual devices.

NVD hand scopes

Fine for surveillance, but requires a dedicated hand. Choose goggles instead, especially for tactical needs. If you want a hand scope, check out TNT's selection.

NVD goggles

This should be your *first* NVD, as it's the most versatile because of the hands-free headmount. Coupled with an IR gunsight, you won't need a night vision scope.

3rd Gen goggles
ITT PVS-7B (ITT, 800-448-8678)

Absolutely *the* coolest thing you can buy for Ø2,500. You can drive, patrol, and shoot at night with these goggles in their headmount. (One guy used his to hot-wire his county's heavy grader at night and build himself a private road. He would top off the fuel tank after each use. Another guy runs his Porsche at night with the lights off down country roads.)

The tubes last 10,000 hours (that's almost 3½ *years* of nightly 8hr use!). They have a small, built-in IR light for increased illumination up to 7yds. The 2 AA batteries will power for 20-40 hours, depending on much you use the IR light. They are warranteed for two years.

I'd get the Ø100 add-on compass, and some IR filters for your Sure-Fire flashlights and 12V spotlights (all from CTD). Commercially, the military PVS-7Bs are called the 5001 series. The Ø2,500 5001Bs have a guaranteed *minimum* lp/mm (line pair per millimeter resolution) of 45 (the newer tubes are often closer to 50); the Ø3,500 5001Js are 58 lp/mm; the Ø4,500 5001Ps are 64+ lp/mm (wow!). **B, J, or P series?** While the 64+ lp/mm 5001P goggles are just fantastic, the 45-50 lp/mm 5001Bs are 90% as clear and sharp for Ø2,000 less money. Unless you're quite wealthy, stick with the 5001Bs.

A few suppliers are N.A.I.T. (800-432-6248), Morovision (800-424-8222), TNT (800-644-4867), and The Camping Supply

Store (800-998-7007; www.campingsupply.com), and Ready Made Resources (800-627-3809).

ITT 210
From TNT. PVS-7B technology in an affordable price.

2nd Gen goggles
ITT 200
2nd gen version of the ITT 210.

Russian Night Owl goggles
By comparison, the Russian stuff is 2nd gen. 34 lp/mm at best. Still, if that's all you can afford, it's certainly better than being totally blind at night. CTD offers the Ø590 Night Owl (designed for helo pilots) with 35,000x amplification and 1x magnification for real-time use. They weigh 2lbs. with headmount, and use 2 AA batteries.

The Russian 2nd gen stuff pales in comparison to the American 3rd gen NVDs. While *any* NVD is better than *none* at all, I'd nevertheless save up for a pair of ITT 3rd generation PVS-7Bs. For night ops, then you need every edge possible.

NVD scopes
Get a pair of PVS-7B goggles *first*. They're *much* more versatile than an NVD scope alone, and you can't search through an NVD scope for very long. If you've still got the money and for a night sniper team, *then* get an NVD scope.

I recently handled a new state-of-the-art Ø8,000 6X scope, courtesy of a friend who is an expert in the industry. With this unit 200yd headshots and 400yd torsoshots are not a problem. The clarity was astounding. What a righteous piece of kit! He finally got it back, though not without my teethmarks on it. Since an Ø8,000 scope is financially out of the question for nearly all of us, what are the more affordable alternatives?

3rd gen NVD scopes
Python (from TNT)
This 3x scope with 36-45 lp/mm sits atop a Hughes Elcan mount (which fits on any flattop base), uses a Duracell 123A battery, and weighs just 0.8lb. Very compact at 5½"x3"--like a fat can of beer. The best scope for the money (about Ø2,000).

Aries MK440
From CTD, it's a pretty good NVD scope for Ø1,100. It's got 34 lp/mm, 4.5x, 50,000x amplification. It's a *much* better de-

vice than the 1st gen MK208 and provides viable tactical performance (50yd headshots; 100yd torsoshots). Has built-in illuminator. It's quite heavy, however.

Cheaper Than Dirt (888-625-3848), America's leading sports discounter, were the pioneers in bringing in Soviet NVDs after the Berlin Wall fell. They offer two scopes which have chevron reticles and internal windage/elevation adjustments, use common batteries, have a two-year warranty, and mount on Weaver bases. An 800 number for service and questions.

2nd gen NVD scopes
DarkStar (from TNT)
Weighing 1¾lb., this Elcan mounted scope (with 4x and 28 lp/mm) is very capable for Ø1,200. Uses 2 AA batteries.

1st gen scopes
AN/PVS-2 (from TNT)
Huge and heavy (2.7lbs.) but only Ø600, and it's Elcan mounted. Uses 4 AA batteries. A cool bit of early 1970s rebuilt surplus which would look great on a wall hanging M1 Carbine.

Aries MK208
From CTD for Ø550, it's 40 lp/mm, 2.6x with 35,000x amplification. It's a pretty basic unit and only 50yd torsoshots are possible. Weighs 1¾lbs--half the weight and size of the PVS-2.

IR laser gunsights
Since even the 62gr .223 is out of gas by 600yds, I don't see how a day scope makes sense with AR15s. The 800m A2 iron sights are fine considering the .223's ballistics.

To me, the point of the mounting systems is to add an IR laser gunsight. When used with ITT's PVS-7B night vision goggles, this system is just amazing. In near total darkness you can hit bad guys out to 200yds. Simply light him up with the IR laser and squeeze the trigger. I tell you, this rig is the *cat's ass*.

An IR laser gunsight has windage/elevation knobs; its specs sticker will read Class IIIb (5-50mW) at **710-850nm**. (The *visible* red lasers operate at *630-680* nanometers with often only 5 milliwatts of Class IIIa product power.) So, if you see a gunsight laser marked 710-850nm, it is IR and you should snap it up *immediately*. All lasers are quite capable of burning corneas, so take care not to blind anyone.

Good luck, however, *finding* an IR laser gunsight as they do not seem readily available to civilians, though I'm aware of no law restricting their availability. You might try Laser Devices (2 Harris Ct., Monterrey, Ca. 93940). Insight Technology (603-626-4800) manufactures the AN/PAQ-4B IR laser gunsight which mounts to the AR15's front sight block.

Mounting systems for gunsights

The best AR15 scope and accessory mounts are by A.R.M.S. from Quality Parts (which is Bushmaster). They use the Swan universal mounting platform, on top of which will fit *any* sighting system (*i.e.*, Weaver, Stanag, and Picatinny).

The Ø60 A.R.M.S. #2 is a carry handle mount.

The Ø60 A.R.M.S. #5 is a see-through multibase used on flat top receivers (alone, or on top of a #19 for zero-hold/QD to raise the optical device above the front sight level).

The Ø140 A.R.M.S. #19 is a zero hold/QD mount that fits on top the #2 or flat top receivers (alone, or under a #5).

I also like the Ø200 helical forestock mount by Knights.

"Gee, these mounts are expensive!" Yeah, they *are,* but just how much is hitting your target *worth* to you? Miss your bad guy repeatedly because of that Ø15 "bargain" mount and congratulate yourself on the Ø45 you saved--*if you live.* When choosing a carry handle mount, I didn't even go for the very good Ø40 Ultralux over the Ø60 A.R.M.S. #2. Saving a whopping Ø20 just wasn't worth it to me. **Get *rid* of cheap thinking, folks!** When it comes to guns and gear, get the very best and you'll never regret it. (I didn't say the very best you could *afford.* Get the very best stuff, *period.* Save money elsewhere.)

KNIVES

A knife is the most basic and most important tool you can own. Besides a rock or club, it's also the most basic weapon. Having a top-quality knife can make the difference between living or dying. Have a knife on you *always*! Finally, *never* skimp on your knives!

Knives fall into two general classes: utility and fighting. No knife will excel at *both*, although some utility knives are fairly good fighters. Avoid bargain production knives as your *main* knife, meaning no Buck, no Gerber, *and certainly no Cold Steel.* Cheaper knives have their place, but don't bet the ranch.

MISCELLANEOUS WEAPONRY

Telescoping batons

A great deep cover concealed weapon. ASP are the best. Coupled with a fighting knife in the other hand (and the training to use them), you'd be very formidable.

PR-24, or Tonfa (hard wood, fiberglass, aluminum)

This is the side-handled baton used by police. A fantastic striking weapon. Buy a training video and practice with it.

Spears

Can be made 4-5' long from green wood, and the sharpened end heated over hot coals to harden it.

OC pepper spray

An excellent non-lethal weapon. Some very rare bad dudes have built up somewhat of a *de facto* tolerance to OC, so don't count on 100% street effectiveness.

Blowguns

While I haven't had much experience with them, some folks really like their blowguns. Good for *very* small pests and birds at *very* close range, but that's about it.

Slingshots

The "WristRocket" slingshots with surgical tubing power bands are quite powerful and accurate. A ¼" steel ball at 200fps packs a real wallop, and can be deadly if well-placed. Stock up on several feet of extra tubing, as there's no substitute for it.

Bow and arrow

A fine weapon, assuming you've the training and practice. I personally prefer a crossbow over a longbow for its superior accuracy and better sighting options. Have *lots* of bolts and tips, as homemade versions can't compare with commercial quality.

WATER

You can live for 3 weeks without food, but 3 days without water. Most water comes to us because of electric pumps. When the electricity goes, you'll be left with only the water you have stored or can find. You should have ample sources of both.

Although we take clean, plentiful water wholly for granted, the Florida victims of 1992 hurricane Andrew paid up to Ø30 per gallon for it. The Des Moines, Iowa flood victims of 1993 had no drinking water for up to *30 days* because the filtration plants had been contaminated by sewage.

High-rise city folks will first drain their waterbeds, then their toilet tanks, and then their toilet *bowls*. If it's safe to venture out in the streets, then they'll have to haul their water from city lakes and rivers. If they live nearby a town water tower, then they'll have pressure until the tower runs dry. Those in the country with their own well (and the power to run the pump) will survive just fine.

STORING WATER

If you foolishly plan on staying in the city during the first months of 2000, then you'll desperately need to store 3-5 gallons per person/day. (One gallon per person/day is considered the *absolute* minimum for the *body's* needs, and does *not* include water needs for dishwashing, bathing, etc.)

To prevent algae in stored water, add one tablespoon (a half ounce) of hydrogen peroxide per gallon.

Static storage containers

These are static because they are too heavy or bulky to move readily. If not several feet above ground for gravity flow, then they'll need their own pumps.

55 gallon water barrels

Since water weighs 8.3lbs./gallon, these barrels will weigh 450+lbs. when full and are hardly movable. Nitro-Pak has a Family Water Package (#2311) for Ø280, which includes four barrels, 5-yr. water stabilizer, hand pump, wrench, and seal caps. This is 2 weeks for a family of four at 4 gal./day/person.

Rain barrels

From a gutter downspout, a 55 gal. barrel can be filled in just two hours in a light drizzle. Netting stretched over the open barrel keeps the water clean and mosquito free.

Waterbeds

A twin size holds 90 gal., queen/135 gal., king/175 gal., but the water must be treated with algicide (not copper-based). If placed on an upper floor, you'll enjoy free gravity flow. Most waterbed plastics are not food-grade, so use this water only for bathing and washing.

Swimming pools

A plastic pool 15' in diameter holds 5,500 gallons and costs only a few hundred dollars. Never use a copper based algicide in your pool (or waterbed), as copper is a blood poison at over .5PPM and no home test kit can measure such low levels.

The stabilizer (cyanuric acid, which acts as a sunscreen for the chlorine so that it doesn't deplete as quickly) is carcinogenic above 100PPM. Normal pool levels are 30-80PPM, but you must test your pool water regularly. If levels are too high, drain some, add fresh water, circulate for 8 hours, and retest.

You might want to Reverse Osmosis (RO) process your pool water to remove particulates and impurities.

This is rather a lot of work for drinking water, so you could simply relegate pool water for washing, etc. *Never* store chlorinated water in *metal* containers, as chlorine is quite corrosive.

Underground fiberglass storage tanks

These hold thousands of gallons and might be the ticket for those without a gushing well. A 3,000 gal. tank is 6'x16' long.

Concrete cistern

These are large and ØØØØ expensive, but might be practical if your property allows an uphill cistern for gravity flow.

Water towers

They hold thousands of gallons, can be automatically topped by low-level triggered pump, and provide gravity flow. Their drawbacks are that they're especially visible, and vulnerable to sabotage.

Mobile storage containers

Fill these from your larger static water containers.

Empty bottles and containers

I'm fond of the pint sized hydrogen peroxide bottles. They are brown (no light allowed) and strong. They make good canteens for backpack or car, or for bartering. Be sure to relabel.

5, 6, and 7 gallon plastic buckets

Plastic buckets (with removable lids) will do fine, but are better utilized for grain, flour, bulk laundry soap, etc. CTD sells the excellent Swiss surplus 5gal water carrier.

3 and 5 gallon plastic water cans

Have as many cans as you are able to move in one trip with all hands helping. Any WalMart has these blue pebble-grain cans for Ø8 each. (Avoid the light green cans which transfer a plastic taste to the water.)

I once was visiting friends in my RV when the neighborhood's water pipe broke. Because I had water cans, I could easily replenish the RV's 50 gallon tank and enjoyed (because of the internal 12V pump) running water, hot showers, dishwashing, etc. (My RV mysteriously became a rather popular place...)

400gal military trailer (called a "Water Buffalo")

If you have to haul water to your place, then such a trailer might make the chore feasible.

When stored water tastes "stale"

Stored water will lose some of its oxygen and taste "stale" but oxygen can be restored by simply rapidly pouring the water back and forth amongst two containers several times.

FINDING WATER

However much water you've stored *will* eventually be used up, so you must know how to *find* water. Water comes from only three sources: air, ground, and underground.

Rain water

Unless there have been nuclear explosions within the previous two weeks, rain water is usually quite safe, though irregular in supply. Roof scuppers and poly tarps will collect the most rain water. One inch of rain falling on 100ft² of surface is about 62 gallons. (Allow 20% loss for evaporation, spillage, etc.) Let it sit several days for the dirt to settle out, unless you can and must filter it for immediate needs.

Surface water

Consider yourself lucky if you have easy access to a stream, pond, river, or lake. While streams and ponds can be sucked dry, rivers and lakes are much more capacious. Strain out grit and foreign matter else you'll trigger your body's gag reflex. *All* surface water needs to be boiled or purified to kill possible parasites (*e.g.*, *Giardia lamblia*) from animal fecal matter.

"Spring" water

This is often actually stream or river water which went underground (sometimes for up to a mile) and emerged again. The reason I mention this is because if it *was* ever surface water then it could be contaminated with parasites. Trust no allegedly "spring" water to be pure and clean, even though it looks so. The *Giardia lamblia* cyst is *4 thousandths of a millimeter*, and nobody's visual acuity is good enough to see the little buggers. **Purify all allegedly "spring" water.**

Well water

There's nothing like sweet and pure well water, which is purified through earth rock like through a gigantic Katadyn filter. If you're in a valley, then your well is probably inexhaustible. As long as you can pump it out of the ground, you'll have water. The best arrangement is the submersible pump, preferably solar powered with a generator backup.

As each 2.3' of elevation translates to 1lb of water pressure, you also want a large tank or cistern at least 58' above ground to provide adequate (25lbs) pressure. The tankless water heaters require a *minimum* of 15lbs. If no such elevation is possible, then a pressure tank is required.

Testing your well water

Send off to Real Goods for a National Testing Laboratories water test kit. NTL tests for 73 items, plus 20 pesticides. Since we're but engines of water, the Ø150 will be money well spent.

PURIFYING WATER

Giardia lamblia

Giardia lamblia is mild form of dysentery (if you'll pardon the contradiction). Contracting *Giardia* will ruin much of your year. Infection leads to months of stomach trouble including chronic diarrhea, abdominal pains, and severe weight loss. The cysts have an incubation period of several weeks, so you probably won't be able to pinpoint *where* you picked it up. Colorado has the highest incidence of *Giardia*, followed by Utah, Oregon, Washington, N.H., and N.Y. Municipal outbreaks (from sewage-contaminated water--*ugh!*) have been reported in Aspen, Rome, N.Y., New Hampshire, and Kentucky.

Treatment (after a likely difficult diagnosis) is with Quinacrine hydrochloride, *Metronidaze,* and *Furazolidone,* which have serious side effects for many people.

All in all, it's best to avoid this bug.

Q: *"So, how do I purify my water?"*

There are four ways: boil it, filter it, treat it, or distill it.

Boiling

A rolling boil for at least 5 minutes (longer at higher altitudes, as water boils at lower temperatures there) will kill any parasite or germ. (Some experts recommend a *20* minute boil, and by all means do so if you've got the inclination, time and fuel.) Reconstitute the oxygen afterwards. Boiling is great, but requires much energy and cooling time.

Filtering

Most portable filters will filter out 99.5+% of the bad things. All filters come with their own pump, and will filter from 1 quart to 1 gallon per minute. A gravity flow is instead recommended for larger quantities, but be patient as this is quite slow. Filtering is impractical for daily needs of more than a few gallons, unless you go to a Reverse Osmosis (RO) system.

Swiss Katadyn

This is the "Mercedes-Benz" of filters, used by the UN, the Red Cross, and dozens of world armies. Its 50psi hand pump pushes contaminated water through a silver-impregnated ceramic element to purify 1,500-14,000 gallons, depending on size, *down to 0.2 microns*. All single-cell bacteria are larger than 0.2 microns, and *Giardia lamblia* cysts are a "whopping" 4 microns (twenty times larger than the pore size of Katadyn filters, thus totally removed, as only a half dozen cysts can infect you). You can use the Katadyn in muddy or algae-ridden water-simply scrape (brush included) the filter element clean if it plugs up. When the element becomes thin enough to pass between its test gauge, replace it. The only routine maintenance needed is to occasionally lube the O-ring with Vaseline. The Combi model will purify 1.2 quarts per minute.

Two drawbacks: They're expensive at Ø185 (from Nitro-Pak, #2004) and their fragile elements *will* crack or break if dropped. Treat them like porcelain. Also, don't let water freeze inside the element. Have several extra elements.

With a Katadyn you can literally drink from a Calcutta sewer (though you'll have to stand in line).

Paper-element and charcoal filters

All other filters rely on multistage pleated-paper elements, and while very effective, their filters are bulky and require *much* more frequent replacement than Katadyn's filter. First Need and Pur Explorer are good brands.

For international travel, I take one of those filter straws, which will filter up to 40gal of clear, contaminated water.

Be sure to strain any muddy or cloudy water first, as these filters will otherwise quickly become clogged with impurities much heavier than they are designed for.

Q: *"So, which filter should I buy?"*

I guess it all comes down to this: How much will you *use* the thing? Where would you rather save your money, in up front costs (with cheaper filters) or in *usage* costs (Katadyn)? Personally, I'd go Katadyn and have the best.

Treating

No additive **5% chlorine bleach** (15 drops/gallon) works well. Chlorox brand has the most consistent chemistry. It'll taste like chlorine (gee, what are odds?!). It's *supposed* to. If you can't taste the chlorine, then the bleach has lost its strength. Bleach weakens over time, so stock up in late 1999.

For water from streams, ponds, etc. I prefer **iodine** over chlorine (and Halazone tablets). A bottle of ordinary liquid iodine antiseptic is only a buck at most stores. Three drops per quart of canteen water will kill most bugs, yet can be drunk indefinitely without ill effects. Shake vigorously, slosh some of the iodized water over the canteen mouth and neck, and let the iodine work for at least 15 minutes before you drink. **Do *not* iodize water if you suffer from thyroid problems.**

You *won't* care for the taste, but the water *will* be clean. While I prefer the Katadyn filter on longer camping/hiking trips, I do carry a bottle of iodine in my "always-with-me" fanny pack, in case I get separated from my backpack.

Water drawn for cooking and hot beverages needn't be treated, as a 5 minute boil will kill all parasites.

Distilling

Water is boiled in a chamber (a 5gal metal container works fine) to condense the resulting steam in a 10' long copper water pipe (or fin heater tubing), which is collected as pure water at the other end. Fill the 5 gallon boiler with 3 gallons of bad water. Build a good fire and bring the water to boil. Permit 10 minutes of uncollected boiling to get rid of unwanted gasses and odors. Now place the collecting container under the pipe.

Solar stills can distill water without fuel, but are much slower than boiling. They will, however, produce enough to keep you hydrated and alive.

LEARN TO USE LESS WATER

Unless you've a good well and the power to pump its water, you will have to accustom yourself to using less water. Having lived in an RV for several years, I got used to taking "Navy showers," and rinsing clean dishes with hot water over dirty ones still in the sink (a habit I've continued at home, to the amusement of my friends). Install an on/off valve in your low-gpm shower to turn off water while soaping up.

WASTE WATER

We must base our next industrial revolution on using our wastes. Wastes are simply useful substances that we do not yet have the wit to use.
     -- Athelstan Spilhaus

This is generally classified in two types: gray water (from washing and bathing), and black water (sewage).

Gray water

This can usually be drained into yards and fields without problem, especially if you use friendly soaps and detergents. Make sure any soaps biodegrade within 24 hours.

Black water

Sewage must be carefully handled, and cannot be simply poured into the open ground without contaminating ground or surface water. This is one subject that must be done right.

City sewage treatment

If the power grids fail, then so do the sewage treatment plants, and these plants are nonetheless still vulnerable to their own internal Y2K problems.

Septic tanks

Expensive at Ø2-6,000, though usually affordable. Still, it's an unkind thing to do to your own land, and the permits are often a costly pain.

Composting toilets

This may be the answer, both ecologically and financially. They are waterless (or low water), clean, and odor-free. At the end of the cycle is bateria-free pure humus for your garden. While they are Ø1,000 to Ø1,500, you avoid the hassle and expense of a septic tank (especially in rocky areas), and you get to recycle your waste. Pretty elegant.

Suppliers

Cottage Toilets   800-461-2461
Envirolet   800-387-5126
Backwoods Solar   208-263-4290   www.backwoodssolar.com
BioLet   800-5BIOLET   www.biolet.com

❖ 6

FOOD

Food is power. We use it to change behavior. Some may call that bribery. We do not apologize.
  -- Catherine Bertini, Exec. Dir. U.N. World Food Program,
     U.N. 4th World Conference on Women, Sept. 1995

Billions of suddenly hungry people in January 2000 will scream bloody murder for the restoration of order. It is supremely likely that the federal government and UN will use Y2K-induced hunger to finally achieve martial control of the populace. Armed, well-fed folks are the only obstacle to this scenario. Make sure that your family and friends have stockpiles of food to see you through the lean times.

> *When I got home* (after hearing on his car radio about the 1962 Cuban Missile Crisis), *I found that the stores were jammed with people buying everything in sight. Many supermarkets in Denver were literally stripped of anything edible, while newspapers reported fights and some minor rioting as everyone translated the frightening news into personal* [re]*action to provide some security. Food was their first instinctive response.*
> -- Howard J. Ruff; *How To Prosper During The Coming Bad Years* (1979), p.249

Typical American behavior. Total apathy about or denial of their vulnerability to thin food reserves, followed by utter panic once crisis occurs. (I've been through enough hurricanes to know this first-hand.) Have your food way in advance and *stay home* when the swarms of locusts descend on the supermarkets.

I'll hit the highlights on nutrition and food alternatives, but know in advance that this chapter is *not* exhaustive. The health aspects of food I cover in the chapter *Health.*

STORED FOOD

Until you are regularly harvesting game and plants, you will need stored food to get you by. You will also need stored food for hikes, camping, patrolling, etc.

Survival Tabs

Developed for the U.S. Special Forces, these tablets are high calorie and 100% RDA sufficient in essential vitamins and minerals. Packed in a 15-day ration plastic bottle which fits in standard issue 1qt. canteen pouches, these malt-ball tasting tabs store for 8-10 years, little affected by cold or heat. Every pack of mine has at least one bottle of these attached to it. From Nitro-Pak (#5700) for Ø22-24, depending on quantity. A must for compact food for those on the move.

Store-bought food

Macaroni and cheese dinners, Ramen noodle soup, whole wheat, powdered milk, tomato juice, honey, granola bars, and raw peanuts (or peanut butter, if kept cool and rotated often) are all good low-cost, nutritious foods that store well enough. (Fish, berries, citrus products, shelled nuts, and other foods will last only 6-12 months.) Store these vermin sensitive foods in plastic containers.

Canned "wetpack" food

Depending on the contents, this will store for at least 6 months (unrotated), and up to 18 months if rotated every 6 months. By two years the nutritional value has greatly deteriorated. Bulky and heavy, but short-term familiar food for your family. Bulging cans you should always throw away unopened (botulism is reportedly no fun).

MREs

Meals Ready to Eat. Each meal is fully cooked (though they'll need heating for better taste), provides up to 1,400 calories, and is packed in a rugged plastic pouch (which is worth saving for emergency water use, etc.). They have a shelf life of up to 5 years if kept cool (not frozen). The current production dates are in tan pouches, have better menus, and come with heaters. I recently bivvied with some Army guys and experienced "MRE Envy" of their new stuff compared to my 1994s.

Tips: Resist the temptation to sort out your least favorite meals before a pack trip, else you'll just end up with a pile of them that you'll never eat. Eat the cracker; it provides necessary carbs. Slit the entreé pouch on the long side to provide better spoon access. Use the Tobasco sauce; some meals aren't all that tasty without it. Fill your canteen or CamelBak with the beverage powder for a Gatorade-like liquid. The cocoa power is surprisingly good and makes a good evening treat. Avoid the "Omelet with Ham"--it's *nasty*. Best meal in my opinion is the "Chicken á la King." Use the heater for best taste on all meals. Put some duct tape on each pouch so that you can keep it folded and closed after opening. Save the case boxes; it's the toughest cardboard on the planet, and good for heavy tools, parts, etc.

Most importantly, chew the gum, as it contains a laxative so vital with these salty, constipating meals. (The laxative gum is not widely known about.) Drink *lots* of water with MREs, else they'll gum you inside. (Once, on a 5-day hike with only MREs, I didn't have to defecate until day *4*.) MREs are *designed* this way so that troops in a protracted battle won't be hampered by daily bowel movements.

Get MREs while you *can*. The feds have put a stop to military surplus MREs, and soldiers caught selling them "U.S. Government Property" face big trouble.

Cheaper Than Dirt has contracted with Star Foods (the military's supplier) for civilian production (without the water-activated heater, which UPS considers hazardous). Cases are Ø45 each, or Ø40 each for ten or more cases. CTD will pay freight on the first 50lbs. (Cases are 14lbs. each; order #MRE-100) This is a *great* deal, folks, and CTD reports selling over 1,000 cases/month, compared to 200/month in 1997. They'll even sell you individual meals (#MRE-200, no choice of meal) for only Ø4. CTD also sells individual, precooked MRE 4oz. ham slices for only Ø10 per dozen (#MRE-410).

For current *military* production MREs, best deals are Ø50-52ppd. (depending on quantity) per case of 12 meals from Sierra Supply (970-259-1822). Tell 'em Boston sent you. Another supplier (though at Ø73ppd.) is Long Life Food Depot (800-601-2833). Emergency Essentials (800-999-1863) sells a case of 72 entreés for Ø125 which is a great deal at Ø1.73 each.

T-Rations

These serve 18 people (6oz. each). Each sealed tin contains 96-106 ounces of a single meal, such as Lasagna, Spaghetti and Meat Balls, and Chicken Breast in Gravy (there are 16 meals to choose from). Just heat and serve. From CTD for Ø15-17 each. The feds hand out T-rats during emergencies.

Air dehydrated food

I bought some dehydrated water, but I don't know what to add.
          -- Steven Wright

This food is one-fourth to one-seventh the weight of its former self. Nitro-packed food has a nutritional shelf life of years, depending on temperature of storage (cooler is better, though *do not freeze*). It is *half* as expensive as freeze-dried food, but takes longer to reconstitute. Supplement with grains, beans, freeze-dried meals for an affordable, balanced and interesting diet.

#10 (1 gallon) cans are fine for grains or powdered milk, but #2½ (1 quart) cans are better for most other foods as there's less to spoil once opened.

Home dehydrated food is fine, though it will not have the same shelf life of commercially nitro-packed food. It'll keep for about 6 months in Zip-Loc bags. Dehydrating is much less work than canning, less expensive, and takes up less space. Dehydrating units are quite affordable at under Ø60, even with fan. Have several and keep 'em working!

Freeze-dried food

98% of the water (thus 90% of the weight) is removed. None of the taste or vitamins and minerals are lost in the process. This is the lightest and highest-quality food, and you simply add hot water for reconstitution easier than air dehydrated food. It's also the most expensive, but to *me* it's well worth it. Post-crash days will be highly stressful, and the convenience of quick, easy, delicious meals (*e.g.*, shrimp creole, beef Stoganoff, etc.) are worth the extra couple of bucks per day. I'll personally have more important things to do than grind wheat, but then I've never been much for cooking.

A well-balanced, inexpensive food storage program will consist of supplements, grains and mostly dehydrated foods with some freeze-dried products. Then you add a few luxury items such as freeze-

dried meat, fish and combination casserole dishes as "reward foods." A more luxurious program would substitute all freeze-dried foods for dehydrated.
As for taste, I give a slight edge to freeze-dried, but not much.
-- Howard J. Ruff; *ibid*, p.309

Alpine Aire
Hands down, they make the best. Their Gourmet Reserves are restaurant quality--you'll forget you're "roughing it." Millennium is also good, and somewhat less expensive.

Bulk food

Beans (pinto, soy, and mung), rice, powdered milk, pasta, honey, wheat, barley, corn, millet, oats, rye, and alfalfa seeds are examples of nutritious bulk foods that store well and can be easily combined to create delicious meals for less than Ø1. (There's no reason for hunger in America. While some families may not be able to afford frozen pizzas and beer, *any* family can afford bulk foods. Food does *not* have to come in a pretty box.) Beans and grains (or rice) together form a complete protein, something Latin Americans have known for centuries.

Beverages

First rule: No soft drinks! Not only are they a ripoff, they are *very* bad for you. What's wrong with iced tea instead? Or a glass of water with a slice of lemon? Store beverage powder rather than constituted drink--it's a better bargain and more space efficient. Try to avoid dextrose based drinks for fructose ones. (Translation: No KoolAid.)

Q: *"How do I order food storage?"*

Call **Jeb Bryant (800-525-9556)** for quotes on Alpine Aire or Millennium products--and tell him Boston sent you. He reports a *tenfold* increase in orders over last year, and expects this itself to double by 1998's end. By mid-1999 he believes low-supplies and high backorders to choke off pre-2000 deliveries. If you don't order your freeze-dried food by spring 1999, you might not ever get any. Suppliers are no longer advertizing as they currently have a 3-6 *month* backlog. Other suppliers/manufacturers include: Ready Made Resources, Nitro-Pak, Major Surplus & Survival, and JRH.

Use my techniques in *Bulletproof Privacy* to order. Ideally, you want no record of your real name and address to be associated with your order, just in case the feds try to compile a master list of "hoarders" from the suppliers. Order under an alias (this is not unlawful), pay with postal M.O.s bought with cash, and have your food shipped to a freight terminus moderately out-of-town (where you're unknown) and pick it up yourself. Paranoid thinking? *Perhaps,* but this food (and the weapons to defend it) is the most important major Y2K purchase you'll make, so do it right. Create no record trail. Don't order with your credit card or check, don't use your real name, and don't have it delivered directly to your home.

Q: *"How much should I buy?"*

I'd have *at least* 3 months per family member, and I consider that an *utter* minimum. 6-12 months is much better, and I'd have 2 years if you can afford it (for friends and family who will be unprepared and hungry). Remember, not only is this *insurance,* but it's insurance you can *eat.* You cannot have enough, as most folks will have little after January 2000. Make sure that your package has at least 2,000 calories/day. Beware packages which don't brag about this.

Q: *"Where do I store it all?"*

Each person/year supply of food will weigh between 400 and 1,500lbs , depending on how much is dehydrated. Storage area will be at least 3'x3'x4' and up to twice as much. A spare bedroom will store most families' needs for up to 12 months. A cool basement is best yet, as long as flooding is not a problem in your area. I *don't* recommend storage units because of their heat and vulnerability to theft or confiscation (expect "hoarding" to become illegal by fall 1999).

Food storage, by Howard J. Ruff

❶   Store a year's supply of food per family member.
❷   Make sure it's nutritionally balanced for anti-stress.
❸   Don't rely on canned or frozen foods.
❹   Rotate your supply and replace as needed.
❺   Don't buy a "junk food" storage program. Eat healthy!
❻   **Buy it now.** This is primary insurance before all else.

Miscellaneous

Even if you're not much of a cook, somebody in your group *will* be and they'll greatly appreciate having cooking oils and a spice rack (I bought mine at Service Merchandise for only Ø40).

Keep your mouth *shut* about your food!

This is *paramount.* Hungry people without lawful recourse to food *will* resort to looting. Unarmed Mormons, for example, will likely suffer raids on their well-known food hoards.

Storing your food

The enemies of your food supply are:

Heat
Light
Air
Moisture
Vermin (weevils, beetles, roaches, moths, mice, rats, etc.)

Storage containers

The 5 gallon plastic buckets are best. Use the Gamma Seal twist-on lids to eliminate the need for a bucket wrench.

Metal cans do not off-gas as non-foodgrade plastics do. Non-foodgrade plastic containers should be lined with clear or white *Glad Bags* by Union Carbide. For best results, use metalized, dual-layered liners and nitrogen-pack the contents.

Keep your food *cool*

Food storage life is drastically reduced when temperatures rise. Take MREs for example. At 60°--130 months. At 100°--22 months. At 120°--only 1 month!

Keep your food between 40° and 60° Fahrenheit. Fats begin to melt at about 95°. Many foods are damaged if frozen, and most insects become active above 48°. Thus, the *ideal* temperature is just above freezing but below 48°--say 40°-45°. Root cellars and basements will come close to this ideal, especially in winter. Have a thermometer in the room to monitor the temp.

Best places to store your food are the basement, crawl space, root cellar, or indoor closet. (Garages are way too hot in summer.) Northern walls are coolest, and closest to the floor is best. (Ceiling areas are hotter.)

Keep your food *dark*

Glass and clear plastic containers must be kept in the dark. #10 double enameled cans are best.

Keep your food *airtight* (vacuum, CO2, nitro-packed)

Vacuum packing you can do yourself with your own equipment (visit your local Mormon cannery to learn how, and to buy bulk food). Dry ice packing you can also do yourself (allow 2-3 hours for the excess CO_2 to dissipate).

Nitrogen packed food is superior still, but only commercial foods are so delivered. Buy your hard red winter wheat in nitro-packed 5 gallon buckets.

Keep your food *dry*

Desiccant packets inside the containers absorb excess moisture and keep food dry. Use Mil Spec packets. Understand that Desiccant packets and oxygen absorber packets (for nitro-packed foods) are *not* to be mixed, as they cancel each other out.

Quality airtight plastic containers are fairly airtight, though they do tend to breathe, so keep fumes and contaminants away. Place food on wooden slats or pallets in case of flooding. A barometer is necessary to monitor room humidity.

Keep your food *vermin-free*

Unless you bought food already vacuum or nitrogen packed, you must fumigate your packed food with dry ice to kill weevils and larvae. (Only sugar, powdered milk, salt, and honey need not be fumigated.) Place a handful of the food in the container's bottom and a couple of cubic inches of dry ice on top of that. Fill the container and leave two inches of headspace. Place, *but do not seal*, the lid on the container to allow the carbon dioxide gas to escape (which requires at least an hour). After the gas has dissipated, attach and seal the lid.

Rock sulphur will fumigate at 1oz. per 5 gallons of container. Contain the sulphur in cheesecloth or nylon stockings.

Those "Curiously Strong" Altoid mints drive off insects. Sprinkle them about shelving and floor.

Mice are persistent, ravenous, little Houdinis. I have seen MRE pouches chewed through by mice. Sprinkle rock sulphur around your storage room's nooks and crannies to keep out rodents. Have a couple of cats around to thin out your local mice, and praise your cats effusively when they present you with their frequent trophies. Or, stock up on the Ø2 *Better Mouse-*

trap, which has only four parts, is easy to set, 99% deadly, and a breeze to clean. For real infestations, build a drowning trap from a water bucket with peanut butter smearing on a fishing line tightrope over the mouth. (To avoid the lethal *Hanta* virus, touch mice only with gloves and destroy or bury them. Find their habitat and sterilize it with disinfectant.)

GROWING FOOD

The very idea of being fed, or a family being fed, by daily supplies has something in it perfectly tormenting.
-- William Cobbett

You may be forced to grow your own food once the supermarkets run dry and cannot be resupplied. Since this is a *huge* subject, I can only hit the basics here. Have a gardening library.

Sprouting

I've become a *big* fan of sprouting. It is *the* cheapest, easiest, quickest (3-5 days) and most productive method of growing high-nutrition food. For example, only 20lbs of grain or seeds will yield *300-400*lbs of live food. All that's needed is water and sunlight. In the sprout stage, the nutritive content is up to *ten times* that of the unsprouted stage. For literally pennies per day a family can grow nourishing food, *indoors*. Gee. With our depleted soil and dead commercial "food," sprouts are vital.

Sprouts can come from grasses, beans (legumes), and grains. For example, **alfalfa** (because of its 100' deep roots) is highest in minerals (iron, calcium, and phosphorous), and offers good vitamins A, B-complex, C, D, E, G, K, and U. **Garbanzos** offer complete protein with many minerals. **Wheat** is high in vitamins A, B-complex, C, and E, and offers good protein.

Pounds of seeds per adult/year, by Rosalie Mason

Seeds	Beans	Grains	Peas
Alfalfa 8	Adzuki 8	Millet 8	Alaskan 12
Chia 8	Black 8	Oats 8	Bl. eyed 12
Flax 8	Lima 8	Rice 8	
Pumpkin 8	Mung 8	Rye 12	
Radish 8	Pinto 20	Wheat 30	
Sesame 8	Red 20		
Sunflower 8	Soy 20		

Best crops for the beginner

Alfalfa, mung or adzuki beans, and wheat. They germinate easily and require no special handling. Soybeans and other legumes (beans) are more difficult.

While some sprouts (alfalfa, lentils, garbanzos, and wheat) are still edible after a week, most other sprouts lose their crispness after only 2-5 days. Your sprout garden should operate in a continuous overlapping cycle of soaking, germinating, and fridge chilling. Then you'll always have fresh sprouts. **Tip:** Use the mineral-rich rinse water to make soup.

Gardens

I had *originally* planned to include a subsection on gardening, but any summary on the subject would be of little value to you all, given the varied climates, soils, etc. So, I will leave this up to your own research. A superb introduction to gardening and food self-sufficiency is *Self Reliant Living* by the McKeevers (Omega Publ., POB 4130, Medford, Oregon 97501).

I *do*, however, discuss hydroponic greenhousing since it is a largely unknown efficient method of growing vegetables.

Greenhouses

While I don't enjoy 800 years of outdoor gardening experience, having the deer and rabbits eat your first bumper crop makes an impression. Greenhouses provide protection from wildlife, and are a *great* place to have your hot-tub.

Hydroponic or not?

Hydroponics merely replaces the inefficient soil medium for a nutrient-enriched inert medium. Since the plant's root system does not have to deal with the natural stresses of poor soil, movement from wind and animals, etc., more of the nutrients go directly to the edible portions of the plant.

In short, hydroponics yield garden quantities in a fraction of the area in about one-third less time. Automatic watering timers free you from daily care, so you can even vacation.

Rooting medium

It must be sterile, inert, pH-neutral, all-natural, water absorbent, and affordable. The best seems to be milled coconut husk fiber, which is superior even to the excellent rockwool (which has, for some, objectionable runoff).

Water

Rainwater and steam distilled water are best. City water has too much calcium, well water often is too mineral saturated (spend Ø150 for a full test from your co-op), and surface water is usually alive with microscopic critters.

Nutrients

Plants need nitrogen (N), potassium (P), and phosphorus (K)--or NPK--plus calcium, magnesium, sulphur, and nickel. Necessary trace elements include chlorine, boron, iron, manganese, zinc, copper, and molybdenum.

Another neat thing about hydroponics is that you can tailor feed your plants for their changing needs. The vegetative stage requires more nitrogen; the stem-developing stage, potassium; and the blooming/fruiting stage, phosphorus. Regular gardening (organic or not) mixes in compost (or fertilizer) and relies on the plants to take more of what they need.

Buy the best--period. Quality In, Quality Out. These plants are feeding only your *body,* folks--which you kind of *need* down here. The three-part FloraGro system from General Hydroponics is regarded as the best.

Lighting

If your greenhouse will not receive ample sunlight, then artificial lighting must be installed. Plants need a minimum of 1000fc (foot candles) for bare photosynthesis and survival. Four 40W full-spectrum GroLite bulbs deliver only 1500fc, and most plants need 2000-5000fc for the leaves. You'd need a bank of 35 100W GroLites to cover 4'x4' of tomato plants with sufficient energy, and running 3.5kWh of bulbs for 16 hours is absurd.

High-intensity discharge (HID) lamps are the only artificial sun option. Each 500W lamp complete fixture costs Ø300 (replacement bulbs are Ø75) and light 16ft^2 of plants. Given a full 16hr photoperiod (8kWh/day), artificial lighting is *rarely* feasible for independent energy systems in low sun areas (unless you've *lots* of micro-hydro). If you're on the grid then HID costs only 50¢/day per 500W.

Such HID lighting does, however, have the advantage of providing great heat to offset other heating energy demands.

Downside to hydroponics

Since its basically a laboratory, it must start out sterile and be *kept* sterile, to avoid algae and fungus gnats. Unique indoor pests such as whiteflies and spider mites are *very* hard to eradicate without using pesticides once they've thrived.

Suppliers
General Hydroponics   www.generalhydroponics.com
Light Manu.   800-669-5483   www.litemanu.com
Worm's Way   800-274-9676
American Hydroponics   707-822-5777
Diamond   800-331-8311
Real Goods   800-762-7325
Hydrofoam   800-634-9990
www.howtohydroponics.com
www.hydroponics.com
www.aqueous.com/aq148.shtml

Beekeeping

During Y2K I think I'll embrace a couple of new careers, such as beer brewing and beekeeping. No other branch of agriculture yields so great a return on so small an investment with so little interference with other activities as beekeeping. Each hive (containing about 30,000 bees) will produce about 50lbs. of yearly surplus honey, which can be kept or sold for up to Ø5/lb. Not only that, bees account for 80% of the nation's pollination and are necessary for your area's crops. Here's an overview.

Beekeeping equipment

Less than Ø200 will get you started. You'll need a hive (which you can build yourself), a smoker to pacify bees when you're working in the hive, a hive tool to pry apart frames, a veil to protect your head and face, gloves, and a feeder to dispense the initial sugar syrup until the bees begin producing their own.

Bees

There only three kinds of bees: the queen, the workers (sterile males who do everything but mate), and the drones (whose only function is to mate with the queen). Each hive has only one queen, who lays as many as 1,000 eggs per day because the worker bees are constantly being replaced (6wk life-span).

The **Italian** strain of bees are the most common in America, as they are hardy, industrious, and relatively gentle. The so-called **Caucasian** strain are even more gentle, but use excessive amounts of propolis in their hives which makes the frames difficult to remove.

Experienced beekeepers can capture a wild swarm to establish in their own hives. For the novice, however, it is much simpler to buy from a beekeeper your queen and a couple of pounds of bees. The best time to establish a new honey bee colony is naturally in the spring when fruit trees and flowers are in bloom. Bees must be near water (a hive can use a gallon per day), and do best if their colony is in the shade.

If you don't want to do the work, simply own the hive and give half the surplus honey to a beekeeper who works it for you.

Where does the honey come from?

Bees feed on nectar from flowers, and transform nectar into honey (through evaporation) to get them through the winters (when no flowers are blooming). Since a colony will produce 100lbs. of honey each year, but need only 50lbs. for the winter, we can enjoy the 50lbs. surplus.

Fish farming

It is virtually self-managing, and twice as productive than cattle in feed conversion. If your pond system is a *polyculture*, the fish mortality drops from 80% (in the wild) to only 10%.

> *Modern homesteaders could do no better than pattern their fish culture after that of the venerable Chinese system. It works and has for some time. Several thousand years ago Chinese farmers perfected pond culture, developing uncanny techniques for water control and dam construction as well. They knew almost everything known today about breeding and stocking fish, pond fertilization, and weed control. Their terraced ponds had many advantages, not the least of which was the separation of the breeding and growing stages of fish development. One of their greatest contributions was the breeding of varieties of one species of fish to live on the various foodstuffs found on the different levels of a balanced aquatic environment. They stocked herbivorous, plankton-eating, and bottom-feeding varieties. They even bred carp to produce varieties of this species that would consume a specific diet at a specific level of the pond.*
>
> -- Barbara & Ken Kern; *The Owner-Built Homestead,* p. 312

The terracing of ponds drains crop nutrients and animal waste into the fish ponds, which is easily digestible by the fish. Everything is used and recycled. The Chinese even provide privies over their ponds, inviting the passersby to stop and relieve themselves, which strikes me as rather elegant. (Crap in somebody's pond *here* and you'll get arrested. I don't think that the "Fertilizer Defense" will hold up in court...)

With the right combination of plants, ducks, and other mutually beneficial life, a fish pond can give you *hundreds* of pounds of fish (a fat/carb free protein) each year with little work or maintenance. Lovely.

HUNTING FOR FOOD

Unless you're in the back country of a very thinly populated state, hunting for *all* one's food in the U.S.A. will be probably untenable. Deer and elk and moose could be reduced to 10% of their populations in a year of unrestricted hunting. We nearly lost our nation's whitetail deer in the 19th century, and they have rebounded only since the 1930s.

So, if you are already experienced at hunting, you won't need my advice--except to not kill them all off. I hunt, and plan to continue hunting my entire life, although I will be careful not to jeopardize my local herd population.

If you've never hunted, don't start, as you're very likely to merely wound a precious animal and forsake it to a miserable death. Start a vegetable garden and be happy with that. Hunting is a science, an art, a skill, and a passion. Don't try to take it up in 2000 because you haven't had a burger in several months.

FISHING FOR FOOD

Since there are only 100 calories per pound of fish, it is not feasible to exist totally on fish alone. Nutritionally, you'll need to supplement a fish diet with carbs and fat, as fish have almost none. Net fishing is the only *practical* method of catching *lots* of fish on an extended basis. Farming fish makes even more sense in the long run, which I've already discussed.

BOOKS TO GET

Seed To Seed,
Best of The Basics, Jim Stevens
Don't Get Caught With Your Pantry Down!, Jim Stevens
Wheat for Man
     A comprehensive cookbook for wheat.

❖ 7

HEALTH

Health is not a stable condition of soundness throughout, like a steel building on a concrete foundation. **Health is a state of balance maintained by perpetual adjustments to forces from within and without.** *Through the years, the days, the hours, both waking and sleeping, we are steadily responding to the conditions of life, to hunger and food, to cold and heat, to fatigue and rest, to anger and pleasure. We must also deal with our ambitions and our fears, with jealousy, with grief, with feelings of inferiority, with defeats as well as victories, and with the inevitable acceptance of aging.* **Health depends on how well the individual as a whole can maintain balance through all these changes.**
-- Arnold A. Hutschnecker, M.D.; *The Will To Live*

What can a sick man say but that he is sick.
-- Samuel Johnson

When a man dies, he does not just die of the disease that he has, **he dies of his whole life.**
-- Péguy

While this chapter *seems* fairly extensive, I've really only hit the highlights. While researching *Boston on Surviving Y2K*, it dawned on me that the bulk of most "survival" and "live free" books was comprised by the subject of health and food--and not so much how to start a fire or build a log home. *Hmmmm.*

I used to breeze through all that health and food stuff. *Until recently.* I've just realized how utterly vital good health is! Since I am not yet even forty years of age, and was blessed with a very good physiology, health had never been much of a concern to me. I'd gradually moved to the simple country life and healthier foods over several years, but I have just this year begun to really appreciate the necessity of pure, wholesome food and the elimination of toxic elements from one's diet (mentally and spiritually, as well as physically). The computer programmers' mantra of GIGO well illustrates the point:

Garbage In, Garbage Out.

To avoid disease, illness, and cancer (Garbage Out), avoid the Garbage *In* (intake of toxins, such as the wrong foods, life-style, attitude, and thinking).

[H]ealth is not really difficult or complicated to achieve. Most of it consists of letting go of things and situations we really don't need. Who need a giant house with a thirty-year mortgage (millstone)? Who needs one of those throwaway cars that must be replaced just as the last payment is made? And who needs to live amidst confusion and congestion when there is so much of the world that is both beautiful and quiet? (at 189)
         -- Bill Kaysing; *Bill Kaysing's Freedom Encyclopedia* (1988)

So, this *Health* chapter will not focus on disease cures, but *prevention*. **And what prevention boils down to is simply avoiding the Garbage In.** Western civilization has bent over backwards to create patently unhealthy food. Probably 98% of God's earthly garden is healthy on its own, yet we manage to poison and deaden all this naturally good food. A mortician friend of mine once told me that the legal imperative to embalm after three days was in practicality no longer necessary because modern DBs (dead bodies) arrive on the slab with ample preservatives in them from the previous owners' diet. We are walking around already *one-third* embalmed! We are just energized corpses, zombies. Walking Twinkies in 33% dead bodies.

This [American] society is insane. All of it--the customs, the work, the hours devoted to work, the way people spoke to each other without looking, the homes they lived in, the streets they walked, the air, the noise, the filth, the bread--all the basics.
         -- Elia Kazan; *The Arrangement*

"Insane" is not too harsh of a word. If we employ the definition of insanity as a disassociation with reality, then our society *is* insane. We eat Death instead of Life. We worship fictional characters on TV and ignore the true heroes among us. Sport figures are paid millions per year, while the best grade school teacher in the country can't break Ø50K. We tolerate a morally autistic President, as long as the economy seems strong. We fuel the stock market full of vaporish corporations with infinite

P/E ratios, and allow gold to languish at Ø285 an ounce. We long for retirement after 40 years of shouldering the grindstone, yet can't figure out what to do on a rainy Sunday afternoon. And we train our children to be just like us. **We *are* insane.** Our modern civilization is a tawdry play, and its actors are living it as though it were real life. We don't even have a sense of self-preservation.

Example: About 90% of America's supermarket foods come from just two dozen mega-corporations, such as General Mills. **What they are *really* selling us is *Death*, in a colorful cardboard box.** (Whoever thought up *Tombstone* pizza understood his business precisely.) Death By "Food" is forestalled by the ingestion of FDA-approved drugs. (And we're surprised that one of us in *four* dies of *cancer*--which simpler societies and wildlife don't experience.) An excellent research project for the brave of heart is to explore the murky cooperation and interlocking directorates between the *food* corporations and the *pharmaceutical* corporations. If you're in the Poison business, it makes perfect sense to also be in the *Antidote* business--however, the pharmaceutical "antidote" is actually an even worse *poison* than processed foods.

As Dr. Arnold A. Hutschnecker wrote, good health derives from maintaining a proper balance of important elements. Bill Kaysing listed the most important ones:

Diet	(mega-corp Death--or natural Life?)
Environment	(toxic city--or clean country?)
Your Attitude	(philosophy, religion, family, friends)
Exercise	(Inaction breeds stagnation.)
Occupation	(Rat Race--or Rewarding Leisure?)
Recreation	(Harried--or relaxing?)
Vitamins, Minerals, Supplements and Herbs	

Kaysing amplified this with his Two Best Health Guarantees:

1. Create an interesting life for yourself. Eliminate boredom. Do what you want to do, not what other people tell you that you should do. Remember, to be is to do, and vice versa. All the organic food in the world won't help if you're trapped in some boring office job or routine office slot. Nor will diet help if you are constantly under emotional stresses or financial pressure.

This is the most important aspect of health, as I have learned by actual living experiences. Everything else is subordinate to what you are doing inside your head on a day-to-day basis. If you are

frustrated, uncreative, bored and thwarted in self-fulfillment, then don't expect to be healthy no matter what else you do.
2. **Your body is constantly being rebuilt from the foods you eat, the water you drink, and the air you breathe.** *Through cell replacement, you get a new heart every two months, so be sure that it is built from quality ingredients. ...The easy way out is a packaged goodie from the local convenience store, but your body knows the difference and will soon tell you about it in the form of severe complaints. So take the time and trouble to put the best food you can possibly get into your body.* (ibid, at 206-207)

If you create an interesting life for yourself and maintain a good diet, good health *will* follow. Why this is not more obvious or logical to people is because of their incessant brainwashing. **Dare to be *contrarian*!** The masses are nearly always wrong, and about 80% of humanity lead lives of quiet desperation as they slowly kill themselves with their diet of Death. Take that road "less travelled by" to discover Truth and Life.

What you need is a little madness.
You must cut the rope to be free.
    -- Zorba the Greek

Comedian Drake Sather (a wonderfully dry and sick wit) made a joke of dog biscuits which freshened Fido's breath: *"You know, if a dog wanted fresher breath, you'd think he'd stop eating his own sh*t! That would sort of get the 'fresh-breath-ball' rolling."*

Similarly, if people wanted better health, you'd think they'd stop eating such crap! You cannot have Life by consuming *Death.* I call it *DIDO*--Death In, Death Out. People spend more attention to the quality of the oil in their car's crankcase than they do to the quality of the food in their own stomach.

CANCER

Cancer cells *naturally* occur in our bodies, and are actually part of a defense system to eat away damaged tissue. It is only when they proliferate at an abnormally high rate that such is called cancer. Cancer cells wrap a protein coat around themselves to repel like-charged white cells. What *normally* keeps the number of cancer cells in check are enzymes (pancreatic, mostly) which dissolve away this protein coat and allow the white cells to do their job.

Two things get out of balance to cause cancer cell proliferation: Excessive damaged tissue (from the sun, smoking, etc.) which causes excessive cancer cells, and pancreatic enzymes diminished from abnormal digestion requirements of unhealthy foods (*e.g.*, pork). If one's diet consists of less meat and more raw foods, grains, and legumes (beans), cancer cells are kept in check naturally. That's why simple cultures and wildlife *don't* get cancer, and we *do*. **It's all *diet*, folks. Death In, Death Out.**

This has been understood since the 1930s, but any doctor treating patients accordingly had been jailed and/or run out of the country. **You see, there's no money in *healthy* people...** Because the human body is a marvelous machine that is *designed* to work long and well with little incident, doctors *ought* to be as *unbusy* as the MayTag repairman. The body really does require a *lot* of abuse and poisoning before it fails.

> *Look after the causes of things; the effects will take care of themselves.*
> -- Eric Gill

The "cut/burn/poison" treatments kill more people than the cancer, and one is statistically better off avoiding such for natural cures. I lost my favorite grandfather to their chemo and radiation treatments, so don't get me started on these *butchers*. They might as well go back to mercury and leeches.

NUTRITIONAL BASICS

The Red Cross has calculated 1,858 calories as the adult minimum per day. The following table is a rough guide:

Adult Male	2000-3500
Adult Female	1800-2500
Teenagers	2000-3000
Children under 12	1000-2000

Any family food storage program that figures on an average of 2000-2500 calories per person/day will be about right, unless you've many teenagers (who eat about as much as dad does).

Howard Ruff placed the following list in concentric target rings, and claimed that one could remain alive and healthy (though culinarily bored) by eating from just ❶ and ❷.

❶ Protein, Vitamins, Essential Fatty Acids, Minerals

Protein supplement

This will likely be in the form of a powder. It should:

    taste good
    have a high Protein Efficiency Ration (P.E.R.) of over 2
    mix well with little/no grit factor
    be high in lysine & tryptophan (casein should be the first ingredient)
    be low in milk powder (which you'll buy in that form)
    have fructose and not glucose (which requires insulin to metabolize).

Vitamins and Minerals

They should: be an all-natural formula, be in a soft gelatin capsule (for better shelf life and digestion), have essential fatty acids (lipids and sterols), be canned for long-term storage.

Vitamin C should be separate due to the volume of recommended consumption. Under periods of stress you will need more well-balanced animal protein and vitamin C. (A half-hour of stress or fear can deplete all the vitamin C in your blood stream, and a day can deplete all the vitamin C stored in your adrenal cortex. Carry vitamin C geltabs when on patrols or missions.) Use a natural form of C (concentrate citrus fruit, rose hips and acerola cherries). You'll need 200-500mg per day, and more for therapeutic (or mega) doses.

Calcium tablets (with hydrochloric acid) are vital. (Calcium deficiencies can lead to leg cramps, nervousness, and heart irregularities.)

❷ Wheat, Dry Milk, Beans, Sprouting Seeds

Wheat

It's highly versatile, extremely well-balanced, and keeps forever. Wheat found in King Tut's pyramid tomb even germinated after over 2,500 years. Just keep it cool and dry. Half of yours should be in bulk, the other half in one gallon cans.

Wheat is low in Lysine (an essential amino acid, which beans, milk, and TVP provide). Man cannot live by bread alone.

Dry Milk

Provides substantial protein, good carbs, and calories. Very useful in food preparation.

I like the Swiss Whey milk from Country Fresh Farms (503-620-0700). It's delicious and mixes well. It's available in cans for 5 year shelf life, and the price/gallon is no more than store-bought milk (which tastes gross in comparison).

Beans
They provide a complimentary protein to wheat and should be eaten in the same meal. They both also provide some complex carbohydrates, essential fatty acids, and vitamin Bs.

Sprouting Seeds
Provide high-quality vitamins and minerals, as if by magic. No cooking is required, and little handling. Great for city folks. I've read of a family of seven who survived in perfect health *six months* of snowbound winter on nothing but sprouts.

❸ TVP, Honey, Dried Fruits, Salt, Dried Vegetables

TVP (Textured Vegetable Protein)
This is basically soy bean meat imitation (though not a meat *substitute*). High in Lysine to complement wheat's lack.

Honey
Much higher in fructose than table sugar (sucrose) and better for you. Contains traces of minerals and B vitamins. It keeps forever, as bacteria cannot exist in honey.

Dried Fruits
After 2000, it may be quite a while until we see bananas, oranges, etc. again. Dehydrate a bunch to tide you over.

Salt
Vital for nutrition, cooking, and the preservation of food. If you want the most *natural* salt available, then REALSALT is for you. Mined from a 150 million year old seawater deposit in Utah, REALSALT is free from chemical additives (*e.g.*, Silico Aluminate, Potassium Iodide, Tri-calcium Phosphate, Magnesium Carbonate, etc.) and heat processing. It tastes great (not bitter like regular table salt) and you can even buy it in bulk. From Redmond Minerals (800-367-7258).

❹ Canned Goods, Frozen Food, Home Dehydration

Familiar supplements to the first three groups.

FOOD IS THE BEST MEDICINE

We consume about 30 tons of food in our lifetimes, and it has profound effects on our health, attitude, and well-being. In Kaysing's *Freedom Encyclopedia*, he quotes several pioneering doctors (Bieler, McKenzie, Sydenham, and Boerhaave) in a sequentially explanatory order. To paraphrase:

1. Diseases are the result of long-developing processes which begin early in life and finally lead to body saturation with toxins.

2. Improper eating, living and thinking habits are the prime cause of this degeneration.

3. The same type of toxin when localized in a joint causes arthritis; when localized in the liver, hepatitis; in the kidneys, nephritis; in the skin, dermatitis; in the pancreas, diabetes; in the brain, insanity.

4. Disease is nothing else but an attempt on the part of the body to rid itself of morbific matter.

5. Disease is cured with the help of nature by neutralization and excretion of morbific matter.

In his *Food Is Your Best Medicine*, Dr. Bieler summarized:

I have reached three conclusions:
1. The primary cause of disease is toxemia caused by improper foods which results in cellular impairment and breakdown.
2. The use of drugs to treat patients is harmful. Drugs often cause serious side effects and sometimes cause new diseases.
3. Disease can be cured by the use of correct foods.

What to *avoid*

Avoid the Death *In,* and you won't see its Death *Out.* Would you put 85 octane watery gasoline in your Porsche? No? Then why are you putting the equivalent in your *body*?

White (sugar, flour/bread, margarine, etc.)

Foods are not white in nature. We refine them with bleaches to make them white, and thus *appearing* clean.

Baby foods

Mostly water and sugar, to get your child hooked on sweets for life (so he can "graduate" to colas, desserts, etc.).

Supermarket white bread

It's made from devitalized flour and chemicals. Rats die from it, and weevils avoid it. Not life supporting.

Foods that are canned, preserved, or irradiated

This kills most natural nutrients.

Foods that have been sprayed, coated, or treated

Might as well sprinkle DDT on your dinner plate.

Coffee

Coffee has been statistically linked to heart disease, and one cup is equal to .01 roentgens of radiation. Go for herb teas instead. If you must have that coffee taste, try pearled barley oven roasted at 350° (for about 30 min. until deep brown), ground and mixed 50/50 with chicory, and brewed.

Table salt

Use natural sea salt, which has no additives.

Artificial sweetners

White sugar is actually better for you than *NutraSweet.*

Margarine

It's one atom away from being a plastic. *Mmmm.*

Fluoridated water

Instead of government and the AMA encouraging a rational debate "hear the other side," the *antis* were ridiculed as paranoid simpletons even though most European countries have outlawed the fluoridation of drinking water. Fluoride, a by-product of making aluminum, is the active ingredient in rat poison. Gee. It has been proven to stunt intelligence and foment mental lethargy.

Drink well or distilled water only--even when travelling.

Soft drinks

Gross! Liquid Death. Your body leaches calcium from your bones to neutralize the acid.

In a checkout aisle I perused a tabloid article about a couple who met over their love for, of all things, *Plaza Cola.* (Talk about *slumming* it.) Together, they drink a couple of gallons of it every day. Their basement was stocked nearly to the ceiling with cases of it. They were some of the most flabby, pasty, unhealthy people I ever saw.

Save your money *and* your life--avoid soft drinks. What's wrong with iced tea, or water with a slice of lemon?

Pork

Dr. Royal Rife, the medical scientist who cured cancer in the 1930s, wrote that after eating pork (or chicken skin) a patient's blood picture looked cancerous for several hours. Pork is a food that requires *lots* of pancreatic enzymes for digestion, which means fewer left over for keeping cancer cells in check.

I'll miss bacon and sausage, but my health is more important. (Turkey substitutes taste fine.)

Junk food
No more Pop Tarts, Pringles (the "fiber-board" of chips), and Twinkies! You might also cut out the Lucky Charms cereal... The box they come is probably better for you.

Pasteurized/homogenized dairy products
I won't go into what they do to cows for increased milk production. Drink powdered milk or fresh dairy milk, please.

Preparing healthy food
The fresher the better, and the less cooking the better. Remember, Life In--Life Out.

No microwave ovens!
Radiation kills many of the nutrients, leaving you with hot, tasty, *dead* food. Yes, they *are* quick, but Death is always quicker and easier than Life. LILO/DIDO, folks, Pay with time and money for *health*.

Grow in fertile soil, eat it whole, directly from source
This is the "secret" of healthy societies, none of them existing in the Western world.

Cook as little as possible
Water soluble vitamins, such as C and B-complex, cannot survive their twin evils of heat and water. Vitamin C losses can be as much as 75% during meal preparation and cooking. Protein is best cooked quickly (if at all) by broiling or quick searing, to avoid deteriorating amino acids and Vitamin B.

The best method of cooking is the Chinese *wok*, which quickly stir-fries food with a minimum of cellular change and nutritional loss.

Vita-Mix machines
Many folks swear by the Vita-Mix (800-848-2649) machines, which juice, cook, freeze, chop, puree, mix, grind/knead, blend, and crack. Then, it cleans itself in less than 90 seconds. While they are hideously expensive, they make nutritious food, and your body and mind might be worth it. Please tell your friends about my books so I can afford my own Vita-Mix!

DENTAL

A friend of mine has been a heavy smoker for over 40 years. His teeth are fine, but his *gums* won't hold, and his jawbone is receding. During a restaurant dinner, one of his teeth simply fell out onto his plate--to the horror and revulsion of all present. He quickly began a regimen of vitamins, mouthwash, flossing, etc., but the damage had too much of a head start. He now has only half of his teeth. (I asked him if he could get new *gums* and jawbone. He didn't think that was very funny...) You've seen those old guys with their bottom jaw lost from mouth cancer--they look like space aliens.

Start taking care of your teeth and gums! If you clean your teeth as you clean your dishes, you'll have no trouble. An ounce of prevention is worth a *ton* of cure, later. Cut back, or quit, heavy smoking, coffee drinking, and sweets.

Even in normal times, dental problems are miserable. After 2000, when professional dental care may be sporadic or nonexistent, an exposed nerve or gum infection could prove utterly debilitating or fatal.

I mix anti-plaque mouthwash and hydrogen peroxide 50/50, and use it several times a day to keep the bacterial chain broken up. I go through 2¼oz. of this each day, for only Ø3.50 per month. A *year's* supply would be 17 bottles of 24oz. mouthwash, and 26 bottles of 16oz. hydrogen peroxide for only Ø42.

HYGIENE

Good health requires good hygiene. The hippies of Haight-Ashbury district of San Francisco found this out in the 1960s. Forsaking all personal hygiene as "cramping their style" and unnatural, they stopped bathing entirely. Soon, they besieged their local free clinics with an assortment of ailments, rots, rashes, and itches never seen by the doctors (which were finally identified from medical books on ancient diseases).

While soap and washcloths are inexpensive and easy to use, they seem to be too costly and complex for too many people.

EXERCISE

Cardiovascular

For its health, the heart must be "revved up" for an uninterrupted 20 minutes, at least every other day. Jogging, skipping rope (excellent CV exercise), rebounding, whatever--just get your heart rate up three times a week.

Muscle tone

An expensive gym membership is not necessary. *Regular* walking and upper body calisthenics (chin ups, push ups, sit ups, etc.) will keep most folks in shape. I like rowing a small boat on a lake. Stretching like a cat and isometrics are also a real boon to fitness. Simple regularity of basic exercise is more effective than irregular quality workouts. However you exercise, pick something you that *like* doing, and do it daily.

PROTECTION FROM INJURY

It's a lot easier to *avoid* injuries than it is to *repair* them--and a lot less painless. We've all done stupid things to cause injury to ourselves, and that's only natural. Wisdom means m is a lack of *repeat* performances. You cannot afford to take a chance during 2000 with injury as hospitals, staff, and supplies will be reduced.

Avoid injury from exercise

Stretch before strenuous exercise. There's no excuse for torn ligaments and shinsplints if you stretch beforehand. The older you get, the more important this becomes. (I'm learning firsthand that I'm no longer "Superman.")

Avoid mechanical injury

Cut *away* from you, not towards you. Wear gloves. Protect your eyes. Turn off and unplug devices *before* working on them. A friend of mine, a master knifemaker and craftsman, removed nearly his entire thumb with his bandsaw because he did not turn it off before he attempted to dislodge some material. Experience also breeds cockiness. Stay alert and humble.

Eyes

Wear safety glasses *religiously* with *all* power tools and hand tools (saws, hammers, etc.). Insist on only industrial grade safety glasses with an ANSI Z87.1 certification (it'll be on the frame or legs) for superior IR and UV protection (for the sun). Do not trust the little "99% UV" stickers on the cheapies' lenses. True Z87.1 standards will be so certified on the frame.

I highly recommend the polycarbonate glasses from Pro-Tech (800-500-4739) by the dozen for only a few dollars apiece. These glasses are *far* better than gas station/supermarket cheapies, and as good (or better) than expensive brands. GPT glasses even *look* good, too.

In short, pick *high-quality* glasses, and wear them *often*. Have several pairs sprinkled about (car, home, shed, shop, etc.) so that you'll never be far from a pair. Don't ever chop wood, drill metal, etc. "just this once" without your glasses. It takes only a small sliver to blind you for life.

Take no chances with your eyes, especially since simply wearing glasses offers all the protection they need. Have spare contacts and eyeglasses, if you were them.

Ears

Millions of microscopic *cilia*, like fields of wheat in the wind, wave with sound pressure and transmit such as hearing. These *cilia* are very fragile and get broken off from extreme pressure. They *don't* grow back, and they can't be transplanted. "Hearing aids" merely amplify sound to the remaining *cilia* at their optimum frequency. Given the complexity of the human ear, we'll see cybernetic *eyes* long before artificial ears.

Protect your ears. Wear earplugs religiously when exposed for than 5 minutes to any noise level above 85 decibels. I have worn earplugs for years while motorcycling, flying, etc., and my hearing is now much more acute than my peers'.

Knees

Knees are very fragile and extremely expensive to repair. Ask any pro football player. Stretch and warm up your tendons before strenuous use, and wear quality footwear for work, hiking, or any other activity which is notoriously hard on knees.

Feet

Wear heavy boots (steel toe if necessary). Broken feet are amongst the most painful and debilitating of all injuries. A broken metatarsal bone will take you off your feet immediately.

SUPPLIES

Hygiene

Basic supplies will go a long way in providing at least modest hygiene. Think ahead for all the supplies you take for granted, and stock up. Making soaps and toothbrushes is, I hear, not much fun.

Dental

waxed floss (have lots, as there is no good substitute)
toothbrush (stock up, as substitutes pale in comparison)
toothpaste (preferably fluoride-free and natural)
mouthwash, used several times a day to break up bacterial chain
     (I mix hydrogen peroxide and anti-plaque mouthwash 50/50.)
dental mirror
dental picks (for regular plaque scaling)
cold sore medication
mirror
dentures, and related supplies

Face

Keep your face clean and free of oil buildup. Also, protect your face from the sun! *Moderate* tanning is O.K., but use sunscreen religiously to avoid skin cancer later (*e.g.*, on the nose).

milk mud pack (2 tablespoons dry milk powder with 1 tbls. water)
cleanser/astringent (50/50 rubbing alcohol and Witch Hazel)
baby wipes or other moistened towelettes (for outdoors)

Skin

soap
polypropylene "loofah" sponge (have used one for years)

Feet

This is the most neglected part of the human body, besides the brain. Keep your toenails neat and trimmed--don't let them get like goat's hooves. Keep your feet clean and aired out, and they won't fail you. Keep a bit of callus on the soles, in case you're forced to be barefoot over rough terrain.

toenail clippers
pads for corns, blisters, etc.

First aid

An orange paramedic kit (often called a Thompson pack) can be had from Nitro-Pak (and others), and would be vital in a trauma situation. They are expensive (Ø300), but totally self-contained.

Tools and books

First aid book
ice pack
hot water bottles
scalpel and replaceable blades
scissors
tweezers
eye dropper
eye glass (to wash eyes)
thermometers (oral and rectal)
blood pressure gauge
clamps, forceps, etc.
tourniquets (belt, surgical tubing, etc.) and twisting stick
splints (strips of wood, or inflatable splint)
snake bite kit
bed pan
flashlight
measuring cup and spoons
needles and safety pins (for sutures)

Consumables

black silk thread or suture thread
sterile 4"x4" pads
gauze
sheets and towels (for slings and dressings)
Q-Tips
Ace bandages; 2", 3", 4"
assorted Band-Aids
adhesive tape, 1" wide
roll cotton, 1lb.
matches and candles
Melaleuca (Pain-A-Trate, Mela-Gel, and T36-C7)
Vaseline, in 1lb. jars
Murine, or other eye wash
boric acid crystals, powder and ointment
Epsom salts (to reduce swellings)
Erogophene Ointment (drawing salve)

oil of cloves (toothache drops)
ethyl alcohol 70% (rubbing and sterilizing)
hydrogen peroxide (for sterilization and water storage)
baking soda (for insect bites and tooth powder)
dry mustard (an emetic)
syrup of Ipecac (induces vomiting in case of poisoning)
Imodium or any generic Loperamide hydrochloride (for diarrhea)
Mentholatum
Paregoric (need prescription)
Aspirin, 1000 tablet size (Upjohn Libby is best. Others break down.)
Iodine (for sterilization of wounds and surface water)
tincture of green soap
Merthiolate (antiseptic and gemicide)
table salt
cornstarch (for scalding or chaffing)
Cayenne pepper (cuts, sore throat, ulcers)
Milk Magnesia
nasal spray
antacid tablets or liquid
cold medicine
allergy medicine
cough medicine (*e.g.*, Robitussin-DM)
lip balm
sunscreen (use very high SPF of 15-40)
Purex
D.M.S.O. (from vet supply house or ag store)
vitamins and minerals (long storage variety)

Melaleuca is a plant which grows only in Australia. Tea made from the leaves...and an oil pressed from it have been known to have incredible healing and cleansing properties. During WWII, every Australian soldier carried a vial of Melaleuca oil in the first aid kit in his backpack. It was found to be exceptionally effective on burns, skin problems, poisonous insect bites and various fungal and bacterial infections. In addition, it was found to have the following beneficial properties: soothing, natural antiseptic and fungicide, penetrating, non-caustic, aromatic, natural solvent. (Note: Melaleuca products are available from Alpine, 800-453-7453. BTP)
　　　-- Dr. James McKeever; *Self-Reliant Living,* p.54

I do *not* recommend painkillers other than aspirin (which comes from willow tree bark). Modern substitutes can be harmful to your organs (the liver and kidneys, in particular).

A large plastic tool or fishing tackle box can be used as your first aid box. Liquid containers should be placed in their own small Zip-Loc bags in case of leakage.

PERSONNEL

Herbalists & Nutritionists
The Western World is finally appreciating the centuries of health wisdom from the East. While we are superb at trauma medicine and corrective surgery, we have little idea on how to *be* healthy. I used to mildly scoff at herbalists and nutritionists, but no longer. A East/West synthesis is happening, one long overdue. In short, try to *be* healthy without pharmaceuticals and look first to natural herbs, oils, etc. for the non-life threatening issues. Herbals are valuable people in your group or area, especially if they make their own tinctures, teas, etc.

American Botanical Pharmacy (310-453-1987) is an excellent source of high-quality/high-strength herbs.

Midwifes
Most of the world's babies are born under the supervision of merely a midwife. (Many births have not even *that*, according to Monty Python's *The Meaning of Life*.) I know of a midwife with over 1,000 births of experience. Unless the pregnancy and delivery are severely problematic, a good midwife can handle nearly any birth without doctors or hospitals (but consider having such on "standby" if possible).

Trauma medics
If there's any civil unrest and shooting, you could need a trauma medic to save your life. Somebody in your group might be a paramedic, RN, or combat vet. Have s/he train your people quickly, as this talent is one to be widely duplicated.

Dentists
They get highly specialized training that not even doctors have. While one dentist can service hundreds of patients, good ones seem hard to find (especially in rural areas and small towns), so get to work *now* finding one for your locale.

GP Doctors
Sometimes, only a doctor will do. Medics and nurses can accomplish a lot, but at some point a doctor must be called for. I

know of many who are leaving organized practice and all its bureaucratic hassles for the country-doctor life. (If we are ever cursed with a national "health care" system, then their exodus will dramatically increase.) I also know of many doctors are happy to provide "black market" service, even under the auspices of their normal office.

Start to cultivate these doctors quickly. Since they are highly specialized people with little country life experience, enticing them to your area is easier than you may think. Most likely, they *love* being doctors and would continue to *be* doctors in the right environment. They don't want to totally give such up for agriculture or laying bricks.

Surgeons

Surgeons are one worthwhile thing that very large cities have over everywhere else. Some surgical procedures can be performed *only* by internationally renowned surgeons who live in NYC, Chicago, L.A., etc. and practice in huge hospitals which can afford the necessary equipment and staff. I see little chance of such a person and equipment being available near your homestead at Bear Dropping, Alaska.

BOOKS TO GET

When There Is No Doctor and *Where There Is No Dentist*
For 3rd World areas, which we might emulate for awhile. This is very comprehensive and well-illustrated. Ideal for the layman. A must in every home and car.

American Red Cross First Aid Guide
This can be found at thrift stores for 25¢. Buy them all, so that every vehicle, backpack, and building can have their own.

The Merck Manual
The standard text for medical professionals. It covers all medical disorders from abdominojugular reflex to zoophilia, their symptoms, and their recommended treatments.

Survivalist's Medicine Chest, Ragnar Benson
How to use veterinary medicines to treat yourself. From Paladin Press.

◆ 8

ENERGY

I'm going to classify energy needs into three categories: heat (air and water), electricity (renewable or generated sources), and refrigeration (air and food).

Besides food and health, the subject I learned the most during this book's research was energy. What I've concluded are two things, the first a probability and the second a *certainty*.

First, the power grids will *very likely* go down for most of you, and stay down for weeks or months. This has been amply proven, I believe, in *Why Disaster Looms*.

Second, to plan for this likelihood and maintain at least a semblance of modern life with electric light, appliances, and refrigeration will require a *minimum* of Ø10,000 (even for an RV with gas appliances), and more likely well over Ø20,000 to account for new and highly efficient replacements for your current wasteful refrigerator, freezer, washer, etc.

While the public is now just beginning to understand that the power grids are vulnerable to Y2K, what they do *not* yet comprehend is their utter reliance on cheap 8¢kWh electricity, and that independent power sources (except micro-hydro) simply *cannot* meet their present demand of 35-100kWh per day. Even if they bought a 6-8kWh generator, it'd have to run *12* hours every day *just* for their 3.6kWh/day fridge's duty cycle.

Y2K will likely be the death of America's unique waste of water, heat, and electricity. Japan and Germany are *decades* ahead of use with tankless water heaters and superefficient refrigerators--the *price* of which are about three times more than our piggy units, but the running *cost* being less than one fourth. **Americans know all about *price*, but not about *cost*.** It's our exorbitant *cost* of American living that is combining with other factors to drag us, whimpering, into the Second World. No ship can be full of just passengers, and no society can survive merely as an amusement park. We have to snap out of our pleasant fog and realize that the party is *over*. We have less than 20 years to change course, else the dead anchor weight of our wastefulness will pull us down to the ocean floor of Nature.

Accordingly, Y2K could turn out to be an indirect *blessing*. We are not gently awoken through patient scientific reasoning or the inexorable decay of our land. What we need is a slap in the face--a Pearl Harbor. Y2K may very well prove to be both.

HEAT

If you're in the Northern Hemisphere, then January 2000 will mean being in the middle of winter. I imagine you'll want to stay warm? A frozen home is a *real* drag; I returned to one a few winters ago (the furnace's pilot light had gone out). It took days for all the pantry goods to thaw. Joy. Have your heating needs well ironed out in advance.

Wood

A wood stove (not a fireplace) is the cheapest way to heat your home, and can also be used for cooking and boiling water. Oil *has* come way down in price, but will not likely be in reliable supply during Y2K.

Q: *"What kind of woodstove?"*

Most stoves large enough to heat $1,500ft^2$ will cost at least Ø800. While certified stoves do cost much more, you can rarely insure your home with an uncertified model, and fire insurance is something I'd rather not do without.

Spend the extra money for a stove with catalytic converter which raises efficiency and reduces creosote. Soapstone is the best material for stoves, as it absorbs twice as much heat as metal and releases it more steadily and evenly.

A very helpful website for buyers is **www.gulland.ca**.

Woodstove suppliers

JØTUL   207-797-5912   www.hearth.com/jotul
Woodstock Soapstone   800-866-4344

Taylor Manu.   800-545-2293
Waterford   603-298-5030   www.waterfordstoves.com

Wood-fired water heater

Heat with wood, corn cobs, pine cones, cow chips, packaging waste, whatever. **Hotpro** (707-444-1311; www.hotpro.com) offers a good one. Or, only Ø230 (with liquid fuel attachment), the simple **Pronto** 15 gallon water heater easily adapts as a distillery for drinking water. Made in Mexico, from Backwoods Solar.

Wood-fired hot tub

Use a 24" galvanized stock tank as the tub, and surround with wood slats. The **Chofu** (Japan) is only Ø600 and takes 17" wood. Heats to 108° in just 2½ hours. Lots of satisfied owners. From Backwoods Solar.

The **Snorkel** (www.snorkel.com) hot tub stove, which sits *inside* the water for larger surface area and quicker heating.

Pellets

Yes, pellet stoves are *highly* efficient (over 80%, vs. 60% for the best wood stoves) and clean burning, however, them pellets don't grow on trees. Also, pellet stoves use electricity (impractical for off-grid living), and don't burn wood logs (although the reverse is true). Stick with a woodstove.

Gas

While gas is clean burning and great for heating water or cooking, it is (unless you've your own NG well) too expensive for general furnace heating--even in an RV at 1-2 gallons per day. Propane vent heaters (from Northern, Backwoods Solar, Real Goods, etc.) are the best option if you *must* heat with LP.

Propane (LP)

Heat with wood instead, and save propane for freezers, refrigerators, water heaters, stoves, and generators.

It stores well and is affordable at <Ø1.00/gallon. It also transmits well via underground pipe. (Have an extra tank flex hose.) I'd have at least a 500 gallon tank (preferably a 1,000 gallon, or two), situated away from plain view of the road, yet not visible from the house (so you don't have to look at it, and so the gas guy can't see your house).

I'd install the pump, fittings, and weight scale necessary to fill up smaller tanks, just like your local LP dealer.

Natural gas

If you have a gas well on your property, then *yee hah!* You can run your heater, generator and other gas equipment.

Gas water heaters

Would you keep your car running 24hrs a day just in case you needed it all of a sudden? That's what Americans do with hot water. Silly, huh? We get away with it only because of the low *price* of grid power (though not at a low *cost*).

Gas water heaters should be the on-demand tankless versions instead of the wasteful American tank models. The Paloma (Japan) is the most popular and easiest to install (from Backwoods Solar or Real Goods). All three models provide a 50°-100° degree increase and give 1, 2, or 3 gpm for about Ø445, Ø755, or Ø1,230 respectively. RV users can get by with the 1/gpm model, though 2/gpm is recommended.

Another brand, AquaStar (www.cechot.com; 800-642-3199) by Bosch is also good.

Yes, up front price is much higher, but this is amortized after a few years by *much* lower usage costs. It's sad that we've been spoiled by hitherto cheap energy and wasteful appliances. This must change. I'd urge you to think *long-term* and pay for highly-efficient appliances.

Kerosene

While kerosene stoves are efficient and cost effective (especially for out buildings, garages, etc.), they are a *tad* stinky, especially during start up. You'll get use to it. Buy only Grade 1 kerosene for clean burning indoor use. It costs about as much as gasoline, and is available from your local co-op or ag supply. Keep a 55gal drum with hand pump.

Passive solar collectors

Moderate up front cost; almost zero usage cost. Since heating water is so energy piggish, solar is the way to go if you live in 200+ sunshine day years. Inexpensive systems can be built from common construction materials, and plans abound, or buy a complete system (all from Real Goods).

For Ø12 you can buy a 5 gallon Solar Shower for camping. On a 70°F day the Solar Shower will heat 60° water to 108° in only 3 hours. For another Ø29 you can buy the 12V cigarette lighter pump for washing dishes, etc.

ELECTRICITY
The basics of electricity
If you already know this, then skip to the next subsection. If not, then read on, because your survival depends on it. Electricity is like most things in Life--mysterious until understood.

AC and DC
Electricity comes in only two forms, alternating current or direct current.

Alternating current (AC)
Alternating current is called that because the electron flow actually changes *directions*--60 times each second (which is called 60 cycles). AC is produced by an *alternator* which is turned at high speed by some mechanical source (engine, wind/water turbine, or human/animal effort). An alternator in reverse (*i.e.*, one *receiving* electricity) produces *mechanical* energy in a rotating shaft--and we call this a *motor*.

We can thank Nikola Tesla for inventing poly-phase AC motors and alternators. Until he arrived on our shores in 1884, we were stuck with the limitations of direct current, whose dynamos were inefficient and tedious. (The baseball team, the Brooklyn Dodgers, got their name from Brooklynites constantly dodging the sparking tramcars' DC motors.) In 1888, Tesla demonstrated that a magnetic field could be made to rotate by supplying two coils (they amplify Voltage, or electrical pressure) at right angles with alternating currents of different phases. The poly-phase concept is what made the difference. Imagine a one-legged man trying to pedal a bicycle; he cannot maintain the primary gear's rotation. He needs a second leg to independently bring the first pedal *up* to be pushed down again. Tesla's poly-phase innovation was like giving that one-legged AC man a second leg for "poly-legged" pedaling! (It's been said that only the genius can see the obvious.)

The main advantage of alternating current (besides its more efficient production from mechanically-driven alternators) is its transmitability over long distances without boosting. It's not uncommon for people to use power produced in another state, 1,500 miles away from another grid. Thus, areas without proper sites for wind or hydro power, or the money for a steam turbine power plant (the heat from coal, gas, or nuclear) can get their power from a faraway plant.

AC's main *disadvantage* is that it cannot be effectively stored. It must be used as AC, or converted into storable DC.

Direct current (DC)

Chemical reactions produce DC. Your body is humming with minute DC. A lemon will make DC with two different electrodes in it. Solar modules produce DC from the photon excitement of silicon wafers. DC can be stored in batteries, like water is stored in containers.

The trouble with DC is that it cannot be cheaply transmitted over long distances (over several hundred feet). With wind and micro-hydro generators, it often happens that their site is too far from the point of use, so their DC must be inverted into AC, transmitted to the house, and *re*converted into DC for the battery bank. Such loses 25% in efficiency, but some sites are worth it given their favorable wind and water drops.

Volts, Amps, and Watts

Electricity is best explained analogously to water. Like water, electricity has pressure, flow, and volume.

Pressure (psi)	=	Voltage	described in **Volts**
Flow (gal/min.)	=	Current	described in **Amps**
Volume (gallons)	=	Power	described in **Watts**

Volts

The higher the Volts, the higher the electrical *pressure*. Automotive coils increase the alternator's 12V to over 40,000V because that much *pressure* is needed to make electricity jump across a spark plug's electrode gap of 0.030 inch. *Lots* of Volts are required to force electricity through "pipes" (wires) of high "friction" (resistance) or long distance. High-tension power lines require *thousands* of Volts because so much pressure is needed to send AC electricity thousands of miles.

Think of your thumb on a garden hose end to increase pressure, thus increasing distance of output.

Amps

Electrical current is like water *flow,* or gallons per minute. You've heard the saying *"It's not the Volts, it's the Amps!"* Similarly, the cattle prods and defensive shockers produce lots of electrical *pressure* (7,000+V) to get the recipient's attention, yet with little *flow* (Amps) to avoid injury and death.

Amps are expressed in Amps/hour, or **Ah.**

Watts

To measure the "volume" of electricity, we multiply Volts times Amps to get Watts, which describe the *amount* of energy being used or generated. Watts are Watts, no matter if AC or DC, and is the way to compare dissimilar electrical systems of different Volts and/or Amps.

Watts are expressed by the 1000 in kiloWatts, or **kW.** When you seen an "h" after **kWh,** it means kiloWatts/hour.

The need for electrical efficiency

Most homes currently draw at *least* 1,000kW/month (35kWh/day) at only 8-12¢/kWh. After 12/31/1999 you will *not* be able to enjoy 35+kWh of power per *day* at *any* price, and certainly *not* at today's 8¢/kWh. Much of any electricity in 2000 will be desperately needed for restarting neighboring power plants. (Remember, it takes electricity to make electricity.) Next in line will be government and industry. Your poor little household concerns run a *very* distant fourth. Don't expect much, or any, power in 2000 for at least 3-6 months (longer if you're in the Northeast).

Compounding all this is the *grotesquely inefficient* American home. For example, much of our current electricity usage is due to refrigeration and A/C. Air conditioners will be *out* in the summer of 2000--there just *won't* be enough juice from your local power grid (if any), and you won't be able to produce enough on your own (except for micro-hydro). So, it'll be swamp coolers at best (and they only work in less than 75% humidity).

Your current *highly* inefficient 300kWh refrigerator (which runs 12 hours out of every 24) will be too expensive in 2000. Assuming off-line grids, you simply will not be able to produce 3.6+kWh/day just for your old refrigerator. *"What about the 'energy efficient' refrigerators?"* They save only 25%, and 2.7kWh/day is still far, far too hoggish. American refrigerators (with less than 2" of insulation) are made to be affordable to *buy*. (They old low price/high cost problem.) They are moderately affordable to run *only* when you're hooked up to a utility company at 8-15¢/kWh. 2.7kWh/day for a fridge just won't cut it. (With solar and LP it is possible *live* on 2.7kWh/day.)

To enjoy refrigerated and frozen foods in 2000, you must dump your piggy "KennethMore" on some sucker, and replace it with a highly efficient (600-900Wh/day; at least *one-fourth* the energy of a normal fridge), very expensive (Ø2,420) Sunfrost model. Ditto for your chest freezer, washing machine, and many other appliances. *Gone* will be your:

air conditioner	for a swamp cooler
electric heat	for a wood stove
electric water heater	for a LP tankless model
electric stove	for a gas stove
electric clothes dryer	for a clothes line
electric hair dryer	for air drying
incandescent bulbs	for fluorescent bulbs

These appliances account for 80% of your electric bill, and it is coincidentally a reduction of 80% in your electricity usage that will make independent power not only feasible, but affordable. Y2K will force America to become more energy efficient, and it's about time. The average middle-class home will have to learn to live on just 6-18kWh/day from an affordable solar system.

What I'm saying is this: to maintain a reasonable facsimile of your current modern and convenient life-style (*i.e.*, with lights, TV, stereo, appliances, refrigerator and freezer, computer, etc.), you must add an expensive solar system and replace most of your larger appliances with more efficient models. Prepare to acquire and install before mid-1999:

1000Wh solar system	Ø12,000
6.6kW generator	Ø 1,500
300 gallon fuel tank	Ø 300
Sunfrost R-10 fridge	Ø 2,420
Vestfrost chest freezer	Ø 695
12V DC evaporative cooler	Ø 465
Staber clothes washer	Ø 1,170
misc. 12V DC appliances, lights, etc.	Ø 1,000
Paloma PH12 tankless water heater	Ø 755
500 gallons of LP	Ø 400
	Ø20,705

And folks, that's with a *very* modest 1000Wh solar system (you may need a 2000Wh or 3000Wh system), and no budgeting for a well pump, piping, cistern and pressure tanks. If you need all *that* as well, then add another Ø5,000+. I'm also assuming that you're *already* using LP and have no electric appliances to replace. If not, then add up to *another* Ø5,000.

So, unless you want to live in cave, you're in for Ø20-30K to maintain 20th century comfort into the 21st century. Still unconvinced? Let me put it in another perspective.

Even in my RV (with LP fridge, hot water, stove, oven, and furnace), I still used 5kWh/day. As little as 5kWh/day (and its Ø12/month electric bill) seems by today's standards, to generate that much independent power I would need to spend *Ø13,500* for a 1000W system and a generator! This is what solar experts use for an "active family solar home"--and I used *that* much power in a 30' RV with LP heat and cooking! Are you getting the picture now? The few modern 120V AC appliances I used (*e.g.*, TV, VCR, computer, laser printer, space heater, swamp cooler, blender, toaster, hair dryer, and incandescent light bulbs) would combine for an *unachievable* power demand in 2000 (if the grids are down).

To reiterate: in 2000, a single man living frugally in an *RV* with *gas* heating and cooking, will *not* have sufficient electricity from the grids. **If this guy,** *needing only 5kWh/day* **is out of luck, then what kind of sorry shape will** *your* **family be in?** If *he* has to shell out *Ø13,500* for independent power (with no appliance changes or reduction in energy usage) for his puny needs, then how many more *tens* of thousands of dollars will *you* have to spend? (Pretty sobering stuff, eh?)

Folks, we can suffer spotty telecommunications or banking collapse, but if the power grids stay down for more than a week, this country will begin to disassemble at the commercial level first, and then at the family level. You simply *must* begin to acquire efficient appliances and independent power (for refrigeration and modest electrical needs, at the very least).

GENERATED ELECTRICITY

So, unless you want to live by candlelight with 1850-style amenities, then you'll need *some* kind of *independent* source for electricity. This can be very basic or very involved, or anything in between. It's just a matter of your tastes and finances.

On the basic side, I read of a guy who wired his rustic cabin for 12V DC lighting and simply powered it with his pickup truck battery each night, to be recharged the next day whilst driving. (The Unabomber, Ted Kaczynski rejected even *this* "extravagant" level of technology and lived without 12V DC.)

In the middle would be a 600-3000W solar system and battery storage, supplemented with a generator. The high end of the spectrum is a 5+kWh micro-hydro (or wind) system which produces *so* much grid quality power that the excess can be sold to the utility company.

Whatever your system, it is almost sure to rely *in part* on *some* kind of generator, whether it be a pickup's alternator, a diesel generator, or a naturally-driven turbine. Dynamos are powered by IC (internal combustion) engines, or turbines (wind or micro-hydro, which I'll cover later).

Some general comments about IC engine generators

IC engine generators are powered by some form of fossil fuel (*i.e.*, gasoline, diesel, propane, or natural gas). Generators vary quite widely in quality, output, purchase cost, usage cost, and maintenance cost. You can spend as little as Ø400 or as much as Ø12,000 (or more).

The two general uses for generators

Again, think of electricity like water. Most often you want to merely want to have a drink, but sometimes you need to fight a fire. The problem with generators is that they produce as if they're always fighting a fire. *Half* load is the *least* they'll do; there is no "trickle" output if you simply want a glass of water.

Well, since drinking out of a firehose is wasteful, and since generators can't produce a faucet's flow--what to do? Simple, you let the generator produce at its firehose rate of flow, and *store* what you don't immediately need in a reservoir. This reservoir is called a battery. Batteries allow you to capture most of a generator's firehose rate of flow to use for later, say, when you want that cup of water.

When you need to power items too large for batteries, such as big pumps, welders, circular saws, washing machines, etc. you drive them directly off the generator. Otherwise, you "drink" from your battery storage system, and use the generator to occasionally and quickly recharge the batteries.

So, a generator's full output *will* be used, either directly, or to quickly top off the batteries for indirect use later.

How does the storage cycle work? Generators produce 120V AC, which is converted by the battery charger into 30+ Amp 12V DC. When you need 120V AC again, an inverter reconverts it from batteries' 12V DC. In *each* conversion process nearly 13% is lost, which means that getting inverted 120V AC from batteries (instead of directly from the generator) costs about 25%. This is simply the cost of DC storage, as AC can't be stored. Think of excess 120V AC like leftover food that must be "frozen" (in 12V DC battery form) for a later (120V AC) meal.

In my discussion of solar systems, I'll thoroughly cover batteries, high-amp chargers, inverters, etc.

"It's about power, Man!"

Output is expressed in Watts, and usually in peak or surge figures (which are 10-20% over continuous Watts). For example, a generator which produces 8000 Watts continuously will *briefly* produce 9000 Watts on surge demand. Sellers will *call* it a 9000 Watt generator, even though its continuous output is only 8000. (This is kind of like TV manufacturers describing a 12"x16" screen as a *19"* diagonal. Facts may be true, but they are not necessarily the *truth*.) In this book I refer to all generators in their *continuous* output because I feel it's more honest and useful to describe such versus surge output.

The rated output of a generator assumes *sea level*. For each 1,000' of altitude, derate the output by 3.5%. For example, a 10000W generator operating at 7,000' must be derated by *24.5%* and will output only 7550W. So, if you're in the mountains, you must "overbuy" for output, sorry. (Everything about the mountains is more expensive, but most folks there think it's worth it.) **For LP, derate *another* 10% overall.**

A rule of thumb is that each 500W continuous of juice needs one horsepower of engine (at sea level). The larger the engine, the larger the output, and the higher the fuel costs. Because generators come in so many increments of output, choosing the most appropriate size for your needs can be confusing. Two mistakes are common: *Under*buying a generator (to "save" money) and thus running it to death for tasks much too large, or *over*buying and spending more money in purchase and running costs than necessary.

Calculate your needs, and add another 20-30% for extra loads, then add for altitude and/or LP fuel.

What to look for in generators

Pay attention to the output *per circuit*. If 2kW is distributed on two outlets, that means each outlet is only 1000W-- which won't power a 2000W tool. You want *full* Wattage output available on *each* circuit (or at least on *one* of them, which is typically a 120/240V twistlock outlet). Other features to look for are: electric/auto start, high motor starting (extra surge power for induction and capacitor motors), inherent voltage regulation, and auto idle control (for no load running).

Before shopping for a generator you must have calculated your expected needs, else you won't likely pick what you really need. To give you a decent start, here follows a rough guide to the various classes of generators. From there, ask around, compare, and consult the *Consumer's Guide*.

Judging the engine quality with my W/Ø ratio

To give you a coarse comparison within the bewildering array of generators, I've come up with a power/purchase price ratio of continuous Watts/Ø price. This W/Ø ratio does *not* take into account *usage costs* of fuel, or maintenance/rebuilding *costs*. W/Ø ratios run from 2.1 to 8.8.

On it *face*, it seems that higher is better, but that's *not* usually the case. A lower ratio means a more expensive generator, and this is invariably due to higher *quality* components (especially the engine). It's the *price vs. cost* issue, as I discussed earlier in this chapter. For example, let's compare various 8hp and 18hp horizontal shaft generator engines (from Northern):

8hp (3kW)		**18hp** (11kW)	
Tecumseh	Ø269	Briggs Vanguard	Ø 990
Briggs & Stratton	Ø370	Robin	Ø1,000
Robin (by Subaru)	Ø430	Honda GX	Ø1,050
Briggs Vanguard	Ø464	Kohler Command	Ø1,080
Kohler Magnum	Ø468	Onan	Ø1,143
Honda GX	Ø523		

Honda 5hp engines are *twice* as expensive as 500hr Tecumsehs, and *worth* it since you'll get more than 3x the life. Any Honda powered generator with a W/Ø of 4.0 or more is a *bargain* (they're usually around 2.3). In the larger engines, Tecumseh and Briggs & Stratton drop out of the field entirely, and the manufacturers are much more even in quality.

Comparing gallons per hour (gph) and kW/gallon

Smaller engines naturally use fewer gph, but they also produce less power. Often I'll quote gph figures (for ½, ¾, or full loads), but this is only meaningful when comparing generators of an *identical* output. Lower gph is better.

A more useful ratio is my output/fuel usage--kWh/gallon. This ratio measures the efficiency of both the engine *and* the generator head (which produces 120V AC), and ranges from 4.5 to 8kWh/gallon. Higher kWh/gal. is better.

An outstanding generator in this respect is the NorthStar 5500 Watt PPG which, at half load, produces 2.25kW at 0.49gph, for a ratio of *8.67*kWh/gal. At full load it'll give 4.5kW at 0.71gph for 6.37kWh/gal. Its bigger brother, the 8000 Watt PPG, gives at full load 6.6kW at 0.93gph, or 7.11kWh/gal. (The 5500 is most efficient at half load; the 8000 at full load--a fact that would *not* be obvious without calculating the kWh/gal. ratio.) Most other generators in the 4.5-6.6kW range have ratios of about 5.5kWh/gal., so anything 6kWh/gal. and above is superior. *7+* is great!

Features to look for

OHV (Overhead Valve) engines run cooler and more efficiently. A low oil shutdown I consider a *must*. Positive full-pressure lubrication (usually found only in 8+hp engines) extends engine life. Stellite® exhaust valves (last almost 5 times longer) and nickel-silicon cylinder walls *greatly* increase engine life. Most engines 16hp and up are V-twins, which start easier and run much smoother.

Any generator to be automatically started by a low-battery sensor or inside house switch must have an electric start. A wheel kit is a must for heavier generators which much be moved (usually a Ø100 option).

The best engines

Best smaller engines are the Honda GX. For 16+hp, Honda GX, Kohler Command, and Onan. (The 16hp Briggs Vanguard V-2 is *very* good, perhaps better than the Honda which sometimes suffer a front main bearing failure.)

Quality of electricity

Certain items like some computers (Macs), microprocessors, audio amplifiers, nicad battery chargers, and other voltage-sensitive equipment require *very* clean power, meaning no more than 8% harmonic waveform distortion. If you plan on running such equipment *directly* off the generator then check out Northern's generators (<6% THD from Northstar, and <8% THD from Northern Pro). If a generator's juice is *this* clean, the seller *will* brag about it; if not, then utter silence on THD specs.

If, however, you will run such sensitive equipment off battery storage *inverter* 120V AC, then save money on a more "dirty" generator as the inverter can produce the clean juice you need. The battery storage system really is the way to go if your generator plan is off-grid (rather than supplementing the grid when it temporarily goes down for a few hours or days).

Price, wattage, and engine quality being the same, always give the nod to cleaner output.

Internal Combustion (IC) generators

These come in several different flavors: gasoline, diesel, and gas (propane and natural). Each have their pros and cons.

Gasoline powered

Pros: Lowest purchase cost. Easy maintenance. High output.
Cons: Lowest engine life. Fuel volatile, stores poorly.
Best for: Portable and/or incidental (task oriented) use.

The tiny 2kW generators are fine for camping, but cannot handle heavier demands. Try to use one daily to power your home and you'll run it into the ground real fast. I bought a used (like new) 2kW Coleman (5hp Briggs & Stratton) at a garage sale for only Ø250, which is perfect for camping or light power tools. It is *not*, however, capable of extended or heavy use. I wouldn't have *chosen* this generator if looking for a new one, but the price made it irresistible.

The 4-6kW models have much longer lasting engines, and often come with electric start. These provide very viable power. The 8kW generators are often not much more expensive the 6kW models. The 10kW generators begin at Ø2,000. Generators larger than 10-12kW should be diesel or propane powered for longer engine life and easier fuel storage.

The cheapest engines are the Tecumseh and Briggs & Stratton. They are basically lawn-mower engines: simple, heavy, and decidedly short-lived at only 200-500hrs. **It must have low a oil shutdown feature.** If you need an inexpensive generator for *nonextended* use, then a Coleman, Homelite, or Generac will do fine. (Just don't wear it out treating it like a

Honda.) Get at least a 4000 Watt model. I wouldn't buy a 5.5kW or larger generator in this lower quality range, even though such is only Ø690-Ø1,200. Spend a bit more and get one with a *Honda* motor (*e.g.*, Northern's 6.6kW NorthStar for Ø1400) that'll last 4x as long and provide clean 6% THD power.

Better engines are the Vanguard, and Kohler Magnum. Your generator should be powered by at least one of these, which will give you perhaps 2000 hours before rebuilding.

Best engines are the Honda, Kohler Command, and Onan. O.K., for my Boston T. Party picks. All of them have at least a Vanguard engine (if not a Honda), and most have good W/Ø ratios of 4.0+ (rare for Honda engines). While I have not *utterly* scoured the planet and reviewed every single generator, here's enough good groundwork (from the Northern catalog, primarily) to get you started. You can't go wrong with any of these. Best features are in bold:

2.4kW   NorthStar 2700 Watt (**5hp Honda**), **88lbs**
(5.3 W/Ø)   **Ø450** from Northern (#165912-C131)
Note: Best value on a *quality* small generator, and highly portable.

4.5kW   NorthStar 5500 Watt PPG (**9hp Honda**), **6% THD**
(4.5 W/Ø)   **13.4hrs on ½ load** (0.49gph), 9hrs on full; 180lbs
    Ø1,000 from Northern (#165911-C131)
Note: Good usable power, 6% THD, Honda engine--for Ø1,000!

5.5kW   Dyna 6000 Watt (**11hp Honda**)
(4.0 W/Ø)   **Uses gasoline, propane, or natural gas**
    electric start, 1.1gph propane at ½ load; 195lbs
    Ø1,640 from Northern (#160061-F701)
Note: Wow! Tri-fuel, Honda engine, and electric start! Hard to beat.

6.6kW   NorthStar 8000 Watt PPG (**13hp Honda**), 210lbs
(4.7 W/Ø)   **9hrs on ½ load** (0.71gph), 7hrs on full; **6% THD**
    Ø1,400 from Northern (#165914-C131)
Note: Very clean 6% THD power, and lots of it for only Ø1,400.

Between the Dyna 6000 and the NorthStar 8000, they both have excellent Honda engines. The Dyna has tri-fuel versatility, electric start, and is 15lbs lighter, whereas the NorthStar has 1100W more with only 6%THD and is Ø240 cheaper.

Unless you truly need low THD power for *direct* use (unlikely) or the extra 1100W in a midsize generator, the tri-fuel versatility and electric start give the nod to the Dyna 6000.

8.0kW	Dyna 9000 Watt (16hp Vanguard V-2)
(4.3 W/Ø)	**Uses gasoline, propane, or natural gas electric start** at ½ load 5.0kW/gal., 260lbs
	Ø1,860 from Northern (#160061-F701)

Note: Tri-fuel versatility, big power, and electric start. A bargain.

8.5kW	NorthStar 10000 Watt PPG (16hp Vanguard V-2)
(4.9 W/Ø)	**5% THD, electric start**; at ½ load 4.7kW/gal.
	Ø1,750 from Northern (#165917-C131), 335lbs

Note: Gobs of very clean power, electric start, and high W/Ø.

Between the Dyna 9000 and the NorthStar 10000, they both have the same engines. The Dyna uses all three fuels, has a higher kW/gal., and is 75lbs lighter, whereas the NorthStar is Ø110 cheaper, 500 Watts more power with only 5% THD.

Since engines, output, electric start, and price are common to both it's really a matter of *which* is more important to you: tri-fuel versatility or 5% THD clean power? As fuel availability will be uncertain after 2000, I'd probably go with the Dyna 9000. Propane engines run cooler, cleaner, and start without choke in the winter.

Since I chose the Dyna both times, which is the better one? Get the larger 9000 Dyna; for an extra Ø300 you can have 2.5kW more power. Also know that output is *derated* about 10% for propane and 20% for natural gas, so the Dyna 6000 produces 5300/LP and 4400/NG, and the Dyna 9000 produces 7200/LP and 6400/NG. As 6kW is generally considered the minimum size for home use (for well pumps, fast battery charging, and larger power tools), only the Dyna 9000 will produce such when running on LP or NG.

If you don't need the 5% THD power or tri-fuel versatility, then Dyna's 10000 Watt (8kW cont.) with the same 16hp Vanguard V-2 and electric start is a real bargain at Ø1,550 (5.2 W/Ø). From Northern (#160010-F701).

10.5kW	NorthStar 13000 Watt (**20hp Honda V-2**)
(3.2 W/Ø)	**electric start, <5% THD**, 10gal. tank; 375lbs.
	Ø3,300 from Northern (#165923-C131).

Note: Great motor with tons of power. No wheels, though.

11kW	Northern Pro 12000 Watt (**20hp Honda V-2**)
(3.3 W/Ø)	**electric start, 6% THD**, 8gal. tank, **wheels incl.**
	Ø3,300 from Northern (#161461-C131), 325lbs.

Note: Great motor with tons of power, *and wheels* (Ø100).

As engine, THD, price, and output are identical--would you sacrifice the NorthStar's 2 extra gallons of tank capacity and extra 1000W of *surge* power for the Ø100 wheel set and extra 500W of *continuous* output of the Northern Pro? Too close for me to tell--your call. If you're going to be moving it often, the Northern Pro is 50lbs lighter and already has wheels.

13.5kW	NorthStar 15000 Watt **(25hp Kohler V-2)**
(3.8 W/Ø)	**electric start, 6% THD**, 10gal. tank; 460lbs.
	Ø3,600 from Northern (#165925-C131).

Note: Great motor with tons of power. No wheels, though.

14kW	Northern Pro 15000 Watt **(25hp Kohler V-2)**
(3.9 W/Ø)	**electric start, 6% THD**, 8gal. tank, **wheels incl.**
	Ø3,600 from Northern (#161457-C131); 357lbs.

Note: Great motor with tons of power, *and wheels* (Ø100).

Same dilemma as the previous pair. Both have the superb Kohler V-2 (with nickel-silicon plated cylinders for outstanding cylinder wall life--a BMW innovation). Go Northern Pro as it's already got the wheel kit, and it's (inexplicably) 103lbs lighter. These generators will start a 5hp, code G electric motor.

Finally, why buy one of the 11kW generators when you can have *3kW more* output for only Ø300? No where else can you get 3000W for just Ø300.

For power output greater than 14kW, you'll need to go diesel or propane/NG. We're done here with gasoline.

Gasoline engine DC battery chargers

These produce only 12V DC power. *If* you absolutely *don't* need 2kW of 120V AC for a well pump, appliances, or power tools, then a small 5-6.5hp engine driving a Delco 50-75A alternator can be bought for Ø648-Ø1,285.

A 5hp/45A rig will give 540Wh of 12V DC at .25gph. Assuming a two-set Trojan T-105 battery system with 440A and 5280Wh depleted to 50%, this charger will make up the missing 2640W in 4.9 hours with 1.2 gallons of gas.

This same job done by a *generator* (and fast battery charger) is a bit more expensive in both purchase and running costs. **Figure on at least 2kW of output per 60A 12V DC.** A small 2.4kW NorthStar 2700 Watt generator at 0.32pgh behind a 45A charger will take the same 4.9hrs but with 1.6 gallons of gas. This generator costs Ø450, and the 60A charger (switchable to lower rates) is Ø280--for a total cost of Ø730.

Backwoods Solar wants Ø648 for their DC charging rig (though you can build it for much less), which will save you Ø82 up front and 50¢ in gas each time you recharge 50% on cloudy days. Is this savings worth *not* having a generator's 120V AC and the concurrent powering of other tools? I rather doubt it, especially if your battery system goes down, and you will not be able to generate AC power with a mere DC charger.

Backwoods Solar also offers the Genny DC charger which uses a 6.5hp Honda OHV engine for 75A at .30gph. It's pricey at Ø1,285 (Ø1,525 for propane). Since charging rate is limited to 10% of the batteries' amp hour reading, such a high-amp system would be worthwhile for only a 4-set T-105 880Ah (Ø600) or 2-set L-16HC 790Ah (Ø840) battery bank (*i.e.*, a 600W solar system big enough to demand a generator anyway).

Even though these DC chargers don't blow *my* skirt up, do the math on this non-generator option for your own needs. If you could build the charger yourself from scrounged parts and are sure *not* to need AC power, then it might make economic sense for those on a tight budget. Still, you'd miss not having a real 120V AC generator (for power tools if nothing else).

Diesel generators
Pros: Longest engine life. Lower maintenance. Safer fuel.
Cons: Highest cost. Hardest to start. Noisy, heavy, and dirty.
Best for: Dedicated, set-and-forget, long service.

What you want ideally is an 1800rpm industrial diesel (*e.g.*, Perkins, Ford, Yanmar, or China Diesel). Such will chug out power for *15,000* hours before rebuild. That's *thirty years* of power at 500hrs/year (a generous figure assuming good sun and a decent PV system--even 200hrs/year is feasible).

While smaller 3600rpm diesels exist, they have only half the life of their more leisurely big brothers. Still, 7,000 hours of engine life is 3-4x more than even the best gasoline models. Here are a few of some available:

5.5kW (2.1 W/Ø)	Northern Pro 6000 Watt 10hp Yanmar **electric start; 8¾hrs at ¾ load, 0.57pgh** Ø2,580 from Northern (#161454-C131), 215lbs.
6kW (0.85 W/Ø)	Kohler 6ROY (Yanmar 3-cyl. liquid-cool), 674lbs. **electric start** Ø7,050 from Backwoods Solar (#G-6ROY)

8.5kW (2.3 W/Ø)	Northern Pro 8500 Watt 16hp Deutz-Ruggerini **electric start; 5½hrs at ¾ load, 0.91pgh** Ø3,700 from Northern (#161455-C131), 316lbs.
10kW (1.21 W/Ø)	Kohler 10ROY (Yanmar 3-cyl. liquid-cool), 758lbs. **electric start** Ø8,250 from Backwoods Solar (#G-10ROY)
11.5kW (2.4 W/Ø)	Northern Pro 11500 Watt 21hp **electric start; 5.8hrs at ¾ load, 1.38pgh** Ø4,800 from Northern (#161468-C131), 385lbs.
15kW (3.5 W/Ø)	China Diesel Imports Ø4,300
15kW (1.47 W/Ø)	Kohler 15ROY (Yanmar 4-cyl. liquid-cool), 872lbs. **electric start** Ø10,200 from Backwoods Solar (#G-15ROY)

These four generators use an 1800rpm liquid-cooled Perkins.

20kW (2.3 W/Ø)	Northern Pro 44hp, 1310lbs. Ø8,600 from Northern (#161460-C131).
25kW (2.8 W/Ø)	Northern Pro 44hp, 1375lbs. Ø9,000 from Northern (#161470-C131).
30kW (3.2 W/Ø)	Northern Pro 64hp, 1775lbs. Ø9,400 from Northern (#161471-C131).
40kW (4.1 W/Ø)	Northern Pro 64hp, 1600lbs. Ø9,800 from Northern (#161462-C131).

Propane (LP) or natural gas (NG)

Pros: Best storing fuel. Runs off main LP tank, for less hassle.
Engine, oil, and exhaust clean. No filters to replace.
No odor. Starts in winter w/o choke. Best auto start.
50-100% more engine life of gasoline. Can use NG.

Cons: Less output than gasoline or diesel. Bulky fuel storage.

Best for: Auto/remote start systems. Winter and residential.
Smaller tri-fuel generators useful anywhere.

I like LP generators a lot. If your fridge, freezer, stove, and water heater are LP, then it's quite convenient to power your generator with LP, too (eliminating a huge gasoline tank).

The only real drawback to LP engines is their 10% reduced output. A small gasoline engine will produce about 4.6kW per Ø in fuel, whereas a small LP engine only 3-4kW/Ø.

(The larger LP engines give up to 6.25kW/Ø.) The smaller (under 24hp) LP engines just aren't that efficient, sadly. Still, the clean fuel and longer engine life are probably worth it. The Kohler 1800rpm Ford 4-cyl. engines from Backwoods Solar are rated at 7,000hrs. This is the next best to a diesel's 15,000hr life, yet with no problems of fuel management and winter starting. A good mix of longevity and overall convenience. *Very* expensive, however. The other propane engines are 3600rpm with half the life of the 1800rpm units, but they are *much* more affordable and are fine for smaller applications.

5.3kW DYNA 6000 Watt (**11hp Honda**)
(3.23 W/Ø) **Uses gasoline, propane, or natural gas electric start**; 1.1gph/LP at ½ load; 195lbs
Ø1,640 from Northern (#160061-F701)
Note: Tri-fuel, Honda engine, and electric start! Small output.

7.2kW DYNA 9000 Watt (16hp Vanguard V-2)
(**3.87 W/Ø**) **Uses gasoline, propane, or natural gas electric start**; (0.80gph--petrol), 260lbs
Ø1,860 from Northern (#160061-F701)
Note: Tri-fuel versatility, big power, and electric start. A bargain.

8kW DYNA (16hp Vanguard V-2), LP (7.1kW/NG)
(1.90 W/Ø) **electric start**;1.3gph/LP ½ load, 2.2gph full
Ø4,200 from Northern (#164431-C131), 455lbs.

8.5kW Northern Pro 10000 Watt (18hp Vanguard V-2)
(2.94 W/Ø) **electric start, 6% THD, 2.6gph/LP, 185cf/NG**
Ø2,900, Northern (#161453-C131), 360lbs.

10kW Kohler (**1800rpm Ford 4-cyl. liquid-cooled/LP**)
(1.46 W/Ø) **electric start**
Ø6,850, Backwoods Solar (#G-10RY), 580lbs.

12kW DYNA (24hp Onan V-2), LP (10.1kW/NG)
(1.94 W/Ø) **electric start**; 3.1gph/LP full load
Ø6,200 from Northern (#16445-C131), 850lbs.

12kW Kohler (**1800rpm Ford 4-cyl. liquid-cooled/LP**)
(1.53 W/Ø) **electric start**
Ø7,850, Backwoods Solar (#G-12RY).

12.5kW Northern Pro 13500 Watt (23hp Kohler V-2)
(3.13 W/Ø) **electric start, 6% THD, 3.7gph/LP, 260cf/NG**
Ø4,000, Northern (#161453-C131), 385lbs.

20kW	DYNA (**35hp Ford**), LP (18kW/NG)
(2.38 W/Ø)	**electric start**, 2.5gph/LP ½ load, 4.0gph full
	Ø8,400 from Northern (#16444-C131), 800lbs.
20kW	Kohler (**1800rpm Ford 4-cyl. liquid-cooled/LP**)
(2.01 W/Ø)	**electric start**
	Ø9,950, Backwoods Solar (#G-20RY).

For it's worth, I lean towards LP generators, since I'm not a big fan of diesel engines and their fuel which I wouldn't otherwise have to mess with. (I once owned a diesel VW, and didn't like it.)

Final comments on IC engine generators

Go diesel or gas (natural or LP) 8-10kW. These are expensive rigs and best shared by 2 or more households with staggered use. This should be your first major purchase, and *hurry*. Used models can be found in your local *Thrifty Nickel*. Pay cash and save your *Hallelujahs*, as these used generators will disappear by summer 1999 along with the new ones.

I'd go ahead and buy the rebuild kit and pre-rebuild maintenance items. It's best to have all this in stock.

How to use your generator

The rule is to buy the best you can afford for your needs, and then use it as little as possible. As I'll prove later in this chapter, it is not feasible to use your generator as the *sole* energy producer.

If you're powering multiple loads, start with the *largest* load and work down to the smallest. There is a high start-up load in most applications (especially large pumps and motors), so get the largest loads up first.

Shop around for your generator

Remember, time and space did not allow me to research every generator available. (This chapter already took long enough to write--25% of my time for 12% of the book.) You might indeed find better units than I discussed, and if so, please let me know and I'll post them on our Website.

Wind turbines

These have become very high-tech and efficient. They are much more productive in the winter than solar modules. The higher the turbine, the better (for smoother and faster wind). It needs to be at least 30' higher than any obstacle within a 300' radius. Horizontal axis turbines are a bit more efficient than vertical axis turbines (necessary only in variable-direction wind areas). They start turning at about 7mph, reach rated power (500-1500W in 12/24/48V DC) at 25-28mph, and survive winds up to 120mph. 12V can be transmitted 200', 24V up to 800', and 48V over 2400'. (Voltage means *pressure,* remember?)

Its tower (44-104') is usually made up of conventional 2-4" galvanized steel pipe with guy wires. Never mount the turbine or any part of its tower to your house, which will act as a giant sounding diaphragm for the vibration. One or two small turbines could be an excellent system for a stand-alone building, cabin, or RV too far from your other systems.

Windpower's downside

While a viable option for many, turbines are highly conspicuous (as is solar). Cold and hungry people seeing your windmill in the distance and imagining your pleasant island of electricity just may conjure up some unpleasant ideas for you and your family. Be prepared to aggressively repel boarders.

Suppliers

Penryn Farm   800-556-1644
Southwest Windpower 520-779-9463x10 www.windenergy.com
Windstream Power Systems   802-658-0075
Delivered Solutions 800-929-0448 www.deliveredSolutions.com
Sierra Solar   800-51-SOLAR   www.sierrasolar.com
Kansas Wind Power   785-364-4407

Micro-hydro turbines

I have a friend who dammed up his small unnavigable river to produce 20kW of electricity. It powers his home and ranch year round, and he sells the unused juice back to the power company. Pretty elegant. Not everybody enjoys the location for this option, but if you do, you're foolish not to use it.

The average micro-hydro generator makes power for as little as one-tenth as much as solar, and can even be cheaper than grid power. Solar generates power only when the sun is shining (figure on 6-8 hours of full power per sunny day), while hydro generates power 24 hours a day.

Depending on the volume and fall to your site, Burkhardt/Harris turbines will produce from 1kWh (1,000 kilowatt hours) to 30kWh per day. The typical American home consumes 10kWh to 15kWh per

day with no particular energy conservation, so with a good site it's pretty easy to live a totally conventional life style with hydro power.
-- Doug Pratt; *Real Good News*, February 1994, p.11

Micro-hydro is suitable only for low-volume/high-head installations. Volume is gallons per minute, and head is vertical drop in feet. The turbines can handle a maximum of 200gpm. You need a *minimum* of 20' head for any useful power. Your fall doesn't have to occur all in one place. You can build a small collection dam at one end of your property and pipe the water to a lower point, collecting head along the way. Apparently, it's not unusual to have 2,000 to 4,000 feet of pipe in micro-hydro.

If you've got a high-volume/low-head site

Micro-hydro turbines are made to handle high pressure/low volume water. Water is *heavy* and high volume means *heavy* impellers. You could have Mississippi River frontage, but all that high *volume* water will do you no good.

Still, contact the National Appropriate Technology Assistance Service at 800-428-2525 for lots of free information.

The alternators

Micro-hydro generators are 1960s-1970s Delco 12V DC alternators with custom wound windings. Brushes and bearings are replaced every 1-5 years depending on use and available at any auto parts store. Each alternator can produce up to 750W in 12V, or 1500W in 24V.

Micro-hydro's operational downside

It produces DC current, which does not transmit over 500' without expensive large-gauge wires or technical wizardry. If your home is more than 500' from the turbines, you could place the AC inverter with the batteries and transmit 120V AC power more efficiently.

For more information and site analysis

Contact Backwoods Solar or Real Goods. They will need to know your site's head, flow in gpm, size/type/length of any installed pipe, and wire distance from turbine to point of use.

SOLAR POWER

If you will learn to live "lightly" on the Earth, then solar is perfectly viable and (painfully) affordable. The best buy is to get the most efficient end-use devices, and *then* just enough renewable energy supply to meet that greatly reduced demand. Solar systems can be built which can power even clothes dryers, although this is hideously expensive and grossly extravagant.

RVs, for example, already come with 12V systems so it's a simple matter to hook them up to solar panels and deep-cycle batteries. Coupled with a heating stove (wood or kerosene) and large propane tank, a solar RV would provide perfectly comfortable shelter for less than Ø20,000 (maybe as low as Ø8,000 if you budgeted things well).

I expect solar systems to *dramatically* increase in price starting spring 1999 (assuming availability), so move quickly. After late-1999, they might be unavailable at *any* price.

Solar system suppliers
Real Goods   800-762-7325
In Ukiah, California, they are a well regarded equipment vendor for all independent power systems. You simply *must* get their *Alternative Energy Sourcebook* to grasp the breadth of independent energy options and products.

Backwoods Solar   208-263-4290   www.backwoodssolar.com
More casual than Real Goods, yet quite knowledgeable.

Siemens Solar   www.siemenssolar.com
Delivered Solutions   800-929-0448   www.deliveredSolutions.com
Sierra Solar   800-51-SOLAR   www.sierrasolar.com
New England Solar   413-238-5974
Sunelco   406-363-6924
EMI   888-MR-SOLAR   www.emi4solar.com
Solar Electric   800-842-5678   www.solarelectric.com
Kent Morgan   317-465-8496   smorgan@saver.com

The solar power system--an overview
There's nothing mysterious about solar power:

solar panels,
called a PV (photovoltaic) array, collect the sunlight and convert it (at only a 10% efficiency) to direct current (DC). This DC power is sent to the...

charge controller,
a wall-mounted unit, which regulates the flow to the...

batteries,

which store as a reservoir the power in 12V DC form. When DC is needed, it comes right off the batteries, however, when 120V AC is required, such is converted by the...

inverter,

in amounts ranging from 100 to 5500Wh, released to the circuit breaker, and then to the AC powered appliances. The inverter is the major electronic component of a power system, and can cost Ø2-4,000, though most systems do fine on models costing Ø650-940.

Most systems are designed to be *off*-grid, so the battery recharging comes from the...

generator,

which, properly used, is only a backup for solar shortfall, or for temporary need of additional power (as in construction projects, guests, or the breakdown of other equipment). The generator's output is *not* connected to the house breaker box, but to the AC INPUT terminals of the inverter. Such 120V AC power must be converted to 12V DC through either a fast battery charger or a standby inverter/charger.

Some low cost DC generators are available, which send 12V DC directly to the battery, thus avoiding the need for a separate charger. These generators will not, however, produce 120V AC power and are thus useless for such needs.

The solar modules

Since modules will easily last 30 years or more with virtually no maintenance, only your "cover charge" is expensive--the banquet inside is free. **Every 100W of solar costs about Ø600 in modules.** Modules produce 50-90+W each, depending on size. Siemens (Germany) and Solarex (Japan) are the most well-regarded brands. We *could* make solar modules in America, but the factories are too busy making video games. (American solar manufacturers should be income tax *exempt,* in my opinion. Some states offer ØØØØ rebates on PV systems.)

The most practical plan is to meet 85-90% of your reduced and efficient power needs with solar generation. To meet 100% in some winter areas would require 10 times more solar and battery capacity, thus the best compromise is to use an engine generator with a *fast* battery charger to make up for winter days. The basic rule is to buy a *good* generator, and then use it as little as possible. Also, a generator could occasionally be necessary for unexpected high demand (guests, pumping water to fight a fire, a 3hp deep-well pump, or an air compressor.)

So, don't skimp on your solar panels. Start with at *least* one-half of the necessary panels, else you'll simply be running your generator far too much.

Positioning the modules

Since 95% of full power is produced within 20° of the sun direction, precise aim is not required. Modules aimed at the noon sun give virtually full power from 10AM to 2PM. From sunrise till 10AM and from 2PM till sunset give the equivalent of 2 hours of full sun--for a total of 6 hours of full rated power from a fixed mount, adjusted twice a year.

Heliotropism

Automatic tracking mounts use solar heated Freon to move the modules with no motors or mechanism. Zorchy stuff. Power is increased 35-50% in the summer (but only 7-9% in winter). In the summer, tracker can give you an extra *4* hours of full power with the same modules. Using an eight-module Zomeworks Track Rack is like having 1.6 extra modules in the winter and 3.2 in the summer. I consider them a must, as they amortize themselves very quickly, and because...they're so *cool!*

Wet cell batteries

No matter how electricity is acquired, the source will be intermittent (and expensive, if IC engine generated), so batteries must be used for power storage. All dynamo generators produce AC power which is converted to 12V DC for battery storage, and then inverted *back* again to 120V AC for modern appliances (unless you're totally on a 12V DC system). For every 1A used off the batteries, 1.25A must be supplied to them.

Go for a *large* battery bank. The bigger the bank, the more the storage, the more infrequent the recharging, and the longer the life. Remember, pay a high *price* to get a lower *cost.* Also, larger battery banks give you more "autonomy" in which you can tolerate longer periods of sunless weather. A working business may want 10 days of autonomy; a residence 5; a vacation cabin only 1-2 days.

Once your battery bank is at 90% or less remaining life, do not add new batteries to it, as they just get dragged down to the others' lower level.

Your car battery

It has thin plates and lead-calcium grids, and is designed for less than 20% discharge and prompt recharging. (Cat, auto, and truck batteries are *not* deep cycle and *will not last* in home power systems.) *"Don't try this at home!"*

RV/Marine "deep cycle" batteries

They are designed about half way between a *true* deep cycle and a shallow cycle car battery, and have a 18-24 month life. If you can't get the 6V Trojans, these will work in a *pinch* if you keep the discharge level no greater than 35%.

The true deep cycle battery

Can handle frequent and heavy (normally 50%, and up to 80% in emergencies) charge/discharge cycles. They have thicker plates and **lead-antimony** or pure lead support grids.

The plain old golf-cart battery is what you want. It's 6V, 220Ah capacity, and weighs 65lbs. They are pair wired in *series* (+ to -) to increase voltage, then parallel wired (+ to +) to increase amps. They have a life of 3-6 years, depending on care and usage. The commonly used **Trojan T-105** is Ø75, which has the best price per amp-hour of any quality battery.

A better battery is the **Trojan L-16HC**, with 6V/395Ah. They are about Ø210 each and weigh 120lbs., but have 80% more ampacity, lower maintenance requirements, and will last for 7-11 years. Is 80% more ampacity and twice the life *worth* 2.8 times the price? At first, probably not, but lots of users go to the L-16HC on the second round. When battery *storage* space for large (1000-2000Ah) systems is at a premium, then this battery is the way to go.

Buy a ton of them (dry if possible, as they'll store forever that way), and introduce the electrolyte only when the batteries are needed on-line. Sam's Club usually has good deals on inexpensive Interstate brand of 6V golf-cart batteries. Or, try to find a nearby outlet for Trojan and save on the freight. (Wet batteries cannot be shipped UPS for hazmat concerns.)

Gell cell batteries

They are 12V, sealed, maintenance-free, leakproof, tolerant of extreme cold (because the electrolyte is totally gelled) with a life expectancy of 3-5 years. They can be 100% discharged for 30 days with no damage. They don't emit gas or fumes. They are used most commonly in UPS power packs.

Downside: They're very expensive, and they damage easily from overcharging and thus need constant type charge control for their lower 13.7-14.1V. Not often recommended for most homes unless *extreme* cold is an issue.

Nicad batteries

While deep discharging and failure to recharge do not shorten battery life, cost is 8 times higher than lead, voltage swings are higher, charge efficiency is only 60%, and disposal/recycling costs is high. Surplus railroad batteries are often overpriced and defective. Pass on nicads.

Chloride batteries

From Pacific Chloride, these supply 420-1690Ah, can last 15-20 years with proper maintenance while providing 1,500 cycles to 80% depth of discharge (which means less frequent generator rechargings). Since their ampacity is so high, fewer batteries are needed for total capacity.

They're *very* expensive, however. A 1160Ah battery bank, for example, will run you Ø2,595. A similar 1185Ah bank of 6 L-16HCs is priced at only Ø1,260, but there are many more cables, much more maintenance, and they last only 50% as long (at best) for 49% of the price.

Thus, the chloride batteries with their life of up to 20 years and much lower maintenance make the best *very* long run sense. These are the Mercedes-Benz of batteries. *Price vs. cost.*

Fiber nickel-cadmium (FNC) batteries

These have no graphite filler of nicads which clogs up from carbonate formation. They have outstanding life, low maintenance, superior high current performance, high efficiency, wide temperature range, and indifference to full discharges. At 15,000 cycles of 40% discharge, they'll last 30 years!

They are *very* expensive. From Real Goods.

Battery maintenance

Don't skimp here. Your little oasis of civilization will depend on your batteries.

The PulseTech Battery Recover/Maintenance products are worth a look. Lead plates are desulfated by a patented device that emits carefully tuned pulses of electricity at regular intervals into the battery. Reported benefits are extending battery life *3-5 times*, virtually eliminating water loss, maintaining full rated charging capacity, and providing at full charge a freeze point of -83° F. Key Maintenance (800-303-5902).

Inverters
The standby option
Some of the better inverters have a built in battery charger and transfer relay. This so-called "standby" inverter/charger acts like a traffic cop for AC. When AC is coming in from the outside (the generator or the grid), the standby inverter stops producing AC from the batteries and transfers the outside AC straight through to the house. At the same time, it uses that outside power to recharge the batteries. Some standby inverters even auto-start the generator when the battery charge becomes too low.

The sine-wave inverter
The basic and intermediate inverters produce what is called "modified sine-wave" (MSW) power, which is a rough approximation of true sine-wave power. This is good enough for most appliances, except for cordless tool rechargers, some Macintosh computers, and other likewise sensitive equipment. If your pure sine-wave needs are few, then a small sine-wave inverter in *addition* to the larger MSW inverter will suffice.

However, many solar systems with larger sine-wave power needs use one larger sine-wave inverter for *all* AC inversion. This is simple and elegant, though *twice* as costly as a modified sine-wave inverter. Such an inverter is usually a "graduation present" to a more powerful system after a few years of experimentation and familiarization with solar power.

DRY-CELL BATTERIES
No, you can't run your home on these, but you'll them for small portable devices. Here's the scoop:

Carbon-zinc
We use over two billion disposble batteries a year, which is wasteful and ecologically taxing. Forsake these for at least alkalines, or truly rechargeables (nicad or metal hydride).

Alkaline-manganese

A much better value than carbon-zinc, but not as good as true rechargeables. **There is, however, no reason to throw out expensive alkalines after only *one* use.** Did you know that they can be *recharged*? 9V batteries can get 2½x more life, Cs 4x more, AAs 7 x more, and Ds 9x times more life--all for less than a penny per charge. A *very* low-rate (*e.g.*, 75mAh) charger is the key, as the faster nicad chargers (120mAh) are too powerful for alkalines.

I once stayed at a hotel in which all the room door's electric locks were being replaced. In each lock unit was a battery pack of 8 AA alkaline batteries, and there were *dozens* of these units in the trash. I helped myself to several *pounds* of AA batteries, and recharged them at home (with a Ø3 battery charger I found at a flea market). At the first sign of weakness, they go back into the charger for 5 hours @ 75mAh for many resuses. I haven't had to buy new AAs for going on two years.

There is no need to buy those expensive "rechargeable" alkalines, as *all* alkalines can be successfully recharged.

CTD (who else?) has a great deal on military AAs.

Nickel-cadmium (nicad)

These often provide on 1.2V instead of a normal battery's initial 1.5V, so their use is limited to flashlights and other non-picky devices. They take up to 1000 rechargings, but must be often (2x per month) completely drained to clear their "memory." Nicads, however, are far inferior to metal hydrides.

Metal hydride

These could be called 2nd gen rechargeable batteries, which last two-thirds as long as alkalines, and do not have the "memory" problem of nicads. They also recharge more quickly, and have no toxic elements (such as cadmium, lead, mercury, or lithium). They have nearly *twice* capacity than even the best nicads: AA (1100 vs. 700mAh); C (3500 vs. 1800mAh)

Lithium ion

Even better than metal hydrides, as they give more power and recharge more quickly. Too expensive but for laptops.

Battery rechargers

There are many battery rechargers available, from solar to car 12V to 120V AC. Real Goods has a selection. A built-in battery strength meter and auto shut-off are very nice features.

FOOD REFRIGERATION

Unless you plan to eat only dehydrated, freeze-dried, or MRE food during the grid power outage, you'll need some kind of *efficient* refrigeration. After 1/1/2000, your present fridge will an "8mpg" dinosaur best tossed in the scrap yard. (A booming business will be in scavenging the freon refrigerant.)

Gas or electric?

Refrigerator compressors are either gas or electric. Between a gas fridge and a typically wasteful (3600Wh/day) electric fridge, get a gas model (which are also perfectly silent).

Between a gas fridge and an *efficient* (<1200Wh/day) electric model, it depends on *if* you plan to install solar, wind, or micro-hydro. If *so*, then go efficient electric, *especially* if you're betting on the Y2K meltdown to last over several years (beyond which LP tank storage runs into thousands of gallons).

If *not*, then an LP fridge will serve fine. LP fridges and freezers are *very* economical, using only 1½-3 gallons per week, and lasting for 30+ years. You'd better have at least a 500 gallon LP tank on your property, if not a 1,000 gallon.

Gas (propane)

I've an LP fridge that's 25 years old and still works great. It's only 7.5ft³ (6+1.5), but that's fine for 1-2 people.

Gas fridges are the way to go for remote cabins, RVs, and out buildings which are not practical to wire for solar, etc. A good fridge is the 7.7ft³ (6+1.7) Servel 400 for Ø1,185 from Backwoods Solar. At just ¼ gallon/day (less than 1½/week) this will maintain 6° freezer/39° fridge with 110° outside. 500 gallons of propane will keep your food for 2,000 days, which is almost 5½ years--a 1,000 gallon tank for almost 11 years. (After that, you'd better hope that you could refill your tank...)

In summary, for just Ø1,600 you can have an LP fridge and over five years of fuel. This may be the answer for many folks. I've included a gas fridge/freezer in my plan, and a solar system (on trackers) to provide 1500Wh for up to 15kWh/day.

Real Goods sells the Frostek propane freezer with 8.5ft³ for Ø1,785, which uses only 1.8-2.5gal./week.

A 12V DC Sunfrost 10ft³ RF-12 (8+2), on the other hand, costs Ø1,840, and solar system just to power it Ø6,100-8,600 (not counting a generator to top off the batteries on cloudy days). Thus, to put up solar for food refrigeration *alone* is not practical. Even to *add* a DC fridge to existing solar means another Ø3,600-6,600 in module cost (at the current Ø6/Watt for 600-1100W), another Ø150 in batteries, plus possibly a larger inverter. Wow.

Dometic makes the Explorer camping fridges and freezer that work off those tiny 16oz. propane bottles. The 1.6ft³ Explorer FP50 holds five six-packs and uses about 8oz. per day (or you can power it from 120V AC or 12V DC, but read the below). From Ready Made Resources.

Not gas/electric!

There's no such thing from an efficiency's perspective. These hybrid fridges (usually in RVs and boats) are actually *gas* compressor models (which are efficient enough with *extra* insulation). They have an electric heating element which, when plugged into 120V AC, substitutes for the gas flame heat source. **This heating element is *extremely* inefficient** and should be used *only* at an RV park where electricity comes with the space rent. Use it at home and you'll quickly be amazed at your electric bill. Let this be a lesson to you that hybrid designs usually have a hidden high cost for their versatility.

120V AC or 12V DC fridge?

If you've decided on a 600+W solar/wind/micro-hydro system that will also power your fridge, then the only question is which *voltage*--12V DC or 120V AC?

Even though you'll need an inverter regardless, you can use a *smaller* (*i.e.*, cheaper) one if your fridge is 12V DC. You'll also save 5-15% in power from avoiding the 120V AC inverter inefficiency. 12V DC fridge/freezers are quite expensive to buy, but cheap to *run*--contrary to the American appliance "penny wise and pound foolish" philosophy.

Some appliances, however, are either much cheaper in 12V DC or only available in 120V AC, and that's O.K., since the above inverter issue is really no big deal. The superb Vestfrost (7.5ft³) chest freezer from Denmark, for example, is 120V AC only, but is efficient enough (450-900Wh/day) even through an inverter. It's also affordable at only Ø695. (Much more later on the Vestfrost.)

Two of my homemade ratios will be helpful here. In both, the *lower* the number the *better* the ratio.

Ø/ft³ = **purchase price/cubic feet**--measures *purchase value.*
Typical refrigerators (w/o freezer) are   143-166 Ø/ft³
Typical freezers are   93-180 Ø/ft³
Typical refrigerator/freezers are   162-184 Ø/ft³

W/ft³ = **Watts hours per day/cubic feet**--measures *efficiency.*
Typical refrigerators (w/o freezer) are   22- 41 Wh/ft³
Typical freezers are   79-106 Wh/ft³
Typical refrigerator/freezers are   36- 67 Wh/ft³

Prices are from Backwoods Solar, without freight. You might save money shopping around. Best values are in bold.

Refrigerators (w/o freezer)

Sunfrost R-10	Ø1515	9.1ft³	200-325Wh/day
	Ø166/ft³		**22-36Wh/ft³**
Sunfrost R-19	Ø2290	**16ft³**	390-650Wh/day
	Ø143/ft³		24-41Wh/ft³

Freezers

Vestfrost	Ø695	7.5ft³	450-893Wh/day
	Ø93/ft³		**60**-119Wh/ft³
Sunfrost F-10	Ø1635	9.1ft³	715-910Wh/day
	Ø180/ft³		79-**100W/hft³**
Sunfrost F-19	Ø2643	**16ft³**	1300-1700Wh/day
	Ø166/ft³		81-106Wh/ft³

The Vestfrost is the *whopping* bargain. While slightly more costly in summer, it's cheapest when the room is around 50°.
If you need 15ft³ of freezer, why not buy *two* Vestfrosts? Versus the F-19 you'll lose 1ft³, but you'll *save* Ø1,253 up front for about the same running costs:

2 Vestfrosts	Ø1390	15ft³	900-1786Wh/day
	Ø93/ft³		60-119W/ft³

Refrigerator/freezers

Sunfrost RF-12	Ø1840	10ft³	360-590Wh/day
(8+2)	Ø184/ft³		**36-59Wh/ft³**
Sunfrost RF-16	Ø2420	13.9ft³	200-325Wh/day
(10+3.9)	Ø174/ft³		42-61Wh/ft³
Sunfrost RF-19	Ø2584	**16ft³**	800-1066Wh/day
(8+8)	**Ø162/ft³**		50-67Wh/ft³

The above R/Fs are fairly equal in efficiency, and come down in Ø/ft³ in the larger models (typical).

Instead of the Sunfrost RF-19, consider buying an R-10 and Vestfrost freezer to give you a combined 0.6 more ft³ for Ø374 less, and about the same efficiency. (If the Sunfrost RF-19 were the same 16.6ft³ it would use 830-1106Wh/day.)

R-10/Vestfrost	Ø2210	**16.6ft³**	650-1218Wh/day
(8+8)	**Ø133/ft³**		39-73Wh/ft³

Such a combination is also only Ø370 more than an RF-12 (with its tiny 2ft³ freezer) and Ø51/ft³ cheaper, with *6ft ³more* space.

In summary

Buying a Sunfrost refrigerator *and* a Vestfrost freezer is the best deal. The Sunfrost refrigerator/freezer units just can't compare in value. Or, you could use the Vestfrost freezer in conjunction with a propane fridge/freezer.

ENERGY-EFFICIENT APPLIANCES

These could easily go into the *Shelter* chapter, however, I put it here as you need to know about them now so we can compare energy systems in this chapter.

Washing machine

The Staber electronic washer is the way to go. Uses only 200Wh, which is ¼ of a regular washer. Low surge (no starting problems). Top loading, its horizontally tumbling stainless steel hexagon drum (no reciprocating parts) washes 16-18lbs of clothes with only 1½ oz. of detergent, and less than half the water per load as agitator type washers. Made in Ohio. From Backwoods Solar for Ø1170. (Ask for factory brochure.)

Light bulbs

Incandescent bulbs use gobs of power to heat their element until it glows. Crude, brute force stuff. Modern fluorescent bulbs use ¼ the power for the same output and 10x the life. They don't have to hum or flicker, with electronic ballasting. Comparative brightness equals 4x wattage. There are now affordable bulbs for any application. Real Goods has the best selection.

Bed warmers

12V for no AC magnetic field. Use to preheat your bed. You sleep *on* it, not under it (makes sense, as heat rises). Running current is only 2-5A. From Ø56 to Ø90, depending on size.

ENERGY SYSTEMS

Now it's time to put it all together. Know that I can only hit the highlights here, and that planning and design requires much research and consultation with experts. The folks at Real Goods or Backwoods Solar will get you going, and their phone time is free *if you buy your system from them*--which is only fair.

Calculating electrical demand

Multiply Watts times expected length of daily use. A power tool may be rated 240Wh, but is used only 15 minutes each day, so its demand is 240Wh x 0.25 = 60Wh/day. A computer and its monitor draw 45Wh times 5 hours, or 225Wh/day.

Add up your DC Watts and add 30% for system losses. Add up your AC Watts and add 40% for system losses (the extra 10% is for the inverter). Total the DC and AC demands.

Your battery bank should handle the total expected demand times some number of sunless days (say 3-5), times two (because you only want to discharge to 50%).

Running on generator/batteries alone

I've spoken with many folks who plan to do this since they "can't afford" natural electricity (solar, wind, micro-hydro), or they don't foresee the power grids being down for more than a few weeks or months.

If your area's power plant comes back online after a relatively short while, then you'll be lucky and a generator/battery bank will suffice. Still, don't plan on much power being available, since your plant will probably have to help restart the grid. (AC can be transmitted for over 1,500 miles.)

Why generators are too expensive for the *long* haul

Even still, it remains too expensive to produce power *solely* from an IC engine generator for longer than a few weeks.

Depending on the generator's efficiency, it takes a gallon of fuel per hour to produce 4.5-8kW (4500-8000 Watts) of electricity. (This is *fuel* cost only, *not* purchase or maintenance costs.) Let's call it Ø1.20/5.5kW in fuel. Figure in Ø1,500 for a 6kW generator, with a life of 2,000 hours before rebuild, and that's another Ø0.75 per hour (not counting maintenance). Add another Ø0.30/hour for maintenance, and we've arrived at Ø2.25 per 6kWh (or 41¢/kWh for fuel, engine wear, and maintenance). We'll forget about the time to refill the fuel tank, maintenance time, hassle, etc.

Most homes go through at least 1000kWh each month, or 35kWh per day. They pay about 8¢/kWh, which is Ø2.80/day and Ø80/month. Generator power (not counting expensive fast battery chargers, a necessary battery storage system, inverter, powercenter, wiring, etc.) is at least *5 times* more expensive. You'd pay Ø410/month in *running costs alone*, plus you'd have to *listen* to the thing for 6 hours a day, *every day*. Most homes, at present usage, would need even *bigger* generators than 6kW.

Given a Honda engine's 2,000 hour life before rebuild, you'd only get 11 months of daily use out of it at most. (The smaller Briggs & Stratton or Tecumseh engines will last only 500hrs., or just 3 months use at 6hrs/day.) LP generators will see almost twice the life, though at longer running time and higher fuel costs given LP's lower energy content. Expensive diesel generators (1800rpm engines) can run 15,000 hours before rebuild and use cheaper fuel, but even *they* are cost prohibitive to use as your *sole* source of power.

Understand that "only" 35kWh/day, though *modest* usage for most homes, would mean a *Ø42,000* solar system (producing 6kWh for six hours a day). Regardless of solar or generator, you're going to have to live on just 3-12kWh/day for *affordability's* sake. An 18kWh/day solar system (without Ø2,000 generator) will run you Ø27,000.

Still, can we *skip* solar and live on a generator alone?

So, with highly efficient appliances and pairing everything down to a demand of, say 6kWh/day--is it *feasible* to live on generator alone, and save the Ø6,500 in solar modules?

You'll *still* need a large battery bank, which saves generator time, else the thing would have to run for even the slightest demand. 10 L-16HCs (Ø2,100) will give you 1975Ah for a total of 23.7kWh. Since you'll plan on only a 50% discharge (deeper than that begins to really lower battery life), 11.85kWh will give you two days of 6kWh/day between generator charging. You won't, however, get *nearly* as much life out of your batteries by recharging them as often as every two days, as most solar systems produce enough power to keep the batteries at 75+% even overnight, and require recharging only weekly.

Batteries can only be charged at 10% of their capacity-- thus, your 1975Ah battery bank can take only a 200Ah charger. Meaning if you use 50% of battery capacity, it'll take you at least 5 hours (5x10% charging rate) to refill them, and that *doesn't* assume the taper charge factor as the batteries approach 100%.

So, figure *7 hours* of 8kW generator charging every two days, at 1.5 gal/hr, for 158 gal/month. At that rate, your generator (not accounting for incidental power tool use, etc.) will run 1,281hrs/year, which will be 60% of engine life for most generators (and 256% for the 500hr cheapy engines). You'll use about 1,922 gallons of gasoline/year, in which your Ø6,500 solar modules would have paid for themselves (in gasoline alone) after just 3 years (assuming they provide 80% of your power needs).

So, even with the "firehose" problem of IC engine generated electricity solved with batteries and inverters, a generator remains too expensive for the *bulk* of one's power needs. For that we must look to solar, wind, or micro-hydro. Even those systems will need a generator for extraordinary demand, or for when the naturally-driven dynamo is off-line. Therefore, a generator is (or will become) a necessary *part* of your energy system, but it cannot reasonably be *the* energy system.

Some sample *generator-only* systems

Since many of you will not believe that solar modules are really necessary, I'll discuss several sample systems on generator alone. Because nobody will want to run their generator for all real-time power needs (down to mere lighting), these systems *still* require all of a solar system's hardware (such as battery bank, inverter, powercenter, etc.) except for the modules.

A typical home system with ample power for luxury--6kWh/day

I recommend a 150Ah charger/2500W inverter by Trace (which saves you Ø705 in buying three fast battery chargers), and gives you true sine wave power as well.

NorthStar 10000 Watt (8.5kW cont.) generator	Ø1,750
Powercenter	Ø1,750
10 Trojan L-16HC (1975Ah; 23.7kWh)	Ø2,100
SW2512 sine wave inverter/charger	Ø2,585

Sunfrost R-10/Vestfrost freezer	Ø2,210
300 gallon fuel tank	Ø 300
12V DC evaporative cooler	Ø 465
Staber clothes washer	Ø1,170
misc. 12V DC appliances, lights, etc.	Ø1,000
Paloma PH12 tankless water heater	Ø 755
500 gallons of LP	Ø 400
	Ø14,485

For an extra Ø6,500, you could have 1000Wh of solar modules.

What if I'm using *far* less power and an LP fridge?

Say you'll only use 3kWh/day. A bank of 6 L-16HCs will give you 7.1kWh at 50% discharge. A DR2412 inverter will give you 120Ah of charging power. A NorthStar 5500 Watt generator will do just fine for only Ø1,000 (or you could get a tri-fuel DYNA 9000 Watt generator for Ø1,640).

NorthStar 5500 Watt (4.5kW cont.) generator	Ø1,000
Powercenter	Ø1,450
6 Trojan L-16HC (1185Ah; 14.2kWh)	Ø1,260
DR2412 inverter/charger	Ø1,325
300 gallon fuel tank	Ø 300
12V DC evaporative cooler	Ø 465
Staber clothes washer	Ø1,170
misc. 12V DC appliances, lights, etc.	Ø 500
Norcold LP fridge	Ø1,265
Paloma PH12 tankless water heater	Ø 755
500 gallons of LP	Ø 400
	Ø9,890

For just Ø3,900, 600Wh of solar modules could be added.

The economical couple

Again, you'll have a propane fridge, stove, etc. Power demand is 2.5-3kWh/day here, which means inverter-powered lighting, TV, VCR, stereo, DC water pump, vacuum, hand tools, computer, blender, etc. The generator must be fired up for large appliances like clothes washer, deep well pump, and table saw.

Some items for comfort and convenience (to keep *Madam* around) were left in, such as the clothes washer, evaporative cooler, and mid-size water heater.

NorthStar 5500 Watt (4.5kW cont.) generator	Ø1,000
10 Trojan L-105 (1100Ah; 13.2kWh)	Ø 750
Charge control, meters, hardware	Ø 450

DR1500 inverter/charger	Ø 995
300 gallon fuel tank	Ø 300
12V DC evaporative cooler	Ø 465
Staber clothes washer	Ø1,170
misc. 12V DC appliances, lights, etc.	Ø 300
Norcold LP fridge	Ø1,265
Paloma PH12 tankless water heater	Ø 755
500 gallons of LP	Ø 400
	Ø7,850

For only Ø2,700 you could add 450Wh of solar modules and save your generator from much use. Highly recommended. For another Ø510 they could have 6 Trojan L-16HCs instead, for twice the battery life at 70% of the yearly battery cost.

What if I'm a *real* frugal guy?

I say guy, meaning male and alone, because you won't likely find a woman who will enjoy the following low budget system (although it beats living in the dark and cold, ladies). We're talking about 2kWh/day here. This would be a good RV system.

While he *could* get by with a Ø450 NorthStar 2.4kW generator, I *highly* recommend the larger NorthStar which can simultaneously handle heavier tools, a deep-well pump, etc.

He could also save Ø225 on a UX1112-SB inverter, but the DR1512's 70Ah charge rate is worth saving generator time.

He'll have to wash his clothes at a friend's house.

NorthStar 5500 Watt (4.5kW cont.) generator	Ø1,000
4 Trojan T-105 (880Ah; 10.56kWh)	Ø 600
Charge control and meters	Ø 400
Hardware	Ø 100
DR1512 inverter/charger	Ø1,325
300 fuel tank	Ø 300
misc. 12V DC appliances, lights, etc.	Ø 200
Norcold LP fridge	Ø1,265
Paloma PH6 tankless water heater	Ø 445
500 gallons of LP	Ø 400
	Ø6,035

You'd be foolish not to spring Ø2,000 for solar modules here, which would give him 300Wh for 1.8kWh/day (300Wh x 6hrs).

A *dirt cheap* system

Suitable for only a hermit's RV or cabin at 1-1.5kWh/day. He could get by with less inverter (or none at all), but I threw one in as his only luxury for an 120V TV and small appliances.

NorthStar 2700 Watt (2.4kW cont.) generator	Ø 450
30amp. battery charger	Ø 145
4 Trojan L-105 (440Ah; 5.28kWh)	Ø 300
Charge control	Ø 125
DC fuse box	Ø 160
400W inverter	Ø 250
300 gallon fuel tank	Ø 300
misc. 12V DC appliances, lights, etc.	Ø 100
Norcold LP fridge	Ø1,265
Paloma PH6 tankless water heater	Ø 445
500 gallons of LP	Ø 400
	Ø3,940

For Ø330-1,300 you could have 50-200Wh of solar power for 300-1.2kWh/day. So, there you have it--Ø3,940 for about *the* most basic electric self-sufficiency.

So what was my *point* in all this? Given that these systems are 65% as expensive as the whole solar enchilada, why not go the extra 35% for the modules to be "done with it" and also to save all that generator time and expense? (Also know that the above systems did *not* include the several *thousands* of gallons of fuel required for years of generator use.)

I rest my case that a generator-alone system offers little savings in purchase *price,* and is more expensive in running *cost.* Do it right and go solar the first time around, and leave the false economy of generator-alone systems to the less-informed. Here endeth the lesson. (I've always tried to give you, the reader, a high info/Ø ratio, and my editors tell me that this chapter's info is *itself* worth many times the price of the book.)

If you learn one thing from this book, it should be that alternative energy suppliers will be overwhelmed with orders in 1999. If you haven't ordered by April or so, you might not get your order fulfilled in time. No kidding. PV modules are all foreign made, as we have no domestic manufacturers. Great.

❖ **9**

SHELTER

*I do not think that any civilization can be called complete until it has
progressed from sophistication to unsophistication, and made a con-
scious return to simplicity of thinking and living.*
   -- Lin Yutang

Where you ride out Y2K is the most important decision you can
make for your family. You want to be out of the reach of the
mobs and martial law. You can't stay in the city.

YOUR COUNTRY RETREAT

As I've already said, you shouldn't try to weather out Y2K
in a city over 100,000 people. I personally wouldn't be caught
during Y2K in any city with a population over 30,000, as they
have (though on a smaller scale) nearly identical problems and
the same scummy people as big cities.

Unless you savor incredible drama (or target-rich environments), leave the city as soon as possible. Leave meaning
move. You'll need to establish roots and relationships early on,
while things are relatively calm and stable. Don't think you can
drive up to your country vacation cabin on 31 December 1999
and say *"Hi, we're the Johnsons from Los Angeles! Boy that Y2K
thing's gonna be a mess--we barely got out of there! By the way,
got any firewood and toilet paper you can spare?"* Country folks
develop friendships very cautiously. Don't be surprised if they
take a year or three to sniff you out. They must be satisfied
that: ❶ You can pull your own weight. ❷ You mind your own
business. ❸

You don't try to remake their bucolic area into Van Nuys with 7-11s on every other block. Get there *early*. Learn to *relax*. Do things *their* way (*"When in Rome..."*). Lend a hand. Work hard. Don't whine if you can't get a bottle of nasal spray at 3AM, or if the Lobster Thermidor isn't like *"at home."*

Why I love the country
Full moonlight straining through foggy cottonwoods. Bushy tailed squirrels hopping from tree to tree. Robins chasing bugs in full aerial pursuit. The hearty whinnying of horses. The delicate feeding of a doe and her spotted fawns. The stars amongst a quiet night. Chipmunks lazily stretching in the afternoon sun. Raucous crows. Spooky owls. Singing frogs. Hardy, independent people.

I recently visited a friend in her metropolis domicile. City stink. Relentless honking and cries of *"*sshole!"* Choking fumes from diesel buses. The cacophony of wailing car alarms. Otherworldly looking (and acting) people. Traffic jams. On Saturday morning a screaming, mad-as-a-hatter street person woke me at 6AM. The next morning (at 7AM) we were awakened by a *crash!-tinkle* when a guy lost control of his car, jumped a curb (ripping off his oil pan), and knocked down a stop sign. He stomped and swore for several minutes, then hid his car in the nearest parking garage (leaving an oil trail). Once, when my friend wouldn't give a panhandler a quarter, he exposed himself to her. City benefits: We had some nice meals and saw some good plays. *Period.* (Been There. Done That.)

Being there vs. Getting there
I already live in my country retreat, as do many of my friends. You city folks, however, have to decide if you're going to be there in advance (*e.g.*, before Christmas 1999), or if you'll wait and see how January 2000 looks.

Right now, it's October 1998 and too early to tell. By fall 1999 you'll have *plenty* of warning signs to spur you on out of there, assuming that the cities aren't already locked up for some *"national emergency."* I'd get out of the city ASAP, and by summer 1999 at the latest.

*Pre-investigate the locale in which you intend to settle, and **pre-plan the physical move.** Hopefully, you will have enjoyed numerous outings to your site, and you will know the surroundings like the back*

of your hand. Likewise, you should know several ways to get there.
Chances are that when the flag goes down, several roads will be ei-
ther closed or too dangerous to travel, and you will need to know
about alternative travel routes, especially off-road.
   -- *Great Livin' In Grubby Times*, p.77

Yurts and other basic shelters

Back in the 1980s, the Soviet Union made the haughty gesture of sending blankets to Manhattan's homeless people. My Polish friends told me of a guy who, in response, put an ad in the paper reading *"Will trade apartment in Warsaw for blanket in New York City."* (*Touché!* He had some "splaining" to do...)

My point is this: I'd trade my high-rise city apartment or suburban 3/2 home for a tent in the faraway country.

With a woodstove, folks can comfortably weather out an alpine winter in a tent, yurt (a Mongolian design), or teepee. I know people who do so yearly. While *"That's not my bag, baby!"* these shelters can be quite cozy. (Have a cat for the mice.)

The Yurt

"Yurt" is a Turkish word that means "home." The Mongolian horsemen invented the "gher" as a strong and light dwelling which could withstand snow storms. Yurts are more spacious than a tent, lighter than a cabin, and pleasant looking. The only other superior circular dwelling is a geodesic dome.

For prefab yurts, call Pacific Yurts (the oldest firm of the three; www.yurts.com; 541-942-9435), Nesting Bird Yurt Co. (www.nbyurts.com; 360-779-3338), or Borealis Yurts (207-564-3355). To build your own, read *Rustic Retreats* by Stiles.

Recreational Vehicles (RVs)

I've made working study of living the 80/20 Rule (Pareto's Law for you economists). Basically, you can have 80% of the fun and comfort for only 20% of the cost. This concept dawned on me after spending time with a lady friend who knows the secret. She lives in a rural community far from any big city, so she could afford to buy and pay off her Ø25,000 home (on 1 acre). She is a teacher who has summers off, and hits the road every June with her dog in her old Triumph convertible. She's seen the entire country, including Canada and Alaska. She even has her own airplane, an old Piper Cub, which she bips around in.

She enjoys three months of uninterrupted vacation every year, a sports car, an airplane, and a mortgage-free home--*and she's "just" a teacher making Ø28,000 a year!* So, folks, don't tell *me* that a full and interesting life cannot be had unless you're "rich." Although not "rich" she is one of the most *wealthy* people I know. She knows where and how to spend money *efficiently* and for maximum effect. (Sorry, guys, she just got married.)

In part from her example, I embarked on my scheme of becoming a prosperous author out of an RV. It's worked out beautifully. Now I can afford to buy outright my own small home, and not give a penny of interest to the banksters. RV living made it possible--heck, *guaranteed.*

"One receipt for one recreational vehicle, signed by... Boston T. Party." (Yet another *Austin Powers* reference.) Yes, RVs *are* my bag. I've lived/vacationed in them for several years. My monthly lot rent was often free (in exchange for caretaking or general repair work), and never more than Ø225 (on my own quiet ¼ac. lot in the pines). My P.O. box was Ø10 a year, and my pager Ø8 a month. My girlfriends generally thought it cozy and romantic, although one (a spoiled city girl) fairly sniffed her nose at it all. As I owned the RV outright, my fixed monthly costs were never more than a few hundred dollars. If I wanted to take off on a cross-country trip for the whole summer, I did so without some Ø700 rent or Ø1,500 mortgage on my back. The savings I poured into precious metals, tools, and training.

The lower your *fixed* costs, the lower the *opportunity* costs of travel, exploration, and solitude. I could not have written 4 books in just *two* years trapped in some city job and apartment.

While RV living is not for everyone, it suited me just fine, and I'm no worse for wear because of it. It was clean, warm, dry, and cheerful--and all I ever really need is a quiet place to read and think and write. Once, I set up near a ski resort, bought very decent skis/boots/poles at a thrift store for Ø30 and enjoyed an entire ski *season* for what most folks pay for just one *vacation.* I'm done with RV living (needed more space for my books, and a possible family), but I look back on the experience with great fondness. It got me on my author feet without debt.

Two excellent books you must get (from Loompanics) are *Freedom Road* by Hough, and *Travel Trailer Homesteading for Under $5,000* by Kelling. A few families could, on the cheap, go in together on a 5-20 acre parcel of land and set up their own trailer lots on it with a common well, septic tank, etc.--for just a few ØØØØ each. (Tens of thousands of retired couples live this way year round, cheaply though with comfort and style.) Loompanics and Eden Press are your best sources for books on inexpensive, contrarian living. Why work yourself to the bone in some dangerous, unpleasant city for mortgage slavery?

I am constantly amazed at the comfort and modern conveniences that RVs provide. For well under Ø10,000 you can have a mobile, self-contained, fully-equipped (furniture and appliances), versatile home. Yes, they're small, but you're not supposed to spend all day *inside* them!

Your RV should be comfortable enough to make you forget about living in a house.
    -- Harold Hough; *Freedom Road*

I've long recommended having a few travel trailers sprinkled about the country at your favorite places, and visiting them yearly. Your assets are privately geographically diversified, and you'd always have a home of your own to go if ever in trouble. A friend of mine paid just Ø1,000 each for a van and 22' travel trailer, and salted them away at a buddy's in New Mexico. He can leave the city by bike any time for his country digs.

Motor home vs. travel trailer

If you'll be highly mobile (*i.e.*, monthly travel), then I'd get a motor home. They drive, park, and set up easier than a towed rig. The driving and living compartments are not separated, so food may be prepared and drivers spelled without stopping.

If you won't be on the road more than a few times a year and will park your rig for at least a few weeks at a time, then a travel trailer will do fine, especially if you already have a suitable tow vehicle.

Motor homes

They have one big disadvantage: Once set up, your transportation is immobile. Solution: Tow a second vehicle (preferably a 4x4), or mount a motorcycle on the rear bumper.

The neatest setup I ever saw was a medium-sized (about 26') motor home towing a small 4x4 pickup. In the pickup bed were two trail bikes. Above, on a pipe frame rack, was 15' aluminum fishing boat. Here was a "do anything/go anywhere" rig! The boat helped streamline the towed pickup, and also acted as a cover for the motorcycles. *Tres chic.*

If you plan on doing some wilderness camping, then a motor home no longer than 30' should be able to negotiate all but the roughest and tightest dirt road.

Get a Class A (it's on a truck or bus chassis) about 26' long, which is long enough to be comfortable, yet short enough to be affordable and easily driven. (Forget about the monster rigs the size of city buses. For the same money, you can buy a small home.) They'll usually have a 120V generator (the best are the *external* combustion Sterling engine type).

The Class Bs are merely van conversions (*e.g.*, the "Good Times Machine"), and suitable for only weekend trips.

Class C RVs are factory designed on a van chassis and have many of the Class A amenities without the size or price. Since they are necessarily quite cramped, they are suitable only for single people or very tight couples.

Travel trailers

You can use your tow vehicle for transportation when the trailer is set up. They tow and set up easily enough (especially the 5th wheels), but I'd rather have a motor home for *really* frequent travel. Travel trailers do have the added benefit of being about 30% less expensive than motor homes.

If you plan to live in it more than travel in it and don't have your own tow vehicle, then simply borrow a friend's truck or van to occasionally move it. (When I bought mine in a new area, with no tow vehicle or friend to move it, I hired a guy who charged me Ø1/mile. I later bought a pickup to haul it around.)

A word about tow vehicles: don't skimp! You want at least a 350V8, transmission cooler, and *quality* hitch/equalizer/antisway bars. A poorly setup rig can send you off a cliff. Also, make sure your trailer's electric brakes are in good order--there's *nothing* more terrifying than for your rig's brakes to fail.

Size

If you don't anticipate traveling in it much (*i.e.*, no more than once or twice a year), then you might as well get a travel trailer at least 30' long and park it. If, however, you'll be moving about seasonally, then anything over 30' gets to be cumbersome. Anything less than 26' is really too cramped to live in. Best all around size for comfort *and* mobility is about 28'.

Accessories

An awning is a must, providing a dry patio area for a picnic table, BBQ pit, chairs, etc.

Buying an RV
Pick a name brand and test *every* system (*i.e.*, water, gas, and electric) and *every* appliance. (I'd pressurize the water lines for 24hrs and check for leaks.) Make sure the fridge runs on both gas and electric. Look for roof leaks and water damage. Tow it for a few miles and test the brakes.

Weatherproofing
Make sure the roof isn't tarred over to hide defects. (Look for signs of water leakage inside.) If set up for the winter, you'll need to seal the outside of your windows with clear plastic to keep out the drafts and minimize heat loss.

You'll need to install some kind of skirting (corrugated steel, propanel, plywood, etc.) around the outside bottom to keep the wind from whipping underneath. (This will also keep critters from nesting there.) One owner simply jacked up his trailer, placed hay bales under the entire floor, and lowered the trailer on top of them. It's very stable, supremely-well insulated, and forms its own skirting. (A quick egress is prevented, but he wasn't concerned about that.)

Building a rain/snow shed over the RV is recommended if it's to be stationary for years.

Heating
While most larger trailers have a forced-air gas furnace which will heat quite well (at 1-2 gallons/day), a small kerosene heater is cheaper to operate. Travel trailers are unfortunately too small to house a wood stove on 3' square of tile or brick, although I have seen it done. Insulation is very thin, so don't expect your RV to retain its heat well.

I used the gas furnace (for convenience) set at 65° and kept the bathroom toasty warm with an electric space heater. If you use the gas furnace, you'll want to rent a large LP tank as filling up small LP bottles every week gets old quickly.

Other considerations
As long as your RV is not *"readily mobile"* (by virtue of being on blocks and connected to water/power/sewage lines), the courts consider will it a dwelling for purposes of search warrants. Meaning, it escapes the normal *"automobile exception"* to the 4th Amendment (in which no warrant is needed to enter and search, only mobility and *"probable cause"*). If you're concerned about a possible search, then take dated photos of its im-

mobile status beforehand (stored at your lawyer's office, not at home). Get *You & The Police!* for a full discussion on the law.

If you set up on a friend's property, perfectly iron out what is expected of you for the space. Rent and/or electricity money, a helping hand, security--whatever. *"Good contracts make good friends."* as my dad used to say. Resolve all possible issues (*e.g.*, parking, schedules, utilities, etc.) *before* you move in, and honor your part of the bargain *without fail*.

If parked on a friend's property, be aware that some jurisdictions prohibit such a second residence. What constitutes *"residency"* varies, but it's usually continuous habitation for 30 days. If you're ever questioned on this, deny that you've ever stayed there for more than a week or two at one stretch, and that it's not a *"residence."* This may erase any 4th Amendment protection of unwarranted searches, so choose *which* hassle to avoid. In my experience, the "second dwelling" issue will never arise unless there's a snoopy, jerk neighbor involved--so, I'd rather have the full 4th Amendment protection of a *"house."*

Mobile homes

These are great compromise between living in an RV and a proper house. While all the movies show mobile home life as suitable only for dirtbags (and that's often quite true), such doesn't have to be *your* case. Dirtbags will be dirtbags no matter *where* they live, and people of hygiene and dignity can make a tent look palatial.

Quality of construction is often very good these days. I'd look for a used model under Ø20,000, or even Ø15,000. You must pay probably at least Ø8-10,000 to get something clean and decent. Mobiles can be moved once or twice without any problems, but much more than that they begin to loosen up and crack. They are *not* travel trailers, they are homes which can be mobile. They can be moved with all your possessions inside, though you should distribute very heavy items along the axles.

If you purchase it from a dealer in a neighboring state and mail in payment, you should be able to avoid paying any sales tax (especially if the seller transports it across your state line). Buying from a private seller is easier still, although the paperwork usually falls in complexity between a car and a house.

It'll cost you Ø500-1,000+ to move it, depending on distance and difficulty of set up. If in a cold climate, face it towards the south lengthwise. A propanel snowshed might be a good idea. Skirt it immediately. A covered deck adds a *lot.*

Once set up, the county will like some property tax on it, unless you've employed some ingenious means for avoiding it. *If* private movers hauled it out to your land, *and if* you're not on the energy grid, *and if* you've no land line installed, *and if* you've no crappy neighbors, *then* you'll likely avoid the attention of the tax folks. **What they don't *know*, they can't *tax*.** *Heh!* It's worth a try, regardless. Make it into 2000 without their knowledge, and you're probably "home free." (Ha, ha.)

Woodstoves are the best way to heat mobiles.

Rustic cabins
These are usually made of logs. Weatherstripping is much more work than prefab homes, but a rustic cabin can be cheaply and leisurely built by the homesteader.

Homes
A-frame houses
Very quick and inexpensive to build, even by just two people. Great design for alpine climates.
Suppliers
Grayrock 65 High Ridge Rd. #535, Stamford, CT 06905

Straw bale house
A well-built straw bale house is durable, safe, and will last indefinitely. Construction costs are as little as Ø10/ft^2 and walls can be up in a single weekend. Rebar gives the R-50 walls their rigidity, and stucco or adobe provides the finish.
Read *The Straw Bale House* (Ø30 + Ø5.50 S&H, from High Country Enterprise, 800-215-0725).

Underground and bermed homes
These are very quiet, solid, and temperature constant (requiring very little heating and cooling).

Geodesic dome homes
My favorite above-ground edifice. Contains the most volume for the least wall surface, and retain heat the best. Very strong and lightweight.

Suppliers
Oregon Dome   800-572-8943   www.domes.com
Monolithic Dome   800-608-0001   www.monolithicdome.com
GeoDomes   909-787-8800
American Ingenuity   407-638-8777
Architectural Designs, HC01 Box 6201-AB, Palmer, Alaska 99645
Earth Systems Homes   303-247-2100
Timberline Geodesics   800-DOME-HOME www.domehome.com

STORAGE SHELTERS

Necessary for food, tools, etc.

Suppliers
Storm Chasers   817-847-9000
American Steel Span 800-891-6733x1037   www.steelspan.com
Universal Steel   800-993-4660
Port-A-Hut   800-882-4884

HOMESTEADING RESOURCES

Needful Provision Inc.   c/o P.O. Box 246, Cimarron, N.M. 87714
An info-coop club. Membership is only 35 bucks/year.

Tri-Steel Structures   800-TRI-STEEL
Steel framing for fire-resistant and strong homes.

BOOKS

How to Find Your Ideal Country Home, Gene GeRue
Very comprehensive. This book will help you make the break, set goals, make plans, and actually get the country. Ø25/432pp. At any bookstore.

The Modern Survival Retreat, Ragnar Benson
The companion volume to his 1983 classic. Full of typical Bensonian good info and stories. Ø15/106pp. From Paladin.

❖ 10

TRANSPORTATION

HUMAN POWERED

Walking

Have *lots* of shoe leather on hand. I prefer a bicycle over walking whenever possible.

Bicycle

Being a motorcycle enthusiast it's been difficult to get excited about bicycles. You huff and you puff and you go 19mph. Also, certain cities excepted, American roadways are just not set up for them. Still, within limits, bicycles have their place. They are several times faster and more efficient than walking. The Asians can carry up to 300lbs. of cargo on them.

Forget the thin tired "racing" bicycles; mountain bikes are the way to go. I bought a pair of used ones at my local flea market for only Ø110, though I recommend that you spend more and get better bicycles. You don't have to spend Ø3,000. A Ø600 "Rockhopper" is 80% the bicycle for 20% the money. **Stock up on parts:** tires, tubes, spokes, rims, chains, cables, brake pads, and rubber squeeze horns (just kidding).

Unless you've acquired all other crucial survival goods, don't go wild on bike expenditures. I am reminded of the quote:

All bicycles weigh 50 pounds.
A 30 pound bicycle needs a 20 pound lock and chain.
A 40 pound bicycle needs a 10 pound lock and chain.
A 50 pound bicycle needs no lock and chain.

A few words to all you biking mavens: You do *not* have the same rights as cars since you don't pay registration fees and taxes (fuel and excise). You cannot block traffic by riding several abreast at 8mph, and then run red lights when it suits you. Some irate driver will one day nudge you off a hairpin curve or stuff you into a parked truck. Stay to the far right-hand side of the road! Finally, curb your pious attitudes. You're really not all *that* impressive with your silly Buck Rogers helmets, shaved legs, and Lycra butts in the air.

ENGINE POWERED

Since most of you will know of a good horse person, I won't go into horses and mules.

Motorcycle

I've been riding street bikes for twenty years and have over 250,000 miles of road experience in over 20 countries. I *like* motorcycling, although it's not for everybody. Market research indicates that not more than 5% of Americans ride, or ever *will* ride, motorcycles. Still, they do have their place. Even if you don't have a bike or even know how to ride, *learn to ride*. No training is ever wasted, and someday your only way out of some nasty situation may indeed be on a motorcycle.

Street vs. dirt vs. enduro

Street bikes are only for the road, dirt bikes are only for the dirt, and enduros (a dirt bike with lights and on/off road tires) are for both. If you can have only one motorcycle, make it an enduro. 4 out of 5 miles of American roads are *unpaved*, so you'll miss out on 80% of the fun with only a street bike.

Dirt bike vs. ATV

Although ATVs are fine and fun, a good trail bike is much more nimble and can navigate through more congested woods. Have a good 4x4 ATV with rack and trailer for hunting, and an enduro for fun and scouting about.

2-stroke vs. 4-stroke

While two-stroke motors make great power, they are much harder for novice and even intermediate riders to modulate. They're "on" or they're "off." I prefer the more tractable (and *quiet*) four-stroke engines.

Bargain enduros would be, for example, the older Honda XLs and Suzuki DTs, which can be found for under Ø800. I've got a 1974 XL250 that I bought for only Ø300, and it runs great. One of these mounted to a 4x4 pickup with camper makes for a very versatile rig.

Modern enduros are the Kawasaki KLR, Honda TransAlp, BMW GS and Funduro, and Suzuki DR.

Street bikes

If you need an inexpensive road vehicle for running errands, a street bike will do almost as well as a car.

With new street bikes of 650cc beginning at Ø5,000, used bikes are often fantastic bargains. I recommend nothing smaller than 450 or 550cc, the minimum for necessary highway power, speed, and endurance. (Ladies may feel more comfortable handling a 450-550cc, and these are fine for moderate trips under, say, 300 miles.) Unless you travel two-up or for very long distances, you really won't need anything larger than a 750cc. Any 650 or 750 will still give you 40-50mpg, while the 1000s drop down to the 30s.

The very racey "crotch rockets" are great fun, but less comfortable and more expensive to purchase and maintain. A more "plain Jane" bike is much more practical and affordable.

My particular favorites are the stone-reliable Kawasaki KZ (650 and 750), the Honda 700 (Nighthawk) and 750 fours (not the V4 Sabre), the Honda CX500 and CX650 (a bulletproof V-twin popular amongst professional bike couriers), the Yamaha 650 and 750 Seca, and Suzuki GS1000 shaft. Most of these excellent models can be found for under Ø2,000, and some (*e.g.*, a 1980 KZ750, or CX500) for even less than Ø1,000.

The BMW Boxer twins made between 1981 and 1990 are often comparative bargains for Ø1,200 to Ø4,000, and simple to maintain. (The older Beemers before 1980 require a little more fiddling, and parts are more expensive. Still, an old R60 or R75 will provide great service.) My choice would be any Brembo disc-braked R100. The enduro GS80 and GS100 are quite capable offroad, but too heavy for truly aggressive riding.

While BMW's modern K Series are very nice bikes, they are, for our post-Y2K purposes, *far* too complicated with their electronic ignition, fuel injection, and instrumentation. On a bike trip throughout Mexico, a K100 rider had to have his bike carried back in a pickup bed 1,000 miles to Brownsville, Texas because his Ø10 fuel filter split from the high-pressure fuel injection. (He didn't carry a spare. What a bummer.)

Older street bikes might need new steering-head bearings, fork seals, shocks, chains and sprockets, and tires. *Big deal.* Pick up an old KZ750 for Ø800, put another Ø200-350 into it and ride for 30,000 miles with only oil and tire changes. Best deals on tires, chains and sprockets are from mail-order companies (get a copy of *Motorcyclist* or *Cycle* for the ads).

Mopeds

Yes, they get over 100mpg, but with poor brakes and twitchy handling. I'd much rather have a 400cc street bike for 65mpg and true highway capability.

Care and feeding of your motorcycle

Have spare tires and tubes, cables, chains and sprockets, plugs and points, air/gas/oil filters, fork seals and oil, and shocks. I like to install separate in-line fuel filters on my bikes, as the petcock screen is insufficient. Keep a good eye on your chain; don't let it get loose, rusty, or out of line. A Clymer repair manual is necessary, along with a set of metric tools. Keep your bike garaged, or under a cover at least (only Ø5 from CTD, #ZBF-189).

Motorcycle gear

Motorcycling is a *sport*, and every sport has its own gear. *Do not* ride in shorts, T-shirt, and sandals--*ever*. While proper Cordura or leather riding gear is hot, *it's cooler than roadrash*. Jeans are ripped through after only 4' of asphalt sliding, and provide little more than a false sense of protection.

I prefer Cordura over leather, because Cordura can be waterproof (with GorTex membrane), dries quicker, is machine-washable, and is lighter than leather. Leather suits are preferable for dedicated street riding in dry weather.

The *AeroStitch* suit from RiderWearhouse (call 800-222-1994 for free catalog) is *the* suit for street or mild enduro riding. Andy Goldfine has spent over ten years developing his suits, with the input from thousands of riders, and it shows. The quality and usability is unsurpassed. Now, everybody else is trying to copy the concept and design--to little avail. In my pants I fit baseball catcher's shin/knee armor backed with sports Temperfoam. (Most spills involving broken bones are broken shins.)

Always **wear gloves**, preferably heavy winter gloves with gauntlet. *Always* **wear boots**. Mine are "Mad Max" style motocross boots with Vibram soles custom installed. *Always* **wear a helmet**, preferably a full-face Snell rated model. Great brands are Shoei, Arai, and AGV. Have extra faceshields, as they scratch easily. *Never* buy a used helmet, as it could easily have undetectable internal damage and thus fail to protect your bargain-oriented brain in a crash.

ATV (Rokon; 3/4 wheeler)
These are very capable vehicles, and better for snow and mud than motorcycles.

Rokon
While noisy and heavy, these 2-wheel drive 200cc bikes will climb a *wall*. They'll climb hills that'd freak a yak. It takes a *lot* of courage to use a Rokon to its full potential.

3 wheeler
These aren't sold anymore because people refused to learn to ride them correctly and crashed with newsworthy regularity. They aren't as stable as 4-wheelers, but you can find some great bargains on the used market.

4 wheeler
These are amazing vehicles. Many of the modern ones come in 4x4 and make great hunting rigs which can pack out even an elk. Downside: they ain't cheap at Ø4,000+.

Car
If you don't yet have a 4x4, sell or trade your car for one if you have to. Consider selling your sports car if you need the money for Y2K preparation. (If no disaster hits in 1999 or 2000, then you can always replace it.) Use an inexpensive street bike at 40-65mpg for those small errands.

Best cars to have are front-wheel drive for better rain and snow driving. A front-wheel drive minivan (*e.g.*, Ford Windstar) makes for a very versatile rig. (Rear-wheel drive minivans are better for towing.)

Although I prefer to buy American, we are unwilling to offer car buyers the inherent quality of a Honda, Nissan, Toyota, or Mazda. I've had many Japanese econoboxes, and they all gave me great service with little maintenance.

Have a set of chains for alpine climates or muddy roads. Stock up on misc. parts (belts, hoses, alternator, water pump, etc.) to go further in a post-2000 world.

Pickup
2-wheel drive vs. 4x4
Unless your pickup is used only for street hauling, you'll want a 4x4. In 1970s models, Ford *might* have an edge over GM, although Ford's 16.5" rims make tire shopping a pain. For 1980s models, I lean towards Chevy. 1990s models all seem pretty comparable, although opinions are fiercely divided.

Motors
Always go V8. I'm a big-block fan, as there's no substitute for cubic inches. (Size *does* matter.) Go Chevy 454 or Ford 460.

Aircraft
I'm a big fan of kit planes. They often have some of the latest design innovations and features, and can be assembled by the moderately handy in as little as a few weeks. (The KitFox comes to mind.)

Gyrocopters
These are fantastic machines, though with an undeservedly poor reputation for safety. What makes them "unsafe" is untrained, inexperienced pilots who overcorrect for PIOs or get into downwind stalls. Gyrocopters are the most inherently stable and safe aircraft to every fly. They will fly *hands off*.

Proper training is *essential*, as they fly differently than anything else and their controls are quite sensitive. A *light* touch is the *key*.

Gyros (with prerotater) can take off in only 100', and can land in less than 50'. They cruise at 60-110mph for 150-300 miles and can carry a 250-500lb. payload. Floats can be added for water landings, and thus a fisherman could hop from one secluded alpine lake to another.

Tactically, gyros make good sense. Watch the *Road Warrior* to get ideas on this. They are the "dirt bikes" of the air. Good for recon, observation, and even light strafing.

❖ 11

MONEY

Money is an information system we use to deploy human effort.
-- Michael Linton, originator of the Local Employment
and Trading System (L.E.T.S.)

"Deploy" is the *precise* word for what money does to human effort. It's derived from the Latin (*dis*, apart + *plicare*, to fold), and means *"to spread out so as to form a wider front."* Read Linton's quote in my expanded form:

Money is an information system we use to spread out human effort so as to form a wider front.

"To form a wider front" against *what*? **Against the relentless forces of *Nature*, of course.** Her formidable regiments are Gravity, Age, Decay, and Entropy. Humans are in perennial war with these forces, and we use money to spread out our effort so as to form a wider front against Nature.

Why do I (A) accept FRNs from readers (B) for my books? Because I am confident that I can directly trade with others (C) for what I want. Money deploys more than human effort in principle--more specifically, money deploys the human effort of *strangers*. This point is not understood *nearly* widely enough.

David Friedman clarifies why people exert effort for others at *all*: out of *Love* (as favors), out of *Force* ("pay taxes or go to jail"), and out of *Trade* (this for that). There is a *limit* to how much we can induce others to work for us out of Love or Force. For example, my Wisconsin printer (meaning all their employees) do not work out of Love, and I certainly can't force them a thousand miles away to print my books. Love and Force take much time and personal contact to *establish* and to *maintain*. They're too expensive and too unreliable.

Only Trade can deploy the effort of *thousands of distant strangers* to work *in concert* for *my* benefit, and there can *be* no such Trade without money.

The novel *The White Plague* provides an indirect example. A deranged man needs some "vector" to spread his concocted plague throughout Ireland. He is one man working totally alone, trying to infect millions of Irishmen. How does he do it? He sent by mail £5 notes to thousands of strangers, with a note reading *"Here's that £5 I owed you."* Those infected notes quickly multiplied their contagion as they frequently passed from hand to hand. Clearly, he understood the deployment of human effort *amongst strangers* as money's purpose.

Whenever money, that information system for deployment, is suddenly *lost,* then human effort cannot be effectively deployed. **People then become *unemployed.*** Money is the *mortar* of all civilization. A collapse of civilization has always followed the collapse of its money. When there is no money, *when there is only barter*, there can be only *primitive* society. That is why I cannot accept a purely barter economy in defiance of the Federal Reserve banksters. (In fact, the term "barter economy" is more of an oxymoron than not.) That is why I have been working on for three years a new money for freedom-loving individuals. (David Chaum's DigiCash--www.digicash.com--*could* be the embryo of such a new system.)

Think of money as an army's communications. If communications are interrupted, then squad leaders cannot report up the chain of command. Very soon, the commanding officer is without vital information and cannot deploy his troops. To destroy an army, destroy its communications.

To destroy a *civilization,* destroy its *money.*

When bank credit money (the MØ) is tangled up on Saturday, 1 January 2000, that 92% of the "money" supply which deploys 92% of human effort will evaporate. Right now, your very *life* depends on the organized--*deployed*--effort of *thousands* of strangers, most of them very far away and even overseas.

On 1/1/2000, 92% of them will *cease* working for you.

Not only will you have *11½ times fewer* people to help you, but the 8% remaining will have to be predominantly *local* since post-2000 *money* (cash, cash-like, and commodities) will be local. Remember, an economy is only as wide as its money.

CASH

When the stock market breaks, either before Y2K becomes a major factor or after, we will see a cascade effect. You must be ahead of the avalanche. Like a skier racing down the slope ahead of the mountain of snow, you must get ahead of the mountain of snow, you must get out in front of it early and move very fast.

__Here is how it will probably take place. It will hit the stock market first. Stocks will fall as people sell out.__

__Smart money will move into bonds.__ Long rates will drop. Mortgage money rates will drop--one last opportunity to sell your urban home.

__From bonds, money will move to near-cash assets: T-bills, short-term CD's, money market funds.__

From the money market funds, if there is time (don't count on it), money will move into savings accounts and checking accounts.

__From these accounts, money will move into cash.__

...The government will close the markets. With this announcement may come other emergency orders. The avalanche may end in a few days: closed markets. That will be the end of the information economy. Information--conveyed by prices--will become far less accurate when the markets close, either by default or by government edict. __That's when you had better be in a safe place with most of your assets in usable things or cash__.

The public says what money is. Cash is money. In a complete crash, none of the M's will be money except the cash component. If the fiduciary forms of money disappear in a worldwide rush for cash--the de-monetization of everything--we go back to cash. __All the other M's will disappear.__ So will all contracts written in terms of them. The entire pyramid will topple, from banks to insurance contracts to retirement programs. This society is based on a billion promises to pay. They will all be dead [by January 2000].

So, the credit pyramid will make cash a temporary substitute for gold. We can't have a gold run, but we can have a greenback run. In the transition period from fractional reserve banking to whatever replaces it, cash will be king. This could be several years.

-- Dr. Gary North, 2 January 1998 *Remnant Review*

Dr. Gary North (www.garynorth.com), a respected economist, makes a good case. Because the power grids will go down, the BEP's 34 expensive German printing presses will be dead. Even if they were not, the presses could not possibly replace the evaporated credit MØ (92% of the "money" supply) with cash.

In November 1995 I interviewed Robert Leuver, head for many years of the Bureau of Engraving & Printing in Washington, an now head of the American Numismatic Association. I well remember sitting at supper at Commander's Palace in New Orleans when he started scribbling production figures on an envelope to prove to me that it was not physically possible to print enough money (he meant currency) to replace the U.S. money supply. Even if they started now. Both plants [in Washington, D.C. and Dallas] working flat out can hardly squeeze in the additional work of introducing one new [post-1993] bill at a time.

BEP can print nine billion notes a year. Mr. Leuver doesn't think they could even double that. Say they could; still, 225/18 billion = 12.5 years to print enough money (he meant currency) to cover the entire money supply.

*It's not even close. **There is no way that the Federal government could supply enough currency in a Y2K emergency to carry on normal business.** On the other hand...if 18 billion currency notes are going to have to do the work of 225 billion currency notes, then those [existing] 18 billion must experience a SUBSTANTIAL increase in value. ...[I]t would be mere guesswork to figure out what sort of upvaluation the currency would receive in this emergency, **but at least ten times present value would be a good guess.***

-- Franklin Sanders; *Moneychanger*@compuserve.com

North makes the example of how, after the Russian revolution of 1917, Czarist paper money circulated at a premium over Soviet currency as the old notes were no longer being printed or replaced. If the crash is technological as well as financial, then no new currency will be printed and existing currency will be king until the gold and silver coins emerge widely.

Gold is a commodity. So is silver. In a depression, their commodity value will drop. It may take a lot of time before gold is perceived by the public as money, i.e., cash. It will be used for large purchases. It will be used in organized markets. For a time, there may not be many organized markets.

*Silver coins, maybe. We must pay a premium today for silver coins: 400% over face value. **But how may people know that a silver dime is worth 4 times what a clad dime is worth? Not many.** So, we need some silver coins, but not for the initial stages of delation. We need cash in that phase: copper clad coins and small bills.*

*Think of the time it will take for the world economy to readjust prices to the new conditions. It will take years. Think of what it will take: bankruptcies everywhere--the destruction of contracts. In the interim, cash will be king. **Uncertainty increases the demand for the most marketable asset.***

*For small transactions, I don't want to use gold or silver. I want to use token coins or small bills. Gold and silver are conspicuous; token coins aren't. **You will have to explain what a gold coin is. You will have to explain what a silver coin is. In other words, you will have to deal with a specialist.** These coins are so* *unfamiliar that they will serve as money only when there are developed markets. In the interim, fiat money will be king.*

I had never considered this possibility before, because I never considered the physical limits of fiat money production. I had also not considered the possibility that the Millennium Bug will disrupt the production and distribution of fiat money.

I like coins better than paper money, for this reason. The government may decide to stamp newly printed money with some sort of mark and outlaw earlier money. This is unlikely, but it's a technical possibility. But with token metal coins, this kind of physical alteration seems technically impossible in a short period of time.

-- Dr. Gary North, 2 January 1998 *Remnant Review*

On 29 August 1998, the Fed announced to *USA Today* that it plans to add to the Ø460 billion of cash now in circulation an extra Ø50 billion (in Ø20s and Ø50s) to the already Ø150 billion in extra reserves for 1999. So, there will be a whopping Ø200 billion in *new* cash for 1999, which will increase the cash supply by 46%. This means that the cash *percentage* of the total "money" supply will rise from 8% to almost *12%. Oooooooooh!*

The Fed states that families *may* each need Ø450 to buy food, gas, etc. *while Y2K problems are being fixed.* (If Y2K is a mere hiccup lasting only a few days, then the Fed would be right, *but...*) Ø450 multiplied by 70 million families is only Ø31.5 billion. *Why,* then, is the Fed stocking up on *over 6 times* that much in extra cash if Ø450/family is correct? *Hmmmmm.*

Pre-2000 restrictions on cash withdrawals

I view the likelihood of this at nearly 100%. The Federal government cannot permit a significant portion of the population to become monetarily self-sufficient with cash. (Besides, only 3 in 100 depositors suddenly cashing out their accounts would bring the banking system down.) These restrictions can be required under executive order, limiting cash withdrawals to Ø50 per week. In times of "emergency" or war, anything goes:

After the 1941 bombing of Pearl Harbor, Hawaiians frantically withdrew their savings from banks in fear of the anticipated Japanese invasion. Although the invasion never came, the Hawaiian banks nearly collapsed from the run. Accordingly, one month later, the U.S. military police outlawed the holding of more than Ø200 in cash and violators were subject to fines and imprisonment.

All "surplus" FRNs were to be turned in to the government for "safekeeping" and to enforce this provision, the MPs inspected safety deposit boxes for "contraband" cash and confiscated all that was found. Then, the MPs mandated a currency swap for a new

FRN with the word "Hawaii" imprinted on the reverse. (Any coin dealer can show you one of these bills. When the next FRN swap happens, it will be rather familiar to elderly Hawaiians.)
-- Boston T. Party; *Good-Bye April 15th!,* (1992) p. 15 / 14

I'd count on cash withdrawal restrictions by summer of 1999, if not the spring. (Watch out for any future "cash card" program.)

Q: *"Why hoard cash if it might be outlawed?"*

A fair question. First of all, I doubt that existing FRNs will be, before or shortly after 2000, outlawed, or even discontinued for a new currency. Before either is possible, they would have to have a new currency or currency substitute (electronic "cash" card) ready for the FRNs' replacement. They couldn't eliminate 8% of the total "money" supply overnight without throwing our economy into a sharp recession (and perhaps even the world, considering the dozens of countries which use the FRN as their primary or secondary currency).

Regarding such FRN replacement, a new currency is *not* possible as the BEP just doesn't have the printing capacity.

Electronic "money" (VISA or a new smart card)

There are persistent and credible rumors of Y2K concerns throwing us into a *de facto* cashless society in which the credit card system. First of all, I doubt that the VISA/Mastercard system will be Y2KOK, and certainly their ATMs will not be. Right now cards with a "00" year expiration are randomly wreaking havoc on the system. So, I don't see credit/debit cards becoming our new money in 1999 or 2000.

That leaves only smart card technology in the form of a refillable "cash" card. Such a system is eminently possible technologically, and desirable from a totalitarian standpoint, however, such a vast new system by 1/1/2000 is too ambitious, and *certainly* not soon after. In that way, Y2K will work in our *favor*.

Enforcement will be *impossible*

Outlawing cash is *one* thing--*enforcing* such prohibitions will be another. **Never *forget* that.** They've outlawed drugs, but drugs can still be acquired in *prison*, the most controlled environment possible.

People will use "invalid" currency as cash because it's *familiar* and because it *exists* when little else does. (Worthless Nazi Reichmarks circulated as cash *long* after Hitler's Germany had been defeated and occupied by the Allies.) FRNs *will* be a vital form of post-2000 money, *count on it.*

So, start collecting those greenbacks, **but only *after* your core survival goods have been acquired**. Cash *will* be sought after, but not as much as food, medicine, ammo, liquor, fuel, and cigarettes. Remember, *cash is only money*, and money is only a medium of *exchange* to obtain desirable goods. Have in quantity the desirable goods *before* you have in quantity a medium of exchange *for* those desirable goods. *Get* **it? Without a tradable *surplus* of these crucial goods, a medium of exchange is *moot*.** Nobody is going to trade their *last* can of beans or their *last* bullet for cash for *anything*. Trade first requires a *surplus*. People *without* food and ammo will want food and ammo *much* more desperately than cash.

Q: *"How much cash should I have?"*
A: At least 6 months living expenses, in *small* bills.
Ø100 bills today make up 64% of currency, compared to 18% in 1960. (Over 80% of Ø100 bills immediately go overseas.)
I'd hold 10-20% of your cash in coin (dimes and quarters). Why? Because we will go through something unprecedented in post-WWII history: a prolonged *deflation*. That's when cash becomes worth *more* in value, resulting in *falling* prices. What costs Ø15 today could be Ø3 in 2001 because there's less cash chasing goods. (Ammo, medicine, and other scarce crucial goods would be the only likely exception.) That's why you want only small bills (Ø20s and under) and lots of coins.
Avoid Susan B. Anthony Ø1 coins, which were discontinued for being unpopular, proving that money must be *accepted*. (What do you call a boomerang that doesn't return? A *stick*. Money must be widely accepted to be money, else it's a "stick"--even if the government calls it a "boomerang.") Avoid pennies and nickels for their high weight/low value ratio.
Quarters are best. Make friends with a local car wash owner to discreetly buy quarters with paper money.
Start reducing expenses *now* and begin saving cash.

Using cash once the crash occurs
At first, prices for goods will skyrocket until the free market corrects itself as traders realize just how scarce cash actually *is*. Therefore, you must have enough supplies to ride out the initial panic. This would be a great time to *sell* extra *non-crucial* items for cash. (Everything has a double edge.)

GOLD COINS

Before you go wild and run out to buy a sack of coins, let's again review what these coins are *for*.

Money is *not* wealth -- Money *buys* wealth

People accept gold because they can trade (spend) it later. Comparatively little gold is actually consumed by industry. Gold money is traded and that's what it's for. On this point, the miser Scrooge McDuck has transposed the means with the end. Although gold money indeed has intrinsic worth, its main value is exchangeability. The miser deceives himself that, by having a pile of gold, he is rich. But can he eat, wear, or live in his gold? No. Unless the miser trades some of his gold for food, clothes and shelter, he will die. That's how the infamous miser Hetty Green lived and died in abject squalor despite her $100 million estate. ("Being 'broke' is a state of finances. Being 'poor' is a state of mind.") The miser is an illiterate fool collecting books.

Money is a tool. Like any tool, if money is not used, one might as well not even have it. Clearly, money is meant to be traded (spent), not hoarded in a mattress. **Wealth is not money. Wealth is bought with money. Wealth is things and profit-generating assets.**

-- Boston T. Party; *Good-Bye April 15th!*, (1992) p. 3/4

Moral: Don't go crazy hoarding gold and silver coins. Get your food, guns, and energy first. Remember, to buy something you must first have a *seller*. Sellers must have a *surplus* of the desired goods. Do you *really* believe that in 2000 there will be scads of sellers with the necessary surplus of AR15s, freeze-dried food, and generators that you waited too long to purchase? Walk before running--get your basic and intermediate survival goods *before* you concentrate on stockpiling gold/silver coins.

Which gold coins should I get?

The choice is numismatic (purely collector coins with very high premiums, say above 200%), "semi-numismatic" coins (at least 15% but no more than 200% premium), and bullion coins (having no numismatic value and premiums of less than 15%).

Before I tell you to purchase primarily bullion coins, let me explain why I believe higher premium coins are *not* a good choice for a Y2K-induced crash.

Why I *discourage* numismatics for Y2K

Coin brokers prefer to sell customers "semi-numismatic" gold coins for their (alleged) less risk of confiscation, nonreportability, and profitability from the "double play" on increased numismatic premiums. Let's discuss these one by one.

My coin broker friends won't like or agree with what follows. I've *already* been gently chided on similar comments in *Bulletproof Privacy* (p. 8/6). With all due respect to my friends, I must, however, honestly speak my mind on this matter.

The "confiscation" issue

Telemarketing coin brokers harp on the fact that gold coins *"having a recognized special value to collectors"* were "not confiscated by FDR" so they'll more likely remain safe during the *next* confiscation. FDR's 5 April 1933 Executive Order read:

> *By virtue of the authority vested in me by Section 5(b) of the Act of October 6, 1917, as amended by Section 2 of the Act of March 9, 1933, entitled "An Act to provide relief in the existing national emergency in banking, and for other purposes," in which amendatory Act Congress declared that a serious emergency exists, I, Franklin D. Roosevelt, President of the United States of America, do declare that said national emergency still continues to exist and pursuant to said section **do hereby prohibit the hoarding** of gold coin, gold bullion, and gold certificates within the continental United States by individuals, partnerships, associations and corporations and hereby prescribe the following regulations for carrying out the purposes of this order:*
>
> *Section 1. For the purposes of this regulation, the term "hoarding" means the withdrawal and withholding of gold coin, gold bullion or gold certificates from the recognized and customary channels of trade. The term "person" means any individual, partnership, association or corporation.*
>
> *Section 2. All persons are hereby required to deliver on or before May 1, 1933, to a Federal reserve bank or branch or agency thereof or to any member bank of the Federal Reserve System all gold coin, gold bullion and gold certificates now owned by them or coming into their ownership on or before April 28, 1933, except the following:*

Exempted was the industrial, professional and artistic use of gold, and:

> *(b) Gold coin and gold certificates in an amount* (of face value) *not* **exceeding in the aggregate $100.00** *belonging to any one person, and gold coins having a recognized special value to collectors of rare and unusual coins.*

Fact #1: Gold ownership was *not* "outlawed" under Roosevelt.
The Order did not *outlaw* the "selling, buying or owning" of gold, but the *"hoarding"* of gold (*i.e.*, over $100 per person). Further, of gold coins, only *U.S. monetary* gold coins were affected by the Executive Order, not foreign gold coins.
Yes, I *am* rather splitting hairs as the E.O. *was* a *de facto* prohibition of any *meaningful* gold ownership (*i.e.*, over $100 face value, or 5 ounces). And, yes, I *know* that the Government immediately afterwards devalued the dollar from $20.67 per gold ounce to $35.00, but all that is beside the *point* here: To introduce an indisputable *tincture* of inaccuracy by coin brokers.

Fact #2: Gold coins were *not* "confiscated" under Roosevelt.
To "confiscate" means *"to seize (private property) for the public treasury."* To "seize" is to take forcibly, meaning *without compensation.* Gold was *not* taken without recompense ("confiscated") but *surrendered* in coercive 1-to-1 compensation for paper and silver dollars:

> Section 4. *Upon receipt of gold coin, gold bullion or gold certificates delivered to it in accordance with Sections 2 or 3, the Federal reserve bank or member bank will pay therefor an equivalent amount of any other form of coin or currency coined or issued under the laws of the United States.*

Fact #3: Numismatic immunity *then* doesn't mean immunity *later*.
Finally, just because collector gold coins weren't "confiscated" (*i.e.*, forcibly surrendered for silver dollars and certificates) by FDR in no way *guarantees* that they'll *remain* exempt during the coming "buy back" (or outright confiscation). (Brokers will agree on this obvious truth, though with little enthusiasm.) The "exempt from confiscation" sales pitch comforts wimpy yuppies and quavering old ladies, who will likely lose their coins from their "safety" deposit boxes or trustee warehouses, anyway.
Don't *utterly* trust the security of your crisis wealth on *collector* gold coins. Generals are known for usually fighting the *previous* war (*e.g.*, the Maginot Line of France). *Expect progressions in tyranny.* Think *ahead.* **I will not gamble *my* financial planning on government's modest and erratic self-restraint of its *own* evil. What rational person *would*?** The government tiger is a *carnivore,* and just because it didn't devour *Angora* sheep in the 1930s, doesn't mean that Angoras will remain safe in the future. Quit hiding under Mommy's skirt of *"numismatics weren't confiscated by FDR."*

Another argument why collector coins will more likely escape future confiscation is that the Insider Elite prefer them, so *their* form of gold ownership will be exempted. Since numismatic coins comprise only 5% of the gold coin total, the feds will seize the other 95% (which is in bullion coins), and leave their Insider cronies with the 5% left in numismatics. To me, this argument is rather reaching. The Insider Elite can own *anything* they want, contraband or not. They're the Insider Elite! What IRS agent is going to knock on one of the *Rockefeller's* door to seize his Krugerrands?

Fact #4: Federal agents will not likely spare collector coins.

O.K., imagine the day when gold bullion coins *are* declared contraband. *"Whew!"* you say, because you followed the advice of your tele-gold marketer and bought only MS65 $20 St. Gaudens at Ø1,000 a coin when bullion Eagles were only Ø300. (*"Better safe than sorry!"*) Your neighbor phones the feds and reports you as a illegal gold owner. (You once showed him your coins, but he doesn't know the difference between bullion and rare coins, and doesn't *care*, given the Ø1,000 reward.)

The jack-booted thugs in black break your door down, shove you and your wife to the floor, kick your dog, stomp your cat, and demand with great vulgarity to know where *"them illegal gold coins"* are. Inside, you breath a sigh of relief for you know that your coins remain perfectly legal to own. You lead the half-dozen federal agents to your $20 Saints.

Now, here's the question you *should* have thought of when you paid a Ø700 per coin numismatic "insurance" premium: **Will** those agents say, *"Gosh, Mr. Smith, what an awful mistake! We didn't know you had only collector coins! Golly, are we embarrassed! We're terribly sorry! Here's Ø200 to fix your front door, and, gee, I hope your pets are O.K. Here's my card to send any vet bill. Oh, Mrs. Smith, let me help you up!"*

Or, take some future "black market" parking lot where gold coins (collector and "contraband bullion") are bought and sold. You're there to sell some $20 Liberties and the place gets raided. **Will** those agents say, *"It's a good thing you had only these rare coins, Mr. Smith! You're free to go, but we're arresting these damned Krugerrand sellers!"*

These are the future *fairy tales* that some tele-gold marketers will try to *implicitly* sell you.

Listen to me *very* carefully: If you are not *very* confident that the above absurd scenarios will be likely (if not probable), then why pay so much *extra* money for *rare* coins? This "semi-numismatic" premium is like "protection money" to be left alone in the future when bullion is contraband. *Ain't gonna happen. De jure* (of law) is not *de facto* (of fact, in the real world). I've written two law books, so I ought to know.

When I relayed the above scenarios to some coin dealers, they argued that under such it made no sense to own *any* gold whatsoever since it *all* would be seized, bullion or not. I disagreed, replying *"That's when you shoot them."* At this they laughed (nervously), staring down at their penny loafers.

Nobody is going to confiscate *my* gold, bullion or not. I worked *hard* for it and bought it *honestly*. It's my *crisis* money--it's what I'll be feeding my family with some day. I will never allow anybody to *take* it. They'll be confiscating my *lead* the hard way long before they ever see my gold. *This* should be the attitude of any owner of crisis gold.

Final thoughts on future confiscation

Yes, collector coins *do* enjoy historical precedent of having been exempt from *general* gold seizures, and, *yes*, they *could* remain exempt the *next* time. However, do you want to pay premiums of 70-200% (or more) for a *general* exemption which will *not* help you in an *actual* raid which seizes *everything*?

One dealer tried to justify collector coins as *"providing options"* to his clients to *"buy a year or two of extra time"* before rare coins are seized after bullion. I replied that there is a hidden cost to "playing it safe." When his clients are finally backed into a legal corner where *all* gold and guns are contraband, they will *surrender*. Folks, courage is *not* conjured up out of thin air in a sudden moment of crisis. Courage is like a *muscle*, steadily strengthened over time. You will have in the future *only* what you've earned and paid for in *previous* risk and anxiety.

Whatever you *do*, you *become*. Want to *keep* your guns and gold and freeze-dried food in 2000? You'll have to break the law to do it. This is *inescapable* truth. You will not be an outlaw in 2000 if you've lived some wimpy life, playing it *safe*.

> *Until they become conscious they will never rebel, and until after they have rebelled they cannot become conscious.*
>   -- George Orwell; *1984*

We need to be mentally resisting *every day*. We need to be strengthening our *resolve, not* our shrewd ability to remain legal for just one more day by complying with increasingly arcane and contradictory regulations. If you have no experience in disobeying tyranny when it was *mild*, then you certainly won't do it when tyranny becomes heavy.

My coin dealer friends say that I've painted myself into a bullion corner and have bet my crisis wealth on the "all gold will be contraband" argument. **Yeah, I *have*.** They are horrified that I haven't hedged some of my gold into "semi-numismatics." *"What if you're wrong? You won't have an 'out.'"* they say.

Here's my answer: **I don't *want* an "out."** I don't *want* endless opportunities to be a "good little boy" to evil government. *Compliance* with evil *fuels* evil. As Edmund Burke said:

All that is necessary for triumph of evil is that good men do nothing.

Benjamin Franklin added to that truth with:

They that give up essential liberty to obtain a little temporary safety deserve neither liberty nor safety.

A society of sheep must in time beget a government of wolves.
    -- Betrand de Juvenal

If the government ever declares bullion gold coins to be contraband, that's when the gloves come off. Any "out" from then on is *irrelevant* to me. If I took the collector coin "out" at that point, then how about the .30-30 lever-action "out" for when they come for my AR15? Or the .22LR "out" for when they come for my .30-30? Or the BB gun "out" for when they come for my .22LR? (Not that any of these "outs" are options for me; I discuss them to illustrate the progression to expect.) Folks, if you're going to give up *later,* then save the time and give up *now.* Sell your guns and gold for that peace of mind that only a *slave* can know.

Conversely, if you will *not* be giving up later, then why are you playing it *safe* now? **I don't *want* an "out."** I will not strengthen the wicked organ of cowardice. I want to be morally, mentally, and physically prepared to defend my property, even at its expense, and my life, even at its expense.

The price of freedom is the willingness to do sudden battle, anywhere, anytime, and with utter recklessness.
    -- Robert A. Heinlein

Amen. Instead of paying numismatic premiums, spend that money on a battle rifle and go to Thunder Ranch. C'mon, folks, do the *math*! It's April 2000, the power's been out for months, the big cities look like Beruit, and there are no police. **Which would *you* rather have:** 20oz. of bullion Eagles and your FAL (with TR training)--*or,* 20oz. of 1908 Saints *and no rifle?*

The "reportability" issue

All gold bullion liquidations are reportable (by law) on (IRS) Form 1099 by coin dealers. Coins with a premium above 15% do not have to be reported by dealers. The semi-numismatic Liberty has a premium above 15% and is, therefore, a gold bullion coin which does not have dealer reporting requirements.

-- from a coin broker's flyer

While there is some fact to the above, **it is not the *truth***. Facts may be true, *but facts are not truth*. Truth is a *holistic* concept *represented* by facts. The above assertion doesn't exactly *lie*, but it certainly does not tell the *truth*. It reminds me of a quote on statistics:

Statistics are like a bikini. What they reveal is suggestive, but what they conceal is vital.

-- Aaron Levenstein

What is being *concealed* here *is* vital. IRC §6045 requires brokers to file Form 1099s on sales of *commodities* effected for customers. Gold, silver, platinum, palladium, and U.S. silver coins *can* be, under the right conditions, a reportable *"commodity."* But what exactly *is* this reportable *"commodity"*?

26 CFR §1.6045-1(a)(5)(i)

*(A) Any form or quality of personal property that is deliverable (whether or not subject to price adjustment for form or quality) **in satisfaction of a regulated futures contract** that has been approved for Commodities Futures Trading Commission (whether or not the regulated futures contract is actually traded);*

(B) Any form or quality of lead, palm oil, rapeseed, tea, or tin;

(C) Any form or quality of personal property that the Secretary determines is to be treated as a "commodity" under this section, from and after the date specified in a rule-related notice of such declaration published in the Federal Register;

(D) Any form or quality of personal property a form or quality of which is described [in the above subsection A];

(E) Any interest in personal property that is described [in the above subsections A, B, C, or D].

Under §6045(a)(5)(ii), the term *"commodity"* does *not* include:

*(D) A form of tangible personal property, or an interest therein, gross proceeds from the sale of which **exceed by more than 15 percent** the value on the date of sale of the underlying personal property...*

This is where coin brokers got their cherished "15% Rule." **It has *nothing* whatever to do with differentiating between "nonreportable" collector coins and "reportable" bullion**

coins. IRC §6045 affects precious metals *only* when they are *"deliverable...in satisfaction of a regulated futures contract."* IRC §6045 *does* affect the coin brokers because *they* often engage in futures trading of precious metals. Will, however, the occasional sale of your gold and silver coins be somehow tied to a futures contract? Doubtful. Well, then, how *relevant and applicable* is IRC §6045 to *you* and your liquidation of bullion coins?

Not **relevant.** *Not* **applicable.** *Period.* Folks, there is no distinction in any law (of which *I'm* aware) of what is or isn't a collector coin--or that any such distinction even *matters.*

Further, of gold and silver reportable *as futures commodities*, the IRS itself has specified (in a 22 May 1990 letter) only:

1 oz. Canadian Maple Leaf
1 oz. South African Krugerrand
1 oz. Mexican
Pre-65 Silver Coins
Bullion (bars, or ingots in bar form)

According to the Industry Council for Tangible Assets (ICTA), the reporting *threshold* is any quantity *more* than 24 of the above ounce foreign coins (*i.e.*, more than 2 pounds Troy)--and remember, this is *still* for coins related to some futures contract. (Apparently, the reporting threshold for U.S. silver coins must be *quite* high, as a local coin dealer, who buys several $1,000 each week, has never had to report them.)

Finally, Eagle gold bullion coins are *not* considered by the IRS to be reportable, *even if they are deliverable in satisfaction of a regulated futures contract!* (American Eagles are *certainly not* reportable if *uninvolved* in a futures contract.)

Could the IRS *theoretically* make a case against a coin dealer for not reporting your sale of less-than-15% premium coins, *even though such coins were never part of any futures contract delivery?* I *guess* so, *theoretically*--but it's never happened to the knowledge of anybody I interviewed.

Even if a required Form 1099 is *not* filed, the fine is a whopping Ø50! **Shall we *not* get into a dither about a nonissue which has a *theoretical* penalty of only Ø50?** (One coin dealer compared the "reportability" to being arrested by the "Mattress Police" for tearing off those labels.) Note: the alleged Form 1099 requirement is a *separate* issue from the >Ø3,000 />Ø10,000 *cash* Form 8300 reporting requirements.

Ask your tele-gold broker the following question:

"If bullion coins *are* reportable, does that mean if I walk into my local coin shop to sell a *single* Krugerrand, he's *required by law* to file a Form 1099 on me?"

If he says *"Yes"* then he's either ignorant or lying. More likely, he will hem and haw and not really answer you. Skewer him by demanding he quote the exact law which allegedly requires Form 1099s on bullion coin sales (unrelated to futures). Mr. Glib will then begin to *really* stutter.

Fact #1: Brokers can't make as much commission in bullion coins.

So why *do* coin brokers stress the "reportability" issue to their customers? **Because it sells "semi-numismatic" coins, which earn more commission than bullion coins.** Using the futures commodity regulations to justify the marketing of non-bullion coins is pretty *lame*. The coin brokers didn't *quite* pull the "15% Rule" out of their butt, though *almost*.

While they *could* explain precisely how to legally avoid triggering *any* reporting requirement (bullion or cash), they won't risk giving "structuring" advice over the phone. Although this is perfectly understandable, it "coincidentally" creates a very neat defense: *"We can't push bullion coins because we'd have to risk a 'structuring' charge by explaining how to cash out of them without triggering a Form 1099."* Yeah, whatever.

Fact #2: You might not get your >15% premium *out* of the coin.

Paying over 15% premium is one thing; *getting* over 15% out of the same coin is *another*. Numismatic value could dip, or you might not be a good enough seller to fetch that premium. Either way, a >15% coin at time of your *purchase* could be a <15% bullion coin at time of *sale*.

Or, the spot price of gold could balloon which shrinks the numismatic premium percentage of your coin to 15% or less. With spot at Ø300, a VF20 1914S $20 goes for about Ø400 for a premium of 33%. If spot went to Ø2,000, that same coin would have to fetch over Ø2,300 to retain a >15% premium. Coin brokers anticipate this argument by pushing higher premium coins of at least AU50, and often up to MS65.

Fact #3: That 15% is *not* set in stone.

Assuming a bullion coin reporting requirement outside of futures contracts (and such being *enforced*), it is good to recall two things: The 15% premium is a totally *artificial* demarcation line, and is set by the feds themselves. **What could *prevent* them from moving it *up* to 500% and thus** transforming, *ex post facto*, previously nonreportable semis into *reportable* semis? *Nothing.* My advice on not fighting the last war also applies here.

Fact #4: You don't have to sell bullion coins to a *broker*.
Even if such a reporting requirement *does* exist for gold bullion coins (which it doesn't), and is being *enforced* (which it's *not*), it is only when one sells to a *broker*. So *what?*
You don't have to sell coins to a bonafide broker. Private buyers of your gold coins are *not* required to file an IRS Form 1099 on you any more than *private* buyers of your firearms are *not* required to file a BATF Form 4473. You can get your money out of your Eagles at *any* gun show and *most* flea markets. Or, place an ad listing a voice mail number.

Fact #5: *"Good men must not obey the laws too well. "* (Emerson)
Finally, gold coins should be held for that "rainy decade" and not frittered away during "normal" times through official channels. If you don't know how to avoid this bogus "reporting requirement" *now*, then you're in poor shape to avoid *all* the *post-crash* regulations. *"Gosh, Boston, you're talking about possibly breaking the law!"* Yeah, *no sh*t*. (Note: I'm not trying to be *vulgar*--just *emphatic.*) **Don't be a *woos* about all this.** You will *not* be able to maintain your family's wealth and security if you plan on obeying the coming gold/gun coercive buyback programs or confiscations.
Stocking up on semi-numismatic coins over bullion coins is like stocking up on hair dye in response to a law which demanded that you give up your blond children. If you won't obey instead the *higher* laws of justice, defense, and safety-- then just *off* your wimpy self and let a *real* American have the air. I'm tired of people jumping through all the regulatory hoops like trained seals. If the BATF announced that semi-auto rifles must be pink, gun shows would immediately sell the spray paint. **Folks, at *some* point you're going to have to mark your line in the sand and declare *"No further!"* *I'm* not** paying *double* spot price for "semi-numismatics" because of the largely *imaginary* hobgoblins of bullion coin "confiscation" and "reportability." (I'm not painting my AR15, either...)

The profitability issue
Of the three arguments for "semi-numismatics" (an artificial term concocted by the coin brokers to describe their

>15% premium coins), the issue of profit potential has the most *theoretical* credibility, and truly the *only practical* credibility.

Yes, semi-numismatics have a profit leverage potential much better than bullion, meaning collector coins usually rise in price more quickly than bullion coins. The tactic here is to buy semis instead of bullion and hold them until the semi vs. bullion spread has widened sufficiently to warrant trading semis for bullion, thus owning more bullion *later* than what you would have bought *earlier* (instead of semis). This will work *until* the technological meltdown of 2000.

The "Well Fargo" 1908 No Motto MS66 $20 St. Gaudens

Brokers of "crisis gold coins" will even hawk coins *far* more valuable than semis--true numismatics. The recent sale of the "Wells Fargo" hoard of 1908 No Motto MS66 $20 St. Gaudens coins is a prime example. Bags of these coins were put aside in 1917 and left largely untouched until 1998, when they were brokered out. Yes, the history *is* interesting, and yes, their generations of storage *is* kind of neat, *but* these coins are simply 1908NMs, which are not rare coins since *4,271,551* were minted (the most for any year except 1928). 1908NM is "common date."

What does a *regular* 1908NM in MS66 sell for? A tele-gold marketer will tell you at least Ø2,500, but that is *not* correct. I checked with Scott Sparks, a Level 1 Market Maker for numismatic gold coins. He buys and sells millions of dollars of coins sight unseen every *week*. In August 1998, bid (asking) price was Ø2,260, and the *sale* price of an *actual* coin was Ø2,100. These figures are precise, and no better source exists. (Thank you, Scott, for your time and effort in this matter!)

These "Wells Fargo" variants--*identical in every respect but their Numismatic Guaranty Corp. "pedigree" label*--were being sold for Ø2,750 to Ø3,100! (One broker laughingly called these coins the *"Rodeo Drive Barter Package."*)

Any MS66 St. Gaudens goes *far* beyond the bland category of "semi-numismatics." When gold is under Ø300 an ounce, anybody pushing Ø2,100+ ounce numismatics over bullion is not thinking of *your* best interests, but tacking on an *additional* Ø650-1,000 premium for the "Wells Fargo" pedigree is, well...

Fact #1: The rare coin market rises in *good* times, not in bad.

In well-humming *sophisticated* markets, numismatics are *lovely*. PCGS gradings are widely accepted, and prices (like stock quotes) come out bimonthly (the "Gray Sheets").

QUESTION: *What will make the price of coins rise above today's levels?*

ANSWER: *Of course this is basic economics, but if the number of collectors* (who have disposable income for collecting) *increases then the demand for rare coins will also increase. Now the question becomes: will the number of collectors increase?*
    This seems quite likely. The average citizen is working an ever-shorter week. More and more time is being directed toward leisure activities. Coin collecting is an ideal leisure activity.... **As leisure time activities increase, coin collecting will surely increase also.** (at 63)
    -- Q. David Bowers; *High Profits from Rare Coin Investment*

There you have it. Increasing numismatic premiums require *increasing* economic prosperity, a scenario not very likely during Y2K. (Only when people have *disposable income* do collector markets ever emerge in the first place. We're not selling many MS65 $10 Libs to the poor *Romanians* right now.)

Fact #2A: Collector coins (even a VF20 $20) are still *collectibles*.
Fact #2B: *All* collectibles *drop* in value during a depression.

Yes, semi-numismatics offer good profit potential in most scenarios, *except during a depression when all collectibles suffer*. You see, in a *depression,* people are out of work and often kinda hungry. They will *not* likely be *buying* MS65 $20 Liberties, nor will they be holding out for top numismatic dollar on the ones they're desperately trying to *sell* to afford food.

Moral: During post-crash days, you won't get your premium back. **Not for a *long* while, at least.**

After the crash (Y2K or not), sophisticated markets (commodities, collectibles, whatever) will shrink drastically. **Inherent in *any depression* is the collapse of sophisticated markets.** Do you *really* think that some clodhopper at the flea market in 2000 will have *heard* of PCGS, much less be willing to give you a 200% premium for your MS65 $20 St. Gaudens? The only way he *would* is if he *knew* of somebody who'd give him *250%,* which means a *known market.* Numismatic coins, antiques, etc. require specialized knowledge, and therefore *specialists.* No *non*specialist is going to pay you a hefty numismatic premium just because some *pre-crash* PCGS rate sheet *says* he should. *C'mon folks, think things through!* Moving simple *bullion* coins will be difficult enough at first because of the semi-specialist nature of the trade. Those trying to trade *numismatic* coins will get bullion prices for quite a while.

I've been to enough flea markets and gun shows to know that collectibles take a *big* hickey in value during times of economic trouble. Do you *really* think when people are out of work and looking for food in 2000, that any trader is going to give you an extra Ø275 over its gold value for your 1913 MS60 $20, much less an extra *Ø650* for your 1913S because it has an "S" mint mark? Post-WWII German farmers were trading sacks of potatoes for BMWs and grand pianos. An autograph of Thomas Jefferson goes for about Ø7,000 right now. Who will *care* during a depression? (I would, but not Ø7,000's worth...)

Example: After WWII, Germany lay in tatters. To buy food, German combat veterans often sold to American G.I.s, for basically the silver value, their Knights Cross (the highest decoration for bravery, similar to our Medal of Honor). The G.I.s brought them home and sold them to collectors for not much more. During the 1950s, you could buy a genuine Knights Cross for Ø25. Today they begin at *Ø1,500.* My point is this: if a hungry veteran would sell the equivalent of his Medal of Honor (which he risked his life earning, and was possibly awarded by Hitler himself) for essentially meltdown value because that's all he could get, what do you think will happen during Y2K to that Ø600+ premium in an MS65 $20, which was acquired with no combat risk or patriotic fervor like that Knights Cross?

For quite a while after any financial crash, collectible premiums *plummet.* Why? Because basic needs must *first* be taken care of before luxury needs are satisfied. (If anybody can show me some real exceptions, I'd be happy to mollify my position on this point.) Once society has clawed its way *out* of its depression *and* factories are once again hiring, *then* do antiques and collectibles rebound in perceived value (*e.g.*, rare coins in post-WWII boom of the late '50s/early '60s).

If the next crash (Y2K or not) is as bad as predicted, then people won't have surplus cash for antiques, rare coins and stamps, etc. for quite a while. **The time to *buy* such is *during* a depression, *not* just *before.*** Wait until *"blood is running in the streets"* and you'll be able to pick up common date MS65 $20 coins for spot plus 20-50% (instead of 200% in 1998).

Fact #3: Nobody will have *heard* of your funky 1903 foreign coin.
One last thing about tele-gold that really sticks in my craw is the current "Y2K barter package" consisting of small, obscure foreign coins (such as the French "Rooster"). First of all, these coins are being sold during Ø300 spot at an equivalent

ounce of Ø370-577. Yes, smaller coins *do* have higher premiums and tenth ounce Eagles *are* Ø350 gold coins, but I believe they're worth the 20% premium.

But to pay *30-92%* premiums for "semi-numismatic" foreign coins with *bastard* weights (*i.e.*, not ounce fractional) is *foolish*. When you go to trade or sell your Colombian 5 peso coin on some dusty flea market parking lot in 2000, your buyer will need a copy of *World Coins* (the size of a Houston phone book) to *identify* the thing and its beatnik weight of .2354oz. Will he give you your pre-crash premium out of it? Not hardly, because he'll have to carry around *World Coins* to educate his buyers. Nobody will want the hassle! In times of crisis, the markets get *real* basic. Few will want to catalog your weird coin. Folks, the K.I.S.S. principle applies here: *Keep It Simple, Stupid!*

Pushing "semi-numismatics" for Y2K is bad enough, but pawning off these arcane European bastard-weight coins *really* goes over the line, for me. They *could* push Eagle tenths and quarters, but there is little money in *that*. So, they send their buyers to Europe to scour all of Latvia or wherever for old gold coins being dumped by their government for spot plus 10%.

Boston's summary of "tele-gold" claims for post-Y2K "semi-numismatic" coins vs. bullion coins

"Confiscation exemption" of semis	=	95% fear mongering.
"Reportability of bullion coins"	=	99% B.S.
"Profitability" of semis (post-crash)	=	90% wishful thinking.

Don't ask the barber whether you need a haircut.
-- Daniel S. Greenburg

If you *want* to become a coin *collector,* then subscribe to the Gray Sheets and go to coin shows. But *don't* get suckered in by glossy flyers hawking Buicks at BMW prices. Coin brokers make over 15% on numismatic coins, versus only 5% on bullion coins. Is it any *wonder* why they push numismatics and "justify" their high premiums with fallacious arguments about "confiscation" and "reporting requirements" of bullion? If you call up *this* "barber" and ask whether you need a "haircut" he'll say, *"Sir, not only do you need a haircut, you need a style!"*

Why have I dogged the tele-gold brokers so hard?

Because what they're selling for Y2K *"ain't honest."* Lots of people are now getting into gold and silver for the *first* time, they *don't* have a lot of money, they're *terrified* about the impending depression and Y2K, and they just want to convert paper to precious metals for barter purposes. They don't want to become coin collectors. *If* they *knew* the "confiscation immunity" of collector coins was a silly argument in *practical* terms, *if* they *knew* the truth about §6045 and the nonissue of reportability, and *if* they *understood* that collectible values drop in depressions--**then they would *not* pay 2-3x spot price.**

The *only* reason they pay such is because of the slippery arguments for "semi-numismatics" by phone brokers. For the bad times ahead, we need as many *strong* citizens as possible, all independent in energy, food and weapons. Frittering away their thin capital reserves on needlessly expensive gold is a pretty selfish to do, in my opinion.

Let me post-qualify my discussion with the statement that *not all* coin brokers are so heedless of reality, and many *will* recommend American Eagle bullion coins for Y2K. All I'm saying is *Caveat Emptor*--Let the buyer beware. It's *your* money, and *your* future. Do your homework and don't ask the coin broker *barber* if you need a haircut.

Finally, not only do I have utterly *no* vested financial interest in my position (I don't care *what* you buy), I actually stand to see a few friendships strained. I have already had some mildly heated discussions with my coin broker friends over all this, and the more I box them into a corner, the louder their voices become. *Hmmm.*

> *A recent psychological study disguised as an opinion poll showed that members of individual occupational groups were almost uniformly unwilling to accept any conclusions that implied a loss of income for them,* **no matter how airtight the logic supporting it.**
> -- Davidson and Rees-Mogg; *The Sovereign Individual*

The ironic thing about that quote is that I read it in a coin broker's newsletter! Look, I don't mean to harm anybody's livelihood (especially that of my friends), however, I only just learned that the "reportability of bullion coins" argument is crap, and I can't bear to see a half-truth propagated for gain-- especially before Y2K. I've spent 14 pages (almost 4%) on this matter, because I so strongly believe in its importance.

If *anybody* feels that I have unfairly or incompletely discussed the above to the detriment of truth, then please write me *with the facts* (not just opinion) and I will retract any inaccuracies or apologize for any unfairness.

My whole writing career has been built on (at no small risk and emotional cost) exposing lies, telling the truth, and providing uniquely practical information. I could write better *selling* books, but I can't write more *important* books. (I'm not saying that my books *are* the most important, but that *I personally* cannot write anything more important.)

My *primary* reason for writing *Boston on Surviving Y2K* has been to *help* as many people as possible. I get no commission from the companies mentioned. When I saw that Y2K preparation information was *not* very well organized or synthesized, I knew that I could improve on the existing material. Yes, I'll be pleased to make some money from the book, but that's not *why* I wrote it. I wrote it to help *you.* I did not have a summer 1998, but I'm pretty sure you'll get your twenty bucks worth. So, in short, buy *bullion* coins.

Thoughts on $20 Libs and St. Gaudens coins

They have .9675 oz. of pure gold, and lower premium dates and conditions are fairly abundant. *If* you have a bit of numismatic fever and want some of these lovely old coins; *if* you want to hedge on the ethereal "confiscation exemption/nonreportability" argument yet don't want to see a *huge* post-crash drop in numismatic premiums, then go for *lesser* grades of $20 coins. Coins in EF40 sell for as little as Ø100 over spot, AU50s Ø150 over, and MS60s Ø175 over. Stick with MS60s; they're *much* nicer coins than EF40s for only Ø75 more.

As the MS63-66 coins are bought up, the spread between them and the MS60s will decrease as the MS60 premiums increase. A common date MS60 is still a *very* nice coin and affordable at Ø525. (The same coin in MS65 would be Ø900-1,200.)

Libs I consider *undervalued* are 1875, 1876, **1889**, 1890, 1898, 1902, and 1906. St. Gaudens I consider *undervalued* are 1909D, 1913S, and **1914**. (Only 95,320 coins of 1914 were minted, compared to *1,498,000* of the 1914S, but they both list at Ø525 for MS60. Granted there is probably an identical quantity of MS60 coins in both 1914 and 1914S, to explain their identical value, but I'd bet on faster appreciation of the 1914.)

Stick with *common* bullion coins

I have only a few numismatic coins (MS60), for purely *sentimental* reasons. Nearly all of my gold is in *bullion* coin form, for the reasons expressed above. Bullion coins have lower premiums, so their post-crash downside is lower. (I'm *not* looking at rare coins for crash-days profit potential; I'm looking at food, fuel, and ammo to be the profitable items.)

Now that a black Communist and convicted terrorist is president of South Africa, **Krugerrands** are again legal to import. They have the lowest premium (by only Ø5/oz. vs. Eagles), so they'll give you the most gold for your money.

My other favorites are the **American Eagles**. These are beautiful coins which are minted in tenths, quarters, halves and ounces. One *theoretical* catch is their Ø50/ounce face value. In a coercive buy-back, the government *could* pay you mere face value and claim that you were "compensated." (Funny how you can't go to a bank and *buy* Eagles for Ø50 in cash!) Anybody who *settles* for that *deserves* it, that's why I described the catch as *theoretical*. Nobody's getting *my* Eagles for Ø50 an ounce.

The Canadian Maple Leafs are *pure* gold (meaning no copper is added to harden the coin) and will thus bend or melt at a harsh word. For durability's sake, I'd pass on the Maples and all other .999 coins.

Chinese Pandas (.999), Australian Kangaroos (.9999), Austrian Philharmonics (.9999), British Britannias (.917), Isle of Man Persian Cats (.9999), Mexican (.900), and other foreign bullion coins (all ounce based) are not as well known as Krugs and Eagles, and you don't want to have to educate traders in 2000 (although fineness and weight *is* clearly marked).

Stick with Krugs and Eagles. They both have a durable fineness of .917 (22k) and they both fit in common plastic tubes.

Just in case you run across some other gold bullion coins, consult the table below to learn of their pure gold content. **OGR** means Official Government Restrike (modern copies of older date coins--no numismatic value), **B** means bullion, and **N** means numismatic with premiums over 20%. (Notice how nations had gold coins for the last half of the 19th century, but not much later? Thus began the decline of the Western world.)

There's a current hoard of old Scandinavian gold coins on the market. Some of these are just over ¼oz. and sell for only Ø16 more than a ¼oz. bullion Eagle. Of the foreign "semis," these are the best deal. While they'll nevertheless remain tougher to *recoup* your premium, they're *beautiful* coins.

Pure Gold content of more common non-ounce coins

	Type	Fine	Content
Austrian 1 Ducat	OGR	.9866	.11090 oz.
Austrian 4 Ducats	OGR	.9866	.44380 oz.
Austrian 10 Coronas	OGR	.900	.09800 oz.
Austrian 20 Coronas	OGR	.900	.19600 oz.
Austrian 100 Coronas	OGR	.900	.98020 oz.
Belgian 20 Francs (1866-1882)	N	.900	.18700 oz.
Chilean 100 Pesos (1926-)	N	.900	.58850 oz.
Colombian 5 Pesos (1913-1930)	N	.9166	.23540 oz.
Danish 10 Kroner	N	.9166	.12860 oz.
Danish 20 Kroner	N	.9166	.25920 oz.
Dutch 10 Guilders (1911-1933)	N	.900	.19470 oz.
English Sovereigns (1871-1984)	N	.9166	.23500 oz.
English £5	B	.9166	1.17700 oz.
Finnish 20 Markaa	N	.900	.18670 oz.
French 20 Francs (1861-1915)	N	.900	.18670 oz.
Hungarian 20 Krona	OGR	.900	.19600 oz.
Hungarian 100 Corona	OGR	.900	.98020 oz.
Italian 20 Lire (1861-1897)	N	.900	.18670 oz.
Mexican 2 Peso	OGR	.900	.04822 oz.
Mexican 2½ Peso	OGR	.900	.06028 oz.
Mexican 5 Peso	OGR	.900	.12057 oz.
Mexican 10 Peso	OGR	.900	.24113 oz.
Mexican 20 Peso	OGR	.900	.48230 oz.
Mexican 50 Peso	OGR	.900	1.20570 oz.
Norwegian 20 Kronor	N	.900	.25920 oz.
Peruvian 1 Libra	N	.900	.23540 oz.
Russian 5 Ruble	N	.900	.12440 oz.
Swedish 20 Kroner	N	.900	.25920 oz.
Swiss 20 Francs (1897-1933)	OGR	.900	.18700 oz.
U.S.A. $1 (1849-1889)	N	.900	.04830 oz.
U.S.A. $2½ (1840-1929)	N	.900	.12090 oz.
U.S.A. $5 (1866-1929)	N	.900	.24187 oz.
U.S.A. $10 (1866-1933)	N	.900	.48375 oz.
U.S.A. $20 (1877-1933)	N	.900	.96750 oz.

MTB (800-221-5240) sells a Ø5 color booklet on these coins.

Avoid bullion bars

Gold comes in bars of 1, 5, 10, 32, 100, or 400 ounces. At today's spot of Ø285, a 400 oz. bar would cost Ø114,000! The downside to gold bars is that they are difficult to *sell*, with an assaying fee often required. In post-Y2K days expect unscrupulous folks to gold plate silver and lead bars and stamp them with authentic looking marks. *Caveat emptor!*

Q: "*Which size of bullion gold coins should I buy?*"

The smaller the coin the *higher* the premium. Quarter ounce coins have a 13-15% premium, and tenth ounce coins have a 20% premium. I'd have most coins in ounce form, with maybe 20% in tenths and quarters. (For some reason I don't care for halves, but that's just me.) The tenths are *so* cute, like gold dimes. Get a handful of fifty and you'll feel like Ali Baba.

While gold is cheap (Ø285/oz.) you should aggressively pick up the tenths and quarters, as their high premiums are minimized during cheap gold. Once gold moves above Ø400, start buying the ounce coins.

Pay no sales tax!

In Texas, for example, there is no sales tax for gold coin purchases over Ø1,000. Many other states have no such minimum. If your state charges sales tax, it's likely that a bordering or nearby state does *not*, so drive there to purchase. (Call around to find out.) Don't give the bastards a free 8-12%!

Storing your gold coins

Keep your coins in their plastic tubes for secure and jingle-free storage. I'd separate your hoard and bury most of it.

Great tip #1: A junkyard or other location with lots of ground metal will foil a search with metal detectors.

Great tip #2: Keep valuable papers, gems, and all other *nonmetallic* treasures apart from your gold and silver, just in case the detectors do find your coins.

SILVER COINS

Many experts feel that silver often has a much better upside potential than gold. I tend to agree. While the Ø285/Ø5 gold/silver ratio is now 57 to 1, in 1/1980 it was as low as 17 to 1 (Ø850/Ø50). Just a few years ago it was *114* to 1 (Ø400/Ø3.50), but sharp folks (*e.g.*, Warren Buffet) have moved on silver and driven up spot to its current floor of Ø5 (after a recent peak of Ø7.95). What's the "right" ratio? Who knows--probably about 40 to 1. When gold spikes up, however, terrified investors turn to more affordable silver and proportionally drive up its spot even more than gold's. The days of Ø2,000 gold/Ø100 silver (20 to 1) are probably due within ten years--sooner if a global depression hits.

   Silver's downside: it's *bulky.* At Ø5 spot, Ø4,000 ($1,000 *face* value bag) of 90% junk silver weighs 55lbs, so Ø10,000 in junk silver fills up nearly three shoeboxes and weighs over 130lbs, while that value in gold can be held in a child's hand. (Note: To calculate the face value multiplier of 90% junk silver coins, figure 80% of spot. Even though dimes, quarters, and halves have only .7234 oz. of silver per $1 face value, there is an added 8% premium for their coin form.)

pre-1965 90% junk U.S. silver coins

   Keep it simple. Non-numismatic pre-1965 U.S. dimes, quarters and halves (which are 90%), or "junk" silver, and it sells for X times face value (*e.g.*, Ø5 spot means 4 times face for junk silver). I'd buy as many $1,000 bags as you can afford within the overall plan. Probably 50% of your precious metals stock should be in junk silver. This will serve as your post-2000 trading money once events calm down. (Remember, people will have to be gradually *educated* that silver coins are worth more than clad coins.) I forecast that rifle ammo will sell for a 90% silver dime a round by summer 2000.

   Non-numismatic .999 ounce coins (called "rounds") will also become widely accepted in time. Eagles are the best choice.

Pure Silver content of U.S. coins

Dimes, 1916-1964	.07234 oz.
Quarters, 1916-1964	.18084 oz.
Halves, 1916-1964	.36169 oz.
Kennedy 40%	
Halves, 1965-1970	.14792 oz.
Peace & Morgan	
Dollars, 1878-1935	.77344 oz.
Eisenhower 40% proofs	
Dollars, 1971-1976	.31625 oz.

Astute math types will notice that the Peace and Morgan silver dollars have 6.9% more silver than equivalent face values in dimes, quarters, and halves (which are exactly proportional amongst themselves). Go figure. (The smart thing to have done was to buy silver dollars with silver dimes, quarters, and halves. Even *smarter* was to buy them with clad coins and paper FRNs. People did that until LBJ declared in 1964 that silver was *"too valuable to put into coins"*--which was like saying nutritious calories are too valuable to put into food. The *point* of precious metal coin money *is* their intrinsic value.) Therefore, $1,000 of the $1 coins have *50 more ounces* silver than $1,000 of the smaller coins, not that dealers don't know this.

There's no such thing as "junk" Morgan and Peace dollars. With spot at Ø5 they still fetch Ø9-10 even in poor condition. Thus, I do not recommend Morgan and Peace dollars as your "junk" silver because of the Ø4-5 premium.

Most folks don't like 40% silver and neither do I. 90% silver is bulky enough, but 40% silver is *2½ times* bulkier still.

Numismatic U.S. silver coins

As with gold coins, I do not recommend collector silver coins for the immediate post-crash days. Nobody will be terribly interested in your tube of MS60 1896 Morgans for their (pre-crash) numismatic value of Ø15 per coin (especially when spot was Ø5). A Ø15 MS60 Morgan today has a 200% premium. With the same Ø15 you could have bought nearly three times as much silver in bullion form. Are you catching on here?

If you've nonetheless got numismatic fever (as do I)

MS63 Morgans *are*, however, a relatively inexpensive way to get into numismatics versus the gold coins (and even versus most of the *silver* coins, such as the Liberty halves, Standing Liberty quarters, or Mercury dimes). *Affordable* MS63s run from Ø28 to Ø40, which is *not* a lot of money considering that the same coins in VF20 are Ø12-15. (More rare dates in MS63 run from Ø275 to Ø1,400+. Proof 63s *begin* at Ø1,500.)

What about MS65s? Even in very common dates these will be Ø100-125, which is at least a *2000%* premium over Ø5 spot. (For only a 200% premium over Ø285 gold spot you can get a common date $20 St. Gaudens in the same MS65 condition.) Therefore, I see the MS65 Morgans as a poor bargain, unless you truly have the money to spend and the time to wait. MS65s *will* appreciate more rapidly than MS63s, but you've waited too long to get into MS65s *cheaply* as they're already in strong demand. The MS63s are today's sleepers.

What about common MS60 Morgans for Ø15-20?
That thinking is *too* cheap.   It'll take forever before the
numismatic market begins to demand the "lowly" MS60s, and
for only Ø10-20 more you can have an MS63 coin.

If you pay Ø28 for an MS63 1884O Morgan today (spot silver at Ø5), spot needs to go only to Ø36 for that coin's mere silver content to match your purchase cost. (We briefly saw spot
at Ø50 in 1/80.) What I'm saying is that the numismatic downside to currently inexpensive MS63 Morgans is practically
nonexistent. It is my belief that the MS63 Morgans are the *last*
affordable numismatic precious metal coin, thus their appreciation potential is quite good (once the post-crash days level out).

> No [90%] *silver dollars were minted after 1935... The appeal of
> owning a bright Uncirculated silver dollar of the 19th century caused
> a steady stream of these to flow out of the Treasury vaults. In addi-
> tion, silver dollars were a popular medium of exchange in Nevada
> and certain other western states. By the late 1950's word had
> spread among the public that these "treasures" could be had for
> face value. In the early 1960's the race was on! Long lines formed
> at various Treasury outlets as people eagerly purchased silver dol-
> lars of long ago--paying just face value for them. The appeal...was
> enhanced by the occasional finding of scarce and rare dates among
> common issues!*
>   *The silver dollar situation has been a real windfall for collectors.
> For about $10 you can buy a silver dollar of the 1870's, 1880's, or
> 1890's in condition as nice as the day it was minted!* (Note: This
> was in <u>1977</u>.   BTP) *Needless to say, this appealing situation has
> created tens of thousands of collectors...* (at 138-39)
>   -- Q. David Bowers; *High Profits from Rare Coin Investment*

Most of the 200,000,000 Peace dollars were issued, but millions
of then-abundant Morgan dollars were stored by the Government until the "Great Treasury Raid" of the 1960s. Regarding
MS63 coins, *37* varieties can be had for *Ø50 or less!* These coins
should *begin* at Ø60, not Ø28. With the exception of a few years
(1892, 1893, 1894, 1895), you could assemble a collection of
every year from 1878-1904 (and 1921) in MS63, all PCGS
slabbed, for only Ø800.   I've already got a such a collection in
EF40 for Ø11 each, and am considering one in MS63. *Then* my
numismatic craving will be satisfied, all for less than Ø1,500.

All the earlier gold and silver coins are now *very* high-end
numismatics. A proof 1879 "Stella" Flowing Hair $4 (only 425
minted) sold for Ø650 in 1953, Ø10,000 in 1973, and goes for
Ø65,000+ today. An uncirculated 1795 silver dollar went for
Ø150 in 1953, Ø3,000 in 1973, and goes for Ø160,000+ today.

The post-WWII boom has fueled the collector markets (coins, cars, guns, antiques, etc.). In the 1950s you could buy Ferraris for only Ø5,000 and German Lugers for Ø25. Now Ferraris are Ø200,000+ and nice Lugers *begin* at Ø1,000. It's the same with coins: who can *afford* Ø10,000+ coins, or even Ø100 coins? It's too late to find bargain $5 Libs, so look for the *next* class of coins to shoot up in value: Morgan dollars.

Getting lucky with Grandma's silver hoard

While junk silver has been *thoroughly* searched for rare date or G8+ coins, you could get lucky with some family hoard. Get a current copy of *A Guide Book of U.S. Coins* (known as the "Red Book"). Coins types earlier than the 1916 issues are much more valuable, so consult the Red Book. I'll cover the more common modern (1916-1964) coins, but know in advance that this is a *very* rough guide to help you catch the rarities.

"Mercury" dimes (1916-1945)

Separate the 1931/earlier coins (which are worth at least Ø1.50-3.00 even in G4 condition) from the 1934/later coins .

Very common dates are 1934 to 1945, with two exceptions in 1942 (the 1942, 2 over 1, and the 1942D, 2 over 1).

Moderately rare dates are 1916S, 1917D, 1918, 1919D, 1919S, 1924D, 1925D, 1926S, 1927D, 1928D,

Very rare dates are 1916D, 1921, 1921D, 1931D.

Roosevelt dimes (1946-1964)

There are few rarities. Moderately rare dates (if EF40 or better) are the 1949 and 1949S, and the only *really* rare dates are the 1950S (S over D) and the 1964D (doubled die reverse).

Standing Liberty quarters (1916-1930)

Any coin between 1916 and 1924 is at least moderately rare and should be looked up. In only VF20 condition you could easily have a Ø200 coin. More rare within these dates are 1918D, 1919, 1919D, 1919S, 1920D, 1921, 1923S, and 1924D. The real standouts are 1916 and 1918S (8 over 7).

The recessed date style coins (1925-1930) are still more rare than the average Washington silver quarter. Notable dates are 1926D, 1927D, 1927S, and 1929D.

Washington quarters (1932-1964)

All pre-1940 coins will fetch good premiums, with common dates in VF20 worth Ø4-6. More rare dates to look for are

1932D, 1932S, 1934 (doubled die), 1936S, 1937 (doubled die obverse), 1937D, 1937S, 1938, 1938S, 1939D, 1939S, and 1940D.

Post-1940 coins are generally *quite* common, with the exception of the doubled die obverse coins of 1942D, 1943, and 1943S, plus the 1950D (D over S) and 1950S (S over D).

Liberty Walking halves (1916-1947)

Moderately rare are 1916D (obv.), 1917D (obv.), 1917S (obv.), 1921S, 1938D, 1939D, 1939S, and 1946 (doubled die reverse). More rare still are 1916, 1916S (obv.), 1921, and 1921D.

Franklin halves (1948-1963)

These coins generally have little numismatic value, except for the 1949S, 1953, and 1955 dates.

Kennedy halves (1964)

No numismatic value--junk silver date only.

Morgan dollars (1878-1921)

Most common dates are 1878S, 1879, 1879S (3rd rev.), 1880, 1880S, 1881S, 1882, 1882O, 1882S, 1883, 1883O, 1884, 1884O, 1885, 1885O, 1886, 1887, 1888, 1888O, 1889, 1890, 1891S, 1896, 1897, 1898, 1898O, 1899O, 1900, 1900O, 1901O, 1902O, 1904O, and 1921 (all).

In general, comparatively rare dates are 1878CC, 1880CC, 1882CC, 1883CC, 1884CC, 1884S, 1886S, 1888S, 1880O (doubled die obv.), 1890CC, 1892CC, 1894O, 1894S, 1899, 1899S, 1901, 1901S, 1902S, and 1904.

Very rare dates are 1879CC (CC over CC) 1879CC, 1881CC, 1885CC, 1889CC, 1893, 1893CC, 1893O, 1894, 1895O, 1895S, 1896S, 1901 (dbl. die rev.), 1903O, 1903S, and 1904S.

Extremely rare dates are the 1893S (worth Ø1,400 in only VF20 condition; Ø12,000 in AU50; Ø27,000 in MS60), and the 1895 (Ø12,000 in EF40).

Quick guide: *All* of the CC minted coins (Carson City, Nevada) fetch quite a premium. *Any* coins (regardless of mint) of 1893, 1894, and 1895 are worth *big* bucks.

Peace dollars (1921-1935)

Most of these are semi-numismatics. The only very common dates are 1922 (all), 1923 (all), 1924, 1925, 1926, and 1926S. The rest are worth at least Ø10-16 in VF20 condition.

Comparatively rare dates are 1921 and 1934S. The beautiful high relief coin (made only in 1921) is worth getting in MS60 or 63 (Ø125 and Ø250) if want a very nice collectible.

The *only* very rare date is 1928 (VF20 for Ø100).

MEASURES & WEIGHTS

We use the Troy System, versus the Metric System.

1 Metric Ton	=	1000 Kilograms
1 Kilogram	=	1000 Grams
1 Gram	=	1000 Milligrams
1 Pound Troy	=	12 Ounces Troy
1 Ounce Troy	=	20 Dramweight Troy (dwt)
1 dwt	=	24 Grains

Helpful conversion equivalents in each system are:

1 Ounce Troy	=	31.1033 Grams
	=	480 Grains
	=	20 dwt (Pennyweight)
14.5833 Ounces Troy	=	1 Pound Avoirdupois
0.9114 Ounces Troy	=	1 Ounce Avoirdupois
32.15 Ounces Troy	=	1 Kilogram
1 Gram	=	5.3 Karats
	=	15.432 Grains
	=	0.643 dwt
1.5552 Grams	=	1 dwt
1000 Grams	=	1 Kilogram
28.3495 Grams	=	1 Ounce Avoirdupois
24 Grains	=	1 dwt
5760 Grains	=	1 Pound Troy
15243 Grains	=	1 Kilogram
437.5 Grains	=	1 Ounce Avoirdupois
7000 Grains	=	1 Pound Avoirdupois
1 Grain	=	0.0648 Gram
240 dwt	=	1 Pound Troy
643.01 dwt	=	1 Kilogram
18.2291 dwt	=	1 Ounce Avoirdupois
291.666 dwt	=	1 Pound Avoirdupois
1 Kilogram	=	2.6792 Pounds Troy
	=	35.2740 Ounces Avoirdupois
	=	2.2046 Pounds Avoirdupois
1 Inch	=	25.40 Millimeters
	=	2.54 Centimeters
	=	0.0254 Meter
1 Millimeter	=	0.0394 Inch
1 Centimeter	=	0.3940 Inch
1 Meter	=	39.40 Inches
	=	1.094 Yards

FINENESS & CARAT WEIGHT

Fineness is the actual gold (or silver) content in a coin or bar and is expressed in grams or troy ounces. Each karat weight is a unit of fineness for gold equal to 1/24th part of pure gold in an alloy (usually copper or silver). For example, pure gold, which is 1.000 fine, is 24 karat; a fineness of .750 is 18 karats. Below are the standard karat weight to fineness conversions:

24 karats	=	1.000 fine	(Maple, Kangaroo, Philhar., etc.)
23 karats	=	.9583 fine	
22 karats	=	.9166 fine	(Britannia, Eagle, Krug)
21.6 karats	=	.9000 fine	(95+% of all gold money coins)
21 karats	=	.8750 fine	
20 karats	=	.8333 fine	
18 karats	=	.7500 fine	
16 karats	=	.6666 fine	
14 karats	=	.5833 fine	
10 karats	=	.4166 fine	

OTHER MONEY

I nearly titled this subchapter "Money Substitutes" by mistake, until I remembered something--money is as money *does*. While there will be *Federal Reserve Note* substitutes, as long as people accept something *as* money, it *is* money:

> We should...define money as **any medium of exchange adapted or designed to meet the inadequacy of...simple barter.** Anything that accomplishes this object is "Money."
> -- Bigram, Hugo, and Levy; *The Cause of Business Depressions*, (1914), p.95

How does one commodity become this "medium of exchange" over others? By a community's *agreement*:

> The one quality which is peculiar to money alone is its general acceptability in the market and in the discharge of debts. How does money acquire this specific quality? It is manifestly due solely to **a consensus of the members of the community to accept certain valuable things**, such as coin and certain forms of credit, as mediums of exchange.
> -- *ibid*

Community agreement. Different communities do not *agree* on common money. Nations are communities--communities which determine their *own* money. This is why your local McDonalds won't take French francs, but the McDonalds in Paris will. *Cities* are communities too, and they also determine some of their own money (*e.g.*, by accepting only *local* checks). Even *households* often create their own internal money to deploy their family's effort and to reward or punish behavior.

Local scrip

Any sizeable group anywhere, any day, could start a nonpolitical monetary unit and system. There is no law against it, and no legislation need be invoked.
-- E.C. Riegel, *Flight From Inflation,* p.49

Local communities and even companies have frequently created their own money. Remember, money is necessary to build and maintain civilization. Useful money *will* always be created by the free market, unless severely hampered by government. An excellent book on this subject is *New Money for Healthy Communities* by Thomas H. Greco, Jr. (ISBN 0-9625208-2-9).

Invalid foreign currency (a BTP idea!)

Gold and silver have been successful commodity money for over 6,000 years because they are naturally scarce, difficult to produce, and impossible to fake. Paper, however, is not naturally scarce, and currency is easy to produce and fake, *when the technology exists.*

For some time after 2000, however, that technology *won't* exist, and currency--*any currency*--will be king. Worthless Russian, Polish, Ecuadorian, etc. currency can be bought for practically nothing (ask your local coin dealer). This is high-quality, water-marked, serial-numbered currency *unable to be counterfeited* during the post-crash days which can be used for a community's money. Defunct foreign currency notes will be naturally scarce (the serial numbers could be logged to prevent surprise infusions from unknown caches), and impossible to produce or fake. No local scrip can match foreign currency's uncounterfeitability. Therefore, why *couldn't* invalid foreign currency serve as cash in local insular economies? America may see the irony of having 1980s Soviet Ruble currency being traded on her streets.

❖ 12

COMMODITY BARTER

To survive, we must trade with others for things we cannot make. Even the most reclusive of hermits must trade with others, at least occasionally. Truly, "no man is an island." There are only two possible manners of trading: direct and indirect. Indirect trading is accomplished through money. The direct trade of goods is commonly known as *barter*. The five classic criteria for barter items are:

❶ High consumer demand
❷ Not easily home manufactured
❸ Durable in storage
❹ Divisible in small quantities
❺ Authenticity--easily recognized

I would add a sixth criterion: a lack of substitutes.

The *best* example I can think of is a box of .22LR shells. It perfectly meets every one of the six criteria. Other good examples are: nails, needles, matches, condoms, wheat, ballpoint pens, pencils, fishing line, aluminum foil, motor oil, fuel (gas, diesel, kerosene) and can openers.

BARTERING

Can you even remember when *you* last bartered for something: that is, personally traded something on a direct, equal exchange? It happens very rarely because it's difficult to find someone who wants *exactly* what you *have* and has *exactly* what you *want*--value for value. Thus, the problem with barter is "lack of coincidence of wants" and "indivisibility." A dentist may want some potatoes, but the farmer may not necessarily want any dental work. Even if he did, it would be worth much more than the amount of potatoes the dentist needed. Dental work, as most services, is indivisible in value (there's no pulling just *half* a tooth) so the dentist couldn't make trades for lesser valued things. And if the farmer wanted a *car*, the dealership clearly couldn't accept a huge pile of perishable potatoes.

Invention of the money tool for indirect trading

A medium of exchange (a "middlething," if you will) is needed to facilitate indirect trades. Without a middlething we could never trade between large and small, divisible and indivisible, common and rare, perishable and nonperishable, near and far. We need a middlething which is accepted by dentists, potato farmers, car dealerships and everybody else.

This middlething is called "money." Money is the hub of society, operating as the common denominator between us all-- otherwise, we (as specialists) could hardly trade directly with each other, one on one. Every civilization is based on and requires *indirect* trade. Without indirect trade, the dentist would starve and the farmer's teeth would fall out (and then *he'd* starve!). Without indirect trade we'd all be surviving as primitive savages. Without money there is no indirect trade and without indirect trade there is no civilization.

> *...and in societies of low civilization, there is no money.*
> -- Herbert Spencer

This middlething, this money, must have some intrinsic amount of consistent value. To even *have* value, money must first be an article of commerce--a *commodity*. Commodities are things which many people desire. Money is a certain commodity which nearly *everybody* desires, any time, any place.

> *Historically, many different goods have been used as money: tobacco in colonial Virginia, sugar in the West Indies, salt in Abyssinia, cattle in ancient Greece, nails in Scotland, copper in ancient Egypt, and grain, beads, tea, cowrie shells, and fishhooks. Through the centuries, two commodities: **gold** and **silver**, have emerged as money in the free competition of the market, and displaced the other commodities [as money].*
>
> -- Murray N. Rothbard; *What Has Government Done To Our Money?*

> *The commodity chosen as a medium must be a **luxury**. Human desires for luxuries are unlimited and, therefore, luxury goods are always in demand and will always be acceptable. Wheat is a luxury in underfed civilizations, but not in a prosperous society. Cigarettes*

ordinarily would not serve as money, but they did in post-World War II Europe where they were considered a luxury. The term 'luxury good' implies scarcity and high unit value. Having a high unit value, such a good is easily portable; for instance, an ounce of gold is worth a half-ton of pig iron.
-- Alan Greenspan's 1966 essay *Gold and Economic Freedom;* from Ayn Rand's *Capitalism: The Unknown Ideal*

Money is money only because it's readily exchangeable for something else. And *why* is it readily exchangeable? Because it has a universally recognized *intrinsic* value. Notice that historically, money commodities were useful, everyday items; either *divisible* (tobacco, sugar, salt, copper, tea) or *small* (nails, beads, seashells, fishhooks). In pre-industrial times, these items were also luxury goods. However, the more advanced and prosperous a civilization becomes, the more advanced its luxury goods. By 1900, nails, salt, etc. were no longer luxury goods-- modern industrial technology and manufacturing had relegated them to being cheap and plentiful.

Money is a *means* to an end. Money is rarely an end in itself; few want money for its own sake. For example, in postwar Germany, cigarettes traded as money, even amongst nonsmokers. Why would nonsmokers accept a commodity for which they had no personal use? Because they could easily trade cigarettes for something else which *did* have personal utility. To the nonsmoker, cigarettes were only a means to an end. (To the smoker, cigarettes were *both*.)

Let's cover the many items which will likely become commonly bartered items after 2000.

Alcohol

In the best of times, people want to drink. In the *worst* of times, they'll drink even *more*. When I toured the Soviet bloc countries in the early 1980s, I was constantly having to dodge drunk pedestrians on the roads and even the *highways*. Alcoholism in Poland and the U.S.S.R. was utterly pandemic.

Whether your morals, conscience, or religion can allow you to supply alcohol (and tobacco) to generally miserable post-crash people is a personal matter. There are no doubt consequences to our actions, and you should consider this issue carefully. Granted, people *will* procure alcohol regardless, but you do not necessarily have to help them. Your call.

Vodka

There are few really *poor* vodkas. You don't have to stock up on *Absolut* or *Stolichnaya* (overrated) for vodka to be of good quality and thus desirable. Any decent vodka will be fine.

Jack Daniels

I'd make this the "gold coinage" of your alcohol stockpile. Buy several cases of pints. You can also get it by the gallon and fill up empty bottles. Wild Turkey is popular amongst those who can't afford Jack. Grain alcohols have the advantage of indefinite shelf life.

Single malt Scotch

This is considered superior to any blended malt Scotch.

Tequila

Trade it *and run away quickly*. Tequila seems to bring out the wildest tendencies in folks. *Cuervo Gold* will remain one of the more popular choices.

Beer

It won't keep. The fresher the better. After six months it begins to go flat, even if kept cool.

Better yet, put together a home-brewing kit and become a post-crash brewmaster. You'll need to eventually grow your own hops, barley, and malt. No big deal. Beer has been brewed in quantity since the 14th century.

Wine

This would require a book in itself. Some will store for many years, but all wines peak at *some* age and must then be served else it'll turn into red vinegar. Consult with an expert for your choice of inventory. I'd have wine primarily for my *own* enjoyment rather than for barter purposes.

The box wines (in airless Mylar bladders) will keep for *quite* a while, even after they're "opened." Their blended nature is abhorrent to true wine *connoisseurs* of course, but I'd rather have box wine than none at all.

Tobacco

It's immutable human nature that people will continue to want to smoke during and after a crisis, and will pay dearly to do so. This is highly irrational, but that's one of our bad traits.

I'd always been a proud nonsmoker, until 1997 when somebody offered me a *Monte Cristo #2*. (The *first* one's always "free.") Now, I am an *occasional* (perhaps 8-10 a year) cigar smoker. I can now empathize with smokers--it's an insidiously subtle addiction. I promised myself that I'd only *very* seldom smoke, and then only with friends. (Since I spend more time alone than not, this proviso is an effective governor.) After a year, I was driving down the road and out of nowhere this totally reasonable voice said, *"Wouldn't a cigar be really nice right about now?"* I was rather alarmed. It wasn't some mere amorphic craving, *it was a clear suggestion formed in a perfect sentence.* It didn't light up, and I've never forgotten that voice.

Moral: Don't smoke, and *quit* if you do. It's nasty stuff. Again, it's your call whether or not to store barter tobacco.

Cigarettes

In prisons and postwar societies, cigarettes trade as money. A few dozen cartons of the most common brands, such as Marlboro and Camels, will go far. Ask your local tobacconist which brands have the most universal appeal.

Have good supplies of cigarette tobacco and paper with a rolling machine to manufacture your own cigarettes.

Cigars

You'll need a humidor. Properly stored at their required 70% humidity and 70° temperature, cigars will last for years. I'd stock up on only good quality Dominican Republic and Honduran cigars. Consult your local humidor folks.

Pipe tobacco

Probably the most luxurious of tobacco products, but it will seem indispensable to certain folks. Get this last, if at all.

Coffee

I don't drink the stuff, but most people do. Coffee will always be *big wampum*. Whole beans kept dry and cool (or frozen) will last for many years. You'll need a grinder, and the hand-powered variety is best.

Fuel

We will need mechanized tools to claw our way out of the post-2000 crash, and fuel will trade at a high premium given the greatly reduced output of the refineries.

Gasoline

It's rumored that gasoline is intentionally manufactured so as not to last. I wouldn't be surprised. Untreated, it'll last only 1 year. Treated, 5 years. *That's it.* Therefore, your electric generator and main trucks should be diesel or LP powered.

I'd have some well-hidden 300-500 gallon tanks, and several dozen of the military 5 gallon cans.

I once ran out of gas in the middle of night in the middle of Poland. Sputtering on fumes, I rode through a large bus transit stop and asked in several languages if anybody could sell me some gas. One guy answered in French that he could, hopped on the back of my bike, and we rode to his flat where he had 20 liters in the basement. I gave him Ø10 for it, which was the equivalent of two weeks of his wages. He and his wife served me tea and cake, overjoyed at this monetary windfall. (They looked on the brink of being homeless.) Moral: Have a surplus of gas, and somebody will someday pay you handsomely for it.

Diesel fuel

For fossil fuels, diesel is the way to go. It's not volatile and treated with algicide and anti-humidity agents, diesel will last five years.

Liquid fuel treatment

Ø20 of this will treat 5,000gal of fuel. Could be priceless in the future. Nitro-Pak and many others carry it.

Propane

LP gas is a *marvelous* fuel. It's extremely clean burning and will power vehicles, generators, stoves, refrigerators, freezers, and even lamps.

I'd have the largest tank you can afford to buy and fill. A 500 gallon tank had be had for only Ø275 if you look around. While you can lease tanks for little money, you are then obligated to have them filled by only that company. I'd *own* your tanks and thus be able to shop for the best price and service. (Note: Tanks are becoming a bit hard to find. Hurry.)

Buy your LP during the summer when it's cheapest. Often, gas companies will run "fillup specials" so shop around before you have your new 1,000 gallon tank filled. Right now, propane is running about 75-85¢/gallon. Most alpine homes use about 300-500 gallons/year.

Regarding barter of LP, keep it only for trusted folks, as recipients will have to visit your big tank directly for fillups (unless you swap their empty tanks for full ones of your own).

Ammo

Very few people have "enough" ammo. If *I* don't, then you probably don't. A unloaded pistol is but a "rock" and an unloaded rifle is but a "club." Have ample surplus stocks of the below common calibers, preferably in their original boxes (for the Freudian *"transitional object"* effect on involuntary psychological regression to the previously "normal times"). I'd stock up *quite* heavily on the military calibers of 9mm, .45ACP, .223, and .308. Common *civilian* calibers would be .38 Special, .243, .270, .30-30, etc.

If the city dwellers *are* armed it will probably be with dad's old shotgun, and they will quickly run out shells. A box of shells will be worth *big wampum*, such as rare paintings, jewelry, or nice furniture. Rifled slugs will be *especially* desirable. Forget the 32, 28, 16, and 10 gauges--serves 'em right for choosing such ridiculously uncommon gauges in the first place.

Boston's "Any Gun" ammo pouch

I came up with an idea (originally for caching) that you should consider. In a small belt pouch (the 120rd SKS stripper clip ammo pouch works well--from CTD), waterproof pack 5rds of each of the following calibers:

Handgun ammo (5rds @)
.22LR (box of 50rds)
.25 ACP
.32 ACP
.380 ACP
9mm (9x19)
.38 Special (can be used in .357 Magnums)
.40 S&W
.44 Special (can be used in .44 Magnums)
.45 ACP

Shotgun shells (2 shells @)
.410
20 gauge
12 gauge

Rifle ammo (5rds @)
.223
.243
.270
.30 Carbine
7.62x39
.30-30
.308
.30-06

Such a collection of ammo will cover probably *90%* of all firearms in America (maybe even 95%) and would make an excellent barter package or piece of foraging kit (for when guns are found). Buying ammo in quantity and breaking it down will make each kit (including a Ø5 mag pouch) cost about Ø35.

Yeah, I omitted the 9x18 Makarov, the .357/.41/.44 Mags, the 7mm Rem Mag, the .30-40 Krag, the .303 British, the 8x57, the .300WM, and other fairly common calibers, but remember that we want a *portable* kit, not an exhaustive one. **The *immediate* loading of the *most random* guns is the goal.**

Have a boxes of these other calibers at home. An SKS chest ammo pouch has three times the room if you want to create a *99%* ammo kit for about Ø75.

Final advice: *never* sell ammo or guns to strangers without them first being disarmed or overwhelmingly outgunned. Your safety is more important than the deal.

Weapons & Gear
I'd lay up some trading *wampum* in firearms. Statisically, there's only one gun for every 1.3 Americans. Only one American in four owns guns, which means each gunowner has an average of three firearms. I would estimate that *half* of these are .25ACP pistols, shotguns, .22LR rifles, and other tactically limited weapons. There will be a real demand for reliable and powerful guns. You should have a few extra, if only for your family and friends.

Handguns
You might include a little bit of ammo with these.

A S&W Model 10 .38 Special you bought for Ø125 today could, desiccant shrink-wrapped with 18rds of ammo, fetch a gold coin or two in 2000. The modern Hungarian and Czech .32s, .380s, and 9mms are good bargains and solid pistols.

A Glock with extra mags and 100rds might be worth several gold coins, or a year's food or housing. Colt 1911s are and will remain popular, though requiring more maintenance. (The Argentine "Sistema 1927" is a bargain at Ø250.)

Choose bargain priced guns with good profit potential. Basically, you can't go wrong with *name brand* handguns in *common* calibers. You're *not* going to get your money out of Ø1,600 SIG 210s or Ø2,000 Korth revolvers, however.

Shotguns

These are inefficient in ammo weight/kill ratio, slow to reload, and limited to under 100yds (even with slugs). I'd prefer just about any rifle over a shotgun (unless a CQB team needed a 12 gauge). Stock up on trading rifles instead.

Lots of people, however, will be needing shotgun *shells.*

Rifles

Unarmed folks in 2000 will be lusting after *any* .22LR rifle just as we lust after pre-ban FALs today. Marlin semi-autos can be found by the bushel for only Ø70-90 apiece, and these are perfectly capable of 50yd headshots. Well placed, a .22LR is nothing to sneeze at. Get a dozen of these bargain Marlin rifles.

An SKS with 500rds in stripper clips? To a city dweller, it's probably worth all his fine furniture (grand piano included), and/or the family silver. Nearly the same for a .30-30 lever gun.

Stock up on the Indian-made .308 Lee-Enfields (for Ø70-Ø150 each, depending on configuration). I have come to view these 12rd box mag rifles as proven solid and serviceable. The Indians used better steel to beef up the Enfield action to .308 strength. They are a better bargain than the Spanish FR-8 .308 Mausers were a few years ago at Ø140. Find them in the *Shotgun News.*

An AR15 or FAL with extra mags, parts, and 1,000rds? You could *name* your price: land, vehicles, daughter, whatever.

Nearly the same for a scoped bolt-action. Choose *extremely* common calibers (*e.g.*, .270, .308, and .30-06). No .257 Roberts, please, even though it's a great whitetail caliber.

Gun stuff

Guns are tools which are consumed through use. Also, gear and accessories will be highly sought after in 2000.

Guns parts

Guns are tools, and tools break. Some guns, however, rarely break (like the Glock and the FAL). These you'll want to own for yourself. Most everybody else, however, will not have been so wise and will own less reliable guns.

You could be the "Firing pin Baron" of your area. Marlin lever guns, M1As, 1911s, and other guns break pins more than other guns, for example. Extractors and ejectors do, too. Springs (especially mag and hammer springs) wear out. I'd have an extra trigger assembly for all semi-auto rifles.

Ask your local gunsmith which parts he routinely replaces, as every area has different guns. One locale might be awash in sporterized Krags, another in M98 Mausers, another in M94 Winchester lever-actions. Anticipate your area's needs.

Magazines

Common pistol mags (1911, Glock, Browning M1935, Ruger, etc.). While pre-ban hi-cap mags will trade at a premium, people will also wish they'd stocked up on the 10rd mags. A pistol without a mag is a single shot.

Common "assault rifle" mags (AR15, AK47, Mini14, M1A, FAL, and maybe H&K). Such rifles without mags are mere single shots, and 5rd bolt-actions would then be superior.

Scopes and sights

These will break or fail at the worst possible moment, and without them guns are pretty useless beyond 7yds. Have a modest supply of common sights and 3-9X Tasco scopes.

Slings

Every long gun needs a sling. Everyone will figure that out for themselves after 2000. While ropes and straps will suffice as makeshift slings, have a good supply of QD studs and swivels, and dozens of 1¼" G.I. web slings (from Sierra Supply for Ø3@). These 1¼" slings will fit in 1" swivels if necessary.

Cleaning gear

It's rather difficult to make your own bore cleaner and gun oil. Buy this by the gallon (G.I. stuff works fine). Have lots of copper brushes, rods, ends, and patches. Sierra Supply can set you up.

Caliber converters

These are wonderful devices, allowing you to shoot in a .30-06 rifle, for example, the .32ACP, the .30 Carbine, the 7.62x39, and the .308. .410 and 20ga shotgun shells can be fired in a 12ga. .22LR from a .223. From MCA (760-770-2005).

Knives
Quality name brand knives (and sharpening stones) will be good trading *wampum*. Given their indestructibility, an extra Mad Dog knife or two will be worth *big* money.

Consumables
Items of low price/low margin will be the first things no longer manufactured. Nails, matches, safety needles, pencils, and .22LR ammo require sophisticated industrial machinery and materials. Ever try to make a ballpoint pen on your own?

Matches
One match saves you minutes of time and frustration. Have hundreds of boxes of strike-anywhere matches.

Nails
Buy a barrel of them. People will be scrounging for wood and building shanties.

.22LR ammo
Yeah, I know I already mentioned this, but it's worth repeating. There's no reloading the .22LR rimfire case. It's a testimony to free enterprise how something can cost only 2¢ apiece at WalMart, yet be impossible to manufacture at home.

Trapping for food is fairly unreliable, even when you're good at it. A simple Ø60 Marlin .22LR rifle can take even an elk or moose with the right head shot. A box of .22LRs could mean the difference between starving and eating for some people.

Ballpoint pens and pencils
Pencils write any time, *on* nearly anything. Ballpoint pens will become important items, although pre-crash supplies will last for quite a while.

Salt
Only pennies per pound, salt is necessary for food storage.

Honey
This keeps forever. (Crystalized honey is still perfectly good and needs only to be gently warmed up to reconstitute.)

Toilet paper
There are workable substitutes, but barely. Civilized people quickly become *unhinged* when they are forced to use leaves. Have ample stocks of generic TP.

Straight razors and shaving lotion
 While there will be oodles of disposable razor for a while, the supply *will* run out. Have resharpenable straight razors. CTD has a supply of surplus *Swiss* razors from the 1920s-1940s. They're neat!

Toothbrushes, toothpaste, floss, and mouthwash
 Homemade versions are awful, and healthy gums/teeth will be crucial. (Even in normal times, dental emergencies are painful and highly debilitating.)
 Have a couple hundred toothbrushes. They're cheap and impossible to fashion yourselves. Have 2-3/person per year, plus lots of extras for *wampum*.
 My favorite toothpaste is *Glister* from Amway. It is very soft and doesn't scratch your enamel like *Crest* (which in comparison seems as abrasive as *Comet* cleanser!). Many whole-food toothpastes are good, too. Pick a non-fluoride brand.
 Have *lots* of dental floss. Nothing else works as well.
 I mix half and half generic brand anti-plaque mouthwash and hydrogen peroxide to make a superior mouthwash. The cavity-making bacterial chain requires 18+hrs to form, so if you disinfect your mouth several times a day in addition to regular brushing and flossing, you'll won't likely suffer dental problems.

Condoms
 Birth control will be *very* important in 2000 and beyond. For many couples, an unexpected pregnancy might risk unmanageable health and financial concerns.

Pocket solar calculators
 These have become the modern abacus. Back in 1988, I took a bunch of them to my friends in East Germany and Poland, where they were not only unattainable, but *unheard* of. Costing me only Ø5 each, you'd have thought I was giving away space shuttles. After 2000, they will be indispensable for daily commerce. Have a couple dozen of them (with % function).

Glue, epoxy, duct tape
 Repair of broken tools, appliances, etc. will be a big industry, so have plenty of the above to join parts. I've found JB Weld to be a near miracle epoxy. Loc-Tite products are also great.

Tools
 Even if you aren't mechanically-inclined, somebody else *will* be. Stock up on quality tools (*e.g.*, Craftsman, Proto, etc.).

Books
Bibles, classics (*Atlas Shrugged*), how-to, survival, fix-it, gardening, back-to-basics, medical, encyclopedias, novels.

Storage of your supplies
I expect the storage units to be looted in 2000. At the very first hint of unrest or "anti-hoarding" laws empty yours out.

POST-Y2K HAGGLING

How to haggle as a cash buyer
After the crash, bargaining skills will be extremely important. First rule: Don't appear more prosperous than everybody else. Wear old clothing and no jewelry. Don't be freshly shaven. A little B.O. is good.

Learn to haggle. Never pay the first, or even second, asking price--and often not even the third. Offer a half and pay two-thirds, that kind of thing. Remember, unless buyers are standing in line, there are always more sellers than buyers. You have the leverage, and never forget that. **If his stuff was so choice, then he'd be *keeping* it.**

Inspect the item very carefully. *Caveat emptor!* Once you've decided to bid on it, *put it back on the table.* This is very powerful psychologically--you haven't yet accepted the goods. Find a palpable defect and *harp* on it in disappointed tones.

Act more disinterested than not, and keep looking about as if you're searching for a friend. No seller can stand such "iffyness" and will work harder to reel you in. Before you make your first offer, slowly count your money with a scowl, pull out the offered amount and put it on the table. That makes it easily his with a simple *"Yeah, O.K."* He'll usually chase you down. Here are some of my best buyer lines:

> *"Why are you selling it?*
> *"What repairs does it need now? What will it need later?"*
> *"What's your best cash price, right now?"*
> *"Can you work with me on price?"*
> *"It's something I kind of like, but don't really need."*
> *"Is there anything you need on trade?"*
> *"I don't think I can swing it..."*
> *"Can you sweeten the pot with something?"*

For the hard-core sellers I've come up with a great technique if your bid is firm. Let's say he's asking Ø225 and the most you'll pay is Ø150, and you're not in the mood to haggle. Tell him, *"I'll give you Ø150 right now. That's what it's worth to me."* He'll no doubt counter with Ø200, figuring you'll meet at Ø170-185. You reply with, *"Was I not clear? I told you that it was worth Ø150 to me. That's it. Now it's worth Ø145. My time's is not free."* This will blow him away; no buyer haggles *down!* This is a hard-core tactic, to be used sparingly.

Times will be tough and you must stretch your funds, but *do* try to create only Win-Win deals. Don't haggle some old guy to his bones. Once you've reached a fair price you can happily afford, *pay it.* It's cruel to demand everybody's bottom dollar. Let the seller make a modest profit. **Be *fair* to sellers; you never know when you might be one *yourself.***

Final bit of advice: *Never* divulge how much you paid for something, as doing so might kill the chance of a profit later.

How to haggle as a seller

Same rules apply, but in reverse. Act fairly disinterested, but not overly so (that's rude). If an offer is not even close, don't mull it over or hesitate to reject it (although halfway politely). Only when an offer is "in the ballpark" do you begin to haggle. Never accept a first bid or the buyer will have immediate "cognitive dissonance" by imagining some hidden defect or cursing himself for not offering less. Make him work a bit and he'll be much happier with his purchase.

When he asks why you're *selling* such a treasure, reply that you have two, or that you *"just can't keep everything."* Say or imply nothing to directly disparage your goods, or to communicate that you desperately need the cash.

If he doesn't bite and walks off, don't follow him with your eyes. He'll notice and correctly figure you to be a motivated seller. He's walked off and you've forgotten all about him-- that's your attitude. When he returns (as you knew he would) acting all disinterested, you only faintly remember him.

Here are some of my best seller lines:

"I'd be losing money at Ø100."
"Don't you think Ø125 is fair?"
"Hey, I'm not here for the fun of it!"
"I just got here. I think I'll hear some other offers, thanks."
"Can you sweeten the pot with something?"

❖ 13

COMMUNICATIONS

WALKIE-TALKIES

For ranges within 2 miles, the Motorola TalkAbout Plus (from Cheaper Than Dirt) are great little radios. I have used them skiing and mountain hiking with very good success. They are rugged and only Ø115. Many plug-in mike options available.

CB RADIOS

Buy name brands (*e.g.*, Realistic, Uniden, Maxon, Cobra).

Base units

It must have an SWR (standing wave ratio) meter (to measure antenna efficiency), and be an SSB (single side band) radio (for increased range). It should have a 12V DC jack for car power, in case you want to use it as a mobile unit.

Mobile units

These transmit up to 5 Watts, and are highly portable walkie-talkie size. Their AA batteries drain pretty quickly, so have spares and a solar charger. I like the Maxon radios.

Antennas

A radio is no better than its antenna, any more than a car its tires, a gun its ammo, or a stereo its speakers. An excellent antenna is more important than an excellent radio. Don't skimp on your antennas. Stick with quality gear from K40, Firestik, Hustler, and Realistic.

For best practical efficiency of mobile antennas, a "102-inch" steel whip (which is one quarter of the 27mHz wavelength of 36 feet) is the ticket. The so-called "loaded" shorter antennas work O.K. if at least 40" in length.

For base units, a 5/8 wavelength unit (22' long, with 8' radials) will give the best omnidirectional range. An alternative to such a large unit is the single, vertical "half wave" Antron 99.

Beam antennas on a rotator focus in one direction to dramatically increase range and ignore unwanted signals in the opposite direction.

Use only top quality coaxial cable (e.g., from Belden). Runs less than 50' from antenna to radio can use RG-58, but over that you'll need RG-8 for less signal loss.

Power Packs

They convert more powerful car CBs to mobile use, and contain a 12V battery pack (usually C cells) and have a telescopic antenna. You'll occasionally find these at flea markets and garage sales for Ø10. Snap it up if you find one.

Or, you can make the same thing with either C or D cells, or a small wet-cell motorcycle battery, and adapted antenna.

Get a solar battery charger and 10 nicad batteries for unlimited wilderness transmitting.

Repairs and tinkering

Get *The Screwdriver Expert's Guide to Peaking Out and Repairing CB Radios*, by Lou Franklin (from CBCI, POB 31500, Phoenix, Az. 85046). With this book you'll be able to install and match antennas, rewire a mike, and provide general repair.

Final thoughts on CB radios

Don't spend a lot of money on CBs. If your radio needs are fairly extensive, then go ham radio (with encryption).

HAM RADIOS

Too much to go into here. Contact the American Radio Relay League (203-666-1541) for HRO and equipment info. They publish a good book, *Low Profile Amateur Radio*, by Kearman. Ham radio will be *the* long-distance comm of 2000.

On a related note, have a good scanner. I also recommend the book *Scanners & Secret Frequencies* by Henry L. Eisenson (ISBN 1-56866-038-2).

SECURITY

Here's yet another subject which space cannot permit full discussion. If your security concerns are fairly intense, then you'll need somebody in your group with military training to plan and coordinate matters. Pick a combat vet (*i.e.*, one who has actually *killed* in battle, as there is just no substitute for that kind of experience).

COMMUNITY PERIMETER

Vigilant communities will have little or no trouble from bands of marauders, as there will be plenty of sleepy towns for them to take over.

Overlapping fields of fire from elevated positions of cover should be worked out and then manned at all times. All adults should constantly wear their handguns, if not carry their rifles (or have them within arms' reach). Some prearranged call to arms (town bell, siren, flare, etc.) should be sorted out and practiced with the Order of Battle.

A town may deem it necessary to cordon itself off from outsiders, at least for a short while until the chaos dies down. The 80/20 Rule *really* comes into play here. 80% of the boundaries can be closed off with only 20% of the effort. It's the remaining 20% of "porosity" which costs the 80% of effort. (Ask the former East German border guards.) Since the 100% standing border effort required for a sieged city is wholly impractical, your town will make better use of its people with a few checkpoints and several highly vigilant roving patrols (with NVDs) which can call for immediate reinforcements.

A retired Army or Marine officer with battalion/regiment level field command experience is vital.

During periods of heightened alert, the townfolk should have some sort of *visible* recognition (*e.g.*, hat, shirt, etc.) so that they may quickly spot infiltrators.

Any residents caught aiding and abetting your enemy must be dealt with as harshly as your situation merits.

DISTANT HOME PERIMETER

What I mean by "distant" is up to a mile beyond your property's boundary. Security is made up of concentric rings, and it is fatal to have merely your home buttoned up and allow attackers to camp out on your front lawn. Distance equals time. The further away you can begin to detect and repel boarders, the more costly and fruitless their attack is likely to be. Be like a cactus; your patrols are the needles protecting the more vulnerable and lush center.

If you are surrounded by forest or BLM land, stage regular patrols throughout a wide buffer zone. If you are bordered by neighbors, then work with them to create a *mutual* buffer zone.

Unless radio linked, your patrols should probably be limited to remaining within visual contact of home (and its snipers). If ambushed within 30yds (grenade range), the rule is to rush the ambushers since they won't expect it and you'll be moving *away* from a likely trap to your rear. If ambushed at longer range, seek cover and fall back while returning fire. Small unit tactics and patrolling is quite a science, so get some of the U.S. Army Field Manuals (FMs) and learn the basics.

Part of distant home perimeter security is a long-range sniper team, armed with a 600-1000yd rifle (.308, .30-06, 7mmRM, .300WM, etc.). Even better would be a bolt-action .50BMG sniper rifle, which can disable light vehicles at 1½ miles. There are a dozen affordable choices, which I discussed in *Boston on Guns & Courage*. Like night vision devices and encrypted radios, a .50BMG is equipment which will give you an order of magnitude edge over your enemies.

INTIMATE HOME PERIMETER

What I mean by "intimate" is from your fenceline to the outside walls. If your patrols are overwhelmed or beaten back, then you'll have to fend off an attack from your living room. If you expect this scenario to be possible, then you must fortify your firing positions with sandbags, work out fields of fire, assign duties to every household member, and run practice drills.

Having a clandestine way of escape is always a good idea, one that all burrowing rodents practice. Your house could be set ablaze, or overwhelmed by sheer firepower. Have some way out (probably a tunnel) which exits in the trees or behind a hill. From there you can escape, or counterattack from their rear.

PERSONAL SECURITY

This means individual combat. It can take place rifle to rifle at hundreds of yards, or hand to hand. Regardless the variety, *quality* instruction is vital. Since defensive shooting instruction for civilians will likely be curtailed very shortly, get this *first*. Training with PR-24s, sticks, knives and open hand can come later, as it's quiet, indoors, and there are more instructors. So, get to Thunder Ranch for Urban Rifle 1 and 2 ASAP! Dojo work can be done later. Besides, you need to be acquiring your quality rifles now, while they're affordable and legal to buy.

After you've been through class, continue to practice. School can only train you how to ingrain your athletic memory, which requires hours of practice on your own. A diploma or certificate is *not* competency; it is the *beginning* of competency.

REFUGEES OF 2000

Expect the greatest migration of Americans in recent history, basically from the cities to the country, and from the east to the west. It seems probable that people who are already in the countryside and the western states will not be *gah-gah* about this. Some of this attempted immigration will be physically blocked by armed citizens who feel their actions perfectly legitimate. (I can empathize. I've been in my small town for years, and would resent the sudden arrival of thousands of Millennium refugees, most of whom scoffed at the Y2K alarmists.)

"It's a free country! We have the right to live anywhere in America!" Conceptually, that's true, but... There's *de jure*, and there's *de facto*. Some areas *will* vigorously prevent newcomers from relocating, or even passing through. Whether or not such is right or wrong will be rather moot when a .30-06 is pointed at your chest and you're told to move on.

"How will my city relatives join me in the country?"

Good question. They might not be able to contact you, leave the city, or make a long journey.

Assuming they get out and reach your county line (a likely demarcation to be defended), they need some way of being allowed through any checkpoint. In 1999, send them a photocopy of your driver's license (with your rural address on it), and a handwritten note inviting them to live with you at your full responsibility (for their food, water, etc.). Such might be *the* persuading factor at the barricades.

Before they embark, have them try to contact you (*e.g.,* via ham radio) so you can expect them. Be at the "border crossing" at the appointed time, or inform the personnel of their arrival.

I realize this all sounds dystopian and ridiculous, but we could actually see a Road Warrior society in 2000 and beyond. I'd start envisioning the ramifications of such, and prepare for them while nobody else is thinking that far ahead.

TOOLS, IMPLEMENTS, & CLOTHES

TRACTORS

Usually essential for even the smallest of homesteads. You'll need a tractor if you harvest hay and grains. Tractors can move logs, plow, grade, remove snow, and power through its power take-off water pumps and generators. Draft animals cannot do all this, and even if they *could*, a pair of them consumes 5 acres of produce per year, working or not.

Also, why have *two* diesel engines (in a tractor and a generator) when a 12kW generator head can be PTO run from the tractor's 24hp engine? (A 25kW generator needs 35hp.)

Row-crop tractors

These are high ground-clearance units, often with close-in front wheels. They have a high CoG and are prone to rollovers.

Utility tractors

Unless you are cultivating row crops, you'll need a utility tractor, which is designed to power devices with its PTO, and pull rear-mounted implements. Ground clearance is only 16" so they are not suitable for row-crops grown tall.

Gas vs. diesel

The smaller gas engine tractors are typically older and designed to operate on poor gasoline, gasohol, and even straight grain alcohol. They can be hand-cranked to start, and made for on-the-farm service instead of trained mechanics in a shop.

Diesel fuel is less expensive, and easier/safer to store than gasoline. The newer diesel tractors usually have power steering, hydraulic brakes, and implement lift. New models begin at Ø6,000, whereas an older gas model can be found for Ø3,500, including implements. If you plan on frequently (more than once a week) powering a water pump or generator from the PTO, then go with a diesel tractor for its longer engine life. If your tractor needs are fairly basic and infrequent, then a less expensive gas engine will do fine.

Ford 9N
Made for nearly two generations, with parts widely available and in stock. But for a few castings, an entirely new tractor could be assembled from new spare parts. Has an internal hydraulic implement lift.

China Diesel
They offer a 25hp @ 2000rpm tractor with 8 forward gears with a Category One 3-point hitch (now near-universal), for only Ø6,000 (was only Ø5,000 in 1995). Call 619-669-1995, email them at Cdi@chinadiesel.com, visit at www.chinadiesel.com. While I'm not at all fond of Chinese products, these are good tractors and generators for nearly half the cost.

POWER TOOLS

These will cut your work time by half or more. Essential for large construction projects. The list is endless.

Suppliers
Ultimate Home Shop   800-345-6342
Northern   800-533-5545

HAND TOOLS

Camp axes
Gerber makes very nice camp axes with synthetic handles, as does Glock and Colt.

Speznatz all-purpose survival tool

This 10" high-carbon steel blade will chop, shovel, saw, ax, pry, or ice pick. From Sovietski (Ø69; 800-442-0002).

Knives

Swiss Army knives (Wenger or Victorinox)

A must. While the knife blades are rather brittle, the cornucopia of tools make these knives indispensable. Do *not* buy the cheap copies; insist on the original Swiss brand.

folders

I like the half serrated edge blades for heavier materials. A handle clip is quite useful for pockets and inside waistbands.

The Spidercos are good, but way overpriced, and Japanese. The Gerber folders are a good bargain.

Avoid the cheap copies of the Spiderco, *unless* they are relegated for mere letter opening/box cutting (as are mine for the book business, and I need such a knife in every room).

Mad Dog SEAL A.T.A.K. (520-772-3021/3022fax)

The best utility knife made, *period.* Chosen in the famous 1992 Navy SEAL knife trials. Materials, design, and workmanship are all unsurpassed. Until the U.S. Navy nearly bankrupted him by their slow payments, Mad Dog's A.T.A.K. was the SEAL's sole-source justification knife by grueling trials (in which it beat out 31 competitors, including Buck, SOG, Gerber, etc.). When McClung couldn't be the Navy's "banker" *and* keep up with demand, the Navy in a snit went to SOG. (Many SEALs still order A.T.A.K.s out of their own pocket.)

Any knife is only as good as its materials, design, and workmanship. Mad Dog knives are superior in all three. Kevin uses only Starrett 496-01 high carbon tool steel (selectively hardened and tempered, and industrial hard-chromed), G11 glass epoxy composite handles, and Kydex® for sheaths. Their design is no B.S., no buckskin fringe, real-world stuff. The workmanship is second to none. Kevin is a true materials scientist and knifemaker, not some ex real-estate hairball who sells mass-produced Japanese stuff through saturation marketing as the "Ronald McDonald" of knives.

All of his knives and Kydex® holsters are backed by a no-sniveling lifetime guarantee. You can will them to your great-grandchildren, and the 23rd century paleontologist who digs them up will have quite a usable treasure.

If you want a Mad Dog knife, *hurry*. Get your order in ASAP so that you'll get it in 1999. And tell him Boston sent you.

Bolos

A great field chopping blade for many tasks.

Machetes

Since this will be wielded with great force, make sure the handle is very comfortable with no gaps or sharp ridges. I like a guard on my machete handle. Avoid the cheapy military machetes for a higher quality model.

Misc. cutting tools

Florian ratchet-style garden clippers

Got this tip from Christopher Nyerges. Great for cutting wood for handles, bows, drills, etc.

Pocket saws

These are vital for basic camping woodwork. The Buck folding saw is very good.

Miscellaneous

Wheelbarrow

This is easy to forget. Hugh Farnham in *Farnham's Freehold* made the same oversight, to his regret.

Suppliers

Harbor Freight Tools   800-423-2567
Cumberland General Store   www.cumberlandgeneral.com
Brookstone   800-
Grizzley   800-523-4777   www.grizzleyindustrial.com

BOOKS

The Home Machinist's Handbook, Doug Briney (from Grizzley)
The Pocket Reference (from any hardware store)

PEOPLE

FAMILY

Hermits will not make it through all by their little lonesome. The Lone Wolf will die by himself. We must join together to share our talents and strengths, and for sheer companionship. The family will be the most important social unit in 2000, followed then by neighborhoods and small communities.

If your family is not tight and loving *right now*, then get to work making it so. Talk through misunderstandings. Iron out your differences and grudges (most of them no doubt petty). If your family is irretrievably fractured, then you'd better get "adopted" by another family, real fast. You must have a fairly reliable support mechanism for the approaching storm.

Men

No more prissy, whining, "sensitive" males. You're supposed to be at the helm of your family ship, so start acting with responsibility. No "Captain Bligh" attitude is necessary; just love generously, and behave with calm and wise authority, and your family *will* respect and follow you.

So, you want to be the "King" of your castle? Treat your lady like your "Queen" and she'll gladly *let* you be the King. But, acting like "King" won't get you your crown. You must "serve" before you will be allowed to "rule."

Women

The majority of women, if honest, will admit that they'd rather their man take charge of important family matters.

Guys, this _doesn't_ mean that women want to be _ruled_. It only means that, assuming you're loving, wise, and responsible, most women are happy to ride "shotgun" while you "drive." Conversely, most men prefer to "drive."

Give your lady her space! Women are security minded, and since Y2K is going to derail our short-term future, the women will feel quite adrift (especially the city women). Give her that space she'll need to adjust and sort things out.

Babies

As long as you keep them out of stress-filled moments, they'll never know anything is wrong--and that's as it should be. The first 24 months are crucial for good nutrition, lots of love, and mental stimulation. Don't cheat your baby of this.

Children

Children, however, are _not_ babies and are amazingly perceptive of hidden turmoil. You will need their cooperation, obedience, help, and love--so tell them what they _need_ to know (but no more). Don't be _too_ serious, however. They're still children, so don't be too heavy. We all know that Dad who's too grave:

> _"Son, life is a sucking, swirling eddy of despair, punctuated by cruel moments of false hope, in an ever shrinking universe."_
> _"Gee, Dad, if I can't have a bicycle--just say so!"_
> -- comedian Bill Marr

Keep up a jolly spirit with your children, as we need them to "jump start" us _Olde Phartes_. Also, make sure that have the security of their favorite toys and Teddy bears.

Teenagers

Good luck here. Puberty's a bitch, for the whole family. Three things will make the difference: how _well_ you brought them up as young children, how _strong_ your family is, and how _strong_ any negative influences are (_e.g._, intensely toxic: music, movies, TV, friends, romances, etc.). Poorly brought up teenagers with a weak family structure will usually be lost to the world and its nastiness.

Even well brought up children with loving parents, but with strong negative influences have only a 50% chance, for the world is that pervasive.

To avoid losing your children at their teenage stage, you must bring them up well, you must provide a secure and loving family home for them, and you must limit the negative influences which seek to steal them from you. Succeed at all *three,* and your children will more *likely* grow up to make you proud, although there are sadly no guarantees.

There will be plenty of work to be done for Y2K. Keep your teenagers *busy.* Today, I see high-school kids at the mall spending hundreds of dollars on junk. Do not give your children an allowance; make them *work* for it! This can be "burned on the chip" only when they're young. They must feel a *causality* between work and money. If they get money for free now, they'll expect money to be free later (and vote Democrat as a result).

Couples

No even-numbered group can practice flawless democracy. At times, one half will have to go with the other half. A marriage or couple is made up of only two people, so they cannot always be in perfect agreement with each other.

Men, seek your lady's counsel frequently. Women often have an inherent intuition about many things, especially regarding people. If she *really* doesn't like or trust somebody, *listen to her.* If "something seems wrong," hear her out.

When you don't agree...

In 90% of matters requiring a couple's joint decision, a tight married couple will be in agreement. In the 10% where agreement is not easy, I would recommend the following:

When the matter *isn't* very important, but one of you feels strongly

When he feels *very* strongly about his view and she only mildly disagrees--*and* the matter is not terribly important--go his way. When she feels *very* strongly and he only mildly disagrees--*and* the matter is not terribly important--go her way.

When the matter *isn't* very important, and both opinions are mild

Try this: Assign a value to your position from 1 to 10 (10 being the highest). For example, you're planning a weekend vacation. If she feels an 8 about the beach, and he feels a 7 for the mountains, then go to the beach.

What's to keep them *both* from assigning a *10* to everything? Nothing, really, but such would create perpetual gridlock. Here's an idea. Have three cups and 100 pennies. Each gets 50¢ and puts them in their own cup. When a less-than-earth shattering issue arises in which both of you could go the other's way without bloodshed or tears or pouting, then each of you dips into your own penny jar for 1¢-10¢ as an expression of your position's personal value. Hold them in your fist. When you're both ready, plunk 'em down. Whoever puts down the more pennies "wins." Then, *both* of your pennies are placed in that *third* cup--"spent," so to speak. A finite and dwindling supply of pennies will keep your valuations honest. If you pay 9¢ for a position that really only meant 6¢ to you, you'll probably-win *that* round but you'll have shorted yourself by 3¢ overall, and you could be too "poor" to afford a *real* 9¢ position later. **Meaning, lying *will* catch up with you.** (Only *you* will know it, but sometimes that's *worse*.) In a tie round, go again.

At some point, one of you will be out of pennies and the other will still have a few and win. I haven't thought up a way to cheat at this. If Ed puts down 10¢ five times in a row, and Sally put down 7¢ those five times, Ed will certainly win the *first* five rounds, but then he will be broke. Sally will still have 15¢, **and the game is still played as long as *one* of you still has pennies.** Since a position's minimum value is 1¢, Sally could theoretically win the next *15* rounds if she placed a mere penny per position (although such would no doubt be *fibbing*). Once the last pennies are finally spent and the third cup is again full with the original 100 pennies, they are then divided up again.

Anyway, try this out and let me know if it works for you. As I said, use this tool only when the issue is fairly *trivial* and *neither* of you has leviathan opinions about it. You wouldn't use the Penny Tool to decide, for example, whether or not you have children, or move to Paraguay.

Here's another method by *Freedom Road* author Hough:

> My wife and I were both in the Navy so we brought one Navy tradition to the RV: a captain. Each week at midnight Saturday, the other person becomes skipper for a week. As such, they are the final authority on spending, where we go, and what's served for dinner. Even though we scarcely ever disagree on what to do, a rotating command gives each of us a chance to make all the important decisions. Not only does it eliminate arguments, it has provided many funny moments (Gee, I don't know what to do. I'm not paid to think this week.)

This is great advice, especially for couples dominated by a control freak guy. I have one friend in particular who needs to give his iron grip on life (and his family) a break.

When the matter *isn't* very important, and opinions are strong

Try to lovingly work it out (it gives you practice for the larger issues). If you're still gridlocked, then find an agreeable *third* option. *Avoid strife!* Your love and commitment is far more valuable than egos.

When the matter *is* important, and opinions are strong

Look for a third option, if possible. If there is no third option--*work it out.*

Men, if your lady is *adamantly* opposed to something, there is probably a *very* valid reason *why.* Find out. Try to keep your pride out of it. Get to the heart of her opposition. Adamant opposition based on good reason or solid intuition is *not* the same as sheer stubbornness or disrespect.

Ladies, if you've expressed your feelings clearly and he's understood them (though respectfully disagreed), then it is my general view that you should defer to his choice. Sometimes no third option is possible, and his mind is set. As I warned earlier, perfect democracy is impossible in a couple. Give him the room to take responsibility, even at the risk of him making an error. If he makes a poor choice and you were right, *don't rub it in.* The male ego is not fragile, though it *is* tender.

Elderly

"We don't respect our elderly!" No, we generally *don't,* and the easy half to *why* we don't is because the elderly have *accepted* their disrespect. Like Louise told Thelma, *"You get what you settle for."* They should have been knocking surly kids on the head with their canes years ago. Too late now.

The other (and more unpleasant) half to why is that too many of our elderly do not *deserve* the respect they insist is lacking. In America, respect is not correlated to age alone. This country is, and always *has* been, a *meritocracy*, and people are respected by their accomplishments, not by the number of candles on their birthday cake. (Yes, decades ago the elderly were given a large degree of automatic respect, but my point here is that America is not like Japan.) Less than 5% of Americans older than 65 are financially independent--meaning they own their homes, have a good income, and don't need SS or other government welfare and subsidies. I say to the elderly, respect comes from *respectability.*

The Eskimos have the right attitude. You can live as many years as you want to, provided that you pull your own weight. Become decrepit, and the Eskimos will lovingly cart you out to the tundra for a quiet, merciful death from hypothermia. The Eskimos understand that life is about *survival*, and that if somebody is *not* pulling their *own* weight, then others will have to--and there is no such surplus available for mere passengers. In the Arctic, *everybody's crew*.

Our American system, however, is much different. The national motto of our nursing homes should be *"We care...so you don't have to."* Too many of our elderly believe that society owes them a tax-paid security, simply because they're old. Let's be honest: I don't want to have to support *your* parents any more than you want to support *mine*.

Does this mean that I'm for Euthanasia? No, because it would likely lead to a *Logan's Run* or *Soylent Green* kind of society. But, there must be *some* alternative to elderly people existing in senility for 10+ years only to fill a bedpan.

The best *theoretical* option is for an individual to live in dignity and health for as long as possible, and then to gracefully "check themselves out" when they can no longer live in sufficient dignity and health. (What "sufficient" means should be up to the *individual,* as it would be monstrous for *others* to decide.)

This is what *I* will do. Luxurious and heartless musings of a young man? Possibly, but show me any *other* way that's as fair to everyone.

The elderly will achieve respect by: having lived wisely, independently, and honestly; by having provided for their old age; and by not overstaying their visit. The elderly *should* live by their *own* fortune, health, and wits--or, at the most, by those of their family and friends. *After that*, have the grace to just *go*. Resolve your earthly affairs, host a farewell dinner, speak tender good-byes to your loved ones, and *go*. (Oriental martial arts masters often *will* themselves to pass on in a deep sleep, which strikes me as quite elegant. I guess Americans will have to rely on some sort of pill.)

So, what to *do* about the elderly during Y2K? I make no systemic recommendations. I can't even make any personal ones, but to cherish and honor them while they are alive. If, however, an invalid elderly relative is proving to be a fatal hemorrhage of your family's time and assets, then you'll have some tough issues to ponder.

Y2K will put many folks between hawk and buzzard. Start thinking *now* about what might be *forced* on you later.

FRIENDS

In *Bulletproof Privacy*, I classified friends as "mere," "good," and "best." During Y2K, I think you'll have family and a few "best friends" and everybody else will be demoted to some *utility* class--meaning what can they *do* for you (buyer, seller, service, etc.).

Best friends (and family) are people who keep life liveable. Perhaps the hermits of my readers will disagree, but, to me, best friends make all the difference. As an author, I can live and write *anywhere* on the planet. *Where* I've chosen to ride out Y2K is largely because I've got some best friends here. **What's the *point* of living elsewhere?** Not many other areas would suit me as well, and even if they did, my best friends wouldn't be there and I'd miss them terribly. So, since my life is generally more flexible than theirs, I'm here with them.

Start planning together. Share your funds for those big ticket items (*e.g.*, large generators, fuel tanks, equipment, etc.). Design a mutual support system. (With a large enough group, you could have your own *de facto* town.)

NEIGHBORS

Help your neighbors. It does you no good to have weak neighbors, now or in 2000. Each household is like a cell in the community "organ" and you'll need as many healthy cells as possible. Help to get them aware and more self-reliant.

Like-minded neighbors are rare. Most won't share your Y2K concerns, your passion for the 2nd Amendment, your food storage, or your home-schooling beliefs. If you believe that such neighbors are forever opposite to your beliefs and life-style, then you should immediately begin to *downplay* these differences. Stop rubbing your life-style in their face.

STRANGERS

Most strangers you will encounter in some commercial setting. Keep things sweet and simple. Demand cash and let them take immediate delivery--*"Thank you, good day."*

"To trust, or not to trust?"

Of course you'll want to meet people and make new friends during Y2K. My rule from *Bulletproof Privacy* still stands:

Trust only when you *can*--and then, only when you *have* to.

Another maxim about fresh acquaintances I've taken to heart is:

A new broom sweeps clean.

Any used car will test drive around the block fine. It takes time and pressure to begin to see what people are *really* made of. Usually a *long* time and a *lot* of pressure. Don't be overly impressed with Month One performance. You'd be surprised how long the immature, conniving, or disturbed can hold out. Put new friends to a *long test* before they become good friends.

BUYERS & SELLERS

Keep things merely on a commercial level. Be known as an honest trader, and deal only with like kind. Divulge no more than necessary for the transaction. Make friends *slowly*.

GOVERNMENT OFFICIALS

Heh! These people will finally have to *work* for a living. I don't see much hope for government at the state and federal levels during Y2K. The long arm of Washington, D.C. will be lopped off on 1/1/2000, and it'll take years (if ever) to grow back. Mostly the same for the states. (Many of our states are larger than some *countries*, so they'll have problems national in scope.)

In 2000, local and county government will be all that's in *relevant* power. Know and love your county sheriff. If you don't have a good person in office, then install one, *quickly*.

INTRUDERS

You must be able to deal with intruders quickly and harshly, *else* word will get out that you're "easy." Scumbags are opportunists at heart, and *lazy* ones at that. In the Great Depression of the 1930s, farmers would stand guard on their porch and fire at would-be crop thieves. A bullet whizzing overhead does wonders for keeping thieves off your land. You want a reputation for an *unrelenting* and *merciless* defense of your home and family. You want people at large to gladly prefer jumping into a vat of broken glass than to try to steal from you.

Trust will be difficult enough to rebuild without these roaches about. Take the matter of Pest Control *very* seriously, else your area *will* be overrun with vermin.

THE DEAD

We will see a lot of dead people in 2000. Murders and suicides, primarily, then followed by justifiable homicides, then disease, then starvation. (I don't expect a true *famine* in America, but *many* people will lose a *lot* of weight.) You'll probably need to know how to bury or dispose of dead bodies. Loompanics has a book or two on this grisly subject.

SHARED-DOMICILE LIVING

Since our standard of living peaked in 1973 and has been in decline ever since, Americans have become accustomed to sharing domiciles. Houses have been divided into duplexes and quadplexes, young couples are buying mobiles as their "starter" home, children are moving back in with their parents, and parents are moving in with their children. Few families rattle around by themselves in very large homes anymore.

Y2K will force a lot more people to share accommodations. Space might be limited, and tensions are sure to be high. Communicate and plan matters thoroughly. The coming depression is more likely to be a marathon event (like the last one), so everyone will need to pace themselves.

"COMMUNE" LIVING

This is probably the best option for many folks. Several families on a 50+ acre piece of productive land could really do very well for themselves.

VILLAGE LIVING

This is probably the best option for survival. There will be enough diversity of talent to handle most needs, and everybody will already know each other. A good website on community Y2K preparedness is: www.millennia-bcs.com.

TOWN LIVING

If your city has over 20,000 people, then it will likely have similar problems as a much larger city. Any city over 100,000 people might as well have a million.

As I explained, good neighbors will be vital after 1/2000. Most city folks don't even *know* their neighbors, much less have a working friendship with them. If you will be remaining in the city during Y2K, then get to work *now* on creating relationships. FEMA (www.fema.gov) offers Community Emergency Response Team classes, which are highly recommended.

METROPOLIS LIVING

Don't bother to use the rest of this book's information and advice if you plan on remaining in L.A., etc. Rent *Escape From New York* to get an idea what's in store for large cities.

If your area is gang-infested, *get out!* If you think things are bad *now* when it's *already* their "turf"--just wait until the cops have evaporated by the first week of January.

SERVICES DURING Y2K

Heinlein's *Farnham's Freehold* concludes on page 255:

They lived through the missiles, they lived through the bombs, they lived through the fires, they lived through the epidemics...and they lived through the long period of disorders while civil government writhed like a snake with a broken back. They lived. They went on. Their sign reads:

FARNHAM'S FREEHOLD
TRADING POST & RESTAURANT BAR

American Vodka
Corn Liquor
Pure Spring Water
Grade "A" Milk
Corned Beef & Potatoes
Steak & Fried Potatoes
Butter & some days bread
Smoked Bear Meat
Jerked Quisling
(by the neck)
Crêpes Suzettes to order

!!!!Any BOOK Accepted as Cash!!!
DAY NURSERY
!!FREE KITTENS!!
Blacksmithing, Machine Shop, Sheet Metal Work--
You Supply the Metal
FARNHAM SCHOOL OF CONTRACT BRIDGE
Lessons by Arrangement
Social Evening Every Wednesday

WARNING!!!

Ring Bell. Wait. Advance with your Hands
Up. Stay on path, avoid mines. We lost three
customers last week. We can't afford to lose
YOU. No sales tax.

Hugh & Barbara Farnham & Family
Freeholders

(In case you're wondering what a "Quisling" is, it's a traitor who collaborates with an enemy power occupying his country, named after the fascist Vidkun Quisling who led a puppet regime during the Nazi Occupation of Norway. He was executed for treason in 1945.)

When the computers' clocks think it's 1900, it soon will be.
Any job classification that did not exist in 1945 will probably not have a lot of demand in 2001, with one exception: computer software programming.
-- Dr. Gary North; *Blind Man's Bluff in the Year 2000*

PEOPLE, INFORMATION, THINGS

My point in devoting a whole page to Farnham's sign is to illustrate the many and varied services likely to be required of us after 2000. The Age of Specialization will be over very soon, and most of us will need to become multi-taskers. You'd better become adept at something more than just Turkish history, *real quick*. It all boils down to People, Information, and Things. Here's a half page (15/4) from my *Bulletproof Privacy* (1997):

What *kind* of business?

Whatever we do for money is usually oriented towards:

People (sales, health care, hairstylist, therapy, etc.)
Information (computer programming, research, etc.)
Things (car mechanic, inventor, construction, etc.)

I recommend that you develop marketable skills in *each* of the three areas. For example, an individual competent in tutoring, bookkeeping, and locksmithing could grow a successful business *anywhere* in the country. There is safety in diversity.

Not everybody, however, can be such a generalist. If, for example, you are *not* a "people-person" or mechanically inclined, then only the Information field is open to you. So, if you are clearly attracted to a single area, try to develop several marketable skills *within* your area. Being a plumber is fine, but learn how to fix cars and computers, too.

Whatever it is, *do what you love doing*. That's the only *real* "secret" to success. If you're not doing--*right now*--what you'd *rather* be doing, then change it--*right now*. Probably 90% of people die with deep regret how their lives "went"--and they generally had no excuse for it but themselves. Live *your* life.

Be able to provide many items among (or at least within) the People/Information/Things model. (Also, since many of you might be forced into a career change, why not finally realize some postponed/submerged dreams at the same time?) The Farnhams offered *several* goods *and* services in *all* three:

People:	restaurant & bar, day nursery, social evenings
Information:	bridge lessons, and possibly used books
Things:	blacksmithing, machining, metal work, kittens

Below follows some ideas amongst each category. My list is only a guide and is by no means exhaustible.

PEOPLE

Medical
This will be one of the most important fields, because of its importance and scarce personnel.

Security
While millions of Americans own guns, very few have been trained to use them safely, properly, and effectively. Any graduate of a premiere shooting academy (*e.g.*, Thunder Ranch) will have valuable talent to sell or rent.

Hunting
A good hunter is born *and* made. Such people can hunt for a small group, who take care of his other needs.

Fishing
Same applies as in hunting.

Teaching and tutoring

Learning must increase greatly during Y2K, else the specialists will starve. A tutor is somebody who can help a student learn faster than he could by himself. As I tutored in college, I found out that mastery of the subject was not as important as being able to understand *how* the student was *not* understanding. Discern the student's obstacle, and the learning comes easily. If you can do this, then you'll have a marketable skill.

Cooking

Regular fine meals will be a luxury unless you've got a fine cook who loves the work. Food supplies are likely to be pretty basic, so the talents of a real chef will be put to task.

Entertainment

Comedians, actors, musicians, etc. will have regular (though meager) work during Y2K. Read *The Postman*.

Homemaking

A lost art is about to be rediscovered.

Cleaning, Janitorial

A vital service that children or handicapped can perform.

Sales

If your area has a decent economy, then good salesmen can be put to work.

Therapy

Lots of people will have lots of problems. If you are talented at helping folks talk things out, make yourself known.

Ministry

Spiritual needs will become acute, and they always have been during depressions, wars, natural disasters, etc. A good pastor will be one of the key figures in your community, and he will rely upon his flock's support.

Nursery, baby-sitting

The parents will have their hands quite full with work, so a common nursery in your neighbor will be a blessing.

INFORMATION

Bookkeeping, Accounting, and Filing

If you can handle the paperwork, you'll be set.

Computers

Home/business PCs will be used almost as much as before, as they can easily be powered by solar, etc.

Used books, library services, research

A good librarian/researcher will be very valuable during Y2K, as they were during the siege of Leningrad.

THINGS

Gunsmithing

The spare parts inventories will dry up and gunowners will need custom-made replacements of their broken and missing parts. They will want their 8x57 M98 bolt-actions rechambered to 8-06 so that they can use the more plentiful .30-06 brass. They will want their scoped bolt-action bore sighted since ammo cannot be wasted finding zeros. They will want their post-ban barrels threaded for pre-ban flash suppressors. Etc., etc., etc. Every community needs a competent gunsmith. Find one now or get to work training one.

Blacksmithing

This nearly lost art is about to be rediscovered. Plows, horseshoes, swords, etc. will be in high demand.

Welding

It'll be easier to fix things than to replace them. A good welder with a bit of artist in him can make/fix nearly anything.

Locksmithing

Lots of valuable stuff will be locked up, and knowing how to pick locks, copy keys, etc. will be very useful.

Construction

There will be much new construction going on in 2000. Real experience in this will be priceless.

Carpentry, plumbing, electrical, engine repair

Vital skills for Y2K.

General Handyman
Probably the best skill to have, besides medical.

Sewing
Old clothes will have to make do.

Gardening
This is as much an art as a science. A master gardener with heirloom seeds is vital for every neighborhood.

Well drilling
Call DeepRock (800-333-7762) for an info package.

Inventing
Necessity is the mother of invention, and creative, resourceful people will solve many problems and fill many needs.

Suppliers
The Foley-Belsaw Institute offers correspondence training courses in many of the above services. Other such schools can be found in *Popular Mechanics* and similar zines.

THE "IDEAL" BUSINESS

In his *"Uncle Eric" Talks About...Personal, Career & Financial Security* (from Bluestocking Press), my friend Richard Maybury lists the following excellent guidelines for selecting the "ideal" business:

❶ Call sell anywhere in the world.
❷ No employees--if you need it, contract for it.
❸ No accounts receivable.
❹ All variable costs, no fixed costs (no overhead).
❺ Fast payback (in one year or less to reduce risk).
❻ No inventory (e.g., programmers, consultants, writers).
❼ Easy exit. Business folding cost should be low to reduce risk.

This is *excellent* advice. The only trouble I see with purely service businesses (❻) is their inability to "clone" one's time. There are only 24 hours in a day, and we're awake for only 16-18 of them. The writing business is a wonderful cloner; write it *once,* sell it *forever.* The downside (if you publish your own work) is the rather expensive up-front press runs (to achieve low unit cost of the books).

The ideal *pre*-2000 business is probably selling self-produced videotapes. While the equipment is expensive, you could contract out the actual production. The tapes themselves can be duped in batches of only 30-100 and still have a low unit cost. Wait until orders total a few dozen tapes and *then* have them made. (This is why those TV cassette and CD offers require an 8 week delivery time. They have no inventory on hand.)

8 BASIC SKILLS & KNOWLEDGE

Richard Maybury continues with the following list of the vital skills and knowledge you and your family need:

❶ Austrian economics and Common Law.
❷ How to sell.
❸ Accounting (or bookkeeping)
❹ Uniform Commercial Code, especially contracts.
❺ Typing.
❻ How to use a computer.
❼ Opportunity costs.

I learned them by the time I was 19 years old, which explains my entrepreneurial life history.

Selling I first learned in Kindergarten when I packaged chocolate powder in folded *Big Chief* notebook paper to sell at recess for 3¢. (That is, until my dad started charging me for the Néstles Quik and the sudden increase in materials cost drove me out of business.) I next came up with the scheme of knocking on apartment doors asking for an egg, only to sell it next door for 5¢. (Folks had differing reactions when they later found out they had bought their neighbor's egg...) Later I collected, by farmers' permission, unharvested onions in fields and sold them door-to-door for 10¢. In junior high school, I sold silver and turquoise jewelry at the cheesy local mall from card tables. In high school, I often rented space at the flea market to hawk stuff that I'd bought the week before.

Typing I learned in the 8th grade (a most useful class!). By 18 y/o I "invented" basic double-entry **bookkeeping** on my own, to my later surprise that it had been around for only a hundred years. I tested out of **Contract Law** with a B+ in college, as I had already owned a successful business for several years before college. **Computers** I learned in high school and college.

Therefore, I had to chuckle at Maybury's fine list as I recalled each skill and when I first learned it. Trust me on this; you and your children *must* have and hone these skills and knowledge.

❖ 18

RAISING ANIMALS FOR FOOD

As I knew very little about raising livestock, this chapter was graciously written for me by an expert, author Amelia Porter. Her first book is due in spring 1999:

A Common Sense Approach to Farmstead Livestock

I now turn you over to the wit and expertise of Amelia Porter, and her copyrighted material (© 1998).

WHY LIVESTOCK?

Trying to keep an animal alive while you are trying to keep *yourself* alive may not seem like a winning idea, but there are many reasons why livestock makes sense during Y2K.

The limits to grains, beans, etc.

For one thing, you can't raise beans and rice in the city or suburbs. Sure, you can store them, but how long before you run out? Grains and beans are simply not a renewable commodity in many areas.

They are also *not* the best protein source. I know that vegetarians will disagree, but the fact is that your body can not utilize protein unless it is presented in a form that mimics your bodies absorption pattern. This is what is meant by the term "complete protein;" a protein which your body can use *as protein* not simply convert to fat. Grains and beans must be eaten together in the proper proportions to be usable protein foods, but there are three protein sources (and only three) that are regarded as high quality proteins, meaning those which the human body can utilize most effectively. These are meat, eggs, and milk--all animal products.

In addition to providing superior protein, meat, eggs, and milk counteract appetite fatigue (something we'll all probably become way too familiar with in the times ahead).

Non-food animal products

And if these weren't reason enough, animals also provide many products besides food, such as: leather, wool, oils, pelts, bone, down, and numerous obscure products, such as horn for buttons, gut for instrument strings, and lanolin for skin-care and water repellent needs.

Animals provide emotional comfort

When the whole world is falling apart, wouldn't it be nice to have a fuzzy, care-free friend? (**BTP Note:** This is historical fact. During the 1941-43 Nazi siege of Leningrad *kittens* were prized highly enough to fetch a price equivalent to nearly two pints of vodka.)

Pitfalls to livestock

If you live in the city or suburbs, animals may not be practical for you. I will discuss some livestock options that do well in these situations, but whether or not the animals can survive is not the entire problem. Neighbors and vagrants who see or hear you housing livestock will be that much more eager to target you for begging or looting. You'll need to weigh this risk against the benefits of livestock.

For most people, however, animals provide a perfect complement to other Y2K preparations, and should be given serious consideration.

When to Start?

If you have decided to be involved with livestock during Y2K, the time to get started is *now*. It may seem impractical to jump forward into animals when you have so many other things to learn and do, but remember that learning *any* new skill takes time, and learning animals is no different. You wouldn't decide on a career as a surgeon or a rocket scientist and expect to be proficient at it by tomorrow night, yet that is exactly the attitude most people take when acquiring animals. In reality, it takes time and practice to master the skills and instincts necessary to become a successful livestock keeper.

It also takes time to learn your preferences for equipment and methods. It would be a shame to purchase husbandry tools based on something you read or heard, and then discover during the Y2K collapse (when it was too late to easily change things) that you really hated your system and would get along much better with a different one. **It's best to do experiment now, while there's still time to revise methods and materials.**

In addition to equipment availability, you'll need to consider breeding stock availability. As I write this, good breeding stock is still easy to acquire. But give the masses a few months to wise up, and you may have a difficult time finding what you want, or being able to *afford* it when you *do* find it. Animals can only reproduce so fast, and with less than a year to go to Y2K, your breeding stock choices are pretty much limited to what is already on the ground or will be born spring 1999. With most livestock, it's too late to breed additional numbers for the increased Y2K demand. In the less-common heirloom breeds (such as those I will be recommending here) their scarcity makes the situation even more critical.

Lastly, many aspects of a smooth-running livestock program take time to develop. For example, if you are planning to raise worms under your rabbit cages to use as feed for chickens, you'll need to allow time for rabbit poop to accumulate and the beds to mature before they will support a large worm population. Likewise, if you want milk from a dairy goat, you must have her bred in autumn 1999. If you want chickens, you'll need to order your baby chicks in spring 1999, if not before. There are similar examples with every animal possibility, so get started before you miss the opportunity to make it work.

Butchering

If you have an emotional or spiritual problem with the idea of killing an animal, relax. You don't have to. Many animal products are provided without any pain or inconvenience to the animal whatsoever. These would include eggs, down, limited horn, wool, milk, manure, lanolin, and others.

If this is your stand, then I'd advise you to skip the rest of this section. But if butchering is required for the products you want, and you are willing to learn the skill, then read on.

Most people are not prepared for the strong emotions they will have to conquer to master butchering. Even a seasoned hunter can have a difficult time when the killing must be done up close and personal, as butchering of small livestock requires.

Shooting wild game at a distance is much different than holding a tame animal you have raised in your hands and deliberately breaking its neck. To read books on butchering and assume you will be able to manage this is unrealistic.

Don't wait until your survival depends on killing an animal you have grown attached to. Get a few chickens or rabbits and butcher them now. The first few are always the toughest, and it's best to get it over with on an animal you haven't lived with. *Never, ever, ever* **name or play with animals destined for butchering.** Always think of them only as future food. Personally, I like to keep in mind that the animal has had a good life during its short time with me, in contrast to animals raised commercially, who usually live in horrible conditions and are slaughtered cruelly. This helps me to feel better about my part in the process, and is also why I would rather butcher an animal myself than buy meat from the store.

As for technique, before you get completely discouraged by your first attempts, realize that butchering is one of those skills that improves with practice. Even a little chicken can take you an hour (or more) if you've never done it before. With practice, you can butcher a small animal in less than 5 minutes. It helps enormously to have an experienced person show you the ropes. Often you can find a willing farmer who will let you come and watch when he is butchering, or even try a few times yourself. Butchering is easy and efficient once you get the hang of it. Be patient with yourself and stick to it. And start now!

Meat Preservation

This subject is too extensive to cover in this chapter, but I did want to mention that there are *many* ways to safely preserve surplus meat. Your freezer may not be functional in the year 2000 and even canning might be impractical. But drying, salting, pickling, making jerky, and smoking are all reliable options. A smokehouse can be built easily and cheaply at home, and is one of the best conveniences for this necessity.

Fat does not need to be preserved as meat does. Once rendered into lard or oil, it will keep for months in a cool place. To render fat, simply heat it until the moisture is boiled off (temperature will raise to 255°) and the solids ("cracklings") turn brown and start to sink. Then it is ready, and can be strained through cheesecloth or some other filter, and then stored in a container.

What the veterans know

Before I move on to discussing the animals, there are some universal truths you'll need to know. These are the common-sense principles that every stockman understands down to his bones, but that newcomers often must learn the hard way. The problem is, you don't have time to learn them the hard way, so pay attention!

Rule ❶ If an animal *can* hurt itself, it *will.*

This is the oldest rule in the book. If there is one protruding nail in your corral, some animal is going to find it and it won't be just to cut his hide. It will be a slice across the eye, or a ripped udder, or some other serious injury. (And when it happens it will most likely happen to your *best* animal.) I can't stress enough how diligent you need to be at keeping potential hazards out of your livestock facilities. After awhile you will develop a sixth sense about this, but until you do, get rid of even inconsequential seeming possibilities.

Are you familiar with that orange bailing twine they tie hay with? One strand of it lying in a field doesn't seem like it would cause a problem, does it? Well, I can't count how many times I've seen one of those strings wrapped around a sheep or cow hoof so tightly it had broken the skin and was cutting circulation, or tangled in a duck or goose leg badly enough to drown it, or imbedded between the teeth of a horse, or eaten by a sheep or goat to risk a blocked intestine. I had a calf which almost lost a leg to the stuff. I'm not against orange bailing twine, I'm just using it as one example of many.

The point is, there is no hazard too outlandish for an animal to make something out of it, so go over your cages and pens with a fine-toothed comb, and do it regularly.

Rule ❷ If an animal *can* escape, it *will.*

This is the same basic principle as Rule ❶, just a different application. The potential for grief is sometimes less severe, but why risk it? Poorly constructed or maintained enclosures are a hassle you don't need. If you don't mind your animals wandering around, then open the gate and let them wander. But there are times when for their own safety or yours, you must be able to confine them. When this happens, make sure the area you are confining them to is able to do the job.

Consider, too, that animals are smart. If they find they can escape one time, they will be ever more determined to break out again and you will find yourself playing a one-step-ahead game of increasing difficulty. Construct the pen securely so they can't escape the first time, and you will teach them to respect fences, which makes your job that much easier.

Rule ❸   A bad animal costs as much as a good one.

There is no substitute for good breeding stock. The extra money you spend today will be forgotten long before the daily regret a poor animal causes will be outlived.

In the long run, a poor quality animal always costs you more. The reason may be health problems, poor production qualities, temperament flaws, lessened diversity, or some other failing, but whatever the factors, a poor animal will only provide a constant source of frustration and regret.

A good animal, however, just gets *better*. The babies it produces will carry its good traits forward to the benefit of your entire program, and that can make your endeavor simpler and more rewarding.

In addition to this, the feed, housing, and supplies needed to care for a given animal cost the same no matter what the quality of that animal is. Ditto for the hours of work involved in managing it. I know it isn't always within a person's means to get the best animal, but do *try*. Obtaining an excellent animal isn't always dependent upon money. If you do your homework well enough you will have established some valuable contacts who might be willing to help you out in this. You will also be able to recognize a good bargain when you see one, and can take advantage of it with confidence. Remember, the breeding stock you begin with today lays the groundwork for your success or failure tomorrow. Stack the deck in your favor by starting with the best animals you can find.

Rule ❹   Consider the animal's natural tendencies.

I can't tell you how many people miss this one. It would seem obvious that if dogs eat chickens, you shouldn't pen them together, but you would be amazed at how many people do just that in one form or another. Even zoos will sometimes keep one lone animal in a cage while their little information plaque clearly states that this animal always lives in a colony. How stressful do you think this is for the poor creature?

It is essential that you understand your animals' needs and natural tendencies, and arrange your facilities and management techniques accordingly. Try and consider how the animal would live in the wild. Ask yourself questions like:

What things make it feel threatened?
Does it live alone or in a group?
Is it active in the daytime or at night?
How much privacy does it like?
Who are its natural enemies?
What are its social habits?

The more you can accommodate your animals' natural tendencies, the happier and thus healthier your animals will be.

Rule ❺   Animal trading attracts dishonest people.

I won't delve too deeply in this one, because I think the rule says it all, but just be warned that for some reason, the animal industry attracts more than its share of unscrupulous people. Perhaps it's because animals are helpless against abuse that they attract abusive types, or perhaps some people just see an easy dollar, but whatever the reason, there are many, *many* people out there who will lie to you and take advantage of you. So, buyer beware!

Rule ❻   You are taking a life into your hands.

This is another one that should go without saying, but sometimes it doesn't. There is a grave responsibility that comes along with every animal you acquire. The Bible says *"A righteous man carefully considers the welfare of his animals."* Life is indisputably precious and you are accountable for the well-being of every animal in your charge. To take a life for food or other life-sustaining use is one thing, but to carelessly throw it away out of neglect or ignorance is something else entirely.

I have been appalled at how often I have seen people inflict cruel damage on some innocent creature simply because they did not care enough to do the preliminary research. They'll say it was *"an accident."* **Not so! An accident born of ignorance is *negligence.*** Hold life in high enough esteem that you act responsibly and knowledgeably with living creatures. Do your homework. To any *decent* person, there is no other option.

ANIMAL CHOICES FOR SURVIVAL

There are plenty of books on how to care for animals. As space in this book is limited, this chapter is simply a discussion on which animals make the most sense in the context of Y2K (both as food and beasts of burden), with a brief overview of what is required for maintaining each one.

Experience has taught me that people *will fail* if they don't consider the *human* element as carefully as they consider their animal selections. The most important contribution I can make in these few pages is to teach you how to *think* when it comes to considering your livestock options. In light of this, here are some factors which influenced my livestock picks. My motive is to get people thinking along the lines they will need to in order to succeed during Y2K.

Before you actually go out and purchase any of the animals mentioned, I would strongly encourage you to familiarize yourself with the details of husbandry by visiting those already successfully raising them, and by researching the subject yourself.

People are always asking me, *"If you could pick just one animal as the perfect homestead addition, which one would it be?"* Well, in the context of Y2K, I would answer that it's blatantly unrealistic to pick just *one*. There are as many different types and traits of animals as there are people and situations, and it's largely the *mix* that makes for success or failure--not the choice of animal. Certain geographical regions lend themselves better to certain types of animals, and even more importantly--people are always more apt to excel with animals that match their personal quirks, tastes, and lifestyles. It is foolishness to try and make a success story out of a person paired with an animal that they simply do not enjoy. Animals are time consuming, costly, and often aggravating. To presume you will be able to put up with those hardships for an animal you dislike--especially long term--is just setting yourself up for heartbreak. So my first piece of sagely advice here is:

Get something you *like!*

You'll need to experiment to discover which ones are a good fit for you. Often an animal we have romantic notions about will fall off of its pedestal once the novelty wears off, while an animal we may not have considered can turn out to be much more charming than we imagined. The only way to know for sure is with first-hand experience. Most of the books out there (all, I think!) are written by people who enjoy the creature they are writing about. Human nature, I guess. Unfortunately, this is *not* helpful when you are trying to get a realistic idea about actually living with said beast.

I would suggest visiting a few farms where people are raising the animals you want to consider and asking to walk through their daily routines with them. Make sure they understand this is for research only, so they will not glaze matters in an effort to sell you something. Then, ask a *lot* of questions. Especially, ask questions like:

> *"What things get on your nerves with this animal?"*
> *"What has been the most difficult challenge of this animal?"*
> *"How much effort did becoming proficient with this animal require?"*

And so on. Try to get them to share their personal stories and anecdotes, good and bad.

Farmers who have an assortment of animals are probably a better source for learning, since they have the benefit of being able to compare and contrast from personal experience. *Do* keep in mind that individual breeds and strains within a species can be vastly different in temperament and function, and this accounts for some of the conflicting information you will hear.

With that all said, we must get realistic and understand that within the context of finding something you like, it is also important to encourage your tastes toward animals that are best suited for your purpose.

In the context of Y2K, what matters is *survival*. You need an animal that can provide the *greatest benefit*--both in product quantity and diversity--with the *least amount* of feed and supplies. Ditto for the non-food animals (beasts of burden). Luxury animals, meaning those which are pleasant and/or pretty but don't excel in proliferation or diversity, or those which have an abundance of health or management needs, will not be considered as options for our purposes (though many are fine choices for the non crisis-oriented homestead).

Before I reveal my personal top three Y2K livestock selections, (and a brief discussion of several others) I'd like to present the factors I considered when choosing my top picks:

How much **food** must be stored for this animal, and would that food be easy to come by if I could not buy it?

Does it require any **supplies** which I may not be able to get during a survival crisis (such as shoes for horses)?

How many different **useful products** can it provide me with? (Very important when husbandry supplies are limited!)

Does it **reproduce** itself rapidly and without complications?

Are there non-conventional ways I can use it to increase its usefulness?

What is my margin for **success** with this animal if I am inexperienced? Similarly, how much **time and effort** are required to become proficient in managing it?

How difficult and/or expensive would it be to **house** this animal?

How **quiet** is this animal? (I'm thinking of looters here, and the potential need to maintain seclusion.)

Could this animal present a **danger** or **health threat** to my children?

In light of these considerations, my top three suggestions for Y2K production animals are: **geese, rabbits, and sheep.** A good dairy goat would be my fourth pick. Chickens, ducks and pigs are also excellent choices in certain parts of the country, but not as well suited for regions with a short growing season.

Production animals
Geese
Provide meat (food), eggs (food and offspring), down (bedding and insulation material) and fat (cooking oil, soaps, lotions, etc.). More importantly, being classified as a true grazing animal (the only one in the poultry world), they eat predominantly grass rather than grains and bugs, making them the best choice for no-cost/no storage feeding, especially in winter. They do not fly (so a 30" fence is sufficient for confinement), and they don't scatter (so they can be herded when necessary; no chase & catch scenarios). They also reproduce easily, and require no special tools for butchering (a simple hunting knife does the job).

A goose is not a goose--the different breeds
Yes, I know, you are all now protesting that geese are noisy, aggressive, and obnoxious and I must be out of my mind. But before you call for the men in white coats, let me explain a

little about goose breeds. There are two distinct classifications of geese: the Oriental breeds, and the European breeds.

The **Orientals** (comprising of African, Chinese, and others, usually with decorative knobs on their heads) are the most commonly known geese since they are the more "ornamental" visually. They are also the ones who are prone to hissing, honking, biting, chasing people, and other unseemly carrying-on.

The lesser known **European** breeds, however, (Embden, Toulouse, Sebastopol, Buff, Pilgrim, etc.--no knobs on their heads) are generally calm, quiet, mannerly, and very pleasant to work with. Unfortunately, when you cross the two types (by breeding an Oriental to a European) the aggressive tendencies of the Oriental are usually magnified in the offspring, thus producing...*the goose from hell!* As there seem to be more crossbreds than purebreds wandering around this world, the reputation geese have gotten is understandable. (Note: Feel free to cross Orientals or European's within their own group)

The point is, that choosing the right breed of goose, and the right strain (bloodline), can make all the difference. This precept is true for *all* animals, I think.

As far as bloodlines, I would steer you away from buying commercially-bred geese, which are the ones offered by local feed stores and discount mail-order companies. These are mass-produced, and often grossly inbred with no thought given to temperament. They are also generally smaller (less meat) than show-bred geese, which are bred with better muscle and bone structure, and tremendous consideration given to temperament (poultry must be calm & easy to handle in the show-ring, or the judge may score them down).

Any of the European breeds will do for Y2K purposes (with the exception of the Giant Dewlap breeds), but my personal choices would be Pilgrims and Sebastopols. Both are exceptionally quiet and easy to handle, and produce a good meat carcass.

Pilgrims: are gender apparent from birth, fast growing (10lbs. by 10 weeks of age), small enough for a family to eat in one day (no refrigeration required), and they are excellent natural parents.

Sebastopols: are hardy, reliable and gentle setters (means they will diligently incubate any egg you stick under them) and are the best natural parents of all domestic geese. If egg production is your main goal, however, you may want to consider a laying rather than setting strain, or one of the Oriental breeds (up to 100 eggs per year), or go with ducks or chickens.

Other advantages of geese
When handled as young, they make excellent pets for children as they are gentle and solicitous and can become quite attached to a particular person. (Remember, you won't be butchering your breeding pairs, just the goslings). Goose grease is one of the most advantageous fats produced by livestock. (Emu oil being the best, and pig lard coming in just after goose grease). In addition to down, geese provide feathers which are useful for making quill pens, toothpicks and other small items.

Disadvantages of geese
Geese are strong enough to be difficult to handle when you're trying to butcher them, and they can inflict a few bruises and cuts in the process if you haven't learned how to restrain them properly.

They don't reproduce as generously as chickens or ducks (nor provide as many eggs), so you need a fair sized group if they are to be your only meat source.

Geese have a troublesome habit of making ponds and streams wider and shallower by constantly scraping the banks into the deep part.

Their poop is copious and they leave it everywhere.

From time to time they do decide to make noise, usually around dawn and dusk during breeding season.

When young, they are quite vulnerable to predators.

Recommended stocking rate of geese
If you will be using geese as your primary protein food source, I would recommend keeping 20 to 30 breeding females for a family of four. Whether you'll need to keep as many males, or can breed a single male to several females, will depend on which breed you select and how you choose to contain them. You can find this information in a good goose manual, or ask the "flock manager" at a reputable poultry supply company.

If you will be using geese only to add variety to other protein food sources, subtract according to what percentage of your diet will be provided by the geese.

Recommended breeds
Pilgrims, Sebastopols, and American Buffs. With geese, (as will all poultry) the *strain* within the breed is equally

important. There is certainly nothing wrong with the more common breeds, such as Toulouse and Embden. I omit them simply because it's getting difficult to find good specimens among those breeds since they are predominantly commercially bred these days. Stay with show-bred geese if you can.

If noise is *not* a concern, the Oriental breeds do make good "guard" animals by providing a natural "alarm system" and they are good layers. Some people enjoy their aggressive temperaments (usually those without small children).

Butchering age of geese

Will depend on conditions and environment. Geese are normally butchered at about 10 weeks of age or more (depending on growth and desired weight of carcass), and are considered objectionable after 6 to 12 months of age, depending on personal taste preferences. The older the goose, the stronger the flavor and tougher the meat, with a noticeable difference beginning at about 6 months of age.

Breeding age of geese

Approximately 9 months. You can expect them to begin reproducing during the spring after their first winter. They have a useful breeding lifespan of 10+ years, and an overall lifespan of 10-25 years. (Note: This figure is low because mishaps normally shorten their potential lifespan of 50+ years).

Gestation / number of offspring per year

Varies according to breed and strain, but generally 4-12 goslings per nest. At a rate of two or more nests per season (requires ideal conditions and feed), geese normally will provide 10-30 goslings/year, but the total can be as high as fifty.

Basic needs of geese

To facilitate grazing, geese need quite a bit of room. For this reason, geese are generally left free to roam about the homestead. If you chose this approach, you will need to protect your garden from their curious bills.

Where larger predators are a problem, if they don't have an escape pond you might want to lock them up at night inside a little building of some sort. Small predators, like raccoons and skunks, however, present no problem for adult geese.

In winter, geese will generally dig through light snow to continue grazing, but in climates with heavy snow cover, some grain or good quality hay is necessary.

Geese do *not* require ponds or creeks or other bodies of water as commonly thought, but are happily diverted with a bucket of water tied to the fence (be sure to tie it securely or they'll tip it over in their zeal to play in it). They have no particular desire for shelter except the occasional shady spot in summer, windbreak in the winter, and some secluded place where they can build a nest. Most natural vegetation provides all this adequately.

They appreciate a bit of corn or other grain from time to time, but it is not necessary.

I'm really wracking my brain here, but I just can't come up with *any* goose necessities that require human interference. Case in point about why I picked them, I guess!

Tools and supplies required for geese

Leg bands or some other way of permanently marking them is not necessary, but can be very helpful in preventing excessive inbreeding, and recognizing who gets butchered.

Likewise, a small assortment of portable panels can be helpful when herding them into a confined area for banding or butchering (or to keep new additions from wandering). The only "tool" really necessary is a container to provide drinking water if you've no creek or pond.

Like all poultry, if you are raising them from birth without the mother, you will need some draft free, warm area to house them in when they are little, and plenty of starter (grain mix for baby birds). Be careful not to purchase medicated chick starter for your geese, as most of the antibiotics used on chickens are not safe for use in waterfowl.

Rabbits

Provide meat (food), pelts (clothing, material needs, fly fishing lures), fiber (Angora), and indisputably the most useful poop in the animal kingdom (fertilizer, worm habitat, pasture friendly). Another grazing animal, their food is plentiful year round (although their nutrient requirements are the greatest of any of my 3 picks), and they are easily housed and handled, quiet, take minimal space, and can be butchered without effort.

Rabbits are known for being one of nature's best production animals, and when managed correctly, will pop out babies at a staggering rate. At their normal rate of one litter (6 to 13 babies strong) every 6 to 8 weeks, a single doe can produce 90 offspring in a year (or more), and those babies will be mature enough to follow in this lucrative legacy at only 6 months of age.

If you kept all the female offspring from that one doe, letting them all breed as soon as they were able, and figured on an average of 5 female babies per litter, in just one year's time you could have a whopping 2,260 bunnies--all from starting with a single female! (This is, of course, not a plausible scenario because you would need housing for an awful lot of breeders along the way, and these figures are based on everything going perfectly, but it does give some idea of the rabbits potential for reproduction.)

Unlike most other homestead animals, rabbits are year-round breeders. They are also the most efficient meat-machines of all livestock, producing a white meat that is higher in protein and lower in fat, cholesterol, and calories than any other meat, including chicken and turkey. You can produce 6lbs. of rabbit meat on the feed it takes to produce 1lb. of beef, and a single breeding doe rabbit weighing just 10lbs. can *realistically* produce 250lbs. of meat in one year.

Rabbits are small enough to eat in one day (no refrigeration needed), extremely easy to butcher and skin, and can be managed by relatively young children. Their hides can be processed without heavy tanning (just soak in a brine mixture made from grocery store ingredients), and although too thin for most leather purposes, do provide some light warmth and a decent windbreak.

If you want the added diversity of a fiber animal, you will be impressed to know that a one Angora rabbit can produce as much as 4½lbs. of wool in a year. That's as much as a small sheep! Wool producing breeds, however, do not have as high a meat-producing capacity as the production breeds do.

Other advantages of rabbits

They make wonderful pets for children, and provide comfort for the soul. This last probably sounds a bit squishy, but remember that in times of physical or emotional upheaval, the human need for something warm and cuddly to hold on to increases, especially if that human is a child. Therefore, the comfort a rabbit can offer should not be disregarded.

Rabbit poop is the only type of animal waste that can be used *immediately* in the garden without burning the roots of your plants. All other manures must be carefully aged and composted, but the rabbit variety is born ready. This can be a real advantage when one considers the storage requirements for making large batches of compost, inherent problems with flies, etc. Rabbit poop is also used almost exclusively as habitat for raising certain varieties of worms, which are important for gardening purposes, fish bait, and food for chickens, pigs, and other animals. When I mention "pasture-friendliness," I am referring to manure which is supplied in convenient little pellets that do not adversely affect your pasture (causing die-off within the burn spot), or cause unsightly landscape additions that one must avoid stepping in.

(**BTP Note:** I have to interject the fabulous symmetry of combining an **earthworm** farm underneath your rabbitry. Worms turn manure into nitrogen-rich soil, and are worth several dollars/pound to gardeners and fishermen. Worm farming is probably even *less* labor intensive than even beekeeping or fish farming. O.K., I'm gonna brew beer, keep bees, farm fish, and grow earthworms--and run a used bookstore.)

Disadvantages of rabbits

Unfortunately, rabbits can be very discouraging if conditions are not just right for them. Many would-be rabbit raisers have given up because of constant problems with them either failing to produce or to nurture, or consistently destroying their young. Rabbits are very sensitive to drafts, heat, noise, intrusions, predators, stress, and other common day-to-day occurrences. All of these problems *can* be surmounted, but the would-be rabbit raiser needs to learn the tricks of the trade. It is best to start with proven breeding stock (under 1yr old), and to learn everything you possibly can from several experienced rabbit keepers before you try it yourself.

Rabbits have incisor teeth that grow constantly, and so they do tend to chew things up pretty radically. This must be considered when designing housing and cage furnishings, and can also present a real problem if some escape. (I know of one family whose escaped pet rabbits ate the foundation from under their house over time until they were forced to move!)

Like most livestock, rabbits need salt, which may become hard to obtain in a worldwide collapse. Rabbits very often aggravate dander allergies and asthma.

Rabbits have a relatively high nutrition requirement, and so are more challenging to feed than my other two choices, and are also the most labor-intensive livestock to maintain.

Setting up suitable rabbit facilities is affordable, but *must* be done correctly if you are going to succeed.

Recommended stocking rate of rabbits

If rabbits are going to be your primary protein food source, I would recommend keeping a dozen to a dozen and a half does and two or three bucks per family of four. This figure assumes you will be using one of the larger meat breeds, such as **New Zealand Whites**, so double that number for smaller breeds. If you will be using rabbits only to add variety to other protein food sources, subtract according to what percentage of your diet will be provided by the rabbits.

Recommended breeds of rabbits

Unfortunately, **New Zealand Whites** are still the only top production rabbit, with **Californians** coming in acceptably just behind. There is one breed, the **Altex**, which outperforms the NZ, but these are only kept by large commercial rabbitries, and so may be difficult to obtain.

All other breeds are decidedly less efficient and hardy, including the New Zealand Reds and Blacks. Favorable results can be had by breeding a Californian buck to a NZ doe, but don't keep the offspring for replacement breeding stock.

If you are after the pelts, you might want to toss a few **Rex** in for fun since they produce the most luxurious fur of all breeds (the shearling of the rabbit world). **Satins** also have uniquely lovely pelts, exhibiting a sheen that justifies their name. Both of these breeds are fine for eating, even though they do not possess the superior production qualities of the NZs and CALs.

For fiber, I would recommend the **Giant Angora** as the heaviest wool producer, or the **English Angora** if you prefer the child-sized model. Other Angora breeds require considerably more coat maintenance.

Butchering age of rabbits

Rabbits can be butchered at any age, but are normally butchered between 8 and 12 weeks for fryers, and 6 to 8 months for roasters. Older rabbits are just as tender and flavorful, but rabbits in excess of 16 weeks become more difficult to butcher.

Breeding age of rabbits

Can reproduce as early as 4 months, but it is normally recommended that you wait until they are 6-8 months old, when the doe is more fully developed. They have a useful breeding lifespan of around 3 years, and an overall lifespan of 7-10 years.

Gestation / number of offspring per year

The gestation period for most breeds is 30 days. Babies are normally weaned at 5-8 weeks. One doe will usually have 6 to 8 litters per year, consisting of an average of 6-10 babies, for a yearly total of 40 per doe. I'm being conservative here because of the difficulty inherent in keeping the kits alive. Rabbits are considered year-round breeders, although during the fall and winter they will need some additional light, warmth, and protein to cooperate in this.

Basic needs of rabbits

Rabbits require a draft-free but well ventilated area for their cages where the temperature can be kept mild in summer, and the rain/snow/sun kept out, while offering some privacy/solitude and protection from predators.

So as not to completely confound you with my "draft-free but well ventilated" comment, a draft is defined as a constant source of wind blowing directly on the rabbit. A rabbit housed in an outdoor pole-barn, who gets the occasional breeze or wind ruffling its fur is not considered to be in a "draft," although some shelter from strong winds is advisable. It is important to note that rabbits will start to die above 85°, so shade is essential as is knowledge of hot weather tricks (don't worry; there are many).

Food: Rabbits need water, salt, and high-nutrient roughage--either in the form of fresh veggies, grains and hay, or commercially prepared rabbit food. The commercial pellets are by far the best way to succeed with rabbits and already contain salt, but I mention the alternatives because of potential Y2K storage and availability problems. If you are using fresh stuffs and hay, remember that rabbits need a large percentage of legumes in their diet, such as alfalfa, clover, and other nitrogen-fixing cover crops, and that baby domestic rabbits (and certain adults) can not tolerate fresh greens (they must be dried first). Contrary to the teachings of children's literature, cabbage (and its relatives) is *not* a good food for rabbits.

Tools and supplies needed

At *least* 25 individual cages with a minimum of 24" x 36" of space (36" square is best) and drop-through flooring made from ½"x1" or ¾"x¾" mesh. The drop-through flooring is so important that I'm listing it as a necessity, although technically it is not. Cages are best constructed completely from 14 or 16 gauge wire mesh, not wood. When figuring the number of cages needed, bear in mind that in addition to your breeder cages, you will need sufficient "growing out" cages for the weaned babies until slaughtering time, and for your replacement breeding stock until they are mature.

You will also need climate-appropriate nest boxes for the does, some spill-proof, soak-proof, drown-proof way of dispensing water, a salt lick securely attached to each cage wall, a supply of wood or bone chunks to gnaw on, appropriate nippers (round cutting edge) for clipping overgrown teeth and claws, and tip proof containers for food. The metal J-feeders sold for this purpose are highly recommended, as they pay for themselves immediately by preventing the rabbits from throwing all their food out while cavorting around in their bowls, which is a leading rabbit pastime. Some method of marking individual rabbits (ear tags, tattoo kit) is also helpful, (as are J-Clips and pliers, and flush cutters for building and re-pairing cages), although certainly not required.

One note on water dispensing: Keep in mind that by play-ing with their water containers, animals often waste as much as they use. If you are storing water, this may be a concern. Rab-bits do fine with securely-attached water crocks, but if you want to go with hanging bottles, I would recommend *against* the ball-bearing type bottles sold in pet/discount stores. The tubes on such quickly wear out, leak, and can become clogged. The bet-ter way is a drinking valve used in commercial rabbitries. These are available already installed on 32oz. bottles from the Morton Jones company, and are top-fillable for refilling without removing from the cage. They're also less expensive.

Sheep

Provide meat (food), milk (soap/skincare/paint ingredi-ents, food, beverage), pelts & leather (clothing, material needs), wool (bedding, clothing, insulation), lanolin (water repellent, lotion, soap/skin care ingredient), body heat (you never know), very manageable & pasture friendly manure (fertilizer), and can also be used as beasts of burden, for pulling carts and packing small loads. (I once saw a man driving a full-sized carriage neatly pulled by 8 stout sheep--*really!* Best yet, the sheep were all wearing *hats.*)

At the mention of sheep, I'm sure some of you are shaking your heads vigorously at the prospect of having to shear them every year. But take note: nowhere else in livestock will you find a greater diversity among breeds than in sheep. So if shearing bothers you, take heart; there are breeds of sheep with no wool at all, only short hair. There are also breeds of sheep which shed their wool all by themselves (all at once, how convenient!), and those with wool so long it drags on the ground. There are sheep which produce dairy-quality milk in abundance, sheep which produce whole litters of lambs rather than singles or twins, sheep which breed year-round, and sheep which breed only during the fall. Some sheep produce fatty meat, while others produce meat that is naturally low in fat and cholesterol. There are stupid sheep, clever sheep, tiny sheep (60lbs.), and tremendous sheep (300lbs.), and the list goes on and on. With such mind-bending diversity available in this lone animal, there is undoubtedly a breed suited to your personal needs and preferences. You will need to do a bit of research to determine which breed is best for you.

One note of caution: If you have a lot of potential hazards on your property that can not be fixed, don't pick a stupid sheep. A primitive breed (Mouflon, Romanov, Jacobs, etc.) will be better able to figure their way out of a problem situation. Case in point: I've had many commercial meat breeds manage to get their heads irreversibly stuck in the fence mesh, but never have had a primitive breed do this. Something to consider.

I chose sheep in my picks, not only for their wonderful diversity and the plethora of useful products they supply, but because out of all the larger meat animals (goats, cattle, etc.), they are the easiest and safest to work with. Sheep are very predictable animals, and once you learn their particular idiosyncrasies you can make them do almost anything.

Contrary to popular belief, you do not need a collie or other herding dog in order to manage sheep. In fact, since the training of such dogs is a very specialized skill and a poor dog is a liability, I would recommend against it. The truth is, sheep are easily trained to come when called, and can be moved around very well by using only your voice and presence. This is better for the sheep, too, as it stresses them less. I personally keep about two hundred sheep during the summer months, and the entire herd comes *running* to me when I call. The effect is quite thrilling!

Other advantages of sheep

Another grazing animal, their food is simple to come by in any season. They are easily contained, easily handled, very quiet, gentle enough to be worked by older children, have minimal care requirements, and do not jump, climb, dig, tear, or chew their way out of pens like goats do. Sheep will also fatten on grass alone as they have about the lowest nutrition requirement of all ruminants (zoo animals excepted).

Disadvantages of sheep

When compared to other large meat animals, none. But in comparison with poultry and rabbits, sheep require a large fenced area (unless a human or a good livestock guard dog stays with them), and produce a quantity of meat which will require the use of a freezer, smoker, or processing in some manner to preserve the surplus.

They also require salt and loose minerals, which might be hard to obtain in a survival crisis. Sheep occasionally need to have their hooves trimmed, wool producing breeds need to be sheared or pulled (pulling is only an option for naturally shedding breeds), certain strains have intelligence problems which require you to check up on them semi-frequently, and certain breeds and strains have a tendency toward difficult births. (For goodness sake, stay away from these last two tendencies when selecting your Y2K stock!)

Rams (uncastrated males) in some breeds can be dangerous, depending on the way they were handled as babies (never make a pet out of a ram). All sheep are vulnerable to larger predators, such as mountain lions, coyotes, and stray dogs). Certain breeds of sheep panic easily presenting a potential hazard to children, and sheep do have a tendency to scatter under duress which can be aggravating as heck!

Lastly, the lanolin present in most breeds tends to make their sheepy smell stick to you long after you've finished handling them. This, however, is easily removed from your hands with baking soda, and washes out of clothing without difficulty.

Recommended stocking rate of sheep

If sheep are to be your primary protein source, and you have some manner of preserving surplus meat, I would recommend 3-6 ewes (depending on breed) and one ram (better yet, borrow the neighbor's ram) for a family of four. Because of their strong herding instincts, I would not recommend you keep less than three sheep in any case.

Recommended breeds of sheep

Too diverse to council you here! Personally, I have **Romanovs.** They are small, hardy, clever, early maturing, prettily marked, shed their wool, produce large litters year round, stay where you put them, are excellent mothers, have ample milk, and provide naturally lean, low cholesterol meat of superior flavor. When I want a bigger meat carcass I cross them with a **Dorset** ram. I also keep a few **Cottswold** crosses for wool. Selecting sheep is a very personal thing, and everyone will tell you their breed is the best. Have fun deciding!

Butchering age of sheep

Usually 5-8 months for lamb, and up to 2 years for Mutton. ("Mutton" refers to meat from a sheep over one year of age. It has a stronger flavor than lamb.) Considered objectionable by mutton haters at approximately 10 months, and by mutton lovers after about 3½ years.

Breeding age of sheep

Varies. Primitives and year round breeders generally will breed starting at around 4 months, while more conventional breeds will breed in the Autumn after their first winter (at around 7 months). Sheep have a useful breeding lifespan of 8 to 10 years, and an overall lifespan of about 12 years.

Gestation of sheep

5 months, give or take a few days, depending on breed.

Number of offspring per year of sheep

Varies greatly. There are seasonal breeders that produce only one lamb per year, and year-round breeders who produce 3 to 8 lambs per litter twice a year, and then there's everything in between. Most of the conventional breeds (Columbia, Suffolk, etc.) will produce 2 lambs per year, while the prolific breeds (Fins, Romanovs, etc.) normally produce 3-5 lambs per year, or 6-10 if they are bred twice, but most people don't do this because of the extra management requirements.

Basic needs of sheep

Sheep need grass or hay to eat, still water to drink, loose minerals (very important to stockpile before Y2K), access to shade in summer, and a windbreak in winter. They need to have you present when they are lambing (most breeds). It is nice to have some corn or other grain around for lactating ewes, although if your pasture is good and you breed late (Dec/Jan) this is not essential. Sheep are not too particular about shelter, but young lambs should have some place to get out of heavy rain, and newborns require a draft free area in colder months.

Sheep do not do well confined in a fully enclosed barn, as they need a lot of fresh air to avoid respiratory problems.

Tools and supplies needed for sheep

An assortment of small pens or portable panels are handy for moving and working sheep, and for providing newborns with a private place to get to know mom for the first few days.

It is a good idea to have some bottles and feeding tubes around for weak or excess lambs. Milk replacer that is specifically formulated for sheep is a wonderful and worthwhile convenience, but not essential as you can always milk your ewes or other dairy animals.

Sheep are great wasters of hay if it is not kept up off the ground, so you'll want some type of hay feeder. Do *not* use hay nets for this purpose, as they are like magnets to lambs with suicidal tendencies. You'll want some Iodine for the lambs navels, a castration device for your ram lambs (not essential, but makes management much simpler), some goat-style hoof trimmers.

If I could stockpile any medicine for sheep and other livestock, I would keep a supply of injectable penicillin (with corresponding needles), a supply of uterine boluses (to prevent infection from assisted births), some antibiotic salve, and a supply of Ivermectin injectable wormer.

Thick, soft rope also comes in very handy when working with sheep, as do lassos and shepherd crooks.

Animals worthy of mention

Although they did not make my top three, chickens, ducks, goats, and pigs deserve some discussion.

Chickens

In some areas of the country, chickens are ideal. They provide an abundance of eggs almost year-round, and also can be butchered for their meat. Like rabbits and small geese, their carcass is modest enough that refrigeration is not necessary, and if you must store water, chickens use less of it than any other livestock.

The reason I left them out was because they lack in product diversity, can be noisy (roosters), and because they have special requirements in winter, namely, supplemental feed and a sheltered roosting place (their feet and combs tend toward frostbite).

If you live in an area where grain is prevalent, or where the ground not freeze solid, chickens are an excellent choice. In other regions, grain would need to be stored to get them through the winter (they'll forage for bugs the rest of the year). Allowing some leeway for variations in breed and environment, flock of 12 layers (sufficient for a family of four) will require approximately 75lbs. of grain per month, so 3 large metal trash cans will hold enough for one winter for 12 birds.

Of course, grain is not the only winter feed suitable for chickens. If you'll have any leftover food scraps or butchering waste, the chickens will be delighted to give up some of their grain ration for it, and so your storage needs can be reduced accordingly. They'll especially enjoy picking every scrap of meat off any bones, and feeding them cooked eggshells gives them the vital calcium they need for laying. (**BTP Note:** Chickens do not much care for orange rinds or banana peels--assuming you'll *have* any fresh oranges and bananas during Y2K...)

Another trick for supplementing a chicken's diet is to stick a lightbulb or candle (protected inside wire mesh) in their pen at night to attract moths and other bugs. Flies drawn to cage manure will also serve the same purpose.

When it comes to creative feeding, chickens are comparable to pigs in that they can thrive on almost anything. In fact, studies have shown that a diet of 25% flies, 50% weeds, and 25% grain will allow them to produce as many eggs as chickens raised entirely on commercial feed.

You do not need a rooster to get eggs--hens will lay them either way, but you do need one if you are hoping to raise chicks for meat or replacement layers. Laying hens have a useful production life of only about 2-3 years. As for breeds, be aware that most high egg production breeds will not set (incubate eggs), and so you'll need a setting breed (*e.g.*, Cochin or Silkie) to hatch chicks, or put the eggs under your Sebastopol goose. For egg production only, I would recommend **Egyptian Fayoumis**, **Kraienkoppes**, or **Lakenvelders** for their superior foraging skills, disease resistance, & ability to avoid predators.

I would also add a few **Dorkings** to my flock for off-season eggs and meat. Unlike the more common dual-purpose breeds (Barred Rocks, RI Reds, etc.), Dorkings are exceptional 3-season foragers and are also reliable in raising and protecting their young. The more common chicken breeds *do* produce more eggs per year than others, but for a survival situation I gave the emphasis to disease resistance, longer lifespan, and heightened ability to forage feed.

You should be aware, that unlike ducks and geese, chickens from show lines are *not* the best choice for Y2K purposes. They are bred only for correct body and feather type, and the production qualities are often sacrificed. Rather, try to purchase chickens from a reputable breeder who focuses on breeding birds for high production in a homestead environment. The Kraienkoppes and Famous mentioned above are great for this because they have not been bred for anything *except* production and good survival skills.

Ducks

Like all waterfowl, ducks have the advantage of being exceptionally hardy in inclement weather. Winter ice and snow present no hardship to ducks or geese, which are both willing to forage for their food year-round. The disadvantage of ducks is that, like chickens, they need bugs or grain in their diet and so will require some supplemental food in winter in most climates. Their feed conversion ratio is not as efficient as chickens, so they do require more grain, but they can be excellent year-round egg producers (egg-bred ducks consistently outperform chickens). Ducks are usually wonderful natural parents, which also provide meat, fat, and limited down.

They do not roost at night like chickens, or herd like geese, so catching them can be a real adventure! Requiring them to walk inside an enclosed small pen to access their grain each day is effort well spent when it comes time to apprehend one. Like chickens, they can be trained to lay in a pre-determined nesting area, so no "egg hunts" are necessary.

For egg production, I recommend Khaki Campbells; for meat, Pekings; and the best all-around homestead ducks are the **Muscovies**, who are silent, wonderful setters, excellent meat birds, yet are still wild enough to have the uncivilized advantages.

Goats

There is no question that dairy goats are the best choice for milk. In nutrient quality and digestibility, goat milk is *far* superior to cow milk. Also, many people who are allergic to cow milk can drink goat milk without incident. Contrary to popular belief, if you choose the right breed and individual, goat milk flavor cannot be distinguished from cow milk flavor (don't taste the stuff sold at stores--yuk!).

In addition to providing abundant milk (normally a gallon per day), goats can be used for meat and hide, wet-nurses for other livestock, and are very willing beasts of burden. They have pasture-friendly poop, are normally gentle and easy to work with, and have the added perk of keeping your land clear of poison ivy, which goats consider delicious.

The disadvantages of goats are the noise, difficulty in confining them, necessity of having a (smelly) buck available to facilitate milk production, and, in certain breeds, their headstrong nature. Because they have high nutritional requirements and don't graze, they browse for leafy plants and legumes, so they will need grain during winter (most climates) and during lactation.

If you have decided to get a goat, I would steer you away from the popular (and admittedly darling) Nubian breed for Y2K purposes, because they are the most *noisy* breed and generally do not have a very long lactation cycle (period when milk is produced). Swiss breeds are known for their long lactation cycles, higher production (up to 2 gallons/day or more) and certain strains within this group can even be milked for several years without having to be re-bred (a definite advantage when buck's may be hard to find).

If you are wondering what you'd do with all that milk, consider that takes at least a gallon to make just a few ounces of cheese (which can be stored indefinitely), and milk is a basic ingredient for many household products, as well as an excellent food (curdled) for chickens, pigs, dogs, and other animals.

One last thought is that certain breeds of goat are also fiber animals. Admittedly, their milk production is not as great (approx. ½ gallon/day), but if you want diversity, consider that Mohair and Cashmere are both produced by goats.

Pigs

Pigs deserve a mention because they produce an abundance of usable fat (essential in a survival crisis), and they will eat almost *anything*. Classified as an omnivore, they can happily thrive on everything from leaves and roots to road kill, and will gracefully dispose of your butchering waste for you. (**BTP Note:** Read *Unintended Consequences* to appreciate their omnivore quality.) This ease in feeding is what has made them one of the more popular homestead animals.

In addition to fat and meat, pigs provide very tough and versatile hide, which can be made into strong rope and string. Pigs are exceptionally intelligent and can be trained as beasts of burden or guard animals.

Because pigs do not have sweat glands, they must regulate their body heat by keeping wet during hot weather by rolling in mud. This has led to the image of pigs as a dirty animal, when in truth they are very clean if given access to streams or other renewable sources of water.

The main disadvantage of pigs is that they are outrageously strong. So strong that they can root your fence posts right out of the ground. This attribute makes them very difficult to keep confined. While it's true that pigs do quite well raised free in a pasture where they can forage for their own food, their tendency to kill and eat small animals (such as your chickens and rabbits) and cause havoc in the garden make this method challenging for most homesteaders. To fence pigs either in or out of an area, requires *very* stout fencing that is solid all the way down to the ground. If they can get their mighty snouts underneath any part of it, they will pull it up and out of their way with a lack of effort that will astonish you. Electric fencing works tolerably well for pigs, but in a Y2K context might not be practical. Concrete block is also used frequently. Putting a ring through their nose will solve this problem, but will prevent them from foraging food.

The only other disadvantages are that they are difficult to restrain bodily (for vet care or butchering), can exchange illnesses with humans (*e.g.*, they can catch your cold, and visa versa--most animals can't), and if angered, they are capable of inflicting fatal injuries on adults as well as children and pets. Having said this, I need to add that this is rare, since pigs are decidedly amiable and affectionate creatures.

Amusing Anecdote: I once knew a lady who kept a cordial 900lb. hog as a house pet. One day she came home to find that her oversized refrigerator had been relocated to her dining room. Fortunately, it was not damaged, and thanks to a series of door bolts she had been forced to install when the creature was young, the contents were all accounted for.

(**BTP Note:** The European Wild Boar (*sus scrofa*) are incredibly hardy and prolific, have superior immune systems, and can handle cold weather with their wooly/bristle coats. For more info, send a SASE to the North American European Wild Boar Asso., POB 133, Lake Spring, Mo. 65532.)

Other animals

It is hard for an animal lover like me to completely omit *any* species, since each one has its own peculiar charms. As I have mercilessly written this, I have been squirming in my seat at the prospect of enthusiasts of the omitted animals feeling outraged or heartbroken that their dear ones were not included. In light of this...

Cattle

Cattle were ruled out because of their size, reproductive limitations, and handling challenges.

Cattle are available in most breeds as miniatures, and these do warrant strong consideration (meat, fat, hides, horn, bone, milk, beasts of burden). **Miniature cattle** (called "lesser cattle" in the Bible) are almost twice as efficient in regard to meat production as their full sized cousins, are docile, and though considerably more difficult to handle than sheep, provide the added benefit of being substantial beasts of burden while producing about as much milk as a dairy goat. Unfortunately, they carry a hefty price tag at present. If you decide to go with miniature cattle, I would recommend the **Kentshire** or **Dexter** breeds for their versatility. You might be interested to know that the Amish are presently buying up all the Kentshire miniature cattle.

Homestead dogs

I also did not discuss homestead dogs, but it stands to reason that if you are going to expend the effort of feeding a dog during Y2K, you should put a bit of thought into choosing one that is useful to you. The livestock guarding breeds make the most sense to me in this regard, because they keep predators at bay (both 2 legged and 4), are normally quiet (if raised so), and are large enough to be adequate beasts of burden, especially with respect to pulling carts. A small and cunning dog might also be useful as an alarm system, and game finder, as long as it generally remains quiet.

Emus

Emus were ruled out because of their expense, handling challenges, and because if you have a problem with them, there aren't a lot of knowledgeable people around who can give you advice. Emus, however, are worthy of a word or two because they appeal to Boston's eccentric tastes, and also because they provide a wealth of excellent products and unique advantages, and will manage on food scraps and garbage as readily as chickens and pigs will. They also adapt to every climate, needing only shade and a decent windbreak even in snowy weather, and can be raised successfully with limited space.

Predators are not a problem for emus, who often have the advantage in strength, speed, and fighting technique, and yet they are very tame and friendly toward humans if handled regularly. In fact, many people keep emus as pets.

Emus produce a red meat, similar to beef, that is 97% fat free and naturally low in cholesterol. Their oil (fat) has medicinal properties, and in addition to being a skin care favorite and transdermal carrier, is used as an effective treatment for muscle aches, arthritis, and skin rashes. They produce 35-50 three pound eggs per year, and fine quality hide that is strong and versatile. The white lab coat guys in Australia also use emu eyeballs for human cornea replacements, and emu hearts for human heart transplants, but I wouldn't suggest attempting this on your own during Y2K!

Another advantage to emus is their breeding habit. Emus make their nests and hatch young during the winter rather than in spring and summer like other poultry. This can be a wonderful plus if you're worried about having fresh winter food. It does, of course, require you to have feed or a forage area available for the youngsters (yes, they'll forage in winter), but if it's just the eggs you're after you will not be disappointed.

Emus are not normally butchered before 1½ years of age, so that their valuable fat layer will have time to deepen. You can butcher them as early as 10 months, however, if you are just after the meat.

The down side to emus is that they are expensive, can jump out of pens under 8' tall (though *rarely* will), and if not handled regularly, can be tricky (and dangerous) to capture and restrain. The most well-known drawback is actually the flip side of an advantage: the speed at which they reproduce. Emus are so prolific that the sheer quantity of food and offspring they provide often overwhelms people. Picture the reproductive ease of a rabbit in an animal whose babies grow to 120 lbs. See what I mean? A single pair of emus raising chicks will produce 1,500 to 2,000 pounds of meat in a year. And all those growing babies must be fed. This is something you'll need to plan for if you decide on emus.

Bees

Honey can be stored indefinitely, but even so, a few of you might want to consider keeping bees. They provide wax, bee-pollen, and royal jelly as well as honey, all of which are good barter items. In addition to these familiar products, bees provide: propolis, valuable for its antibacterial and fungicidal properties; bee venom, used in treating certain ailments (including arthritis); and high-protein larvae, which in Asian countries is considered a food delicacy.

Bees require only seasonal maintenance, and so are pretty carefree for most of the year. Many people don't realize, that as with livestock, bees have been selectively bred for man's purposes. The defensive nature of the wild bee has been reduced in commercial bee strains, who also have been cultivated to produce more honey and wax, and greater resistance to disease. Many of the bee races can be handled quite confidently without protective clothing by an experienced keeper. Bees are inexpensive to purchase and set up, and are easily managed. If you are frightened of bees, and want a strain without much sting in them, I would recommend starting with Carniolans, Italians or a similarly gentle race, depending on your climate.

ADAPTING LIVESTOCK TO THE CITY

I don't know if Boston has yet convinced you to sell everything and move to the country, but just in case some of you must stay put I figured I should mention a few methods for adapting livestock to the suburbs and city.

For this application, your choices are obviously going to be more limited, but keeping animals is still an option. The biggest hurdle here will be *water*. If you have a well, nearby creek, or some other source for water, you are in pretty good shape. If, however, you are relying on a *stored* water supply, you'll have to weigh the extra water use against the benefits provided by your animal/s.

Rabbits

Rabbits are an obvious choice for the city & suburbs, because of their high productivity, minimal space requirements, and absolute silence. However, rabbits consume an awful lot of water! Just one 10lb. rabbit will drink 16-32oz. of water a day, and that amount can more than *quadruple* for a nursing doe and her litter. So, if you must rely on stored water, I would recommend chickens as the best choice.

Chickens

Chickens can be kept in cages, just like rabbits, and they only drink about 8oz. of water per bird per day. Chickens do have the disadvantage of getting dust (dander) and feathers all over everything--so keep them well away from your living quarters, and in some well-ventilated area that can be disinfected occasionally.

City breeds

The breeds I recommended earlier, however, would *not* be suitable choices for the city or suburbs. Foraging skills and predator avoidance are both traits of very active, alert type birds, and such creatures do not handle confinement well. In contrast, city chickens need to be docile, calm, easily handled birds who don't care if they are caged. In other words, couch potato chickens.

For this application, feel free to choose between some of the more common commercial varieties available from feed stores and mail order catalogs. Most breed description blurbs will tell you if the bird takes confinement well.

I would also advise you to pay attention to the *strains* here (specific families within a breed) and try to find one known to have a long productive life-span. Most commercial chickens are bred to give very high production for a year or two and then quit altogether. For Y2K, it would be better to have a strain that will produce a few less eggs per year, but keep going for a long time. A knowledgeable flock manager or breeder is likely to have this information on his strains.

Most of the chicken breeds come in a bantam variety, which means miniature, and these are just as well-suited for your purposes as their full-sized cousins. Bantams yield less meat, of course, but 3 bantam eggs are equivalent to two regular sized eggs, and their flavor is excellent.

Whatever breed you choose, stay away from any chicken with the word "game" in its name. These are the old fighting cock breeds, and their obstinate and aggressive temperaments can make your life hell. The wild stories you hear about some rogue rooster attacking people and terrorizing pets, etc. are generally based on encounters with chickens from this breed group. Some of them are wonderfully sweet, of course, but why risk it? They also are not the best choice for production.

Game birds
While we're discussing poultry, I should add that small game birds such as quail and partridge are extremely prolific and are often raised in garages and basements. The eggs and carcasses are not as large, of course, but depending on your space limitations, their size might be an advantage.

Pigeons and doves also warrant some consideration, as they can be trained to forage their own food around the neighborhood, but come home to roost and raise young in your attic or some other convenient spot. They are not very prolific, however, raising only 2 to 4 young per nest.

Sheep
If water is not a concern and you would like to try sheep, you will be happy to know that there are several breeds of miniature sheep available, and they can be managed in about ½ the space required for the full sized varieties.

Two popular breeds are the **Brecknock Hill Cheviot** and the **Babydoll Southdown**. Shetland sheep, while not classified as true miniatures, are sometimes just as small as the miniatures and they have very charming personalities as well as fine and colorful wool. (Shetland sheep come in 11 different colors and some 30 patterns!)

Goats
Along this vein, I would recommend goats over sheep for city living, because the miniature breeds of goat come in smaller packages, and while providing similar meat and fiber benefits to sheep, have the added advantage (in certain breeds) of being true dairy animals. Goats also take better to solitary living when there are people around, whereas sheep tend to always need other sheep.

If you live in a completely urban area, you will be happy to learn that miniature goats can be housebroken, and get along quite well in apartments. Like their larger counterparts, they have no body odor (unless they are bucks) and do not shed nearly as much as dogs. They do tend to leave hoof-shaped bruises when they make a running jump onto your lap, so you may want to discourage this habit when they are young.

For milk production, I would recommend the Nigerian Dwarf goat, for fiber the Pygora, and for meat, the African Pygmy. Pygmy goats also give wonderful milk, but their teat structure makes them more difficult to milk than the Nigerians, who have slightly higher production.

One note of caution: If you are hoping to use miniature goats for meat, you will need nerves of steel. The babies are absolutely adorable and by the time they are butchering age they will have completely won you over. I've butchered hundreds of animals throughout my lifetime, but in truth I would *not* be able to bring myself to butcher a young miniature goat whom I had lived with. I think I'd starve first. A factor to consider.

Pigs

Since a few of you must be wondering about Pot-Bellied pigs as food animals, I should briefly note that the Pot-bellied pig is actually a lard-type beast and not a meat animal. Since fat is essential in a survival crisis, I would not rule them out, just be aware that you'll get more fat than meat out of them.

Most of the creatures being sold as true Pot-bellieds these days are actually crossbreeds which should, however, improve the meat quality considerably. For urban living applications, pigs are very easy to litterbox train, have little or no body odor (except boars), cannot get fleas (skin too thick), and do not shed.

They are generally very good around the house as long as you NEVER, EVER, EVEN ONCE *spoil* them. Pigs are extremely smart, and if you let them get the best of you even one time, they will be incorrigible for life. Even miniature pigs are extremely strong and are single-minded about food, so if you plan on keeping a house pig, plan also on bolting shut the door to your food storage area.

One final comment about pigs. They are capable of emitting a bloodcurdling wail that is literally louder than the Concorde at takeoff. This is no exaggeration, but documented *fact*. They generally will not do this unless they are pretty upset, but depending on how permissively you've raised them, they could get that upset over not being given a chocolate chip cookie. If you are hiding out in an urban area where such a noise could threaten your well being, you should either rule out pigs or take me very seriously when I say don't spoil them. A good-natured and well trained pig would most likely never raise such an ungodly racket, but you'll need to consider the possibility when making plans for slaughtering time. Also, because a pig's skin is very tough and the fat layer thick, they are difficult to kill without a gun.

BEASTS OF BURDEN

Horses

Most people I know are planning to keep a few horses in the event of transportation needs, but few are thinking about the potential need for animal power in more industrial applications. The fact is, that if this Y2K global meltdown lasts for any length of time, and liquid fuel is not available, we may all be using animal brawn to run small engines, dig wells, haul logs, pump water, harvest hay, and other heavy tasks too numerous to mention.

I hate to ruin a good fantasy here, but if things come down to that, your lovely horse is not going to be of much use to you. Light, riding-type horses do not have the strength or endurance necessary to perform extremely heavy tasks. In addition to this, their relatively fragile feet require regular attention, their spirited temperaments can be counter productive, they are prone to injuries, and their feed-to-energy ratio, pound for pound, is not terribly efficient. Yes, their magnificent presence, flowing manes, winning personalities, and soft noses will always keep them in high esteem, but for the biggest bang per buck, you really need to consider mules and oxen.

(Note: Draft horses are in a different class entirely, but because they are less durable than mules and oxen, and require more hoof maintenance, I won't be covering them here, even though they do a wonderful job of such work.)

On a side note, if your heart is really set on using a horse for transportation, I would guide you toward the native wild horses (Mustangs), because they are much hardier, sounder, more feed-efficient, have keener instincts, and their hooves do not require shoes or scheduled maintenance.

Mules

For those who don't know, a mule is the hybrid cross between a Jackass (male donkey) and a mare (female horse). Mules can be male or female, but all are sterile.

One of nature's most handy creations, mules are considerably stronger than horses, live longer, require proportionately less food, are less prone to health problems and injuries, and have hooves that need neither shoes nor trimming (provided you have some rocky areas around). They can be ridden like horses, driven as draft animals, are quiet, and are probably the best all around beast of burden to be had.

Mules tend to be expensive to buy and challenging to train, but the payoff makes these temporary inconveniences well worth the trouble. Contrary to popular belief, mules are not "stubborn," but simply possess a strong instinct of self-preservation. The truth is, mules can be extremely willing and dependable if handled properly, and are vastly loyal to their handlers. If you are inexperienced, purchase a mule that is already working well. Don't be too concerned about age as mules can have a realistic working life of over 30 years! They come in many sizes, but a larger mule (15 to 16 hands) is arguably the most versatile.

Oxen

Oxen are not for everyone. Their extreme size and strength make them impractical for most small farms, but if you have a lot of hay to mow, or can foresee a need for an excessive amount of power, it's hard to improve on an ox.

For those of you who don't know, an ox (also called a "bullock") is simply a mature domestic steer (castrated bull) that has been trained in a very specific manner from a tender age, usually since it was 4 to 6 months old. It does not receive the designation of "ox" until it is four years old.

Oxen can be created from any type of cattle, but there are certain breeds that lend themselves better to the application, with dairy breeds being the traditional favorite because of their meek and cooperative natures. Despite the awesome stature of an ox, they are generally very gentle and are careful not to injure their human friends. Surprisingly, they are also quite affectionate. The familiar knocking over people/fences type of behavior exhibited by most cattle is almost unheard of in oxen. In light of this, they are much safer to work around than many breeds of cattle.

Oxen are cloven-hoofed animals, and so don't require hoof care (except for the odd trim), have no particular needs for shelter (shade in summer, windbreak in winter), eat grass and hay, and need salt and minerals in their diet. Like mules, they have a better feed conversion ratio than horses, are extremely hardy and disease resistant, and are not prone to injury.

Technically, only castrated males can be called oxen, but there have been many very successful cases of cows (females) being trained to the yoke as well. If you need a beast of burden and are after milk but don't want goats, this idea might be worth consideration. The **American Milking Devon** breed was used extensively as oxen in the pioneer days, and as their name suggests, they are also a dairy breed useless for milk. A **Dexter** is another good choice, as are the **Florida Cracker**, **Pineywood**, and **Milking Shorthorn**.

One additional point about oxen, is that they can be fashioned from the miniature cattle breeds as well. So, if you like the idea of an ox but don't want the size or need as much strength, this approach might be and option for you.

Beasts of burden in conclusion

If all this draft animal stuff sounds overwhelming and you already miss your tractor just thinking about it, here are a few small points you might want to consider:

Draft animals cost less than mechanized equipment (both to purchase and to maintain); they don't depreciate as rapidly or break down as often.

They work well in hilly terrain that defies a tractor.

They can work soil that's wet enough to bog down machinery.

They let you work without human helpers, as a properly trained team will pull ahead on voice command while you gather firewood, etc.

Their slower pace gives you plenty of time to think, making you less likely to get hurt in an accident.

Nobody develops the rapport with a rototiller or tractor that a teamster inevitably has with his team.

So there you have it. Six good reasons why draft animals rule!

MISCELLANEOUS INFO
Mixing Your Own Medications

Many commonly-used livestock medications and preparations can be made cheaply by buying the key (active) ingredient and mixing up your own. For example, if you buy a jug of *Novalsan* disinfectant (a brand name of chlorhexadine diacetate, a key ingredient in many veterinary preparations), you can add a bit to liquid soap to make surgical scrub, to petroleum jelly to make a waterproof salve, to KY jelly to make water-soluble salve, to a spray bottle with water to make udder wash or disinfectant, etc., allowing you to get a lot of different products from just one bottle of *Novalsan*. This is not only a lot less costly, but if you run out of something, you can mix up more on the spot.

Active ingredients are generally expensive, but a little goes a long way. If the price shocks you, just add up what you would have to spend to buy all those products separately and you'll find you'd have to pay that much or more, anyway. By purchasing the active ingredient instead, you will only need to use a tiny portion of your investment to formulate many preparations, and so will have an ample supply left over well beyond the time when the assortment of individual products would have been used up.

Most key ingredients *do* sport an expiration date, but that is usually more of a marketing strategy than a fact. After all, if it's "dead" you'll go buy more, right? Some products do expire, of course, so you'll need to be savvy. Veterinarians usually have the correct bottom line on this, since they often find themselves in situations where the only bottle a person has of something "expired" 3 years ago. A willing vet or chemist can be your best source for actual expiration dates. The company who made the product would be your *worst* source, as their insurance requires them to stand behind the dates given. The reason I bring all this up, is that most key ingredients never expire, regardless of what the bottle says, which may help you to feel better about the initial cost.

Some of my favorite key ingredients for livestock are:

Novalsan Disinfectant, gentle on skin, no bad fumes. Used to make surgical scrub, various salves, udder wash, wound irrigation, germicidal hand soap, etc.

Chlorox Broadest spectrum disinfectant and wound cleanser. One advantage is that unlike *Novalsan, Chlorox* dissipates completely with exposure and so does not require rinsing. This quality makes it impractical for scrubs & salves, however. Use unscented name brand to avoid potential toxic fillers.

Ivermectin Very safe wormer for all animals, from canaries to cattle; anti lice/mite/mange/ked/fluke remedy, heartworm preventative in dogs, tick killer, ear mite cure, etc. Safe for use in most pregnant animals. Very broad spectrum.

Iodine The classic navel dip. Same uses as *Novalsan,* but not as broad a germicidal and is much cheaper.

Some other products that are handy to have in your livestock medicine chest are: hydrogen peroxide, Epsom salts, baking soda, Apple cider vinegar, Probiotic powder, Electrolyte powder, Vitamin B Complex (powder or injectable), Gerber (or similar) dry baby cereal (preferably oatmeal), and a few bags of Lactated Ringers with 5% dextrose (IV solution, same as they use for humans).

The Lactated Ringer is for hydrating animals who have lost fluids either through diarrhea or starvation (usually newborns). In animals that are too weak to swallow and/or digest, it can be injected just under the skin in several places until enough has been given, or injected directly into the abdominal cavity once you've learned how to do that. Either way allows quick absorption. Not many people know this trick, but it is the deciding edge in many cases, and one of the most valuable techniques I know. The baby cereal is indispensable for convalescent feeding of small animals or newborns, and the rest you can probably learn through your livestock books.

Syringes & Needles
It goes without saying that if you are going to be injecting things, you'll need appropriate sized syringes and needles.

These are available through the livestock supply companies. Watch the price there can be a dramatic range. If you are worried that your needle supply will run out so soon as to be impractical to store, keep in mind that most uses for hypodermics do not require a sterile needle. Yes, people usually use one since they are readily available, but that is primarily to prevent the spread of disease from one animal to another and to keep the medicine bottle from becoming contaminated. If you are using an injectable wormer or vitamin for example, you can pour a bit out into a cup and draw it into the needle from there. The needle can then be used on several animals just fine. The risk that one of the animals will be carrying some tissue-borne disease and will thus spread it to others is pretty slim in subcutaneous (just below the skin) injections.   Also, most needles and syringes can be boiled.

For most of the animals I've mentioned, a supply of #22 and #20 needles an inch or more long, and a supply of 3cc and 10cc syringes will work fine for everything. If you will be getting into the heavier animals, such as cattle, mules, or full-sized hogs, you will need to add some #16 or #18x2½ needles and bump the 10cc syringe up to a 12cc. Larger syringes, such as 60cc and 140cc are also good to have for tube feeding and wound irrigation purposes.

Although dependence on needles and syringes and modern medical products may not sound like the best idea for Y2K, storing just a smallish selection of these items will probably last you through the next 5 years, at least. Medicine is for animals that are sick. You will not be using these things as regular maintenance on your healthy animals. Buy a box of 100 syringes with needles, keep them for emergency use only, and you'll probably be set for a decade or so. Better yet, buy 2 boxes and use them for barter. Keep in mind that many of these products can save human lives, too! (**BTP Note:** Ragnar Benson's *Survivalist Medicine ToolBox* covers this. From Paladin.)

Medical Perks

While we're on the subject of medications, I would be remiss if I did not tell you about a few of the drug perks you'll be privy to through livestock supply vendors. Many prescription medications used in humans can be bought right over the counter from veterinary supply catalogs and cheaply, too!

Certain cancer medications come to mind, as do all the well known antibiotics. The large-animal catalogs usually only carry injectable antibiotics, but the small-animal vendors will carry the same encapsulated amoxycillin, penicillin, sulfa, terramycin, tetracycline, and other familiar antibiotics in the same milligram size your doctor gives you, for about one zillionth the price. (The bottles, usually 1000 capsules, will be labeled for aquarium use only. Of course, I am only suggesting you stick to the labeled application. I know there will be many hard-up tropical fish enthusiasts with an extreme need for massive quantities of antibiotics during the Y2K crisis, so I wanted to let them know about this wonderful source.)

Most antibiotics (not all) loose potency at the rate of 10% for every year exceeding the expiration date on the bottle. So if the need arises to medicate your fishtank many years into Y2K, remember to adjust the dosage accordingly.

Antibiotics may be in short supply during Y2K, but trained doctors perhaps will not be. If you are going to use one of your aquarium antibiotics on something other than an aquarium, it would be best to seek the advice of a doctor or veterinarian first (Yes, vet. They study primates [monkeys and *us*] in vet school.). Antibiotics can be very damaging if used incorrectly, so it is unwise to experiment with them if you do not know exactly how to determine when they are essential. Remember, these modern pharmaceuticals were brought to us by the same people who are selling chemotherapy as a happy option! Another point to mention, is that not all livestock medications are safe for use in humans, so do your homework before stocking up.

Disease Control

I feel obligated to add a few thoughts on this subject because the vast quantity of books out there frighten many people with their warnings about disinfecting everything from your cages and pens to your boots and feed tubs. What you need to realize, is that the majority of books available on livestock care were written with the large commercial operation in mind, or were *based on* the information found in such books.

In a homestead situation, you are keeping only a few animals and they are not subjected to the overcrowding, horribly filthy conditions, high turnover, and stresses associated with commercial establishments.

Because of this, you don't need to worry about disinfecting everything your animal comes into contact with any more than you would worry about disinfecting your children's hairbrush and schoolbooks every day, or spraying down the walls of their bedrooms. Diseases are out there, yes. And animals, like humans, are exposed to them every day. A healthy animal's immune system will keep them from getting sick from the germs commonly found in their surroundings, and through constant contact will actually build up a resistance to the illnesses caused by them if we don't interfere by disinfecting everything. The healthiest animals are the ones who get a natural exposure to frequently present germs and through this can build up their immunity.

There are, of course, exceptions. *Occasional* disinfecting of pens and cages is good management, and specific contagious ailments will sometimes get into your livestock that do need to be carefully controlled and prevented from spreading. These specifics will be addressed in the various livestock books, but for now, simply know that any area that is clean enough for you to be comfortable in is probably clean enough for your animals. If you keep the accumulated poop to a minimum, have fresh food, water, and dry bedding available in a roomy, well-ventilated area, you should not worry about constant disinfecting.

SUMMARY

Well, I hope this brief overview on Y2K livestock has at least given you some things to think about. When researching breeds, *do not* overlook the minor (traditional) breeds. These are the heirloom foundation stock that today's commercial production animals descended from. As a group, they are much more hardy, and are generally better suited to the needs of a small farm, especially a survival oriented one.

Today's industrial livestock breeds were carefully engineered to deliver the greatest possible production yield in a carefully controlled environment. (Yes, it's about money; what a surprise!) But in achieving this goal, the natural stamina and vigor had to be sacrificed (due to excessive inbreeding), and in many cases, were eventually lost. This is one reason why commercial farms of today keep all their animals on maintenance antibiotics. Many of the modern breeds have brittle bones, low fertility, birthing problems, poor maternal instincts, respiratory and organ weakness, poor foraging ability, and little resistance to diseases and parasites.

The traditional heirloom breeds, however, are the same as they were when our great-grandparents depended on them for life. This is why most savvy homesteaders are going back to the minor (foundational) breeds when choosing livestock. This just might be a good idea for you, too.

In case you are wondering, all of the breeds I recommended in this chapter are heirloom breeds.

For more information, consult the various livestock associations and clubs as well as a number of books, and talk to as many experienced stockman as you can. Since there are as many successful methods for keeping livestock as there are successful livestock keepers, it is best to gather an abundance of information and then pick and choose those techniques which are best suited to your life-style.

HELPFUL LIVESTOCK RESOURCES

Associations

American Livestock Breeds Conservancy (excellent!)
    P.O. Box 477, Pittsboro, NC. 27312 - (919) 542-5704
    www.albc-usa.org
American Rabbit Breeders Association
    P.O. Box 426, Bloomington, Ill. 61702 - (309) 664-7500
    www.members.aol.com/arbanet/arba/web/index.html
Society for the Preservation of Poultry Antiquities
    1878 230th St., Calamus, IA. 52729
International Miniature Cattle Breeders Association
    (253) 631-1191 / http://www.minicattle.com

Magazines and publications

Countryside & Small Stock Journal
    715-785-7414   www.countrysidemag.com
    Best homesteading zine. Very Y2K preparedness oriented.

Rural Heritage
931-268-0655   www.ruralheritage.com
Deals with using draft animals for power, and homesteading.
National Poultry News
P.O. Box 1647, Easley, SC. 29641
Alternative livestock & minor breeds as well as poultry.
Good source for related classifieds and reputable breeders.
Sheep Magazine
P.O. Box 10, Lake Mills, WI. 53551
Homey format with reader tips, etc. Good ad section.

Equipment & supplies
Jeffers Livestock Supply (wholesale prices)
1-800-JEFFERS (533-3377)
Best all around wholesale distributor. Great selection & prices.
Hoegger Supply (Home Dairy Supplies)   1-800-221-4628
Dair goat supplies. Cheese and soap making. Harnesses & carts.
Klubertanz Equipment Co. 1-800-237-3899
Supplies for rabbits & other small animals at wholesale prices.
Morton Jones Cages & Supplies 1-800-443-5769
Manufactures a top fill valve-system water bottle for rabbits that is
FAR superior to the common ball-bearing type. Wholesale prices.
Cutters Pheasant Supply 1-810-657-9450
Don't let the name fool you! Only source for wooden nest eggs, etc.
Smith Poultry & Game Bird Supply 1-913-879-2587
Good selection / wholesale prices.
Mann Lake Limited 1-800-233-6663
Beekeeping Supplies. Vast selection ÷ wholesale prices.
Premier Sheep Supply 1-800-282-6631
Hard-to-find & innovative products. Very helpful staff.

Reputable Poultry Suppliers
Note: All good breeders have limited stock. Associations
can recommend others.

Holderreads Waterfowl Preservation Center
Exceptional quality waterfowl (ducks & geese). Heirloom breeds.
Sand Hill Preservation Center (phone in residence, so prefers mail)
1878 230th St. Calamus, IA. 52729
Heirloom breeds of poultry. Glen breeds for optimum survival
instincts & good production. Very knowledgeable.

Recommended Books
Encyclopedia of Country Living, Carla Emery
> Excellent beginner instruction in homesteading skills.

A Common Sense Approach to Farmstead Livestock, Amelia Porter
> Husbandry made simple. Thoroughly covers each animal and is filled with insider tricks & secrets, many never before published. Due spring of 1999.

Basic Butchering of Livestock & Game, John J. Mettler, Jr.
> Best book on the subject. Includes section on meat preservation.

Keeping Livestock Healthy, N. Bruce Haynes
The Book of Geese, Dave Holderread
Raising the Home Duck Flock, Dave Holderread
Guide to Raising Chickens, Gail Damerow
Raising Rabbits the Modern Way, Bob Bennett
Raising Rabbits, Anne Kanable
Raising Fishworms with Rabbits, Howard "Lucky" Mays
Sheep Raiser's Manual, William K. Kruesi
Raising Sheep the Modern Way, Paula Simmons
How to Raise Rabbits & Chickens in Urban Areas, Javites & Perry
> Ecology Ctr, 2179 Allston Way, Berkley, CA. 94704

The New Complete Guide to Beekeeping, Roger Morse

Surf's up!
Urban Agriculture www.cityfarmer.org
> Focus on food self-sufficiency in the city. Includes city livestock.

Homesteader   www.homesteader.org
> Best all-around home base to surf from. Exhaustive resources

Special thanks to everyone who gave their time and expertise to me while researching this chapter. Draft animal "points to consider" borrowed from Gail Damerow's *Rural Heritage* article called *Horse Power vs. Horsepower*.

(BTP Note: This concludes Amelia Porter's excellent coverage. I thank her for such a valuable contribution to my book!)

RECREATION

Fun and excitement are inside the mind, not the amusement park.
-- Boston T. Party

I will *not* employ the word "amusement" in this chapter. To "muse" (from the Old French *muser*) is to *ponder* or *think*. When the "a" prefix is used with nouns or verbs, the *opposite* is meant. **Thus, to be "amused" means *not to think*.** It's my opinion that relaxing recreation needn't be *unthinking* activity (like watching TV). Yes, the mind needs a break just like the body, but that's what sleeping and dreaming are for. If I want to mentally relax and unwind, I read a good novel. (Everybody is different; perhaps my mind has a "fast idle.") Point of this being, don't make your recreation mindless. You will need your mind to be its sharpest in the months to come.

Also, try to combine your recreation with *productive* activities as much as possible. With imagination, this is easier than you might think. Chores could be transformed into fun races between individuals or teams, with a tantalizing prize (special food, a box of ammo, extra hot tub use, relief from other normal duties as "King" or "Queen" For A Day, etc.).

SOLITARY RECREATION

Reading
I have acquired from thrift stores, flea markets and garage sales enough mysteries, suspense thrillers, and spy novels to last me 10 or 15 years. Usually I paid only 10-50¢ apiece for them. After I've read them, they go into my swap/sell pile.

There's nothing more refreshing than to hole up in some quiet place with no people, and devour a good book.

Puzzles
I don't mean jig-saw puzzles, I mean word problems and brain teasers.

Art
Pencils, ink pens, crayons, etc. and butcher's paper can provide hours of quiet, refreshing entertainment. I look forward to mining what I think is my hidden talent for drawing.

Music
I'm also looking forward to polishing my piano playing, and learning the guitar. Playing music can provide hours of free and enjoyable entertainment alone.

GROUP RECREATION
This is necessary for group bonding and cohesion. All work and no play makes for a very dull group. Every group will see its own "activity director" emerge to get things going.

Songfests
Since about 10% of the population is musically inclined enough to play an instrument, there should be plenty of talent in your group. A couple of guitar players will make the evening.

Skits & Plays
This takes more artistic talent, but is great fun to pull off. Try to involve the entire group in the cast, if only for cameos.

Sports
Football, baseball, basketball, soccer, frisbee golf, etc. are all excellent team sports, though highly competitive. I've heard of a game from Israel whose object is to make the other players look good, but I don't know any more about it.

Games
You're limited only by imagination. There are thousands of games requiring little or no equipment.

Cards

Some of the most fun I had in 1998 was playing Spoons, B.S., and Indian Head poker with a dozen friends (whom I see only once a year). The fun of a group is more than the singular fun of the individuals. Synergy works for many things.

Board games

Remember, the fun is not in the game, but in the hidden fun brought *out* by the participants. Even tired old games like *Clue* or *Monopoly* are fun with the right people.

Trivial Pursuit

The most fun are the facetious "Hollywood Square" type of answers. Also, we dispense with the board and ask each person the entire card, keeping a running score.

Pictionary

This is great fun with a bunch of rowdy players.

Scavenger hunt

When I was 18 y/o, a local businessman and his wife were having several couples over for a weekend, and were wondering what they could all do for fun. I offered to set up a scavenger hunt encompassing the entire *county*. A buddy and I drove around and notated landmarks, colors of buildings, phone numbers on poster, and other visible trivia. One store was known to be the only supplier of some trinket, so buying one of them was on the list.

We then listed, in random order, sparse directions to each (on a clue basis). Thus, the trick to finding them all first was both *perception* (in deciphering the clues) and *organization* (of time and travel for maximum efficiency).

It was an all-day hunt. By late afternoon, the couples began to trickle in, all bubbly about what they'd found, the route they took, how they followed other couples until they were shaken loose, etc. One couple was particularly enterprising and figured out how to *telephone* one place for the same information which everybody else had driven for. They had a *great* time and talked about it all night! My buddy and I were a big hit (and we each made Ø200 plus some good tips and a big dinner).

Something like this could be arranged for your group, using landnav techniques, etc.

Movies

There are home movie projectors for sale that connect to your VCR and project on a large enough wall or screen for many people to view comfortably. Granted, such will take electricity, but probably only 300Wh, including the VCR.

Stock up on lots of comedies, as laughs will be sorely appreciated in the rough times ahead.

Group projects

The Amish barnraisings come to mind. Fifty people can accomplish more together in day than they can on their own in 50 days. It's sociologically vital that people put in effort in each other's needs. This is what builds communities.

Final comments

I would have loved to expound on this chapter more, but this book is already "over budget" as it is. Sorry.

❖ 20

IF I WERE A LOOTER

While you may not experience armed marauders, you *will* suffer from the plague of any catastrophe--looters. Although the law does not generally support the use of deadly force against criminals of property, I feel that looting goes *beyond* crimes of property because it foments a mob insanity, which, once energized and focussed can destroy whole cities.

There are certainly things you must "nip in the bud" at once, else you'll be overwhelmed later. Looting is one of them. Thus, it is my belief that bands of looters should be *shot.*

WHAT I'D LOOK FOR

Like packs of coyotes, looters will scout out the terrain. Show the first sign of a downed guard and they'll be on you. Therefore, the trick is not so much never to let down your guard, but to never *appear* as if you have.

Visible and audible signs of life, wealth, and productivity is what they'll be searching for, coupled with lax security.

Lax security

As Clint Smith of Thunder Ranch is fond of saying, *"If you look like food, you'll be eaten."* Larcenous hearts are inherently cowardly and lazy, which translates into coarse opportunism. Remain vigilant and armed, and you'll most likely *never* have a problem with them. Part of being vigilant and armed is *appearing* so. That's why rape prevention classes teach women to walk with purpose and confidence.

Noisy generators

When New York and Canada had that bad ice storm a couple of winters ago, knocking out power for weeks, thieves stole generators within minutes of their start up. Yours should be in a well-insulated shed and not heard beyond your property.

Shut down your generator before outsiders visit. What they don't know, *they don't know*. Keep it that way.

Solar panels and wind generators

While quiet, these are highly visible and highly evocative. Some cold, hungry, unbathed larceny-type seeing your fantastic array of solar modules will visualize your clean, warm, well-lit home--and it'll probably drive him to desperation. He could then enlist the help of a couple of dozen fellow hyenas to try to knock you out of your oasis.

Moral: Keep these devices hidden from general view.

High profile lighting

Light means civilization. In the video *Yanni Live At The Acropolis*, Yanni got all dreamy about an astronaut's claim that from space it was difficult to make out the national boundaries on earth. *"These lines exist only in our minds,"* Yanni oozed. (My girlfriend at the time quipped, *"Yeah, try to build your house on one."*) If you'd ever been to Eastern Europe before 1990, you know that this claim is B.S. *Anybody* could pick out the "GDR" and Poland from space because they were all dark compared to Germany and Austria. (Poland was the darkest country I've ever been to. Warsaw, the capital, had but *one* gas station open 24 hours. *Belgium,* on the other hand, has argon lamps on its entire *highway* system!) **Light means *civilization*.**

Remember, you're not "supposed" to have reliable power in early 2000. A well-lit "compound" when everybody else in your county is huddling over candles is a big "no-no." Blackout curtains should be installed in your windows.

For outside security, infrared spotlights and cameras are superior to normal floodlights (which can be easily seen for *miles*). IR light cannot be seen by humans or animals, and requires the use of an NVD. Wire the IR lights on a motion or heat sensor so they won't be on all night.

Hustle and bustle

Sounds of power tools, backhoes, generators, music, people, etc. or sights of vehicles coming and going and vigorous human activity all signal *prosperity*. No outsider should know of your prosperity. Keep your activity at a discreet level.

Your trash

If you take any garbage to the dump, be careful what you throw away. Packaging from freeze-dried food, AA batteries, ammo, etc. are unmistakable clues to your quality of life. Such "incriminating" evidence you should burn, if possible.

Also, any paperwork, plans, notes, etc., you should also burn so as not to provide any intelligence to outsiders.

KEEP YOUR MOUTH *SHUT!*

This is the simplest and most effective security measure, but the hardest for most people to do. You're "supposed" to be as down and out as the general populace, so don't brag about your micro-hydro power system which generates so much juice that you can even use your electric clothes dryer. Word of such *will* get around. Gossip will be a major pastime in 2000, so give them nothing about yourself to talk about.

HOW TO BUY PRIVATELY

Sensitive items such as food storage, generators, solar energy equipment, ammo, *American Survival Guide* magazines, etc. should *never* be delivered to your home. Use my general techniques in *Bulletproof Privacy* to set up alternate voice mail numbers, shipping addresses, and payment by money orders.

Draw up a list of anything which your neighbors might be envious of, or the government unhappy about--and buy these things discreetly. An ounce of prevention is worth....

HOW TO STOCKPILE PRIVATELY

So, where to stockpile all your stuff? *Not* in a storage unit (not after 11/99, that's for sure). Not in a city (too many eyes). The best place is on a farm or ranch with no visible neighbors.

Since most things should be kept cool and dry, I'd recommend an underground or buried storage container. These 6'x20' or 6'x40' refurbished heavy steel shipping containers are well coated/painted for corrosion resistance. They will easily take 3' of dirt on the roof, and have solid, lockable swinging rear doors. Tell the supplier that it's for company document storage, which sounds a *lot* more boring and forgettable than: root cellar, armory, desperado hideout, or bomb shelter.

Large fuel tanks should be placed out of general view, yet where they can be refilled without the driver be able to see much (or any) of your buildings.

Understand that much of Y2K preparedness will be expensive and/or offbeat, and will require the services of local contractors to deliver, install, service, etc. Underground tunnels, huge generators, and PV arrays will be, trust me, *the* topic of 1999 conversation down at the Rusty Udder--*so cool it!* Have a benign explanation for all this stuff. Also, notate the names and license plate numbers of your contractors just in case they exhibit a year 2000 criminal interest in your setup.

HOW TO LIVE PRIVATELY

If you'll spend some time thinking in "reverse" for what looters, snoops, and government officials will be looking for and lower your profile accordingly, then you shouldn't have much trouble. There will be plenty of more conspicuous targets than you. Live wisely and discreetly, and your standard of living will hardly be affected.

As "they" say, *"Living well is the best revenge."*

As I say, *"Live hidden, happy, and free."*

IF I WERE A GOVERNMENT OFFICIAL

The biggest "sin" of independent citizens is not to need governmental "services." Don't imagine that government (at any level) is going to be happy about your greenhouse, solar system, or home-schooled children. Government must insure the *equality of misery* in order to create its own "customers," so prepare for officialdom's (feeble) Y2K knock at your door.

Here's *how* they'll *try* to find you.

GOSSIPS & SNITCHES

Never underestimate the power of these worms. They are hard to squelch, as fear has a very short half life when you're not constantly around to reinforce it. The best tactic is to never let anybody know anything juicy or compromising about yourself. What they don't know, they can't *tell*.

CUSTOMER LISTS

You might have in your area some fairly enterprising "crats" or investigators who could actually conduct some decent field work. Assuming such is fairly likely, it's best to organize your affairs so that records lead *nowhere*.

The neat thing about databases is that they only "know" what they've been *told*. If, for example, you ordered your food storage under an assumed name, paid with a money order (bought with cash), had it shipped to Mail Boxes Etc. or the freight terminus in another town where you're not personally known, and took delivery discreetly--then your supplier's order records will offer nothing but *dead ends.* It will be as though the order disappeared into thin air. Trust me on this--I've done this for many years, and no picture can possibly be assembled of my buying history. You can do it, too.

Food

I wouldn't be at all surprised if the major suppliers of food storage (MREs, bulk grains, dehydrated, freeze-dried, etc.) will be contacted in 1999 or 2000 by state and federal officials for their list of food "hoarders."

Fuel

Officials will likely check the customer lists of local fuel depots for owners of large quantities of gasoline, diesel, kerosene, and propane.

A *very* sneaky approach

If such fuel is delivered directly to your property, then your address will unfortunately be on the receipt. This can be countered with a bit of ingenuity. On the day of deliver, simply swap your house number sign with a replica. The replica sign has a false number within the permutation gap on your road. For example, along your road are the numbers 72, 73, 77, and 80. Change your number from 73 to, say, 76, and call for service under an alias. The false 76 will be noted on the order form/receipt. The deliveryman finds your place without problem, and is paid in cash. Once he leaves, put the correct 73 back on. Any investigator will have only a list of addresses to go on, and if he can't find 76 later on he will probably skip it and go down to his next entry on his list.

I used this very technique years ago to have a phone line hooked up to an address that did not exist.

A reader of mine told me his secret for beating his frequent bogus speeding tickets. He would plead Not Guilty and request a trial. The court clerk would get the trial request form started, give it him to complete, and return to other business. Complete it he did. On the form was a space for the officer's badge number, already filled in by the clerk.. (As the state's only witness, he is required to appear for trial.) While she wasn't looking, he would change a digit of the badge number before filling out his portion of the form. The computer system would automatically send an appearance notice to the officer--the *wrong* officer. He shows up in court for a case he's not involved in, and my defendant reader demands a dismissal since he had to take off from work, *yaada, yaada, yaada*. It always worked! Maybe other defendants also figured this out since the clerk had the form itself changed to include the officer's name for cross referencing. Still, my enterprising reader had gotten rid of several tickets that way, and had already found another crack in the system to exploit. (I only recently heard of this, else I might have put in my 1996 book, *You & The Police!*)

Moral: Databases--including paper receipts--are *dumb*. They "know" only what they're told.

Ammo

Until 1986, ammo sellers had to notate the buyer's name and DL number with every purchase. As of 1998, you can order thousands of rounds of quality bargain ammo with no paper trail. While many mail-order suppliers insist on your faxing them a copy of your DL, a few do not. Besides, you can get almost the same deal at gun shows and pay cash for anonymity.

Three things will be coin of the realm in 2000: food, fuel, and ammo. Stock up on all three, and you'll be able to trade for *anything* you want. But stock up without leaving a paper trail.

Guns & Gear

As listed in *Boston on Guns & Courage*, in 24 states no record is kept of private sales (which are *intrastate* and thus unregulated by the feds). Gun shows, flea markets, and garage sales in those states are where you should buy your guns.

Out-of-state purchasing--*Cuidado!*

Under federal law, you must be a resident of that state to directly purchase any firearm (even one sold privately), else you'll fall under the *interstate* regulatory grasp of Title 18. If you get busted for buying out-of-state as a nonresident, claim that you live there, *and then clam up*. It's easy enough to later "prove" that you do (*i.e.*, a friend could say that you just moved in with him), and it's *worth* doing so in order to beat a *felony* rap based on violating some cheesy interstate commerce regulation.

(I *don't* advocate breaking crimes which are *mala in se*, or evil in themselves. However, *mala prohibitum*, or wrongs prohibited, are fair game in my book and I can think of better example of such than interstate commerce gun control regulations.)

To lessen the risk of being targeted, park your out-of-state car blocks away from the gun show (or go with a local friend), and remove all home state ID and papers from your person (which will deny the BATF agent of any presumptive evidence). Actually, have no ID at all. You do not have to carry ID with you in America (read my *You & The Police!* on this point). If you give the fed no way to unravel your claim of residency, then he cannot easily concoct probable cause for any arrest.

If asked, answer that you live there, and say/offer/explain/amplify nothing else. He'll ask for your full name, some ID, an address, how long you've lived there--*do not answer!* Reply that if he's got probable cause, then he's welcome to arrest you, and regardless of an arrest or not, you've got *nothing* to say without your attorney present. **Remember, you *cannot* be forced to give testimony about *yourself!*** The out-of-state bust is *very* rare, and you'll have to draw inordinate attention to yourself to become noticed at all, so don't get all paranoid over the out-of-state thing.

Your local gun club

Don't have your real name, address, and phone on their membership list. Sign up under an alias, if possible, or go as a guest. I used to send a local gun club their Ø50/year as an anonymous M.O. and get the gate combo from a friend.

Solar & Wind/Hydro Generators

Independent electricity means independent people. The nice suppliers who walked you through your fancy system shouldn't know your real name, phone number, or address. (Don't pay with check or credit card, no matter how convenient.)

Wood Stoves

You could *probably* get by without purchase discretion for a wood stove, but why take a chance?

Gold & Silver coins

Buy in coin shops with cash. You are not required to show ID (though some shops like to write you out a receipt with your name, whatever it is then...). Expect some future coercive buy-back program or confiscation scheme, so there should be no records of your precious metal purchases. Even the fact that you've bought "semi-numismatics" could make an agent figure you more likely to own future contraband bullion coins. (The same rationale also applies to registered gun owners and likely *unregistered* guns.)

Home-schooling suppliers/organizations

The government *loathes* the home-schooling movement. Over one million children are free from public school disassemblies of their minds, and it is *these* children who comprise our nation's hope, assuming it *has* any.

If you home-school, do so *without* the local school district *knowing* about it. Support the many excellent home-schooling organizations, but through an alias and mail-drop only.

Census 2000

Hah! Good luck! I expect the census taker drones to be dormant this go-around. If for some reason they are not and you actually get a visit, say that you are just house-sitting for a property management company and you know nothing about the owners or where they are. Do not fill out that invasive form.

THE FBI & Y2K

The feds are quite nervous over the prospect of losing control. Instead of orchestrating repairs which *could* have begun in 1989, they are speaking of shadowy individuals and groups:

With fewer than 500 days left before the year 2000, law enforcement officials are increasingly concerned that widespread paranoia about the millennium could touch off a clash between the government and domestic terrorists.

"I worry that every day something could happen somewhere," said Robert Blitzer, section chief of the FBI's domestic terrorism unit. Recent attacks on U.S. embassies in Africa have raised concerns about foreign terrorism, but the potential for violence from within the

United States has also increased. *At any given time, Blitzer said, his agents are working nearly 1,000 cases of potential domestic terrorist activity, a workload that has grown as the end of the century nears.*

The cases, spread around the country, range from a single threatening letter mailed to Washington to the unsolved theft this summer of 25 tons of ammonium nitrate from a West Virginia farm supply business. The amount of stolen fertilizer is more than 12 times the quantity used in the bombing of the federal building in Oklahoma City that killed 168 people in 1995.

Federal officials have begun working with local police agencies to investigate terrorist activity. "As we get closer to 2000, we'll probably see more people coming out of the woodwork," Blitzer said. "Some of these groups have an apocalyptic vision, and they may go violent." Many have already come out of the shadows. At a recent three-day "Preparedness Expo" in Puyallup, Wash., to plan for the coming clashes, conventioneers sold books and pamphlets, hawked camping equipment and survivalist gear and offered ammo cans, hunting knives and the newest rage: blowguns that fire poisoned darts. (**BTP Note:** I go to these shows, which are primarily attended by normal folks, black and white, who share a common desire to reduce their family's vulnerability to natural and man-made disasters. Blowguns are sold, but no poisoned darts--and neither are by any stretch of truth *"the newest rage."* Dan Chittock of Preparedness Shows deserves our thanks for hosting these unique forums for alternative information and goods on health, energy, finances, and many other areas.]

All of it, they say, represents the basic necessities for outlasting the millennium, when many who were here believe that the government will attack American citizens. Others predicted that 2000 will see the takeover of the United States by a "new world order" of foreign despots. Still others claimed that the projected Y2K, or Year 2000, computer meltdown is government hokum to enslave the people. All of them warned that it is time for a second revolution to take back America. (**BTP Note:** Absolutely false. The exhibitors and attendees having been trying to come up with peaceful ways to influence government. Such methods have been, for example, new political parties, radio, petitions, rallies, etc. While there is a revolutionary fervor to some people there, so what? We live under a regime several times as oppressive as the British in the 1770s, and such fervor is understandable, if not justified.)

To gauge the potential threat represented by these predictions, Blitzer said, the FBI early next year will launch an ambitious nationwide assessment to determine what to expect on, before and after Jan. 1, 2000. For authorities, the threat comes in two forms, and both are difficult to track.

The first lies behind closed doors, most likely from within some Christian compound like those that have arisen in areas around the

Ozarks, the desert Southwest and the Pacific Northwest. There, members practice guerrilla war tactics, are often heavily armed and study under the spell of self-styled prophets who warn of a coming fury with the federal government. (**BTP Note:** The same was said by the British press about the Massachusetts Militia of 1775.) *These fortresses are often impregnable to law enforcement undercover agents.* (**BTP Note:** Notice the evocative words: compound, guerrilla war tactics, heavily armed, fury, spell, fortresses, impregnable. Rent the movie *Wag The Dog* sometime for a behind the scenes look at the spin doctors.) *And the militancy of the rhetoric of such extremists becomes clear only when they choose to expose themselves to the outside world.*

David Koresh spoke with messianic fervor during the federal siege of his Branch Davidian compound near Waco, Texas, in 1993. Koresh preached to the outside world via radio hookups that the U.S. government was Satan loosed upon the land. (**BTP Note:** So what? The feds should have peacefully questioned Koresh during his morning jogs, or simply left the Davidians alone--thus not becoming part of a "self-fulfilled" prophecy of disaster. Buy a copy of the film *Waco: The Rules of Engagement*, which was nominated in 1998 for Best Documentary. From Laissez-Faire Books.)

Exactly two years after Koresh and scores of his followers died fiery deaths in a confrontation with federal agents, Richard Snell, a white supremacist, was executed in Arkansas for the murder of a police officer. Walking to the death chamber, he warned: "Look over your shoulder. Justice is coming!"

That same day, April 19, 1995, the federal building in Oklahoma City was destroyed in the worst terrorist attack ever on American soil. It was the work of Timothy McVeigh, who has become the model for the second form of threat the FBI fears, that of the solitary malcontent, or the small terrorist cell of two or three members unknown to federal officials.

"I worry most about the lone nut coming out and doing something," Blitzer said. "And right after that there are these really key groups that are planning and engaging, and they are very hard to penetrate."

-- *Fear 2000: Home-grown terrorism*, Richard A. Serrano, *Los Angeles Times*, 26 August 1998

I don't often interject my own comments so vigorously, but Serrano's article was quite atrocious. Ancient proverb: *Hear the other side.* Go to a Preparedness Expo (801-265-8828) near you and hear the other side.

These people are not McVeigh apologists. The Oklahoma City bombing(s) was/were horrible, but the public never learned the real truth behind it all. Several explosives experts (including retired Air Force Brigadier General Ben Partin of the "Star Wars" testing) publicly stated that an ANFO truck bomb could *not* have brought down the Murrah Building, and that such was caused by high-explosives placed directly on concrete pillars *inside* the building--a feat incapable by McVeigh and Nichols.

The FBI Crime Lab mishandled the case evidence so badly that it looked intentional.

In *The Secret Life of Bill Clinton*, Andreas Strassmeier all but admitted (from safety in his native Berlin) to author Ambrose Evans-Pritchard that he was an *agent provocateur* planted by the BATF in Elohim City to whip up anger and terrorist action against the Government. Oh, and *who* was John Doe #2 and *where* is he now?

Folks, the public truth is rarely the *whole* truth. These days it is perilous to take much a face value, so dig around. Don't believe me and don't believe "them." Check things out for yourself. **Follow the money, and always ask yourself, *'Who benefits by this event?"***

❖ 22

RULES FOR Y2K

Prepare for the *worst*-case scenario, *without* irreversibly degrading your life *if* the best occurs.

While you cannot have it both ways, you don't have to cut all ties, close your business and move to an island in the South Pacific, either. A hedge for the non-worst is recommended. Dave Saleh of Double Eagle Investments makes a good point, *"The more committed you are to a single scenario coming true, the less likely it will come to pass."*

This is probably good advice, yet I'd be happy to bet all on Y2K and it *not* come to pass. I have planned for the worst, but if the power and phones *do* stay up on 1/1/2000 and no depression occurs, then I'm still in the book business and can enjoy international travel.

Don't expect government to solve the problem.

The feds have known about Y2K since at least 1989, when the SSA did some 21st century calculations and their computers shut down. The globalists will use Y2K turmoil to usher in the centralized control of their New World Order.

Don't expect government to help you.

They might, but it's not likely. There will be too many people in more need of help than you, assuming government had the will and resources to do much of anything, anyway.

Plan as if you'll be totally on your *own*.

Because you quite likely will be. Local help, and very little of it, is about all you can reasonably expect. Far flung friends won't be able to do much for you, and local ones will be quite busy with their own problems. Plan on utter self-sufficiency, and any help that you do receive will be the gravy.

Cease to be a *creditor.*
2000 will be a technologically induced Jubilee. *"A debt is always paid, if not by the borrower, then by the lender."* There-fore, it's not just the borrowers who are in debt, but also the *lenders.* Offer great exit terms to your borrowers or sell the paper and get out of all accounts receivables.

Can you prove on *paper* that he owes it to you?
Get paper proof of SSA and pension streams. Get proof of court judgments, contracts, and accounts receivables.

Get a paper backup to all records.
School and college transcripts, medical/dental records, Eagle Scout award, work history, everything. Do not trust other peoples' computers to retain *your* vital records. Have a quality fireproof safe for these priceless records, and store them off-site from your home and business.

Get out of the stock market, now!
As of fall 1998, we've seen a half-dozen "sucker rallies" to pull in new money to replace the more savvy money which has bailed out. With many P/Es at 30 or 60 or infinity, there is no longer any connection between stock prices and true value. It's "tulipmania" all over again. Take your profits and run.

This is also part of no longer being a creditor. Stock mar-ket investors are lenders to millions of unknown debtors.

Cease to be a borrower.
Loans should be short-term, for a low-risk investment, with a specific source for repayment.
-- Mark Skousen, *High Finance on a Low Budget,* p.129

I've heard from many people that they plan to max out their credit cards in 1999 to pay for Y2K necessities (with little or no expectation of ever paying VISA *et al* back). There are two is-sues involved here: moral and financial. Is such an action something you can live with shamelessly, and what will you do if the Crash is not as bad as expected and VISA hounds you for payment? I can't advise you on either issue, but I will say that I do not expect to max out *my* cards for Y2K.

Start collecting cash.
There will be a rush for liquidity in 1999, and cash will be king. If there are cash withdrawal restrictions by summer 1999, then you'll wish you had been collecting cash.

Don't suddenly drain out your account (as such might look suspicious to the bank), but *do* begin to discreetly and steadily cash checks and make modest cash withdrawals.

Convert phantom assets to real assets.

Phantom assets will evaporate while real assets will likely save your life. Pretty simple math. Remember that the point of investments (phantom assets) is to be able to buy more real assets, so you'll have to exit phantom for real sometime, anyway. That time is now, before the rush for the door.

Buy the best. Pay cash. Take delivery.

-- Max Blumert, Camino Coin Co., Burlingame, California

Self explanatory. Most people buy crap on credit, and then replace it with *more* crap when it doesn't last, or have it repossessed when they can't make payments.

If you can't afford to buy it outright with cash, then you don't deserve it. Paying interest on non-income producing items is not only a financial sin, but will degrade your character by destroying your ability to delay gratification.

I always pay cash and take delivery, and I *usually* buy the best, except where I calculate that less-than-best will do--like this keyboard, for example. It was Ø20 less a Ø20 rebate. *Free* keyboard! Yeah, well it *just* went out on me after only 10 months and corrupted this chapter enough to require an hour of rebuilding. Fortunately, I could borrow a spare keyboard, but the event illustrated the wisdom of buying the best. No more "free" keyboards for this author.

We'll need communities, not hermits.
Begin to work together.

While survival planning is largely an individual/family effort, working through the Y2K aftermath must be a *community* effort else America will regress into a "Road Warrior" society. Civilization is a very fragile project which takes centuries to achieve, and we must not allow it all to implode. I'm already trying to imagine and plan for the recovery, and so should you.

Secure your shelter.

I would not want to rent in 2000 and thus be vulnerable to squirrelly landlords who might want to boot you out (lease or not) and move in family or friends. *Own* your domicile.

Have some means of independent electricity.

While it may be 1950 or 1920 for many months, it doesn't have to be *1850*. You'll need electricity for the rebuilding.

Have at least 9 months of food per person.

Gardens won't be producing until July at the earliest. Wild game will be quickly thinned out.

Be in a safe place with most of your assets in usable things & cash.

Self-explanatory. Or, would you rather be in a perilous big city with unreachable bank accounts and no usable things?

Decide your level of self-defense vigor.

Since this is not an issue for me, and I'm as egocentric as the next guy, such only dawned on me after I read it in the McKeevers' *Preparing For Emergencies*. The Amish, and the Quakers, some of the Mormons, and others--though living a healthy, basic life with ample food storage--may have philosophic qualms about defending themselves.

First of all, the correct Hebrew translation of *Thou shalt not kill* is *Thou shalt not murder*--a different matter entirely than justifiable homicide during self-defense. Numbers 35:16-29 explains the difference between killing and murder.

Secondly, Jesus in Luke 22:36 admonished his disciples to buy a sword, even if they had to sell their *coat* to afford it.

In the Garden of Gesthemene, Peter sliced off the Roman soldier's ear with his sword, a personal weapon *already* on Peter's person. Jesus's rebuke of *Those who live by the sword shall die by the sword* had to do with Peter's *substitution* of a weapon for his lack of faith and his lack of understanding of God's sacrificial plan for Jesus. If Jesus had disapproved of general sword *carrying* by His disciples, it then follows Peter would *not* have been allowed to be armed in the Garden.

Even the Talmud and the Koran plainly say that it's no sin to kill a killer, so I really can't see anybody can have, after must study and thought, a problem with self-defense.

But, this is a deeply personal issue, so resolve it yourself *in advance*, before it becomes an actual issue.

Arm yourself, your family, and your friends.

Ten men in 4,000 are *very* bad dudes, with *lots* of practice at mugging, raping, robbing, and murdering. Only *half* of them are in prison at any given time. The rest are out plying their nefarious trades. A Y2K crash will be springtime for them.

I've written not only a chapter in this book, but an entire book, *Boston on Guns & Courage* (which is said to be the best *one* book for most people).

Inventory. Set goals. Assess needs. Make plan.

Where are you now/what do you have? Where do you want to be. What do you need to get there? Make your plan with priorities clearly outlined. Start with A's, not C's.

Take no *counsel* of your fears.

This does not mean "do not be afraid." It means do not let fear organize and energize behavior to the contrary of your philosophy and previously decided actions. Know in advance what is the honorable and correct action, and *commit* yourself to seeing it *through*. Yes, you'll be afraid during Y2K, but fear is a normal and (within reason) healthy part of being human. Only psychopaths have no fear.

Do not be in jail or prison on 1/1/2000.

You certainly won't be able to make phone calls. You might not be able to get out. You might be caught in a riot. Your facility might get stormed by irate citizens, as it is already rumored that the security systems of prisons might automatically *open* doors during Y2K.

If incarcerated, try to be *out* by 12/31/1999. If free, try not be incarcerated into 2000.

Get right with your family and neighbors.

Learn to communicate and sincerely apologize. We will need each other like never before. 2000 will have little room for stupid egos and hypersensitivity. Get real and get honest.

Get right spiritually.

It has been my experience that a simple and honest faith in the Lord and the saving sacrifice of His son Jesus has been a bottomless well of peace and joy. While I am greatly concerned with worldly matters and loath today's wickedness, I try to put such into perspective by reminding myself that my Kingdom is not of this earth. I also often remind myself of Ephesians 6:12:

> *For we do not wrestle against flesh and blood, but against principalities, against powers, against the rulers of the darkness of this age, against spiritual hosts of wickedness in the heavenly places.*

Translation: America's problems do not *stem* from the UN, the Federal Reserve, the IMF, Janet Reno, or Bill Clinton. While these are certainly nasty organizations and people, such are merely *tools* of a spiritual evil being played out on Earth.

I'm not trying to overtly "witness" to my readers, as such is not the mission of the Boston T. Party books, but given the very rough times ahead, I would be grossly remiss not to at least mention my faith and the priceless value it has brought me. This is all I will say here on spiritual matters. Anyone having any questions or comments on such may write me.

It was said that there were no atheists in the foxholes of Bataan. I doubt there will be many during the next Depression, which will interrupt man's perennial attempt to exist in a spiritual vacuum as his own god.

Mankind never learns the *big* lessons.

❖ 23

GET GOING, *NOW!*

RELOCATE!

If you currently live in a city of over 100,000--*get out!* Dump your property on some Pollyanna and get to the country. If the Y2K debacle is only half as bad as most experts believe, then relocating will be the most important action you can take for your family's security. Sell any property within 50 miles of a major city before values plummet (and they will).

Where to go? Preferably to an area where friends and family are already situated, for stronger mutual support. Which in-laws, the husband's or the wife's? Whichever believe more strongly in the likelihood of a Y2K-induced collapse and are better prepared for it.

DATA & RECORDS

Data

Backup your data! It's cheap, yet invaluable. Data storage media have come way down in cost, and are affordable for all.

For example, the 100Mb ZIP drive is only Ø120, with replaceable disks only Ø16. (My first computer, an IBM 8088 clone had a whopping 80Mb hard drive.) One ZIP disk (the physical size of two stacked floppies) holds all of my books (six published, and five working) in their DTP software form, while a second holds all my business correspondence. File retrieval and storage operations are quite fast (though not as fast as a hard drive), yet each disk holds the data equivalent of nearly *70*

1.44Mb floppies. All sensitive files and data should be on a ZIP disk (and probably encrypted), keeping your computer's hard drive "squeaky clean" in case of theft, raid, etc. Hide the disk somewhere really clever between use.

Tape drive backups are now several *gigabytes* if you need that much storage.

Records

Get paper copies of all your records pertaining to yourself, your family, and your business. Do it *now*, as the real rush will begin in the spring of 1999 which will likely overwhelm the agencies. I'd have at least two copies; one for home, and another for storage offsite. Matthew Lesko's book *Info-Power III* explains exactly how to go about it. More important records would be from the following:

> Military service and V.A.
> Hospital
> Last seven years of federal and state tax returns
> Loan applications (bank, SBA, student, mortgage, etc.)
> Court documents
> Passport and applications
> Social Security Statement of Benefits Earned
> Business contracts, etc.
> Licenses (driver's, pilot's, professional, etc.)
> Patent, trademark, and copyright applications

FINANCES

Pay off your credit cards!

The interest fees are horrendous, and will hemorrhage your cash flow. Some folks plan to max out their cards on survival gear and let the card companies get stuck with the bill. VISA *et al* must have also already figured this out, and will after Christmas 1998 begin to really clamp down on this. Expect frozen or reduced credit limits, especially if you're a slow payer.

When your cards are paid off, cancel all but the bargain APR and fee cards. If you can't bear to cancel your unneeded cards, then place them in a jar of water and store in your freezer for a forced "cooling off" period.

Dump your paper investments

Remember, paper investments are not real, tangible assets. They come and they go, and they are more based on illusion and mass perception than solid fact. Y2K will be a reality check for this largely groundless bull market.

Stocks, bonds, and mutuals

They exist only while market confidence exists. Market confidence will vanish sometime in 1999. It's October 1998 right now, and already the market is "fibrillating" with monthly drops of 200-500+ points. I expect the bottom to fall out in the spring of 1999--fall at the latest. Don't get caught with the Old Maid. If you've already realized a paper profit, then take that profit and run! **You can never lose money taking a profit.** As John D. Rockefeller once quipped, *"Only suckers hold out for top dollar."* **Get out, *now*!**

Bank accounts

Cash in the bank is far better than paper equity in the market, but I'd still yank your funds while cash withdrawals are still allowed.

If you withdraw Ø3,000 or more in a single day (or slightly less than Ø3,000 on several consecutive days), you will be required to fill out an IRS form. The bank teller (or manager) will likely inquire the reason for cleaning out your account, so respond that your financial investors have convinced you that your local banks are inherently unstable.

Empty out your retirement accounts

"Oh, but I'll have to pay an early withdrawal 10% penalty!" Remember that these congressionally created 401ks, Keoghs, and IRAs *always* had *some* kind of "exit fee" built in.

Many folks are planning not to clean out these accounts until 1999, thus avoiding taxation until the following year when the IRS is expected to have cratered. **Don't you think the feds have *realized* this?** Expect them to head this off by new regulations in 1999 which limit (or prohibit) withdrawals, or which make withdrawals immediately tax-withholdable by the fiduciary. In short, the feds simply cannot allow the panicky public of 1999 to suddenly empty these corrals of capital.

I'd get out by 1998, or spring 1999 at the very latest. The door will slam shut once the market crashes, if not before. Yeah, you'll pay a penalty to cash out early, but would you rather have XX% in 1998, or 0% in 1999? Should you quit your doomed career early in order to cash out your 401k in 1999? I'd seriously consider it if I were you.

Start demanding cash payment

Get your customers more accustomed to paying in cash. Offer a 10-20% discount for cash--*that'll* get their attention. You'll need the pre-2000 cash liquidity to buy sensitive (or outlawed) goods. After 1/1/2000, cash will be king (until gold and silver coins begin to circulate). Start stockpiling cash.

MAXIMIZE YOUR SPENDING CAPITAL

You must *immediately* begin to change your spending habits. Quit shopping by yourself for single quantities. Quit paying retail and sales tax--that's for suckers.

Start demanding cash discounts!

If there is no issue of warranty or return, then I crack a tough nut by saying, *"Here's cash for a 20% discount, and no receipt."* If refused, I say, *"See? It's easy to lose business!"*

By paying cash, you should be able to get at least a 20% discount from the smaller entrepreneurs. No discount--no business. That's the rule. Anybody too wimpy to take cash off the books or too stupid to appreciate "under the table" receipts doesn't deserve your patronage. Find a guerrilla capitalist who understands Life. Cash oriented folks must support each other.

Stop paying retail!

Paying retail is throwing away 40+% of your buying power. Buy through your business, or through somebody else's. Since I'm in the book business, I get books for 40-55% off retail, and I pass this along to my friends. They, in turn, allow me to buy through *their* company wholesale discounts.

Start a retail business if you have to in order to get a state resale number and sales tax exemption. At year's end, you, *gosh!*, didn't make a profit since sales were lousy--or you sold to out-of-state customers who were tax exempt. Darn it.

Stop paying sales tax!

Sales tax is against my "personal religion" and I avoid it whenever possible. You can co-op purchase articles through your church or other charitable entity, or you can buy through a business with a sales tax exemption.

Tell the clerk, *before* s/he enters the first item, that this is a tax exempt purchase. There will sometimes be a form or simple line registry to fill out. Larger local companies will already have any forms already on file, and who's to say that you're not with ABC Construction buying something with petty cash? (If the store has given ABC their own number, remember it for future use in case you ever need it during a sticky transaction.)

Half the time this will be the clerk's first tax exempt transaction, and a manager will be called. (Once you've found a friendly clerk who handles it without hassle, always use them.) Sometimes you'll need to produce proof of your entity's status, but this isn't difficult to procure. Any state form, already typed in and signed, claiming federal 501c(3) status will work. Occasionally, your ID# is also notated with the purchase record, so be careful if your paperwork isn't up to snuff.

Pay with cash, smile, and leave. You've just saved 7-12% that the state never deserved, anyway.

Mail-order

Even with the shipping costs, mail-order is often less expensive than buying locally.

Also, out-of-state mail order purchases are (so far) exempt from sales tax, but this won't last for much longer. Once we go to a mail-order tax or a national sales tax, you'll need to have some kind of exemption (business or charitable).

Co-ops & Sam's Clubs

Have your business or charitable organization join to avoid the sales tax. This accomplished, shop away! Tires, batteries, bulk food, etc. are real bargain here. Let your friends join you on shopping days as your guest.

Bulk purchasing

Learn this now: *Buy In Quantity!* Onesy, Twosy purchases are for suckers. John Pugsley thoroughly explained this "mini-warehousing" strategy in his OP book *The Alpha Strategy.* Since you are fairly certain to need about 100 rolls of toilet paper over the next 10 years, why not buy them all at one time? The higher the quantity, the lower the unit cost. Also, FRN currency is buying less and less, so spend it when you get it.

All this makes great sense from a tax standpoint, too. Let's say inflation is 10%, bank account interest is 11%, and the capital gains tax is 25%. You put Ø1,000 in the bank for a year and it grows to Ø1,100. Minus that 25% tax, you get to keep only Ø75 of that Ø100 interest income, so your actual balance is only Ø1,075. *But,* since prices have increase by 10%, that Ø1,000 worth of stuff now costs Ø1,100. **You have *lost Ø25* in purchasing power, just as if you threw it out the window.**

You would have been better off buying future essentials in bulk with that original Ø1,000. By doing so, you wouldn't have lost any purchasing power, you wouldn't have given the Government Ø25 it didn't deserve, you would have avoided illiquidity from a bank failure, and you would have had in your own possession goods which will only go up in price (and someday decrease in availability). You win--the Government loses!

Joint purchase of big ticket items

The following will cost Ø20,000+ and are generally unaffordable for individual households. Besides, these items can seldom needed on a daily basis and can be shared by several people or even families. Go in with your buddies or partners and combine your wealth. Companies are doing exactly this by buying time shares of executive jets.

Ø200-500   300+ gallon diesel fuel tank

I consider a 300 gallon tank to be the minimum, and would feel much better with at least 1,000 gallons.

Ø200-500   300+ gallon gasoline tank

Same comments as the diesel tank above.

Ø689   AC powered colloidal silver generator

This "ounce" of prevention is worth a *ton* of cure. Makes up to 6 gallons/day of 10-12ppm colloidal silver which will not fall out of suspension, but store forever. Draws only 2A (250W) which any small generator provides. From CS Pro Systems (888-710-2773; www.csprosystems.com). Have plenty of steam distilled water on hand, and .999 silver electrodes.

Ø1,000   1,000 gallon propane tank
This will hold 800 gallons of LP and cost about Ø650 to fill. Any tanks larger than 120 gallons must be placed at least 20' away (often on concrete foundations) and have underground lines. 500gal tanks can often be found for only Ø250, so it might make better sense to combine these over a 1,000gal tank, especially if more than one building requires LP.

Ø2,500+   1,000yd countersniper rifle
This should be in at least .30-06 (I don't see the .308 as a reliable 1,000yd caliber, although it's often done). 7mmRM would be better, .300WM better still, and .338 Lapua the best. This rifle will handle 98% of all threats, so don't skimp on it.

Ø2,500+   ITT PVS-7B night vision goggles
The civilian version are the 5001 series. The Bs cost Ø2,500, the Js Ø3,500, and the Ps at least Ø4,000. Try to have at least one rifle with an IR laser and vortex flash suppressor.

Ø4,000+   .50BMG countersniper rifle
Any group of 10 or more should have one to deter motorized assaults on their property.

Ø4,000+   8-10kw diesel generator
This is the minimum output for a household. A larger ranch with 2-3 homes would need at least 20kw of power. The batteries, circuit breakers, lines , etc. also add up.

Ø6,000+   diesel tractor
A must for every ranch. Make sure it has a Power Take Off (PTO) for *common* attachments.

Ø10,000+   quality, modern 4x4 (*e.g.*, Suburban)
Every country family ought to have one of these.

Pay *through* 1/31/2000 for phone/utilities
Many folks will have paid up to only 12/31/99, figuring that they will pay for January only if they have service. While this is sound reasoning on its *face*, let's think things through a bit more. Consider the likely situation facing thousands of local

phone and utility companies on 3 January 2000. To *whom* will they first reinstate or ration service: those whose accounts are overdue and/or on credit, *or* those who have prepaid *through* the entire month of January and have the receipts to *prove* it?

You want to have the *leverage of prepayment* to force the continuation of existing services, such as phone, water, electricity, and gas. Force yourself to the front of the line and make the clerks start a separate line for those who have prepaid and can prove it. Convince the manager to compile a list of all prepaid customers and have their service reinstated first. (You may want to meet with such managers in December 1999, before the mob arrives in January.)

START BUYING SURVIVAL GOODS

Once the public begins to panic by summer 1999, many of the below vital goods will be scarce or even unattainable. Start at the top of this list (an adaptation of the pp.275-76 list from Dr. Gary North's *Government by Emergency*) and work down. You may disagree about the order, but no guide is universal.

Food
6 months (12 is *much* better) of dehydrated food per family member
Katadyn water purifier and water storage containers
propane or 12V DC fridge and freezer

Weapons (see pp. 11/1-2 in my *BoG&C* for a longer list)
.308 "assault rifle" (FAL, AR10, M1A) w/30+ mags
reliable handgun (Glock, Colt, etc.) in 9mm, .40, or .45; w/15+ mags
1,000rds per handgun; 2,000rds per rifle

Heat
Kerosene or wood stove with months of fuel

Money
$500 (face value) in pre-1965 U.S. silver coins (per member)
Ø1,000 in cash (10¢, 25¢, bills ≤Ø10) per member

Home
Chemical toilet
Survival stove
Fire extinguishers (car and home)

Communications
Motorola TalkAbout Plus radio for each member
Shortwave radio (digital display and presets)
CB radio with SSBs
Scanner (hand-held, 200 channels; *e.g.*, Radio Shack PRO-43)

Weapons
.223 "assault rifle" (AR15 or similar) w/5,000rds and 30 mags
.22LR rifle (Ruger or Marlin) and handgun (Ruger)
10,000rds of copper-plated .22LR ammo
.177 pellet rifle and 10,000 pellets (mostly hunting)
quality 7" fixed blade knife in Kydex sheath
reloading equipment

Health
high quality (Ø200+) First Aid kit (*e.g.*, Thompson Pack); manual
bulletproof vest (at least IIA rating)
highly soluble vitamins and minerals (colloidal are best)
preventative medical (*e.g.*, dental, appendix, etc.)

Tools & Implements
16"-20" chainsaw
8-10kW generator, with ample fuel

Maintenance
Lubricants for all equipment (personal and business)
Tools for self-sufficiency
spare parts for all your vehicles and equipment
spare tires for your work truck or 4x4 rig

Food
Vegetable seeds for growing (non-hybrid, heirloom *only*)
Sprouting seeds
Gardening equipment and books
dehydrator
canning equipment

Barter items
ammo (9mm, .45, .223, .308, .30-06, 12ga.)
Coffee (50lbs in 1lb cans or jars)
100 6oz. tins of cigarette tobacco, papers, rolling machine
Case of Jack Daniels

Clothing
extra pairs of warm and waterproof boots for every member

extra warm clothing for every member
durable work clothing for working adults
camouflage BDUs for every member
extra socks and underwear for every member

Money
5 1oz. gold bullion coins (American Eagles or Krugerrands)
10 ¼oz. gold bullion coins (Eagles)

Weapons
bolt-action, scoped rifle (.308, .30-06), 500rds of 180gr. GameKing
night vision goggles (the best you can *painfully* afford, preferably ITT)
.22LR Ruger Mk.II pistol (preferably stainless), w/10 mags

Barter items
inexpensive *quality* handguns (*e.g.,* S&W 10, Makarov, Browning P35)
ammo (.40S&W, .243, .270, 7.62x39, .30-30, 20ga.)
20lbs of inexpensive pipe tobacco
case of Vodka
foreign army surplus wool blankets (from CTD)

Weapons
semi-auto rifle in 7.62x39 (SKS, AK clone), w/5,000rds in stripper clips
second handgun as your first, w/10+ mags
.30-30 Marlin lever-action, w/500rds (170gr.)
12ga. Rem 870 w/20" Remchoked bbl., ghost ring sights, 500 shells

Barter items
extra fuel (gasoline, diesel, kerosene, propane)
Katadyn water purifiers
Books (Bibles, gardening, repair, survival, classic novels, etc.)
inexpensive consumables (razors, toothbrushes, soap, TP, oil, etc.)
batteries (dry 12V car and marine; AA & D cells, Duracell 123A lithiums)

Communication
Ham radio
2-5W walkie-talkies

Yeah, it's an *overwhelming* list, and I only scratched the surface. (Post-press ideas I'll post on www.javelinpress.com. Write me with your ideas and comments.)

> *Obviously, these items could consume a big chunk of your capital. You may not be able to afford everything you want, so you have to do the best you can and make choices. In the early stages of the [price] controls (or shortages), or even before the controls are officially declared, **buy the items that the government is most likely***

to ban, ration, or otherwise control. (BTP Note: These would likely <u>first</u> be guns, ammo, freeze-dried food, NVGs, etc.) ***Stay two jumps ahead of each shortage.*** (at 239)

You should already have stocked your home and business with emergency goods by this stage to avoid the charge of "hoarding." "Hoarding" is a nasty term for saving. It really means "buying more than your fair share of scarce goods in competition with others." ***Buying in advance of shortages is not "hoarding."*** (at 240)

Your top priority is dehydrated food. *You should have a bit of land to grow more food. You need extra supplies to help friends and for barter. In the great inflations* (and wars, and natural disasters) *of this century,* ***without exception, the most important single investment was food. In second place was fuel.*** *Finally, you need clothing. But food is primary.* (at 241)

-- Howard J. Ruff; *How To Prosper During The Coming Bad Years* (1979)

STAY HOME DURING SPIKE DATES

Spike dates are those on which Y2K testing or rollovers will take place. In the chapter *Why Disaster Looms*, I discussed the well-known Spike Dates of 1999 and 2000. The biggest ones are, in my opinion, 1 July in which 46 states rollover to fiscal 2000, and 1 October when the federal government rolls over. These two dates will almost assuredly cause damage or shutdown to many government agencies. You do not want to be travelling (for *whatever* the reason) around any Spike Date (especially 1 July and 1 October), and you *certainly* don't want to be out of state. Avoid traffic, building, and public transportation problems then by staying home with your family. If you live at home alone, get "adopted" by friends for the day.

Jim Lord urges not making telephone calls or going online on Spike Dates, and to double-check your bills (utilities, telephone, cable TV, etc.) during Spike Date months for erroneous charges. Definitely stay out of jail or prison during such months, else they might lose your records and hold you indefinitely as more important problems are addressed.

LEARN NEW SKILLS

A new friend of mine who's only 24 y/o aggressively learns new skills, likening them to new tools in the toolbox of his mind.

This is precisely the attitude to have. Put a boot through your TV set and go learn how to weld or administer CPR.

In my chapter *Services*, I list many skills which will not only remain in demand from Y2K, but *increase* in demand. Go to night school if you must--we're talking about a scheduled emergency here! *Top* skills to learn on my list would be **medical** (CPR, first aid, trauma medicine, and nutrition).

A close second would be **repair** (welding, plumbing, electrical, electronics, engine, gunsmithing, appliances, locksmithing, carpentry, sewing, etc.).

Next would be related to **food and water** (gardening, hunting, fishing, well digging and repair, food storage).

Next would be **accounting** (filing, etc.) to make up for the shortfall left by corrupted data and dead computers.

Next would be **entertainment** (music, plays, comedy, game coordinator, etc.). Americans are addicted to not only entertainment, but *surrogate* entertainment of watching others. This habit will not be soon broken. In *The Postman*, the main character was a travelling performer who traded his skits and one-man plays for food and lodging.

TEST YOUR PLAN

Y2K will hit us in the middle of winter. You should test your plan and preparations also in winter. Shut off your power suddenly and leave it off for at least 5 days, if not a week or two. Live only on your stored food. Work and read only by non-electric lighting (unless you've installed independent energy).

This "dress rehearsal" will go far in identifying problem areas, but you must actually rehearse. Merely thinking about it won't work. As I recommend to first time travellers, pack your bags and then lug them around your block. Such a distance is typical of airports, and if your luggage is unmanageable around the block, it will doubly so during the stress of making flights.

Moral: Test your plan!

TEST YOUR PC

Your PC's time comes from the CMOS, which goes to the BIOS, then to the OS, and then to the app, and then to the data file. All layers must be compliant, and all must be tested. A good article on this came from www.currents.net/dfw on 3/98.

CMOS

Pentium PCs made from 1997-on shouldn't have a problem, but older Pentiums and all 386s and 486s have two-digit year clocks. Some CMOS modules can be easily unplugged and replaced, while other (with the old AT-style Motorola clock chips) cannot (www.resource800.com has details.

BIOS

Most Pentium BIOS chips since 1994-1995 are compliant, however your post-1994 PC's motherboard could have been assembled with a pre-1994 BIOS chip. You won't know unless you test it. Upgrades for 386s aren't around, but some are for 486s.

OS (Operating System)

Windows 95, NT, DOS (if your computer is on *during* the 2000 rollover), Linux, OS/2 Warp3, and OS/2 Warp 4 are all *reported* to be compliant. Beware if you're on a network, as who knows if your server is compliant.

Windows 3.x

File Manager will show 19:0 instead of 2000, but a fix is available from:

support.microsoft.com/support/kb/articles/q85/5/57.asp

Novell Netware 3.12 and IntraNetWare 4.11

Patches available from:

www.novell.com/p2000/patches.html

Application software

Spreadsheet, database, personal finance, and calender programs all use date-related macros and calculations. Test all your software (without access to sensitive data files).

Data files

After you've tested your hardware, OS, and apps--bring up some suspected app and create a test case of orders, inventory, interest calculations, etc. across the century line.

Certain tools are available from New Art Technologies (www.newarttech.com) which will search through most worksheets for date-related references for immediate editing.

How to test PCs for 2000
This will *not* harm your PC, so test away.

Testing the BIOS
While your computer is on, reset the clock to **23:59** on **12-31-99** and see if it rolls over properly to 2000 one minute later. (This resets the CMOS and passes it on to the BIOS.) If it doesn't, then your BIOS chip cannot take dates past 1999.

If it does, then it's OK and you should next test the CMOS.

Testing the CMOS
Restart Windows 95 and press F8 when you see "Starting Windows 95" message to stop at the DOS prompt. Then type **DATE 12-31-99** and press Enter. Type **TIME 23:59** and press Enter. Turn your PC off for several minutes, then turn it back on, stopping again at the DOS prompt. Type **DATE** and press Enter. The date should be 01-01-2000, and if it's not then the CMOS clock is not compliant.

Your PC *must* hold a valid 2000+ date (interpreted by the BIOS) *after* rebooting, else the BIOS *will* feed an incorrect date to the OS and apps.

If you're too scared to test your PC...
A test program is Test2000.zip from www.rightime.com.

Don't forget to test for 02/29/2000
Since 2000 is a funky leap year century (occurring only every 400 years), many BIOS chips, OSs (*e.g.*, Win31), and apps weren't programmed for it. Set to **23:59** on **02-28-2000** and test as above. Also, test all your date-related apps.

❖ 24

TINY ANSWERS

Although none or little of the following will ever be implemented, the thinker/inventor/theoretician in me can't help but include such, regardless.

Y2K should be treated as an *invasion*

While I am the *last* person to look to the *government* for help or solutions, Y2K is a systemic crisis which cannot be dealt with at the local or even the state level, any more than the Hawaiians could have defeated the Japanese at Pearl Harbor. As a libertarian, I recognize truly *national* concerns to be the primary duty of the national government, and Y2K certainly qualifies. I regret to conclude that we need a *national* coordination of planning, repairs, and resources for surviving Y2K.

Although some (or even much) of this could be voluntary, some of it must be compulsory. If Y2K *is* such an emergency, then the nation needs to *treat* it as such, like any natural disaster, plague or invasion.

Yes, I'm quite aware of the implications of federal intervention in state/local planning. Wartime increases of governmental power have historically been a one-way ratchet, never to resume to prewar levels. *This* time, however, the federal government will be in too sorry a shape to maintain much (or any) of its advances in supra-constitutional control. (Even if they manage to hold onto power, we can deal with them *after* we cross the 1/1/2000 bridge.)

So, if the feds are going "bye-bye" in 2000 anyway, then let's at least use them for a good purpose in 1999.

Technology triage

Since there is just no time to save all, most, or even many of the due-to-fail systems, the only logical plan is this:

Fix the *most* critical systems, in the most *even* dispersion.

It makes no sense for just one state to be fully-powered, while the other 49 wallow in the Stone Age. Every region, if not every state must have for 2000 at least *one* fully compliant power plant (with ample fuel), large airport, trucking fleet, railway line, "War Room" and communications hub. Each of these must be vigorously defended from looters if that region/state is to survive. Along these lines, Harlan Smith's *Synergistic Mitigation & Contingency Planning* (www.itpolicy.gsa.gov/mks/yr2000/paper/16fp.htm) proposal is worth a study.

Increased excise/sales taxes

What?! Boston T. Party recommending *increased* taxes? Yes, but with the simultaneous elimination of all income taxes (federal and state), so that tax payments can be channeled into Y2K survival projects.

Energy

As my *Energy* chapter proved, we need to immediately begin a national drive for efficiency, through the combination of less usage and more efficient appliances. I believe that the nation could get by on perhaps as little as *half* the energy with little reduction in the quality of life.

As there is a hidden cost within our artificially cheap utilities, I propose that such be brought out into the light ASAP. I suggest that all taxes on energy be at least doubled, with the increase relegated only to guaranteeing compliant power plants. If we allow weeks and months of national power blackouts in 2000, then it will take a good *decade* to crawl out of the hole. I'd rather us pay dearly in 1999 to avoid a 2000 Dark Age.

Nonessentials

Whatever is taxed, people will buy less of. Folks need to get their butt in gear, and if a 200% tax on, for example, movie tickets and restaurant dinners helped to focus people's minds on what is important, then I'd be all for it. We've plenty of "amusement" and "entertainment" already, and whatever is taxed into dormancy can be replaced with inexpensive or free substitutes, such as books, games, and sports.

A shocking federal announcement

We cannot simply go on partying on this technological *Titanic* until the icy water floods the dance floor. If, for example, every wooden door on the *Titanic* had been axed off its hinges and used as a raft, probably another 500 people could have been saved. We're not currently ripping doors out of hinges for the Y2K water, and time is running out.

When the Nazi invasion of the U.S.S.R. ground to a halt in the winter of 1941 without reaching Moscow and sending the Soviet government east of the Urals, the German troops were still wearing their summer clothing. Propaganda Minister Joseph Goebbels then issued an urgent appeal to the German people for donations of all spare blankets, coats, boots, etc. for their freezing troops. Answering criticism for his alarm, he explained that only a *shock* effect would energize the people into action. It worked. Furs, boots, and clothing poured in.

Similarly, the American people will not sufficiently prepare without a federal declaration of *"We're screwed, unless..."*

Make Friday 12/31/1999 through Monday 1/3/2000 a national holiday

Only *essential* employees should go to work just before and after 1/1/2000. Folks should generally stay home, and a curfew might be considered to allow emergency personnel unrestricted use of the roads. A curfew would also reduce looting.

Y2K lawsuit moratorium

While I fully support enforcing the responsibility of companies and adults, the impending feeding frenzy by attorneys is likely to drag down our post-Y2K recovery. The Gartner Group projects Ø1 *trillion* in total sought damages (which is a major chunk of our GNP). *Already* there have been at least two dozen Y2K-related lawsuits filed, with defendants including Medical Manager, Quarterdeck, Symantec and Intuit.

What is often forgotten in all this is that the human world is a *closed* system, and seeking Ø1 trillion in damages approaches the absurdity of everybody suing everybody. Too many people are at fault for Y2K, and we simply cannot collect from them all, any more than we could have imprisoned all of Nazi Germany's SS and Gestapo.

The only *practical* thing to do is allow the core lawsuits to go after the key players (*e.g.*, the Nuremberg trials), and to tell everyone else to get on with their lives.

I think it's best that Y2K (and its origin of programming negligence and sloppiness) be generally treated like a natural disaster in the courts. A Japanese maxim comes to mind here:

Fix the problem, not the blame.

Militarize (or militia-ize) the large cities

While I loathe the thought philosophically, such seems necessary to keep them from descending into anarchy. I'd first concentrate on cities with a high gang population, such as Los Angeles, Chicago, and New York City. The gangs are already well-organized and highly motivated paramilitary groups, and they can be stopped only by military troops. There is no more destructive force than a bunch of unemployed young men. Even *France* experienced the wrath of such mobs recently in Paris, where a rampaging mob of young men destroyed 120 cars.

Mandatory storage and warehousing

Because this is an emergency, every home should be mandated to have a *minimum* of 30 days of food and water, fuel for heat and cooking, and household necessities. Official personnel will be busy enough with fixing technical problems and providing security--they don't need to be doling out soup to the foolishly unprepared.

How will people *afford* all this? They *won't*. Most people haven't sufficient savings or disposable income. Since I have already recommended eliminating the income tax, part of it should be *refunded* to each family in the form of a Y2K Kit. This Kit should contain food (MREs or freeze-dried), water barrels, a cookstove with fuel, candles, solar/hand-crank radio, etc. The sale or theft of Y2K Kits should be vigorously prosecuted.

Large regional warehouses should be stocked with vast quantities of food and fuel, in case the crisis lasts beyond 30 days.

❖ 25

RESOURCES

I will go from most current (websites) to least current (books). Buy books to learn the basics, and visit websites for daily developments.

WEBSITES

Y2K & Preparedness Books
Javelin Press   www.javelinpress.com
Loompanics   www.loompanics.com
Paladin Press   www.paladin-press.com
Cheaper Than Dirt   www.cheaperthandirt.com

Y2K Overview
JES & Associates   www.jes.com
Peter de Jager   www.year2000.com
Dr. Gary North   www.garynorth.com
John Westergaard   www.y2ktimebomb.com
Ed Yourdon   www.yourdon.com
Tim Wilson   www.y2knews.com
Dr. Ed Yardeni   www.yardeni.com

Y2K Preparation
Jim Lord   www.SurviveY2K.com
Ken Klein   www.y2knet.com
Karen Anderson   www.y2kwomen.com
Rick Cowles   www.euy2k.com
Pamela O'Riley   www.millennia-bcs.com
James Stevens   www.y2kprep.com

Y2K News

Tony Keyes	www.y2kinvestor.com
Ed Meagher	www.y2ktoday.com
Don McAlvany	www.mcalvany.com
	www.y2kchaos.com
	www.pw2.netcom.com
	comp.software.year-2000
	www.comlinks.com

Y2K Christian & Community Service

	www.believers.com
Tim Wilson	www.y2knews.org
Pamela O'Riley	www.millennia-bcs.com
Jim Rutz	www.openchurch.com
Dennis Peacocke	www.scsnet.org
Pat Robertson	www.cbn.com
Don McAlvany	www.mcalvany.com

Y2K Government & Corporations

Sen. Bob Bennett	www.senate.gov/~bennett
Stephen Horn	www.house.gov/~horn
Sen. Chris Dodd	www.senate.gov/~dodd
John Koskinen	www.y2k.gov
GSA	www.itpolicy.gsa.gov
ITAA	www.itaa.com
Mitre Corp.	www.mitre.com
NERC	www.nerc.com
	www.epri.com/evaly2k/index.html
GAO	www.gao.gov/y2kr.htm

MAGAZINES & NEWSLETTERS

American Survival Guide
Backwoods Home
Countryside
McAlvany Intelligence Advisor

BOOKS
Y2K Preparation

Boston on Surviving Y2K, Boston T. Party
  Info and perspectives you won't find elsewhere.
Bulletproof Privacy, Boston T. Party
  Privacy will be vital in 1999/2000. I show you how.
Boston on Guns & Courage, Boston T. Party
  My book will get you well on your gun-owning way.
Hologram of Liberty, Kenneth W. Royce (a.k.a. Boston T. Party)
  Full of unique political ideas/answers for post-2000.
Don't Get Caught With Your Pantry Down!, James Stevens
  Profiles over 5,000 suppliers. An absolute *must*!
Making the Best of Basics, James Stevens
  Highly useful and thorough. Another must.
Year 2000: Personal Protection Guide, J.R. Morris
  Good info on protecting files, records, etc.
Whatcha Gonna Do If The Grid Goes Down, Susan Robinson
  Very household oriented. Full of checklists.
Time Bomb 2000, Ed Yourdon
  My favorite Y2K Guru.
The Millennium Bug, Michael S. Hyatt
The Year 2000 Computer Crisis, Tony Keyes
  Business oriented for the investor.
Surviving the Y2K Crisis, Jim Lord
  Solid, useful work.
Privileged Information, Ed Bell
Year 2000 Recession?, Dr. Ed Yardeni
Y2K Crisis, Donald S. McAlvany
  A complilation of his excellent Y2K newsletter issues.
900 Days--The Siege of Leningrad, Harrison E. Salisbury
  Learn how big city folks coped with starvation.
Last of the Mountain Men, Sylvan Hart
  City fellow escapes to the bank of the Idaho Salmon River
and carves out a new home and life.
How To Prosper During The Coming Bad Years, Howard J. Ruff
  Out of print, but available at any used bookstore for Ø1.
Some info, suppliers, and prices are out of date, but the basic
message and planning is timeless.

Novels
Since America risks unraveling at her seams, I've included many novels which dramatize political upheavals. Books in bold are my favorites.

Disaster preparation
Lucifer's Hammer, Niven and Pournelle
Farnham's Freehold, Robert Heinlein
Pulling Through, Dean Ing
Malevil,

Resistance movements with at least a somewhat happy ending
Atlas Shrugged, Ayn Rand
The Moon Is A Harsh Mistress, Robert A. Heinlein
Weapons Shops of Isher, A.E. vanVogt
Unintended Consequences, John Ross
Mirror Maze, James P. Hogan
The Gallatin Convergence, L. Neil Smith
Pallas, L. Neil Smith
When The Almond Tree Blossoms, David Aikman
The Postman, David Brin
The *Ashes* novels by William W. Johnstone
The Survival of Freedom, Jerry Pournelle
Kings Of The High Frontier, V. Koman (www.pulpless.com)
Paul Revere's Ride, D.H. Fischer
The Battle of Athens, Tennessee, Byrum

Libertarian utopias
Alongside Night, Perlman
The Probability Broach, L. Neil Smith
Voyage of Yesteryear, James P. Hogan

Resistance movements with a less-than-happy ending
Defiance (also titled *Vandenberg*), Oliver Lange
Animal Farm, George Orwell
Amerika, Pouns
Let Us Prey, Bill Branon
Resistance, Israel Gutman
The Whiskey Rebellion, Thomas Slaughter
Story of Secret State, Jan Karski

Dystopias
This Perfect Day, Ira Levin
1984, George Orwell
Brave New World, Aldous Huxley

Anthem, Ayn Rand
Man In A High Castle, Philip K. Dick
Oath of Fealty, Niven and Pournelle
The Trial, Franz Kafka

SOURCES

Many of the following report 40+% increases of 1998 sales from 1997, and they expect to be overwhelmed in 1999. Get your orders in ASAP, or stand in line in '99!

Brigade Quartermasters 800-338-4327 www.actiongear.com
Tactical gear/clothing. Best selection of boots.
Their Emergency Preparedness Kit #1 is very good.
Campmor 800-226-7667 www.campmor.com
Huge selection of camping/outdoors gear.
China Diesel Imports 619-669-1995 www.chinadiesel.com
Diesel generators and tractors. Good products
CTD 888-750-5234 www.cheaperthandirt.com
America's leading sports discounter. Great folks.
Best source for MREs. Neat catalog!
DSA 847-223-4770 www.dsarms.com
They make the best post-ban FAL on the market.
Double Eagle Investments 800-290-4127
Convert your IRA to gold coins. Solid financial advice.
Eagle Industries 314-343-7547 www.eagleindustries.com
Quality tactical gear.
Emergency Essentials 800-999-1863 www.BePrepared.com
They sell essentials for emergencies.
Gas Masks Inc. 800-742-6275 www.gas-masks.com
They sell...gas masks.
JRH enterprises 904-797-9462 www.logoplex.com/resources/jrh
Good survival gear, bulletproof vests, etc.
Lehman's Non-Electric Catalog, Box 41, Kidron, Ohio 44636
Farm implements, tools, grain grinders, etc.
Long Life Food Depot 800-601-2833
A food storage supplier.
Major Surplus 800-441-8855 www.MajorSurplusNSurvival.com
Survival and outdoor gear.
McAlvany Intelligence Advisor 800-528-0559 www.mcalvany.com
Good monthly newsletter with lots on Y2K.

Millennium Foods   800-500-9893
   Quality freeze-dried foods.
Militia of Montana   406-847-2735   www.logoplex.com/resources/mom
   Great survival books and videos. Nice folks.
Nitro-Pak   800-866-4876
   Finest selection of survival goods, food, and equipment.
Northern   800-533-5545
   Power tools, generators, and lots more.
QP   800-998-7928   www.bushmaster.com
   Best source for AR15 parts and accessories.
Ready Made Resources   800-627-3809   www.cococo.net/rmr
   NVDs, books, food, survial goods, and much more.
Robar   602-581-2648
   Custom gun work. Tactical weapons. Rustproof finishes.
Sierra Supply   970-259-1822
   MREs, sleeping bags, mags, and other surplus.

Note: The listing of the above resources does *not* imply full and unqualified endorsement of the same. *Caveat Emptor!*

ABBREVIATIONS & TERMINOLOLGY

Ø "Federal Reserve Notes" which are no longer redeemable in and masquerade as real $ dollars (gold/silver money). Ancient Chinese proverb (they're *all* ancient, aren't they?): *"The beginning of wisdom is to call things by their right name."* The inverse of that is to stop calling things by their wrong name, which is why I refuse to call FRNs "dollars."

George Orwell made the point that shoddy language results in shoddy politics. He was right. Calling dry "wet" and darkness "light" requires the simultaneous, purposeful mental suspension of truth--a 1/1000th second bit of insanity--and, in my opinion, evil. Once you begin lying to yourself, you must also lie to others. Do this enough times (as did the Nazis and as do the Communists) and one's entire thinking (and thus actions) will become deranged and evil.

Make a firm habit of calling things by what they are, not by what sounds cute, kind, acceptable, "politically correct," or expedient.

§ **section.** You'll see this in law quotations.

AP **armor piercing.** Usually designated with a painted black tip.

BIOS **Binary Operating System** firmware, which is code that resides on a chip on the motherboard. The BIOS tells the computer how to address all the peripherals, such as reading the OS code on the hard disk. The BIOS gets the date from the CMOS.

BoG&C *Boston on Guns & Courage.* My gun book of 1998.

CMOS **Computer Memory Operating System.** This contains a real time clock (RTC) and stores chip settings powered by a small battery. The CMOS maintains a two-digit year, requiring the BIOS to append such to a proper four-digit year that it supplies to the OS. What is important is not the CMOS date (as no common software uses it directly), but what the BIOS does with it.

CQB   **Close quarter battle.** Hand-to-hand fighting.
Cuidado   *"Be careful."*   That's Spanish.
DIY   **Do It Yourself.** A British acronym.
FAL   A semi-auto .308 battle designed by the Belgians and adopted by 93 countries. Superior to the M1A and H&K91.
FRN   **Federal Reserve Note.** Also denoted by the symbol Ø.
Jubilee   The Biblical reference to the canceling of all debt every 50 years. It's never happened, but nevertheless remains a supernaturally wise plan to prevent intergenerational debt slavery to the banksters.
lp/mm   line pair per millimeter. A measurement of resolution in night vision devices. The higher the better.
MOA   **Minute Of Angle,** which is exactly 1.047" at 100yds, though rounded down to 1". At 400yds; 1MOA is 4", ½MOA is 2", etc.
OP   **out of print.** A book no longer available from its publisher.
QD   **quick detach.** Meaning, no tools needed.
rd   **round.** One loaded cartridge. Can also mean a bullet enroute.
spot   The price of a futures contract of a precious metal. Coins and bullion sell at a premium over spot price.
TANSTAAFL   *"There ain't no such thing as a free lunch."*
From Robert A. Heinlein's *The Moon Is A Harsh Mistress*. A catch phrase and motto of many hip Libertarians.
TEOTWAWKI   *The End of the World as We Know It*, pronounced (tee-OH-tawa-kee). Used both in jest and in earnest.

HOW TO ORDER FROM US

NOTE: The Ø symbol denotes "Federal Reserve Notes" which are no longer redeemable in, and masquerade as, real $ gold or silver money.

Good-Bye April 15th!
We are out-of-stock until further notice on our website. Have faith--we'll either reprint it, or put it out on CD. We've just been busy...

You & The Police!
5½"x8½", 128 pages. Published January 1996.
Prices each: *1-5* copies are Ø15; *6-31* copies are Ø9; *32-91* copies are Ø8.40; a case of *92* or more copies are Ø7.50 each.

Bulletproof Privacy
5½"x8½", 160 pages. Published January 1997.
Prices each: *1-5* copies are Ø16; *6-31* copies are Ø10; *32-79* copies are Ø9; a case of *80* or more copies are Ø8 each.

Hologram of Liberty
5½"x8½", 262 pages. Published August 1997.
Prices each: *1-5* copies are Ø20; *6-15* copies are Ø12; *16-39* copies are Ø11.20; a case of *40* or more copies are Ø10 each.

Boston on Guns & Courage
5½"x8½", 192 pages. Published March 1998.
Prices each: *1-5* copies are Ø17; *6-31* copies are Ø10.20; *32-59* copies are Ø9.50; a case of *64* or more copies are Ø8.50 each.

Boston on Surviving Y2K
5½"x8½", 352 pages. Published November 1998.
Prices each: *1-5* copies are Ø22; *6-15* copies are Ø13.20; *16-35* copies are Ø12.30; see our website for case quantity and 50% discount.

Shipping and Handling are *not* included. Book Rate add: Ø3 for first copy and Ø0.25 per additional copy. First Class add: Ø4 and Ø0.50.

These forms of payment *only:*
Cash (Preferred. Cash orders get autographed copies.)
payee blank M.O.s (Which makes them more easily negotiable.)
credit cards (Many of our distributors take them. See our website.)

Unless prior agreement has been made, we do not accept (*and will return*) checks, C.O.D.s, filled-in M.O.s, or any other form of tender. Prices and terms are subject to change without notice. Send orders to:

JAVELIN PRESS
c/o P.O. Box 31F; Ignacio, Colorado. (81137-0031)
www.javelinpress.com

HOW TO ORDER FROM US

NOTE: The Ø symbol denotes "Federal Reserve Notes" which are no longer redeemable in, and masquerade as, real $ gold or silver money.

Good-Bye April 15th!
We are out-of-stock until further notice on our website. Have faith--we'll either reprint it, or put it out on CD. We've just been busy...

You & The Police!
5½"x8½", 128 pages. Published January 1996.
Prices each: *1-5* copies are Ø15; *6-31* copies are Ø9; *32-91* copies are Ø8.40; a case of *92* or more copies are Ø7.50 each.

Bulletproof Privacy
5½"x8½", 160 pages. Published January 1997.
Prices each: *1-5* copies are Ø16; *6-31* copies are Ø10; *32-79* copies are Ø9; a case of *80* or more copies are Ø8 each.

Hologram of Liberty
5½"x8½", 262 pages. Published August 1997.
Prices each: *1-5* copies are Ø20; *6-15* copies are Ø12; *16-39* copies are Ø11.20; a case of *40* or more copies are Ø10 each.

Boston on Guns & Courage
5½"x8½", 192 pages. Published March 1998.
Prices each: *1-5* copies are Ø17; *6-31* copies are Ø10.20; *32-59* copies are Ø9.50; a case of *64* or more copies are Ø8.50 each.

Boston on Surviving Y2K
5½"x8½", 352 pages. Published November 1998.
Prices each: *1-5* copies are Ø22; *6-15* copies are Ø13.20; *16-35* copies are Ø12.30; see our website for case quantity and 50% discount.

Shipping and Handling are *not* included. Book Rate add: Ø3 for first copy and Ø0.25 per additional copy. First Class add: Ø4 and Ø0.50.

These forms of payment *only:*
Cash (Preferred. Cash orders get autographed copies.)
payee blank M.O.s (Which makes them more easily negotiable.)
credit cards (Many of our distributors take them. See our website.)

Unless prior agreement has been made, we do not accept (*and will return*) checks, C.O.D.s, filled-in M.O.s, or any other form of tender. Prices and terms are subject to change without notice. Send orders to:

JAVELIN PRESS
c/o P.O. Box 31F; Ignacio, Colorado. (81137-0031)
www.javelinpress.com